BLUE GUIDE

MEDITERRANEAN TURKEY

from Muğla to Antakya

PAOLA PUGSLEY

**BLUE GUIDE
MEDITERRANEAN TURKEY**

Published by Blue Guides Limited, a Somerset Books Company
Winchester House, Deane Gate Avenue, Taunton, Somerset TA1 2UH

www.blueguides.com

'Blue Guide' is a registered trademark.

Text © Paola Pugsley/Blue Guides 2020
The right of Paola Pugsley to be identified as author of this work
have been asserted by her in accordance with the
Copyright Designs and Patents Act, 1988.

All rights reserved.
No part of this publication may be reproduced or used
in any form or by any means—photographic, electronic
or mechanical—without permission of the publisher.

ISBN 978-1-905131-88-4

The author and publisher have made reasonable efforts to ensure the accuracy of all the information in this book; however, they can accept no responsibility for any loss, injury or inconvenience sustained by any traveller as a result of information or advice contained in the guide.

Every effort has been made to trace the copyright owners of material reproduced in this guide. We would be pleased to hear from any copyright owners we have been unable to reach.

Statement of editorial independence: Blue Guides, their authors and editors, are prohibited from accepting payment from any restaurant, hotel, museum or other establishment for its inclusion in this guide or on www.blueguides.com, or for a more favourable mention than would otherwise have been made.

Maps and plans by Blue Guides and Imre Bába © Blue Guides.

Cover image: Relief (now in the British Museum) from the 5th-century BC Harpy Monument at Xanthus in Lycia.
Photo: Jastrow, Wikimedia Commons.

www.blueguides.com

'Blue Guide' is a registered trademark.

We welcome reader comments, questions and feedback:
editorial@blueguides.com

About the author
Paola Pugsley is a professional archaeologist with an interest in the Mediterranean and particularly in the eastern part of it. She first visited Turkey in 1970 as a tourist, driving all the way to the Nemrut Dağ, which she climbed on a most uncomfortable donkey. She vowed to return—but had to wait until the early 1990s. From then on she has worked on numerous summer excavations, moving steadily east. Her interest lies in bringing to life the visible and invisible past and in encouraging visitors and armchair travellers alike to engage in and see the sites both in their long-term development and physical setting. Other chapters in the series are *Blue Guide Eastern Turkey*, *Blue Guide Southeastern Turkey*, *Blue Guide Central Anatolia*, *Blue Guide Aegean Turkey* and *Blue Guide The Black Sea Coast*.

CONTENTS

Introduction	6
Travel tips	10
Getting around	10
Accommodation	13
Eating and drinking	14
Timeline	15
Glossary	17
Pronunciation guide	21
Early travellers to Mediterranean Turkey	22
Around the Ceramic Gulf	35
Muğla to Marmaris	35
Cnidus and Loryma: A tale of two peninsulas	37
Caunus and Dalyan	45
Practical information	50
Lycia	52
Fethiye and its gulf (Telmessus)	53
The interior north of Fethiye	56
The upper Xanthus Valley (Tlos, Pinara, Sidyma)	63
The lower Xanthus Valley (Xanthus Letoön, Patara)	68
Kaş	84
East of Cape Uluburun: Aperlae, Simena and Cyaneae	85
Between two rivers: the Demre Çay and the Akçay (with ancient Myra)	90
Dereağzı and the interior	100
Back to the coast (Finike Limyra)	101
Arykanda	105
Rhodiapolis	108
Practical information	111
Western Pamphylia	113
Olympus, the Chimaera and Phaselis	113
West and north of Antalya (Trebenna, Termessus, Evdir Hanı Karain Cave)	120
Antalya	126
Practical information	133
The Pisidia Heritage Trail	135
Ariassos, Döşeme Boğazı and Sia	135
Melli and Pednelissos	137
Selge	138
Perge	141
Sillyon	147
Aspendos	150
Lyrbe and the Manavgat Waterfalls	155
Side	156
Practical information	163
Rough Cilicia	164
Approaching Alanya: Alarahan and Şarapsa Han	166
Alanya	167
Laertes, Syedra and Iotape	174
Selinus	176
Antiochia ad Cragum	177
The Anamur headland	178
Kelenderis and its hinterland	182
Silifke and Ayatekla	184
The Göksu valley	189
Uzuncaburç-Olba Diocaesarea	190
Narlıkuyu and environs	194
Ayaş (Elaioussa)	197
Kumkuyu	201
Practical information	203

Smooth Cilicia	205	**Maps and Plans**	
Mezitli (Soli)	205	Atlas of Mediterranean Turkey	259
Mersin and the Çukurova (with Tarsus and Adana)	207	Map A	260
		Map B	261
Practical information	218	Map C	262
		Map D	263
Inland Cilicia: exploring the valleys	220	Ancient provinces of Turkey	264
The Sirkeli relief and Yılankale	220		
Anavarza	221	City and site plans	
Kozan (ancient Sis)	226	Alanya	172
Feke castle	227	Anavarza	224
Kadirli	227	Andriake	98
Karatepe	228	Anemurium	180
Hierapolis Castabala	230	Antakya	247
Practical information	233	Antalya old town	128
		Aspendos	152
Black Cilicia	235	Caunus	47
Kinet Hüyük and the site of the Battle of Issus	235	The Letoön (Xanthus)	77
		Limyra	103
Around the Bay of İskenderun	236	Olympus	115
İskenderun	239	Patara	82
Practical information	240	Perge	145
		Phaselis	118
Antakya and the Hatay district	241	Pinara	66
Antakya	241	Selge	140
Harbiye: ancient Daphne	249	Side	158–9
Seleucia Pieria and Al Mina	250	Sillyon	148
The stylites of Antioch	252	Termessus	123
Practical information	253	Tlos	64
		Uzuncaburç	192
Index	255	Xanthus	70

INTRODUCTION

The Mediterranean coast of Turkey, stretching from Bodrum to Antakya, measures some 800km as the crow flies but is in reality much longer than that, being full of inlets and bays and culminating in two large gulfs (Antalya and İskenderun). It is backed all along its length by high mountains: to the north the Taurus and Anti-Taurus, rising above 3000m, meet the Amanus Mountains (Nur Dağları) to the east, almost at right angles. Such topography has determined the destiny of this region. Plains are a rarity: the Pamphylian Plain is only 20km deep and further east the Çukurova was until very recent times hardly a plain at all, being more of a malaria-ridden swamp. Agriculture had to accommodate itself to these circumstances and deal with the abundance of water from the melting snows of the high mountains, water that sometimes disappeared underground in the karstic matrix of the rock or simply moved around as rivers changed course, slowly meandering and depositing vast quantities of alluvium. The mountain backdrop made communications difficult until very recently, when modern machinery bulldozed its way through, creating motorways where once there were only narrow tracks. A continuous coastal road was only achieved in the 1970s. A sinking coastline, the prevailing easterly winds, treacherous currents plus alluviation and silting, have put many historic harbours out of use. Only Antalya has made it through century after century. Built on solid travertine and without a river to get in the way, Antalya has kept its deep harbour clear, its star never dimming.

This guide begins in the west, where the Troy to Bodrum volume (*Blue Guide Aegean Turkey*) left off and where ancient Ionia and Caria slowly give way to something different: the Tekke Peninsula, the modern name for Lycia; followed by Pamphylia, which corresponds to the modern Antalya Province. The two Cilicias are next: the rugged Cilicia Trachaea, a repeat of Lycia with mountains meeting the sea, runs roughly from Alanya to Silifke. Beyond that, the relief is in retreat and the flat land (Cilicia Pedias or Smooth Cilicia) has only recently been tamed with the help of modern engineering. It borders the Gulf of İskenderun, a liminal zone between Asia Minor and Syria. Indeed the province of Hatay, where this guide terminates, was historically never part of Asia Minor at all. It is only recent political adjustments that have turned Antioch into a Turkish city (Antakya). There is a map of the ancient provinces of Turkey at the end of the book.

Strategically this is a number one zone, especially in the extreme east where the coast bends south. Beyond lie Mesopotamia to the east, and Syria Palestine and ultimately Egypt to the south, but also the Syrian desert and the Amanus Mountains. That is why the narrow plain around the Gulf of İskenderun has a place in history. Here troops could be deployed, the enemy's advance checked, and access to the Amanus passes controlled. Here Alexander met Darius in 333 BC, here the Crusaders and others followed in the same quest to go east. They came from Anatolia and the Gulf of İskenderun was their bottleneck. Before that the bottlenecks were in the

Taurus Mountains, which normally had to be negotiated at the Cilician Gates (Gülek Boğazı), the crossing that was least disturbed by seasonal mishaps such as snowfalls. At just over 1000m, it was the most reliable pass. Other routes were possible but less secure. The location of the Gates determined the destiny of Tarsus, a very ancient settlement only recently overshadowed and in retreat. Going eastwards meant hugging the foothills. That explains why Adana is where it is, the first crossing point of the Seyhan River as it exits the fringes of the Taurus (a topography now much altered by two dams) and beyond the gap at Misis (Yakapınar) where the Ceyhan could be negotiated without getting one's feet wet. The rest of the plain was a swamp.

Being by the Mediterranean, this stretch of coast could not fail to be affected by what was going on on the other side of the sea, i.e. in Africa—which for a long time simply meant Egypt. Normally Egypt is described as treeless, which is not quite true as there are plenty of palm trees—but palm wood is not very good for shipbuilding. The tall stands of pine and cedar beyond the water in Asia Minor proved irresistible, especially when the closer supply in Syria Palestine was exhausted. That created its own economy, ranging from direct control by the Ptolemies in Hellenistic times to looser arrangements with local chieftains (for whom pirates might perhaps be a more accurate term). Later, as Egypt waned, as Roman rule became a thing of the past and Byzantine power retreated, the Arab expansion of the 7th century left its mark in the urban centres of the Pedias or Smooth Cilicia. Here the conquerors turned Tarsus into an Arab city, the base for their yearly raids into Anatolia and all the way to Byzantium. Normally they would have returned home in the cold winter months, but Tarsus's climate was apparently quite clement.

THE ANCIENT PEOPLES OF MEDITERRANEAN TURKEY

Starting from the west, one seems to be dealing with a homogeneous ethnicity: the **Lycians**. With their language, architecture and political organisation, they imparted a very distinctive character to the land they occupied; it is only going north, where the plateau merges into the highlands leading to the Anatolian Plateau, that other ethnic groups appear, but we know little about them.

Going east, things diversify quite quickly. The **Pamphylians**, who occupy the plain, are not very distinctive and have left little in the way of monuments or inscriptions for investigation. Their name means 'all tribes', which again gives no particular impression. It is tempting to imagine **Phoenician** beginnings for Antalya, but where and by whom might these by found? Up in the mountains to the north were the powerful **Pisidians**, better known than the Pamphylians because of their history and the remains they left behind. On the whole, relations between the two were not friendly. The same pattern, opposing coastline and interior, obtains in Rough Cilicia, which follows immediately to the east. Here the number of coastal settlements is limited as mountains meet the sea abruptly and plains are in short supply, but **Cilicians** do exist here, under constant threat from the warlike **Isaurians** of the interior. 'Smooth Cilicia' further east, the land around today's Adana and Tarsus, may be difficult to define ethnically as it was for a long time a land of passage, a bridge between East and West. Serious permanent settlement (which to begin with was forced settlement) attempting to make the land fully productive, came late, with settlers from far afield, which potentially makes the inhabitants of Smooth Cilicia a very mixed population.

THE ARCHAEOLOGY OF THE MEDITERRANEAN COAST
Archaeology came late to the Mediterranean coast. Freya Stark (*p. 32*) sailed around the Lycian shore, for example, but her interest did not stretch much beyond Lycia. She preferred to go inland and follow 'in Alexander's footsteps'. She was probably looking for the same things Greek that had dazzled her on her Ionian Quest, but here the Greek presence is much more subdued and less certain. Other forces are at work, still not yet fully understood. Antiquarians from the very beginning (there is no Pausanias for this stretch of coast) showed limited interest, though those who did, like Beaufort (*p. 23*) or Lanckoroński (*p. 28*), left an enduring legacy.

Apart from the 'excavations' by Charles Fellows (*p. 26*) in 1840s, which resulted in the shipment to the British Museum of the Nereid Monument, archaeological investigations only began after WWII, at the tail end of the Ionian coast at Xanthus. The relentless tourist development since then has had a twin effect. On the one hand things were concreted over or bulldozed before they could be looked at; on the other hand, as antiquities are now a recognised asset to tourism, research has intensified, with many teams at work in the spring/summer months. In a way, what the building of many dams did for upper Mesopotamia, tourism has done for the Mediterranean coast. Most of the time these are not rescue excavations; nonetheless, time is of the essence as sites need to be put to use as soon as possible. The French know this only too well, as they recently lost their franchise at Xanthus (where they had conducted very valuable work) for being 'too slow'. Sites that are made ready to receive tourists tend to be excavated with a different agenda, one which prioritises, for example, a row of re-erected columns over less graceful features that might enable researchers to better understand the site's development. Moreover, exploration of the surrounding territory may be of limited interest to the permit-granting authorities: as they see it, tourists want to be near the refreshment kiosk and the car park. On the bright side, new science-based technologies such as radar and magnetometry open wonderful new paths of discovery. Limyra, in Lycia, is a shining example.

THE PURPOSE OF THIS TRAVEL GUIDE

The purpose of this guide, like the ones that have appeared before in this series, is both to entice and explain.

The Mediterranean coast of Turkey is a comparatively recent visitor destination, only having developed as such in the later 20th century. Initially it offered little more than a 'place-in-the-sun' sort of tourism, but recently interest has shifted away from the beach and is heading more inland. On the one hand this is because the public authorities have been pushing cultural tourism as a way to diversify the economy and distribute the benefits of the holiday industry more widely, but on the other, visitors do welcome a more varied 'menu' for their stay.

This is an old land, with plenty of history and archaeological remains. But simply seeing the ruins, which are sometimes presented in a much 'improved' state, is frequently not enough to help us understand how they come to be here. A lot of work has been done recently, by historians and archaeologists alike, to weave the extant remains into a coherent narrative, joining the results of extensive surveys with an analysis of historical sources and excavation reports. The explanations and digressions in this guide are intended to anchor a visitor's understanding of what is in front of their eyes in a deep and all-absorbing past, often far more revealing than the immediate event. While the commentaries focus on what can be experienced here and now, this guide will also tell you why things are as they are—at least, it will attempt to do so.

In such a short volume it is not possible to give an exhaustive account of the history of the area, but enough information will be on hand when needed, site by site rather than as an appendix at the end labelled 'background', in small print that no one will ever read. Additionally, there is a rough **Timeline** (*p. 15*). In order to keep the text light and readable, italics have been kept to a minimum and Turkish words in the plural have often been given an ungrammatical 's' ending. Some Turkish words have no direct translation, others are so commonly used *in situ* that it makes more sense to use them in this guide as well. Turkish words and technical terms are explained in the **Glossary** (*p. 17*).

The **Pronunciation Guide** (*p. 21*) is exactly what it says, a guide. Its only purpose is to enable travellers to read place names correctly so that they can ask for directions.

TRAVEL TIPS

The area is comparatively new to tourism, certainly compared to the Aegean Coast, and the authorities are keen to foster an extended season that goes beyond the summer months. If you listen to the local tour operators, visitors should come all year round and indeed, even in the winter, the rugged Lycian hinterland and the Taurus Mountains block out the cold north winds. The Seljuk sultans were right to prefer Alanya to Konya. That said, winter can have its problems; December can be very wet. The mid-seasons are very pleasant. It is true that you might not manage to swim or sunbathe, but you will be able to get around without feeling too hot.

Signposted beaches are generally of a reasonable standard. Venturing along an unmarked lane towards the sea might result in the discovery of a beach but it could also lead you to a lot of unwelcome rubbish.

If you go in the summer (hot and dry), avoid Adana, where the heat is truly oppressive, and try to get inland every now and again for a reprieve. History, culture, monuments and natural features have all been pressed into service to entice holidaymakers away from the beach—and with some success. However, the aims are high and ambitious. As a result, there seems to be a little bit of overcapacity fostered by the belief that tourism is the answer to everything, the solution to any economic downturn.

GETTING AROUND

The region is well served by transport facilities.

BY AIR
Five airports serve the region: from the west Dalaman (*map A, 8*), Antalya (*map B, 8*), Alanya/Gazipaşa (*map C, 7*), Adana (*map D, 6*) and Hatay (*map D, 8*). Dalaman, Antalya and Alanya/Gazipaşa have a range of direct international connections; otherwise you will have to go through Istanbul, which has two international airports, one on the European side and another on the Asian.

If your luggage is in transit and you arrive at your final destination on a domestic flight, it will be taken to the international terminal. Staff will be there to help you by the baggage carousel. At the time of writing Alanya/Gazipaşa airport was still quite new and Adana was due for renovation. It is likely that more direct international routes will be added. Onward connections to the city centres are by coach, tram or taxi.

BY COACH
The coach network is quite dense and you can get to a number of destinations either by bus or *dolmuş*. Competition is fierce, which regulates the prices: generally

speaking there is no real need to shop around for different offers. As a foreigner, you will be quickly spotted and staff in the ticket offices will be keen to help. If you are at the wrong booth, they will bodily take you to a colleague covering the area you want.

When you have a ticket, note that it has a *koltuk numarası*, which is your seat number. It is assigned so that women do not sit next to men who are not relatives. The rule is not as strict as it used to be, but it is still implemented; so do not take a different seat unless you wish to start a minor diplomatic incident. The other thing to note on the ticket is the *peron* number. That is the bay your coach goes from. Some coaches leave from unexpected places, outside the coach station. It is a good idea to look as clueless as possible. The staff in the ticket office will help you to get on the right coach.

Coach stations have waiting rooms, shops and eateries to while the time away; if you do not wish to be encumbered with your luggage, ask the ticket office if you can leave it there. It is a good idea to hang around the ticket office anyway, remind the staff of your presence. When you board, your luggage goes in the hold and you are normally given a token with a number so you can reclaim it. Serious valuables should always stay with you.

Coaches tend to be full. There is a lot of supply but also a lot of demand. People take long coach journeys in their stride from an early age. That may explain why the children are so quiet and well behaved.

Coaches have **no toilets on board**. There will be comfort stops at huge roadside cafés every three hours or so. Stops are normally in the region of 20–30mins. The driver will make an announcement containing the word *dakika* (minute); the number preceding it tells you how long you have. Memorise which coach is yours, there will be easily a dozen or so other buses around, all looking very similar. Head for the toilet queue (which may be longer on the female side as that is where all the children go) and have some small change ready. The cafés have everything from self-service restaurants to shops with fresh fruit. Look out for the stalls selling frothy *ayran*, a healthy yoghurt-based drink and freshly made *poğaças, gözlemes* or *böreks*. The coach will leave at the appointed time or thereabouts: it will not wait. Make sure you are on it. There is no head count and no one will notice your absence.

On board some of the coaches there are free cups of sealed chilled water available as well as the occasional cup of tea, coffee, orange or Cola.

For local destinations you will travel by **dolmuş**. These can also be flagged down on the road and if there is room on board they will take you. Note that in a *dolmuş* seating restrictions do not apply and fares are paid to the driver. Pass your cash forward and the change will be returned to you by the same route. *Dolmuş* services may depart from the *ilce otogar* (local coach station), from the main coach station (*otogar*) or from somewhere else in town. Enquire at your hotel.

BY TRAIN
The Turkish train network is limited—though Adana can boast very early beginnings

since it was included in the Berlin–Baghdad rail link started well over one century ago. This connected it to Konya to the north and Aleppo to the south, with branch lines to Mersin and İskenderun. Adana's railway station, the Adana Garı, is a pure example of Ottoman architecture with pointed arches and wide eaves. The original station (decommissioned), now with a pretty wooden balcony, is at the west end of the old settlement in the Kuruköprü district to the south.

ORGANISED TOURS

Tourism is big business on the Mediterranean coast. It has spawned a successful local package tour industry whereby your stay will be interspersed with organised trips, mainly to the interior but also along the coast to visit sites of natural beauty or historic interest. Now that the internet has more or less killed the tourist information kiosk, information about what is on offer is best found through your **hotel** (have a look on the reception desk, among the ubiquitous leaflets about medical tourism) and at the **travel centres** dotted among the souvenir shops. The means of transport are extremely variable, from charabancs to quad bikes. Before booking something, have a good look at a map and work out the distances to be covered. This is a very long coast and there is a limit to the number of hours you want to spend sitting in a moving vehicle.

BY CAR

Finally, travelling by car is an option that gives you freedom, pleasure and enhances your experience since you are in charge. Your own hire car will get you anywhere (though note that driving in the large towns is more challenging). However, distances are vast and that must be taken into account. The car hire industry is much improved and you can now pick your transport up at the airport. Overall standards are good, though make sure you have checked all possible dents and scratches before you set out.

The **road network** is impressive and at the time of writing (2019) in very good shape. Some roads are toll motorways. Normally your car hire contract includes the **toll payment**. Make sure you drive through the right lane when entering a toll motorway (look for the sticker on the windscreen).

The Turkish police's campaign to reduce accidents appears to have been a success. That said, avoid cities and driving at night if you can.

Petrol is available mainly on the coast and inland on the trunk roads, and at the time of writing was quite cheap. If you travel along secondary roads, make sure you set off with a full tank.

To find ancient sites, you will be relying on **signposts**, normally brown. These have a tendency to be placed a mere few metres before the required turning, which can be too late for a vehicle travelling at speed. In addition, the information then peters out after you leave the main road, which can be a challenge. The road network has improved in recent years, but not the signposting, unfortunately.

Maps are a problem, as the best you will find is 1:700,000 meaning that 1cm corresponds to 7km. The whole of Turkey is made to fit on one single sheet, which is often not nearly detailed enough. There are a couple of regional maps available (Fethiye to Antalya and the South Coast) on a larger scale and they can certainly be useful. It might be worth hiring a satnav before you set off, loaded with the maps covering your destination. This will be helpful in the towns; unfortunately the countryside may not be covered in so much detail.

ON FOOT
The **Lycian Way**, running roughly from Fethiye to Antalya, mainly but not exclusively along the coast, links a number of sites and beauty spots that have attracted a host of devotees. It is well organised, with its own markers and guidebook. A newcomer aimed at the same audience is the **Pisidia Heritage Trail** (*p. 135*) covering a much shorter distance and with a stronger focus on archaeology. Both these trails are designed for independent travellers. Walkers can also join a group for other trails like the St Nicholas Way around Demre, and locally-organised outings.

ACCOMMODATION

In the western part of this area, Lycia, the set-up is similar to what you find on the Aegean Coast, with small family-run *pansiyons*. In the Gulf of Antalya and beyond (bearing in mind that the stretch between Alanya and Silifke offers little accommodation on the coast and inland because the area is comparatively sparsely settled), the provision of accommodation reflects the development of the industry, with a multitude of large, impersonal hotels. They are certainly perfectly functional, providing a place to stay with a beach (sometimes on the other side of a busy trunk road that has to be crossed through an underpass) but they are in between the main centres, to all intents and purposes in the middle of nowhere. It is probably a better option to look for accommodation in the smaller towns such as Narlıkuyu or Kızkalesi/Korikos.

Another line of enquiry worth pursuing is the **Öğretmen Evi** (Teacher's House) network, originally started by Atatürk at the time of his far-reaching educational reforms, enabling teachers to get around the country. At present these are open to the general public. Located in the towns, they range from the very basic (Türkoğlu) to the almost luxurious (Kadirli). Prices are competitive.

A very short list of selected places to stay is given at the end of each chapter in this guide.

Breakfast is normally included, but do check. The offering can very variable and you might prefer to find a **kahvaltı salonu** (a breakfast salon) or an **unlu mamulleri** (a place where they sell flour-based products, a patisserie). Check that they have a tables: it means they will serve coffee and tea; moreover, on this stretch of coast **Turkish coffee** is widely available, a pleasant surprise. Make the most of the opportunity. Turkish coffee can be ordered *sade* (plain), *orta* (medium sweet), or *şekerli* (sweet). In terms of what to eat you can expect *böreks*, baklava, biscuits that come in sweet (but not too sweet) and savoury varieties, and buns (*poğaça*).

EATING & DRINKING

The popular resorts can have an oversupply of fast food joints among the souvenir shops, but for genuine local cuisine you need to eat where the locals eat, including the small makeshift outfits that pop up in the streets after dark; it is a great experience. You get a low table and a low seat and plenty of attention because you are a rare foreigner.

As a rule, avoid places that give prices in Euros. They do so because the Lira is fluctuating so much, but locals will not go there. Going to the genuinely local places will mean some strain on your linguistic abilities but you can always look around and see what is on offer. Either order what other people are having or choose from what is displayed on the counter or in pictures on the wall.

A *çorbacı* specialises in soups and Turkish soups are well worth exploring, from the bulgur-based *ezogelin* to the earthy *mercimek çorbası* (lentil soup). Meat tends to come in small quantities, cut up in a kebap with vegetables and bread. Less meaty dishes or fully vegetarian ones come with rice. You will not find fruit or desserts in a *lokanta*. The former are sold by greengrocers (*manav*, there will be one around the corner) and for the latter you need to go to a patisserie (*see above*). *Lokantas* do not normally serve fish: you will need a restaurant for that, and the best way to enjoy it is plain, just grilled.

To accompany your meal, make sure you ask for sealed water (*kapalı su*) and the same for *ayran* (not out of a jug, but sealed, *kapalı ayran*).

TIMELINE

5000–2500 BC Chalcolithic Period, with metal-working, mainly of native copper

2500 BC Beginning of the Bronze Age, with more complex metallurgies, social relations and trade networks

2000–1800 BC Assyria trades with Anatolia, crossing Cilicia Pedias to reach the Cilician Gates

1700–1200 BC Rise and fall of the Hittites. At the height of their power they reach for the Mediterranean and control the Kingdom of Kizzuwatna, leaving clear evidence in Tarsus, and spill over into Syria

Early Iron Age Faint evidence of Greek presence, mainly in mythical foundation legends

Archaic and Classical periods 900–323 BC

911–627 BC Neo-Assyrian empire. Cilicia Pedias is an Assyrian province. In the Lycian hinterland the burials at Elmalı show contacts with the Phrygian north

mid-6th century BC–332 BC Under Persian control but with a light touch

Hellenistic period 334–167 BC

301 BC Battle of Ipsus, in which the heirs of Alexander the Great fight over the spoils of his empire

333 BC Battle of Issus, in which Alexander the Great is victorious over the Persian King of Kings thus opening his way to the East

334–323 BC Alexander the Great's incredible adventure. He ousts the Persian Achaemenids from the coast and the immediate interior but pays little attention to Rough Cilicia, cut off from the world by poor communications. The map of the coast and of the hinterland is redrawn by his successors, the Seleucids, the Ptolemies and the Antigonids

229–219 BC The first Illyrian war. The Roman Republic has its eyes on the East

Roman period 2nd century BC–AD 337

150 BC Foundation of Antalya (Attalea)

133 BC Setting up of the Roman province of Asia, gradually incorporating the coastal region

First half of the 1st century BC Troubles come from pirate raids, a problem finally solved by Pompey the Great

51 BC Cicero is governor of Cilcia and writes home

13 BC Battle of Actium, sealing the power struggle in Rome (Antony and Cleopatra defeated) and bringing peace to its empire. A

time of prosperity begins: the *Pax Romana*. The only upsets are various earthquakes
260 The Goths: a taste of things to come
337 Death of Constantine. The empire is now Byzantine with its capital in Constantinople

Byzantine era–20th century

7th–9th century Arab incursions from the south by land and by sea. They settle in Cilicia Pedias; Emperor Heraclius moves out

9th–11th century Byzantine reconquest, while nomadic Turks are infiltrating from the east

1071 Battle of Manzikert. The Byzantine Empire loses control of its border and of the Mediterranean coast. The Armenians who had been resettled in Anatolia move towards the south coast

1098 Principality of Antioch. The Crusaders arrive

1176 Myriokephalon, the battle that seals the fate of Byzantine power in Anatolia and on the Mediterranean coast: the Byzantines are defeated by the Seljuks, whose Sultanate of Rum is at the height of its power

1216 Conquest of Antalya. The sultan is now lord of the two seas. He has great plans for a revival of the coast and a new harbour, the future Alanya

1243 After the **Battle of Köşedağ** the sultan becomes a vassal of the Mongols until 1308, when the Mongols take direct control. Trade remains firmly in the hands of the Latins

1375 The last Armenian king is taken prisoner of the **Mamluks**, slave soldiers from Egypt. The coast breaks up into several emirates eventually taken over by the Ottomans

1811–12 Captain Beaufort (*p. 23*) is tasked with exploring and charting the Mediterranean coast. He locates and describes many Classical ruins and his *Karamania* is published soon after his return

1840s Charles Fellows (*p. 26*), inspired by Beaufort, explores Lycia, brings back monuments and opens up to the general public a new artistic world beyond Greece

1863 Victor Langlois (*p. 29*) brings to the attention of the French public the plight of the Armenians in the Ottoman Empire (*Les Arméniens de la Turquie et les massacres du Taurus-Revue des deux Mondes*)

1870s The Ottoman reform movement (Tanzimat) centralises power, forming the basis for the reclaiming of the Çukurova (Cilicia): the heyday of the local emir is at an end

1882 Karol Lanckoroński (*p. 28*) conducts a systematic exploration of the area: the basis of much work done today

1923 The **Turkish Republic** comes into being.

GLOSSARY

Acroterion A decorative element, normally of fired clay, mounted on the roof of an ancient public building

Ağa The landowner in a Turkish village

Analemma The retaining wall on the outer edge of a Greek or Roman theatre

Anta A pillar or a post on either side of the doorway of an ancient temple

Antefix Decorative element of a tiled roof

Bedesten A word of Persian origin and connected to cloth, one of the valuable items of merchandise transported by the caravans. It was securely stored with other valuables in a building (the bedesten) in the middle of town, in the heart of the commercial district, and which also offered hospitality to some merchants

Bekçi The Turkish word for the guardian of an archaeological site

Belediye A Turkish municipality, a Town Hall

Bouleuterion A public building for meeting and assemblies in the Classical Greek world

Börek A baked savoury flaky pastry with a meat or cheese filling, a mainstay of Turkish cuisine. Not to be confused with *su böreği*, which resembles macaroni cheese

Chalcolithic Period The very beginning of the Bronze Age, when copper was worked unalloyed

Caravansaray A large building used for trade and storage in town and in the countryside in the east. A safe place for pilgrims and merchants

Cardo Principal urban axis of a Roman city, running north–south

Castellum aquae A building functioning as a tank from which water from an aqueduct is directed to pipes supplying the town

Cavea Semicircular seating arrangement of a Classical theatre, frequently built against the natural slope of a hill

Cella Inner part of a Classical temple

Cilicia Pedias / Smooth Cilicia / Çukurova The delta area of the Seyhan and Ceyhan rivers, east of Mersin

Cilicia Trachaea / Rough Cilicia The mountainous area east of Alanya

Clerestory Additional level in a building (often above the nave of a church) with windows intended to add light to the central portion

Colonia In the Roman world, an outpost in a newly-subjected land, normally implying an input of citizens from the conquering power

Cothon An artificial, protected inner harbour

Cross-in-Square *See Inscribed cross*

Çukurova *See Cilicia*

Cuneus Wedge-shaped section of the seating in an ancient theatre, divided by access passages

Decumanus Principal urban axis of a Roman city, running east–west

Diadochoi Literally 'the successors', a term used to designate the generals who fought over Alexander the Great's conquests after his death

Diazoma In a Greek theatre, the passage dividing the upper from the lower tiers of seats

Dipteros A temple with a double colonnade or surrounded by a double row of columns

Dipylon A double monumental gateway

Dolmuş A type of shared bus or taxi, which picks up passengers until filled to capacity (the word *dolmuş* means 'stuffed'), a cheap and cheerful form of Turkish public transport, with unofficial stops, not normally used for long-distance travel

Dynast Generic term for a pre-Hellenistic ruler in Lycia

Emir A Turkish petty chief, one level below a sultan

Emporium A term derived from the Greek word for 'merchant'. It referred in antiquity to locations where a variety of goods was on offer. These tended to be places by the sea where ships could unload

Euergetism The practice, mainly in Greek and Roman times, whereby wealthy citizens financed high-status public buildings and facilities

Exedra A semicircular recess in a building

Firman A document conveying the sultan's orders (in an Islamic context)

Fondaco A trading post for storage and lodging

Gerousia A council of elders (in a Greek context)

Gözleme A Turkish pancake, full of good things

Hamam A Turkish bath

Han A caravansaray (*qv*)

Heroön A sepulchral monument dedicated to the memory of a hero

Hüyük A man-made elevation, the result of a long sequence of occupations, usually found in conjunction with mud-brick architecture. Also called a tell or a mound

Hypogeum In Classical architecture, an underground feature

İlce otogar A minor bus station in a Turkish town, used for local travel using a minibus (*see Dolmuş*) rather than a long-distance coach

In antis Term used to describe a Classical temple with a recessed porch framed by an extension of the side walls, between which stand the columns

Inscribed cross (also Cross-in-square) A type of church plan that incorporates the shape of an equal-armed cross into its structure

Insula The basic unit of Classical town planning, a city block

İwan A recess closed on three sides in the colonnaded courtyard of a large Islamic public building

Kastron A Byzantine stronghold

Kışla *See Yayla*

Kouros A sculpture of a Greek youth of the Archaic period (700–480 BC), in a standardised full-frontal pose

Külliye A building complex around a mosque and managed as a single institution; it may include a caravansaray (*qv*), a mausoleum, a school, a hospital and baths

Lokanta Turkish word for restaurant

Luwian An extinct Indo-European language of Anatolia, written either in cuneiform or hieroglyphs and spoken from the 2nd/1st millennia to c. 600 BC by a people about whom little is known

Macellum An indoor retail market in antiquity

Manar A tall slim tower. The word itself is Arabic and means 'guiding light', suggesting that it may have referred to a lighthouse

Mansio In the Roman world, a lodging

place or rest house for travellers on official business

Martyrium A church centered on a central element (e.g. the tomb of a martyr), in shape either round, octagonal or cruciform

Megaron The large room of a well-appointed ancient Greek dwelling, although the term is also used in non-Greek contexts

Meze An appetiser

Metope A square ornamental relief, an element of the frieze of a temple of the Doric order

Merlon The raised section of a crenellation in a battlemented wall

Mimber The pulpit in a mosque

Mihrab Niche in the wall of a mosque, indicating the direction of Mecca

Muqarnas A form of three-dimensional decorative vaulting, typical of Islamic architecture and found from Persia to Spain. It is also called honeycombed or stalactite vaulting. It is used as a means of connecting walls with domed or semi-domed ceilings. It can be either structural and made of stone or simply decorative and made of stucco

Neokorate A *neokoros* was originally the warden of a temple but around the 1st century AD the title began to be attributed to whole communities as guardians of a local cult. Soon it became an honour bestowed on cities devoted to the Roman imperial cult, mainly in Asia, a source of immense prestige and expense

Nymphaeum In the Classical world, a natural feature or monument (e.g. an elaborate fountain) sacred to the nymphs and associated with water

Oculus In Latin 'eye'. A circular opening in a dome or roof allowing light (and rain) to enter

Odeion A small, roofed Classical theatre, used for meetings and artistic gatherings

Opus caementicium Durable Roman building aggregate incorporating volcanic ash; the same as Roman concrete

Opus sectile A decorative wall or floor covering made of thin pieces of different types of coloured stone cut into shapes and laid in patterns

Orthostat A worked stone with a rectangular or square section intended to stand upright either as an architectural element, on its own as a monument, or as part of a monument, e.g. a stone circle

Otogar In Turkish, the main coach station of a town (from the French *autogare*)

Palaestra In the Roman world, an exercise yard, often attached to a baths complex

Pansiyon (with various spellings) A small Turkish hotel or guest house

Paradeisos The Greek name for Persian parks and gardens; denoting something grand and prestigious bordering on the otherwordly, hence our 'paradise'

Paşa A high-ranking official in the Ottoman administration and army

Pediment A low-pitched gable surmounting a colonnade or door or window aperture

Peripteros A temple completely surrounded by a colonnade

Peristyle Colonnaded inner courtyard of an ancient house, open to the sky

Pithoi Very large vessels used for storage (singular = pithos)

Portulan A nedieval nautical chart

Pronaos The vestibule at the front of a Classical temple

Prostyle A temple with row of columns

stretching right across the front

Prytaneion The heart and hearth of an ancient Greek city, where the sacred fire, symbol of its vitality, was kept, together with the official weights and measures

Propylon A gateway

Qibla wall The wall in a mosque in which the mihrab (*qv*) is situated, indicating the direction of Mecca

Reconquest In the context of this book, the ill-fated attempt of the Byzantines to seize back control of their empire from the Arabs between the 9th and 11th centuries

Sebasteion A sanctuary of the Roman imperial cult

Scena A decorative backdrop to the stage in a Classical theatre

Sima Part of the roof in a Classical temple which performs the role of a gutter

Società dei Dilettanti A London high-society club whose members had been on the Grand Tour and wished to promote things Classical

Sospensura The arrangement of brick supports beneath the floor of a room intended to be heated in a house or a bath

Spolia Elements of Classical monuments that have been reused as building material or ornaments from Late Antiquity onwards

Stoa In Classical architecture, a covered portico for public use

Stylobate The continuous base on which a row of columns stands

Sympolity A arrangement between city-states whereby they shared citizenship and political institutions

Synthronon Semicircular bench-like structure behind the altar in early churches, with a throne for the bishop and seating for the clergy

Temenos A defined precinct marked off for religious use

Templon A physical separation in a Byzantine church between the nave and the altar area

Tetraconch Of a building, having four apses

Tetrastyle Of a building, having four pillars

Thermae A Roman public bath

Topos A traditional theme in literature

Tholos A small circular building in Classical architecture

Torus A decorative swelling in an architectural element

Triconch A building with three apses

Tripylon A monumental gateway with three openings

Triskele A symbol with a widespread presence and diffuse meaning. The triskele pattern fits into a circle and consists of three spiralling, curving or angled elements joining at the centre and dividing the space in three equal portions

Türkmen A controversial term used here to indicate the nomads who infiltrated Asia Minor from the 10th century, also known as the Yürüks ('those who walk'). According to some, the term should only be used to apply to the descendants of specified Turkish tribes from Central Asia who moved west and remained faithful to their original nomadic lifestyle. They are the 'real Turks' of pure blood. More restrictively, it may be important that they are also Muslims

Velarium The awning stretching over the seating area of a Roman theatre

Yayla/Kışla Turkish terms denoting summer and winter pastures

Yürüks *See Türkmen*

PRONUNCIATION GUIDE

Turkish was originally written in the Arabic script. In 1928 Atatürk introduced a modified Latin alphabet of 29 letters, the modification designed to take into account the specific requirements of the Turkish language. Turkish is phonetic, unlike English; so it is easy to read and pronounce it—especially useful if you need to ask for directions. All letters are sounded; there are no diphthongs. The letters are pronounced as follows:

A a   as in <u>a</u>damant
E e   as in <u>e</u>lephant
İ i   as in <u>I</u>taly
I ı   the 'schwa' sound, like the 'a' in Col<u>a</u>
J j   used in loan words ('projesi') and pronounced like <u>J</u>acques
O o   as in p<u>o</u>nd
Ö ö   as in bl<u>ur</u>
U u   as in l<u>u</u>minous
Ü ü   as in Z<u>ü</u>rich
Ç ç   a soft 'ch', as in <u>ch</u>arming
C c   a soft G, as in <u>G</u>eneva
G g   a hard G, as in <u>G</u>aribaldi
Ğ ğ   a consonant that is not voiced. If it is between two vowels, it separates them and will lengthen the first one. At the end of a word (*dağ*) it is not pronounced
Ş ş   like the 'sh' in di<u>sh</u>
Y y   as in <u>y</u>eti

EARLY TRAVELLERS TO MEDITERRANEAN TURKEY

Ibn Battuta (1304–68/9)

Born in Morocco, Ibn Battuta belongs to the so-called Islamic middle period. The brilliance of the Abassid Caliphate was a thing of the past but Islam was not in decline: it was expanding west with the Turks as well as east to India and Southeast Asia; the Mongols, firmly in control of Central Asia, had recently converted. It was precisely because of the relative calm brought about by the Pax Mongolica that Ibn Battuta was able to roam the world, from China to Spain and down to Ceylon and the Maldives, according to his account. Seeking knowledge has always been an integral part of Islam: knowledge of the Umma, the Islamic community, both in the Abode of Peace and Salvation (Dar al Islam) and of the world outside it. The pilgrimage to Mecca was a way to seek spiritual knowledge. The roaming mystics, the dervishes and the sufis, so very present in the history of the time, also dealt in spiritual knowledge while stirring up trouble on the way. Ibn Battuta was no mystic. He was led by an insatiable curiosity but at the same time liked his comforts. His account shows clearly that he did very well by the Muslim philosophy that extends hospitality, friendship and security to fellow believers. In total he was on the road for 28 years, beginning in 1326 with the Haj, one of three.

When he finally settled back home he was commissioned by the sultan of Morocco to write an account of his travels. This he did with the help of a local literary scholar. He had no notes and had to rely on his memory and other sources, i.e. travel accounts by other people. A number of inconsistencies have been noted by modern scholarship, casting doubt on the veracity of some of his adventures. Plagiarism has been mentioned.

His travel account, *A Gift to Those Who Contemplate the Wonders of Cities and the Marvels of Travelling*, came only comparatively recently to the attention of Western scholars. The French found the manuscript when they conquered Algeria in 1830, translated and published it in the mid-19th century. It was another 100 years before and English translation appeared. Ibn Battuta's greatest gift to all of us is his outlook on the world in which he lived, a world in which, for instance, upper-class women could appear unveiled in public in Anatolia, where a *jullab* (a syrupy concoction) turns out to be the ancestor of the julep and where a large chunk of Eurasia was one single nation by virtue of a shared religion. The poor, the downtrodden, the powerless, the little people get very short shrift in his accounts; and so do his wives (ten of them; apparently he was a serial monogamist), his innumerable concubines and his five children.

George Bean (1903–77)

The son of a self-taught botanist who rose to become curator of Kew Gardens, George Bean trained as a Classicist specialising in ancient Greek. As a young man he taught Classics, using his summer holidays to organise school trips to the Aegean. His breakthrough came during WWII, when he was posted by the government, through the British Council, to teach English at İzmir. Whether this was a far-reaching diplomatic move intended to influence Turkey out of her neutrality, or a coincidence remains to be seen. What was important was that Bean found his spiritual home, soon moving to Istanbul where he was instrumental in setting up the Department of Archaeology at the University. There he remained, as a 'temporary teacher' of Classics, for 24 years: as a foreigner he could not hold a senior position or be given tenure.

Bean is best known for his field work in western Anatolia. Many people (antiquaries, treasure hunters, inquisitive travellers and the like) had been exploring the western and southern coast of Asia Minor through the centuries. Bean brought a new twist to the process: he could speak Turkish. That is no mean feat as Turkish is a complex non-Indo-European language. But there is an upside: if you take the trouble to learn it, you will soon make friends in Turkey. And so it was with George Bean. He would arrive in a village and wait upon the *muhtar* (the village headman), talking about the forthcoming crop or other local preoccupations, engaging, showing empathy, and mentioning antiquities only *en passant*. Eventually, having won the muhtar's confidence, he would be taken to see the local treasures (inscriptions, worked stones, deserted ancient settlements). As an epigraphist Bean took a particular interest in inscriptions, leaving the stones where they were and taking home squeezes. These are reverse copies of an inscribed text made by applying wet filter paper and pushing it in with an appropriate tool. When dry, the paper can be removed and the text can then be read and re-read with different raking lights. However, a squeeze is a difficult thing to take home in a backpack. Things must have become easier when Bean acquired a car in the 1960s. In any case, travelling long distances in those days must have been a challenge.

Bean was just one step ahead of the tourist boom that has brought major changes to the Turkish coast. However, he was always mindful of the possibility of foreign visitors. He wrote a number of tourist guides covering the Aegean and a large part of the Mediterranean shore. Both approachable and authoritative, these still make interesting reading. Things may have changed here but George Bean's observations still hold.

Francis Beaufort (1774–1857)

Irish by birth and of Huguenot ancestry, Francis Beaufort's forefathers had repaired to tolerant Britain in the 16th century after wars of religion had torn France apart. His father was a clergyman with a taste for surveying. He produced a detailed map of Ireland and dedicated it to George III, 'the patron and promoter of every useful science'. Surveying ran in the family. Joining the Navy at barely 14 years of age, Beaufort made an illustrious career, retiring in 1846 with the rank of Rear Admiral. His great breakthrough came in 1811, when he was entrusted with charting and surveying the Mediterranean coast of what was then the Ottoman Empire. The decision came about in a circuitous way. The alliance between Britain and Russia was viewed as hostile by the Ottoman Porte. When Napoleon met the Czar on the famous barge at Tilsit in 1807, he persuaded him to call the alliance off. This presented Britain with an opportunity for a rapprochement with the Ottomans by way of offering naval expertise. The survey of the Mediterranean coast and its naval resources probably suited the Turks and was certainly advantageous to Britain, which at the time was a surging naval power with an expanding empire. Moreover, knowledge of that area could forestall any intrusion by the French, who may still have had their eyes on Egypt.

The survey was to be conducted on the *Frederikstein*, a frigate with 32 guns ready to salute any *ağa* with a flattering number of shots. There was a firman from the Porte, but the remit of the Sultan did not reach all the nooks and crannies of the Empire, as will be apparent below. Beyond mapping the coastline, the survey was to include an observation of the currents, winds, cliffs, harbours, geology, natural history and local resources. Beaufort trained his crew carefully and worked them hard. He led by example and got what he wanted. The practicality of the work was quite complex, requiring the setting up of a base line one metre off the ground (it took the form of a 100-yard steel chain marked by flags and poles) and then proceeding by triangulation. The result is the beautiful map in Beaufort's *Karamania* (as the area was then called); the coastline is extremely detailed and the unexplored hinterland of the Taurus Mountains is marked as 'Snowy peaks in June'. Antiquities came as a sideline, mainly through the interest of William Hamilton, a keen antiquarian. Perhaps he supplied the handwritten translation of the relevant section of Pliny's *Natural History* (14,5), which was in Beaufort's luggage when he set off in 1811. The survey was conducted over two years, beginning roughly at Telmessus (now Fethiye) and ending almost tragically at Ayas in the Gulf of İskenderun. As soon as the expedition reached Patara, the crew was overwhelmed by the profusion of ruined monuments and buildings. Apparently crew and captain spent the entire day there and did not even notice that they had neither food nor water. It all came to an abrupt end in Ayas, when the captain was shot at by armed locals led by a dervish intent on hounding the infidel. He suffered a bad wound but it eventually healed and Beaufort was back on the waves as hydrographer to the Navy, a prestigious position which he held for 26 years. He roamed the seas, conducting well over 100 surveys from China to South America and drawing 1,437 charts. He died in 1857. As well as for his survey work, he is remembered for his system of measuring wind strength. So when we hear 'Gale force 10!' we know exactly what it means. This is the Beaufort Scale.

Gertrude Bell (1868–1926)

Among other distinctions, Gertrude Bell has an insect named after her: *Belliturgula najdica*, a stinging bee of the Arab central plateau where flowers are scarce. It is a creature about which very little is known. And indeed, the same might be said of Gertrude Bell: an intriguing combination of distinguished birth, moneyed background, excellent education and exceptional circumstances. In a way, the world will not soon see her like again.

Born into a well-to-do family (her father a local worthy educated in Edinburgh, the Sorbonne and in Germany; her grandfather an MP and an industrialist starting a tradition of enlightened capitalism—her mother died in childbirth), the young Gertrude acquired a stepmother, Florence Bell, a writer who had been born and brought up in France where her father was physician to the British Embassy. This cosmopolitan and wealthy background led to what was a unique education for the time, culminating in a Modern History degree from Oxford when Gertrude was 19.

Records show that her first foray to the east was in 1892, in the company of an uncle, Sir Frank Lascelles, British Ambassador to Tehran. The in-between times were mostly occupied with some energetic mountaineering in the Alps: the Gertrudspitze in the Bernese Oberland, named after her, is a reminder of her accomplishments. But the East proved to be Bell's destiny: she would travel there as an explorer fluent in all the required languages: French, Ottoman Turkish, Persian and Arabic, acquiring a deeply rooted fundamental knowledge. As a foreigner she was on a par with the local authorities; as a woman she could access hidden, inner worlds.

Bell's encounters on the ground led her to archaeology, though she thought of herself more as an antiquarian. She did not have much training: just a short season with David Hogarth in Greece. Her work remains however invaluable. There are the numerous pictures, plans and notes (now at Newcastle University) showing the state of monuments then, as well as publications such as the *Thousand and One Churches*, (with William Ramsay), now regarded as a classic text on Byzantine architecture, and her work on the Tur Abdin, a Christian enclave in southern Turkey.

With WWI everything changed. Bell's knowledge of the Middle East was extensively used by British intelligence to help them navigate their way around this part of the world, where the Ottoman Empire was dissolving and the British intended to gain a foothold and eventually a deciding influence. This resulted in the creation of the Kingdom of Iraq under Faisal I. In British political circles it was thought that a friendly king would be cheaper than administering a colony. But a country had to be invented. At the time there were Arabs belonging to different tribes and with different religious affiliations. Bell believed that the evidence of a glorious past, then increasingly visible in Mesopotamian archaeology, could be used as a glue to create a sense of identity. The National Museum of Iraq in Baghdad was her creation. It embodied her belief that archaeological finds should remain close to where they had been unearthed. She complemented that achievement with the updating of the local antiquities law, ensuring a fair share for local museums.

Evliya Çelebi (1611–82)

Evliya Çelebi was a typical product of his time, when the Ottoman Empire, still expanding, seemed to be on the ascendant. He died a year before the failed Siege of Vienna, which is now seen as the beginning of the Ottomans' decline. Evliya Çelebi took great pride in being an Ottoman and set out to travel the length and breath of the Empire and describe what he saw for the benefit of less adventurous compatriots. This, in a nutshell, is what his *Seyahatname* (*Book of Travel*) is, all ten volumes of it. It is a grandiose work not yet critically published in full.

Evliya was a traveller by nature with the wanderlust of a dervish; he actually presents himself as a dervish but does not appear to have been attached to any particular lodge. He certainly did not subscribe to other aspects of dervish philosophy such as poverty and the reliance on alms. He was well aware that his chosen lifestyle required being attached to a wealthy patron and kept a very close eye on the state of his own finances. Some of his time was spent looking for patronage. He was assisted in his quest by having an education (from the palace school in Topkapı), by mastering the 'arts of the tongue' (storytelling, Koran reciting and singing), by having some religious training (meaning that he could double up as an iman or a muezzin) and by being the perfect boon companion of high officials and even of the sultan himself; he was the heart of the party. Evliya never took up an official post in the Ottoman hierarchy. It could be that his education was not complete. He did not graduate with the rank of *paşa* or *ağa*, which would have opened the door to high positions, and he was not a military man. He was a 'gentleman', which is the meaning of Çelebi. The name Evliya may have been a homage to his singing master.

His travels took him everywhere including, according to him, far-flung locations like Holland, the Sudan, the Asian steppes and Abyssinia, well beyond the borders of the Empire. There are some doubts about this and also about his accounts of travels closer to home (like the Siege of Candia), where the chronology is just not right. Eventually he retired to Cairo, where he spent his last years writing everything up. A lot of his content bears the echo of his storytelling. It is anecdotal, intended to inform but mainly to entertain, hence the irony, the jokes, the satire. Before the *Seyahatname* was written up there must have been a lot of social story-telling. There he honed his skills: he knew how to capture his audience's attention and did not shy away from summoning the miraculous and the portentous to his aid. His choice of monuments to describe is strictly Ottoman, though he does make an exception for bridges and city walls. There are a lot of mosques and in some of them, for example at Adana in Smooth Cilicia, his signature graffito has been found.

Charles Fellows (1799–1860)

Born into a wealthy family in Nottingham, Charles Fellows exhibited from a very early age those qualities that were to make him such a successful explorer: keen powers of observation, artistic talent and an inquisitive mind. When he was barely 14 he set out to Newstead Abbey to draw the ruins. One of his sketches was later published on the title page of a Life of Byron. Travelling—at first around Britain and later on the continent—was his vocation from very early times. He pioneered a route up Mont Blanc in 1827. After his mother died in 1832, the scope of his travels widened and he spent more and more time in Italy, Greece and the Levant. In 1838 he was in Smyrna and set about exploring the southwest corner of Asia Minor, which was cut off from major routes and at the time was just a blank on maps. This was the first of four major exploration trips that brought to light evidence of an entirely new civilisation. The Lycians had found their bard.

Fellows's extensive publications aroused much interest in official circles and the government intervened with a view to augmenting the collections of the British Museum. The enterprise proved quite taxing. The paperwork was intractable, the manoeuvring of large stones in Xanthus and down its unruly river was not simple, and the ship's captain proved quite uncooperative. Fellows was on the spot throughout, making things happen, drawing plans and maps and funding the whole enterprise.

Eventually the Lycian stones were reassembled in London in a purpose-built wing of the museum. London fell in love with Lycia and the dancing Nereids with their billowing garments. Lycia was the all the rage for a while: people flocked to the exhibition of the new acquisitions and also chose to be buried in Lycian-style tombs with tall ogival lids. Fellows, who had not been consulted, was not happy with the display. The room was too small from the start, the exhibits were set out artistically 'to make them look as Greek as possible', Greece being at the time he accepted canon of aesthetics for ancient works of art. In 1878 the Lycian Room was closed and the material dispersed around the museum. The Nereids are now displayed close to the Parthenon marbles, suggesting an evolutionary path or at least connections, while for Charles Fellows the Lycians and their art stood proudly on their own, testaments to a new and different way of doing things.

John Kinneir (1782–1830)

John MacDonald Kinneir was the illegitimate son of a Scottish laird. We have no idea what sort of education he had, only that at the end of it he entered the army. Posted to Madras, he was later in Persia tasked with travelling and finding out more about the Kurds. In 1824 he joined the East India Company as an envoy and died in Tabriz in 1830.

In 1813 and 1814 Kinneir conducted two separate trips to Asia Minor. As he says himself in the account which he published upon his return, he 'travelled to amuse himself'; however it is legitimate to think that beyond his natural curiosity, he was on an official mission to find out about the people and places of this little-known part of the world. He avoids the Aegean and large parts of the Mediterranean coasts, comparatively better known, and sticks to the interior as far east as Mosul, north to the Black Sea coast and south to Syria.

Kinneir travelled on horseback in a small group: a friend, a Tatar, an Italian servant, possibly a guide and sometimes an escort. As he went he took notice mainly of the land, the agriculture, the temperature and coordinates, styles of housing, including the Armenian houses below ground level with sheep and goats grazing on the roof. Antiquities came as an afterthought, though he dutifully copied inscriptions and published them. He had a grounding in ancient history and knew his Strabo, so he puts label on places, sometimes correctly and sometimes not.

Kinneir was probably fluent in Turkish, which may in those days have been closer to Persian (the Republic was to purge it of foreign influences). That would account for his frequent and unavoidable interaction with the locals. He had to find horses, which was not always easy, as well as adequate accommodation, and that was not simple either. He took notice of and described in some detail antiquities still standing such as the walls of Konya, Giresun, Erzurum and Antioch (which at the time he reckoned occupied one sixth of its wall circuit); they are all now lost and his testimony is important. A lot of ancient remains he dismisses as 'semi-buried shafts, capitals and pillars'. He is at his best in his dealings with the local people, making his account more ethnographic than archaeological; there is plenty of local colour, plenty of miserable hamlets, local feuds and bugs. But there are also bright spots, such as when south of Trabzon on the way to Bayburt, his companion Chavasse inoculated a great number of local children against the smallpox; how did he gain their confidence? To posterity he has left a description of the luxurious mansion of Chapwanoğlus, somewhere southwest of Amasya (*see Blue Guide Turkey: The Black Sea Coast*) in a village that cannot now be located. At the time the head of the family was the most powerful *ayan* in Asia Minor, with immense estates. Two years after hosting Kenneir's party the *ayan* was dead and the sultan confiscated everything; the family was decimated. The memory of the *ayan* only lives on in Kinneir's *Journey through Asia Minor, Armenia and Koordistan*.

Léon de Laborde (1807–69)

Léon de Laborde came of illustrious lineage with roots in Spain and much marked by events of the French Revolution. His grandfather, a banker to Louis XV, lost his head at the time of the Reign of Terror in 1792–3 and his father emigrated, settling in Austria, where he joined the army. With the advent of Napoleon, Laborde's father was back in France serving the French emperor and maintaining connections with the German-speaking world. He was, among other things, instrumental in arranging the marriage of Napoleon to Marie-Louise, the daughter of the Austrian emperor. Young Léon de Laborde grew up in an international milieu, studying Classics at the university of Göttingen. When he was barely 19, his ageing father, by this time retired from politics, decided to embark on a 'grand tour' of the Orient in the footsteps of pilgrims and crusaders. The trip, from 1826 to 1828, took four of them plus servants and porters (the father was not well enough to ride and used a litter requiring two to four bearers) across southern Europe, Asia Minor from İznik to Aphrodisias and eventually through Syria to Egypt. The ensuing publication (*Voyages en Asie Mineure*) is particularly notable for the abundance of fine drawings by the young Laborde himself: drawings of ruins and other features, including a spooky view of the underground course of the river Lycus, as well as of contemporary scenes and settings. The text, which Texier criticised for 'lacking structure', is what you might expect from a very young man with no previous experience. There are, however, interesting observations here and there, such as what he says about Konya and its wall circuit: 'a dwarf in a giant's bed'. In 1830 Laborde was back on the road, this time bound for Petra and its stunning façades. This made him a household name. Laborde had a subsequent career as a diplomat in Rome, as an administrator at the Louvre Museum and as the acclaimed author of a number of wide-ranging art history publications.

Karol Lanckoroński (1848–1933)

Karol Lanckoroński was an aristocrat of Polish descent with strong ties to Vienna, where he was born, and in particular with the court of the Austro-Hungarian Empire, where his father and uncle held important positions.

He received a cosmopolitan education in elite schools, which according to some made him unapproachable, too conscious of his rank and of his intellectual superiority. Nevertheless, something good must have been seeded there. A collector and an art enthusiast with a particular interest in the Italian Primitives, he set out in 1882 (after the obligatory Grand Tour) on a systematic exploration of of Asia Minor, concentrating on the south coast and its hinterland and taking with him an interdisciplinary team of artists, photographers, ethnographers, anthropologists and philologists. His system of 'explore and describe' was meticulous and all-encompassing, approached with great humility and professionalism and a true sense of purpose. Antiquities were drawn as well as 19th-century town houses in Antalya. Excavating was not part of his brief, only recording. Though he was an avid collector, he took nothing home. Members of his team were in charge of acquisition, which is how the Heroön from Trysa ended up in the Kunsthistorisches Museum in Vienna. He financed all the expeditions himself and was therefore not beholden to any museum or subsidising authority. The lavish and prompt publication of his finds, meticulous and precise and again at his own expense, has been a great gift to today's archaeologists, drawing their attention to sites (most prominently Sagalassos; *see Blue Guide Central Anatolia*) and showing the deterioration in their state of preservation which in some instances has brought them near to total extinction (this is the case with the double walls of Antalya, which are now known mainly from Lanckoroński's drawings and plans). Many write-ups of modern excavations and surveys cite Karol Lanckoroński in their bibliographies.

Lanckoroński's last years were difficult. The dismemberment of Austria-Hungary after WWI destroyed his world. He lived his last years in the seclusion of the Lanckoroński Palace, which he had built in Vienna's Landstrasse district to house the collection of the last king of Poland, Stanislas Poniatowski, which had been bequeathed to his grandfather. The collection has been back in Poland since 1994. Lanckoroński's palace, damaged in WWII, was torn down in the 1960s.

Victor Langlois (1829–69)

A Frenchmen from Dieppe, Victor Langlois had an extensive education: first at the École des Chartes (philology and palaeography), then in Oriental languages. At the age of 22 he hit upon the idea of dedicating his newly completed work on Oriental numismatics to the French head of state, the future Napoleon III, who was then at the tail end of his mandate as president of the French Republic. Langlois was granted an audience—much to his surprise—during the course of which he was asked whether he had been to Asia for his research. Within eight days the young man received an official appointment to explore Little Armenia, today's Cilicia. Obviously the President had in mind the impressive achievements of his uncle Napoleon I, who during his Egyptian campaign had established the basis of Egyptology and of the decipherment of hieroglyphics.

Langlois' explorations were extensive, reaching well into the interior and sweeping across the Çukurova, quite a wild area at the time. He had good knowledge of the historical sources, from the ancient writers to more modern authors such as the 16th-century Venetian ambassador Marcantonio Barbaro and his contemporary Beaufort (*see above*). The account of his exploration was soon published: it reads more like the adventure holiday of a twenty-something than a learned tome. There are plenty of vignettes featuring Türkmen tents, hospitable *ağas*, devious Kurds and snake charmers. His observations on the antiquities are of use, mainly adding to our knowledge of the remains at the time. Otherwise, drawings are poor and scarce; maps and plans sorely lacking. The main value of the publication lies in the ethnographic details about the Cilicia of roughly 200 years ago, a world that has practically disappeared. Langlois devoted the rest of his life to Armenia (in 1863 publishing a rare account of early massacres in the Taurus region) and the Armenian language. He allowed archaeology to fall by the wayside—which is just as well since his methods were quite unorthodox. His own description of his exploration of the Donuktaş in Tarsus (*p. 212*) included digging a 2m hole in the structure, filling it with 3–5kg of gunpowder and setting fire to it, 'with the necessary precautions'. The locals thought the end of the world had come, or at least an earthquake. The monument yielded no secrets about its history or purpose.

Roberto Paribeni (1876–1956)

Trained as an ancient historian, Roberto Paribeni did his best work as an archaeologist before WWI. He had had an excellent introduction to the methodology, working with Federico Halbherr in Crete in 1901 and later going on to work in Egypt and Eritrea. He was in Antalya in 1913, when the walls were being pulled down, and made some useful observations which he promptly published. He was there as a member of a mission intended to foster Italian involvement in the archaeology of Asia Minor; unfortunately the Italian government was never able to obtain an excavation permit from the Porte. After the War and with advent of Fascism, Paribeni appears to have given up field archaeology to become an administrator, with a distinct interest in the Roman Imperial past; this chimed very well with the new regime. He was instrumental in organising excavations intended to boost the image of Italy as an aspiring imperial power with a clear, definite presence in the Mediterranean. At home, he did much to raise the standing of the Museo Nazionale, which he directed. He was also involved in the grand project willed by Mussolini to open up the Via dei Fori Imperiali. This was a prestige excavation intended to showcase imperial Rome. It employed 1,500 workers, caused the relocation of 746 families, the destruction of a number of houses and of three ancient churches. It has left no paper trail. There are numerous photos and watercolours, nothing else. Late antique and medieval Rome were wiped off the map. In the mid-1930s Paribeni, now a member of numerous prestigious academies, moved from committee life to teaching. The postwar years were difficult.

Edward Pococke (1604–91)

Edward Pococke was a man of the cloth and an Oxford academic with a bent for Oriental languages. His interest in this new field was kindled by the arrival at Oxford of Mathias Pasor, a refugee academic who had left Heidelberg when the city was sacked in 1622 during the Thirty Years War. Arabic had become particularly important for commercial and political reasons as the East was opening up. Also, as a clergyman, Pococke saw the missionary potential.

To improve his Arabic, Pococke took up the chaplaincy of the newly-founded

Company of the Levant. He was in Aleppo for three years. Upon his return in 1634 he was the first incumbent of the Laudian Chair of Arabic at Oxford. But the East beckoned again, this time for manuscripts. There was the possibility of learning more about the Arabs' achievements in the sciences (medicine, astronomy and mathematics) as well as the distant hope that some lost gem of the Classics, such as the missing books of Livy's *History of Rome*, might turn up, either the originals or at least a copy. Pococke remained in Istanbul from 1637 to 1641.

On his return to England, his career suffered as a result of the Civil War. For a while he worked as a parish priest, then returned to academia, first as a professor of Hebrew (nominated by Charles I, then a prisoner on the Isle of Wight) and then of Arabic.

A linguist first and foremost, Pococke's output was mainly in the form of translations into and from Arabic and other Semitic languages. He also drew attention to Arab historical writing, which Gibbon later incorporated into his *History of the Decline and Fall of the Roman Empire*. On the side Pococke translated topical texts, such as the one on coffee, 'The nature of the drink Kauhi or Coffee', in 1659. The beverage was quite a novelty at the time: the first coffee house in Europe had only opened a few years previously. Pococke's text presents it as a medicine good for smallpox, measles and 'bloudy' pimples. It should not be drunk with milk because of the risk of contracting leprosy.

Pococke spent many years in the Levant, where he must have travelled around out of curiosity or at least in the pursuit of manuscripts. He certainly took notice of some of the monuments he came across but his approach is not systematic in that way that an antiquarian's would be. He was primarily a linguist. It remains to be discovered where his observations were culled from, perhaps from his letters which are, together with many Arab manuscripts he secured for Oxford, at the Bodleian Library.

T.A.B. Spratt (1811–88)

Thomas Abel Brimage Spratt joined the navy at the age of 16. The calling ran in the family: his father had distinguished himself at Trafalgar, when he swam, 'cutlass in his teeth', boarded the French *Aigle* and got into a fight, only to be rescued by the full boarding party. He was badly injured and retired to Teignmouth, where Thomas Abel was born.

Spratt's main contribution to archaeology was in the realm of surveying, providing maps for future work. He worked as a surveyor in the Mediterranean for 38 years, starting in 1832 and covering an area from Malta to Lycia and beyond. In the process he became interested in antiquities and on occasion ventured inland. The *Beacon*, the ship that took him and his party to Lycia in 1842, then left with Charles Fellows and the Nereid Monument, bound for Britain. Spratt ventured on to the less-known northern part (coming across a party sent by the King of Prussia on the same errand) and then east as far as Rhodiapolis, visiting Termessus, Aspendos, Selge and Perge, and more along the way. The accounts of his explorations, written in diary form, are quite wide-ranging and include botany, geology, natural history, inscriptions, ancient coins, local costumes and anything else that caught his attention.

In Crete his geological observations were instrumental in helping us understand long-drawn-out processes affecting settlement. He correctly interpreted ancient wave notches as evidence that the land had risen in the west, helping to make sense of the ancient harbour of Falasarna, now above sea level and 100m inland.

His maps ('Spratt's Maps') remain his glory: and there he had a couple of felicitous hunches. He marked the site of New Ilium as the location of Troy, dispensing with the hot water springs mentioned by Homer. He was right, as Schliemann (who used his map) was to prove. He also directed Charles Newton to the correct spot for the Mausoleum of Halicarnassus. Spratt had been intrigued by some stray worked stones and had marked them on his map as the site of the Mausoleum.

Spratt's sons died in infancy in Malta and in Crete in 1852, suggesting that at the time he was traveling *en famille*.

Freya Stark (1893–1993)

Freya Stark was born in Paris of mixed parentage: an English father and an Italian-born mother with a German and Polish background. She grew up in Italy in the middle-sized town of Asolo in the Veneto, at the foot of the Alps. Her childhood was marked by poor health and an accident that permanently damaged her scalp; as a result she got into the habit of covering her head with a hat or, at times, with something showy and flamboyant, a true reflection of her strong personality.

In her early 30s Stark decided to learn Arabic and later Persian at the School of African and Oriental Studies in London. In due course she also acquired surveyor's skills so that she could make her own maps. Determined to live life on her own terms, she embarked on a number of travels east, including to regions that had not been explored by westerners before. Her *Valley of the Assassins*, about a then little-known Islamic sect, brought fame and recognition. Other publications followed, looking both at the past and at the present of the Arab world. She was at her best in describing people from all walks of life, from tribal leaders to Bedouins to slaves, and her linguistic skills opened many doors, including those of the harems. Her deep knowledge of the people and of the land secured her a place in the British Ministry of Information during WWII with the brief to encourage the Arab states to support the Allies or at least remain neutral.

It was only after the war that she turned her attention to Asia Minor with *Ionia: A Quest* (1954), *The Lycian Shore* (1956) and *Alexander's Path: from Caria to Lycia* (1958). They are a precious testimony to the state of the Classical remains before the tourist boom. In these books in fact, Stark is only interested in Greek material; the Arabs, who so much captivated her earlier on and who dominated these coastal areas for three centuries only to pass them on to another Islamic power, the Turks, are not mentioned; there are no mosques in her descriptions. Her account of peoples and places is nostalgic. To her this is the land of Pindar (who never lived here) and of Herodotus (a native of Halicarnassus but certainty not of today's Bodrum).

Charles Texier (1802–71)

Charles Texier was born in Versailles and trained as an architect. His working life was much influenced by the political atmosphere of his time. France and Great Britain were rivals, not just in Europe but all over the world with their sprawling empires. The quest for moral superiority was part of the struggle; knowledge of far distant lands became a way to enhance the prestige of the nation.

In due course Texier was instructed by the French government to travel east, to explore and report. This he duly did from 1833 to 1837, later publishing a description of Asia Minor, of Armenia, Persia and Mesopotamia (all the way to Baghdad) and a tome on Byzantine architecture. The publishing format was opulent, certainly worthy of an imperial nation. The text unfortunately betrays some weaknesses.

For a start it is short on maps. This makes it difficult to identify some places as the French rendition of Arab/Turkish names is not an exact science and today so many villages have been renamed. Texier's brief was vast and too ambitious. Plans are scarce and not reliable. The plan of Pessinus, where Texier allowed his imagination to soar unchecked, is just one example and causes archaeologists to cast doubt on his other work, like for instance the detailed plan of the wall circuit, complete with bastions, towers, gates and moat, of the old city of Van at the foot of the Kale. It awaits confirmation by remote sensing or excavation. On the other hand his feature drawings show that he was a very skilled draughtsman.

A lot of space is taken up with historical background, which meant mining Herodotus or Xenophon or any other suitable ancient author. This had been done before and Texier was also aware of the recently published *History of the Ottoman Empire* by Von Harman, which combines Byzantine and Ottoman sources for the first time. On the whole, one gets the impression that Texier did not truly enjoy the experience: his heart does not seem to have been in it. He complains about the people (who are un-cooperative or unruly), the food, the mud, the discomfort, the lack of funds, the bugs. Texier was clearly not an outdoor type. He neatly sums up his attitude in his communication to the Ministry of Education in 1841 stating that, after a stay in Urfa, he chose to ignore Syria and Egypt because 'the work done there by the French has already brought to light all there was to be found'.

Wilbrand of Oldenburg (1175–1233)

Born into an aristocratic family, Wilbrand of Oldenburg received a good Classical education; he took Holy Orders and eventually died Bishop of Utrecht. In 1211, when he was a mere canon at Hildesheim in Germany, he was tasked with two other officials to carry out a mission in Cilicia by Otto IV, the Holy Roman Emperor. These were troubled times, following the defeat of the Crusaders at Hattin at the hands of Saladin; it was also important to counteract the increased power of the Franks in the region. In addition, the Cilician Armenians had to be reassured of continuous support from the West and the incumbents in Cyprus, the Lusignans, could be flattered with some new title and investiture. Looming in the background was the basic disagreement between the Holy Roman Emperor and the Pope: the former thought that his Empire should stretch from the Baltic to the Mediterranean; the latter disagreed. As a result, at the time of his mission to Cilicia, both Wilbrand of Oldenburg and Emperor Otto IV were outside the Church, excommunicated. Wilbrand kept a diary of his trip: two slim volumes, the first one on Cilicia, the second covering the Holy Land.

Wilbrand's journey started from southern Italy, possibly Sicily, from where he sailed to Cyprus in late summer 1211, then on to Acre where he spent six weeks and then on to St Simon (the Crusader name for the port of Al Mina), from where he reached Antioch by land, the Orontes being, by the look of it, not navigable. He crossed the Amanus massif at its south end at the Belen Pass and proceeded along the narrow strip of the coast to Misis, Adana and Tarsus, reaching Sis, the Armenian capital, in time for the Epiphany celebrations which he describes in great detail. He left for the Holy Land and then headed home c. 1212 from Cure, today's Korikos.

Given his brief and his training, it is not surprising that Wilbrand pursued two main lines of enquiry. On one hand, he reports about fortifications: what state they are in, how many towers they have, whether or not there is a moat, what the access is like and also tries to give a good idea of distances. However, he is quite selective in his choices as he does not report in detail on Armenian defences (there is nothing on Silifke for instance) but only those that could be of strategic importance, which tend to be in Cyprus and the Levant. On the other hand he notes the religious affiliation of the townspeople, describes gardens and palaces as he comes across them, and when in Antioch lists an impressive number of churches, none of which appears to have survived. Occasionally the odd Classical monument attracts his attention, such as the now lost structure at Portella (*p. 238*).

AROUND THE CERAMIC GULF

The deep Ceramic Gulf, now the Gökova Körfezi (*map A, 5–6*), is right at the heart of the Turkish riviera, more popularly known as the Turquoise (Turkuaz) Coast, promising eternal sunshine, pristine beaches, a perfect tan—and delivering all three. The riviera, according to some, stretches from Çeşme to Alanya and this has fixed the world's attention on the shoreline, somehow neglecting the interior which—as anyone travelling from Bodrum to Marmaris will see—is certainly worth a second look. On the south side of the gulf is the long, narrow Reşadiye Peninsula (the old Cnidus Peninsula, also called the Datça Peninsula). Its current name honours the penultimate Ottoman sultan, Mehmed V Reşad. Here and in the nearby Bozburun Peninsula (sometimes known as the Loryma Peninsula), recent research has cast light on the ancient history of the area and the influence of nearby Rhodes, which in the past was a powerful local player. But first, Muğla and Marmaris.

MUĞLA TO MARMARIS

MUĞLA
Tucked away inland on the western slopes of the Menteşe Dağları, Muğla (*map A, 6*) was never in antiquity a very important place. In the 2nd century BC it was known as Mobolla, from which the present name appears to derive. The ancient remains uncovered on the nearby height of Asar Tepe are not very impressive. Muğla is more worth visiting for its Turkish connections. It was an important Menteşe centre before the emirate was gobbled up by the Ottomans. The old town has several **restored traditional houses**—enough of them to give the feeling of walking into the past. There is some innovative architecture too, such as the **clock tower** built in 1885 in a fetching combination of brick and stone ashlars. The **Muğla Museum** (*open Tues–Sun 8–5*) has ethnographic material and, perhaps the most interesting, ancient animal remains (including elephants and giraffes) that were unearthed locally. The **Thursday market**, not far from the Belediye (Town Hall), is a mouth-watering sight, piled high with local produce.

IDYMA AND CEDREAE
On the way from Muğla to Marmaris past the Sakar Pass (670m) are the **ruins of Idyma** near the village of Akyaka (*map A, 6*). A Carian city with perhaps a Rhodian past (judging by some inscriptions), Idyma flourished at the time of the Roman Empire only to succumb in the insecurity and turbulence that followed its collapse. It was resettled by the Ottomans as soon they had subdued Rhodes and has recently been transformed into the successful holiday resort of Akyaka ('White Shore'). The ruins occupy the slope below the Sakar Pass and include the remains of a medieval

castle, a number of rock-cut tombs and a fantastic view. Numerous trails inland start from Akyaka, a sign that tourism is diversifying. It is well worth enquiring locally to try and get a guide, or at least a detailed map.

Further south, a stunning stretch of Route 400 passes the Sideyri Adası, and island just offshore and home of the ruined settlement of **Cedreae**, which can be accessed by boat from either side of the gulf. The island is also known for its Cleopatra connection, real or invented, according to which one of its beaches, made of crushed seashells, was created by Antony to please his queen, who may or may not have bathed here (NB: Do not be tempted to take any sand home; the authorities are strict about this). Cedreae itself, a possible Carian foundation among the native Lelegians, prompted Xenophon in his *Hellenica* to call its inhabitants 'half barbarians', with all the hubris of a dyed-in-the-wool Greek. The city was conquered by the Spartan Lysander in 405 BC and the inhabitants were auctioned on the slave market. The Rhodian domination that followed was milder and enabled the Cedreans to show that they appreciated things Greek, as evidenced by the little theatre partially carved out of the rock and partially built in local conglomerate. Inscriptions also reveal an enthusiasm for athletic games (three different festivals are named) and there is even talk of a stadium. The Doric Temple of Apollo (later converted into a church, showing that there was life on the island in early Byzantine times) is another piece of evidence. The ruins, including remains of the defences, are at the eastern end of the island facing the mainland, where the necropolis is with its rock-cut tombs and sarcophagi. Everything is gracefully lost among the olive groves. The ultimate demise of Cedreae is attributed either to the Persians or to the Arabs who followed them in the 7th century.

MARMARIS

When Freya Stark visited Marmaris (*map A, 6*) in the 1950s, she gave a rough figure of one thousand houses, took an interest in the communal pump where women filled their amphorae and noted that in the harbour some vessels were moored to stumps of ancient marble columns. She also noticed a certain amount of cement, in readiness for the building of a pier. Since then things have ballooned. Marmaris is a full-blown tourist town, rivalling Bodrum, its past lost and buried in the process of its development (though the earthquake that destroyed it in 1957 was also a factor).

The ancient **Physcus**, the predecessor of Marmaris, is known to have been under the rule of the Rhodians in the 4th century BC when it was assigned to the territory of Lindos on the east coast of Rhodes. The remains of its acropolis were located by the archaeologist Charles Newton in the mid-19th century, on a hill just over 1km to the north; they attest an occupation from Classical and Hellenistic times. Inscriptions were found there confirming the identification. The next millennium or so is a blank until 1522, when Suleyman the Magnificent assembled his fleet in the spacious bay and mounted his successful attack on Rhodes. The **castle** that dominates the marina is his, according to Evliya Çelebi (*p. 25*), built to house his troops. It may hide evidence of Marmaris' past but in the course of its many restorations it has never been investigated. It is now the city **museum** (*open daily 8.30–7; charge*), with a slightly disappointing collection but offering superb views.

CNIDUS & LORYMA: A TALE OF TWO PENINSULAS

West of the territory of Marmaris, two peninsulas stretch out into the Aegean. The long, narrow Cnidus/Reşadiye Peninsula, all 63km of it, points resolutely west into the open sea. To the south of it the Loryma/Bozburun Peninsula, shorter and more compact, points southwest. Both peninsulas, by their location, mark the transition between the Aegean and the Mediterranean shores. They had, however, fundamentally different destinies, a direct consequence of their immediate geographical and historical environment.

The town of Cnidus was a late comer to its present geographical position. When it enters history, with the Dorian colonisation, old Cnidus was on the sheltered south coast of its peninsula. Those same Dorians (who occupied Rhodes and founded three cities there) appreciated the Loryma peninsula—whose tip is just over 30km from Rhodes—more for its strategic value. As a result, Cnidus flourished in the Hellenistic and Roman periods, when the seas were more secure, and its remains date from that time up until the early Byzantine period, after which it was one of the earliest victims of the Arab invasions. On the Loryma peninsula the architectural remains are more military and commercial and come to an end earlier, as Rhodes waned from the political scene.

THE CNIDUS PENINSULA

The Cnidus Peninsula rises to over 1000m in altitude and is extremely narrow in the extreme east, down to 800m at the **isthmus**, the Balıkaşıran (the 'place where the fish jump over'), presumably also the place where, in the mid-6th century BC, the local people tried to thwart the intentions of the invading Persians by attempting to cut through it (*Herodotus 1,174,2*). Local lore also has it that people from the island of Symi would haul their boats across the isthmus to reach the Ceramic Gulf (Gökova Körfezi). Although Captain Spratt (*p. 31*) reported seeing cut marks in the green serpentine, there is no agreement on the matter, mainly because the eastern section of the peninsula is wild, rugged and unproductive, with no water courses and thus hardly worth defending. The north coast was more unwelcoming in the past (though things have changed with modern transport) but it still catches the north wind in the summer. Wherever the cut through the isthmus was attempted, it remained an unfinished job. According to sources, the work proved too dangerous because of flying splinters. An appeal to the Delphic oracle produced a terse answer: the Cnidians should desist in their enterprise because if the gods had wanted the peninsula to be an island, they would have created it as such. The Cnidians dutifully opened their gates to the Persian general Harpagus.

The **earliest artefact** on the peninsula is a stray proto-Aeolian capital meant to fit a pilaster found with no context in the 1940s and dated by style to the 10th–6th century BC. It suggests Syro-Palestinian or Cypriot connections. It is worth remembering at this juncture, that a couple of capitals of the same style and date were identified at Alazeytin on the other side of the Gulf of Gökova (*see Blue Guide Aegean Turkey*); they also remain unexplained.

OLD CNIDUS

Recent research has moved away from the quest for the famous Aphrodite (her statue or her temple or any form of evidence that drew the first archaeologists here) to more mundane matters such as the earlier Cnidus settlement. It is known that after the Persians left in 412 BC, the town was an important naval base for Sparta (*Thucydides 8,109*). The quest for old Cnidus has concentrated around the area of modern Datça (*map A, 7–8*) on the more hospitable south side of the peninsula, where there are a few plains and rivers—and the search has been fruitful: in the town of **Burgaz**, 2km northeast of Datça, investigations have revealed a high concentration of finds showing that the location was occupied from the 8th to well into the 4th century BC. The settlement, laid out on a square grid from the very beginning, included courtyard houses in mud brick on stone foundations, with tiled roofs and separated by cobbled streets. Workshops for weaving, metalwork and oil and wine production have been identified. The settlement was defended and had four harbours with breakwaters. The acropolis may have been on the promontory to the southwest.

Investigations of the Sanctuary of Apollo at **Emecik** to the east, especially on the lower terrace used for ceremonies, have revealed activity from the Late Geometric period as well as far-flung connections with Egypt, the Etruscans and the Phoenicians. That chimes well with what is known from sources, that the Cnidians founded colonies in Corfu, on the north shores of Sicily and on the Lipari Islands, where apparently life was difficult because of the Phoenicians and the ever-present Etruscan pirates.

CNIDUS

The **move to the tip of the peninsula** is roughly dated to the 4th century BC and is still wrapped in mystery. The Burgaz site mentioned above appears to have been in decline at about this time, with a loss of civic buildings, while the Cnidus at the tip of the peninsula does not appear to have many remains earlier than that date. It not clear who would have initiated such a move: Mausolus (the Carian satrap of the famous mausoleum at Halicarnassus, modern Bodrum) casts a long shadow at this time; he is known for his ambitious projects, such as when he moved the capital of his satrapy from Milas to Halicarnassus, becoming an important player in the Greek world, or when he was instrumental in the setting up of Priene. The reason could have been an economic shift from agriculture to seafaring as navigation became more secure. The new foundation certainly prospered, meeting its demise only in the early Byzantine period, when security became a serious concern.

Looking from the top of the acropolis to the northeast, about 300m above sea level, one can see why the site was chosen. The terrain, gently sloping towards the sea, and a rocky headland defended by steep cliffs on the exposed side defined two bodies of water now separated by a narrow isthmus possibly developed from an earlier causeway. The present road comes in from the east at a much lower level but a climb to the acropolis among the myrtle and oleander is possible and well worth it.

According to recent excavations, beneath the theatre by the large harbour was a

5th-century BC spring house. That suggests that the place was not deserted in the 4th century BC. The population of the newly-founded Cnidus could have been the result of the merging of small local communities plus population transfers, something with which Masuolus could well have been associated. Alternatively, the Hellenistic Ptolemies or the Seleucids could have had a hand in it. At any rate, by 188 BC Cnidus was a free town.

FAMOUS CNIDIANS

Like any Graeco-Roman city, Cnidus boasts a few famous individuals who have left their mark on history, although here in an altogether muted way. One of these is **Artemidoros** (p. 42). Much earlier on, Ctesias and Eudoxos, both active in the 4th century BC, betray a wide range of interests. **Ctesias** started as a physician at the Persian court c. 400 BC. Upon his return he settled in Greece and turned historian, producing works covering Assyria, Persia and India and claiming to have had access to Persian archives. What little is left, in a much later Byzantine summary full of court gossip and anecdotes, does not seem to bear this out. **Eudoxos** was an astronomer and mathematician whose works laid the foundations for Euclidean geometry. He is credited with having built an observatory at Cnidus. Finally **Sostratos** may have designed and built, c. 280 BC, the Lighthouse of Alexandria, one of the wonders of the ancient world, though there are dissenting voices. The possibility that Sostratos may also have had a hand in the design and construction of Cnidus' Doric stoa is not confirmed either.

In any case, the most famous Cnidian is not a man, nor even a human, but rather a block of marble in the shape of the goddess **Aphrodite**.

'Where did Praxiteles see me naked?' the divinity apparently quipped. Nudity had been around for at least a couple of centuries, but it was male nudity. The kouros, a product of Archaic Greece, with his sure stride, clenched fists and eyes firmly looking forward, clad in heroic nakedness, was hardly a model for the nude female that was revealed to the world in Praxiteles' work. The statue that Praxiteles sold to the Cnidians for their temple was one of a pair. The other, decently draped, went to Kos and sank without trace. The Cnidians were bolder and defied convention. Their Aphrodite, a first in the Greek world, can be seen as both modest and provocative at the same time. She is either about to get into her bath or just stepping out of it—and is she covering her pudenda, or drawing attention to them? She smiles, but what is the meaning of that smile? Polychromy would have added to the illusion. Fundamentally she is equivocal and plays on different registers, the more so since as time went on and her fame grew, she was conceived as a real woman in a male-dominated world. Lurid tales abound—and the profusion of erotic and pornographic terracottas unearthed around the temple of Aphrodite Euploia suggests that there was some truth in them.

On the whole, Cnidus benefited from the publicity. Already in the mid-3rd century BC King Nicomedes of Bithynia had offered to pay Cnidus' debts in exchange for the image and was turned down. Either a steady stream of 'pilgrims' was already on its way or the debt was not so large.

The original statue is unfortunately lost and the quest for it in Cnidus has proved fruitless. According to sources, the artwork was last seen at the palace of Lausos in Constantinople in AD 476. Constantine's idea of building a new capital involved pillaging the Empire of works with which to adorn it and so the statue was moved there, one of many to share the same destiny. It burnt when the palace went up in flames.

The statue, however, was so popular that it was replicated *ad infinitum* in Hellenistic and Roman times, both in marble like the original as well as in cheaper media like terracotta, for lower-quality copies. The emperor Hadrian had a replica of the temple and of the goddess at his villa at Tivoli, where he liked to be surrounded by visual tokens of his extensive empire.

INVESTIGATIONS AT CNIDUS

The settlement has been the object of investigation ever since the Dilettanti began exploring in the late 18th century. The lure of the famous statue (*see above*) must have proved irresistible; besides, according to accounts, there was still a lot to be seen: streets, porticoes, temples and theatres. The archaeologist Charles Newton rescued the **lion** (the one that now greets visitors in the Great Court of the British Museum, its eyes dull since the glass fittings have been lost, as has the red paint on the tongue). The 18m high Heroön, whose pyramidal roof it crowned, on top of a 60m high cliff 5km southeast of the city, is now no more. Worked stone was haemorrhaging anyway: Newton himself swapped ancient building stone used in the Ulu Cami at Reşadiye for food; more was lost to Ottoman Cairo and to Istanbul (Dolmabahçe); local housing also took its share. The fact is that the site had been deserted for a long time. Captain Beaufort (*p. 23*) reported some shepherds there in the early 19th century. Fifty years later Newton did not even find that, just jackals and wolves and eight Crimean huts. By 1950 the place was deserted. The mixed population of the peninsula—including, according to a recent ethnographic survey, Yürüks, returnees from the Maghreb where they had been forcibly moved by the 16th-century naval commander Turgut Reis, and descendants of Spanish gypsies expelled by Queen Isabella—lived more to the east. The Greeks left with the population exchanges of 1927.

Modern investigations have involved British, German and Turkish teams. Earlier on however, in the late 1960s, a single-minded young American archaeologist in her early 30s, with the right connections to get funding and answering to the predestined name of **Iris Love**, set her spade to the ground with the specific aim of finding the body of Praxiteles' goddess of love. She claimed to have the head already; she had 'identified' it in a battered lump of marble in the dusty stores of the British Museum. Iris Love was not successful in her quest, but though the Aphrodite may still be missing, we know much more about the settlement itself.

CNIDUS: EXPLORING THE SITE

The town of Cnidus stood on the tip of the peninsula and on the Triopian headland, now connected by a sandy isthmus about 100m wide (this may have been cut by a canal in antiquity to allow communication between the two harbours). Both parts of the settlement were walled.

On the mainland the 4km-long **wall**, which is best seen on the acropolis and to the southeast (the most exposed section, which is why the wall is at its thickest here, 4.6m), as well as by the west harbour, follows the topography and takes in swathes of land that were probably never developed. This sort of wall (there are similar examples at Halicarnassus and Heracleia) was only effective if it could be properly manned and would have made high demands on the local population. It was more for prestige than efficiency, as the Cnidians themselves discovered in the 3rd century AD, when the city was disastrously raided, perhaps by the Goths. Sixty-one towers and ten gates and posterns have been identified. According to McNicoll, the towers were not large enough to house catapults. Built of local breccia and limestone and in different styles, it looks very much a local construction, built by a people short of both money and manpower. Walling on the Triopian headland was erected where needed, on the east and west sides. The south approach was defended by high cliffs.

The settlement had **two harbours**. One to the northwest, the small harbour or trireme harbour, and on the other side of the isthmus a large, undefended **commercial harbour**, whose wide opening was narrowed by two moles 30m deep. The north mole, now a shadow under the water, has collapsed under its own weight. The **trireme harbour** was defended by narrowing the entrance, which may have had a chain at some point, and by a beautiful section of the city wall. Its deisgnation as a military harbour comes from Strabo (*14,2,15*), where he talks of a closable harbour capable of housing 20 ships. So far no trireme has been identified but the harbour has not been yet fully investigated. **Shipsheds** have been located on the isthmus.

According to Felix Pirson, the city was laid out to impress visitors sailing in. While **residential quarters** are thought to have been on the north slope of the Triopian headland (which has been little investigated), the slope beneath the acropolis was gridded and set out in terraces covered with public buildings; the layout was determined by the location of the harbours and by the access road skirting the lower reaches of the acropolis from the east.

The main axis, the better-known street, is the so-called **Harbour Way**, a monumental stairway 5m wide with long shallow steps and ornamented in antiquity with statues. It led from the isthmus all the way to a propylon where it met, at right angles, the main east–west road leading out of town. Six other stepped ways have been identified parallel to it, as well as three more east–west thoroughfares. The space so defined was laid out on four terraces with, among other structures, a **bouleuterion**, a Corinthian temple, a Doric stoa and, almost at sea level, the **Temple of Dionysus** and its 120m long **stoa** in local conglomerate, with 25 rooms at the back; it was restored at the time of the Empire with a profusion of marble, including green porphyry from Laconia. Beyond the propylon was the Doric **Temple of Apollo Karneios**. Right at the top of the town, in a choice position well visible from the sea, the base of a round temple in Doric style, 18m in diameter, is believed to be all that remains of the **Temple of Aphrodite Euploia** (of the 'Fair Voyage'). Admittedly the site lacks space for the surrounding gardens planted with cypress, fruit trees and myrtle (if we believe Pseudo Lucian, writing much later) but the profusion of explicit terracottas tells its own story.

Today one mainly sees Cnidus in its Late Antique/Byzantine garb, which accounts for the seven churches so far identified. This may explain the discrepancies in the description of the temple (for instance, the cella should have no walls so that the goddess could be admired from any viewpoint) and its missing garden.

Going east along the main east–west axis, the **gymnasium** long-ago identified by Charles Newton has recently been re-excavated, with evidence of mosaic floors. It does not look like gymnasium, given the lack of a large open space normally associated with this sort of structure, yet the identification is based on an inscription found by Newton honouring **G. Ioulios Artemidoros** with the right of burial 'in the gymnasium', for which structure these ruins seem the most likely candidate. Artemidoros makes it into history via Plutarch (*Life of Caesar 65*), as the man who warns Caesar not to go to the Senate on the Ides of March in 44 BC. Beside the anecdotal value, his life story reveals a Cnidian who moved from peripheral Asia Minor to the centre of things in the last turbulent days of the Roman Republic, possibly in the wake of, or together with, his father Theopompos, a friend of Caesar's.

The 'Temple of the Muses' was identified by Newton on the basis of marble female statuettes that he found during his excavations. A re-evaluation of the site in the 2000s (much hampered by the fact that the structures still standing had in the meantime been infelicitously used as a goat shed) has concluded that far from being a temple of the Muses, it was a **nymphaeum**, adding very important information on the day-to-day working of the town. Located on a terrace completely hewn from the rock, the structure was backed by a tall artificial cliff. The entrance was by steps to the west and led into a peristyle court. To the east a passage gave access to three grottoes exposed by the cutting of the cliff. A system of pipes was designed to collect the water and lead it into a channel running along the rear wall of the fountain. Judging by the pottery, it would seem that it was built c. 300 BC, not much after the city was founded, with later modifications such as the addition of a cistern in the 2nd century AD. By the 5th century the original access was no longer in use and the monument was transformed into a church and finally abandoned around the 7th century.

Further east is the **Temple of Demeter**, from which Newton retrieved, among other things, the famous *Demeter* now in the British Museum. This rare example of an original 4th-century BC building stands within the walls, but just beneath a towering cliff on a terrace with a massive retaining wall.

Two theatres have been identified: a larger one, of which very scanty remains survive, on the way to the acropolis, cut into the rock and with a capacity of c. 20,000; and a slightly smaller one to the east of the Temple of Dionysus by the commercial harbour. It had a Hellenistic antecedent, possibly with a wooden scena, which explains why its west wing was trimmed when the Romans developed the Dionysus stoa and a temple for the Imperial cult. The building immediately north of the breakwater on the north shore of the commercial harbour may have been an **odeion**.

THE LAST DAYS OF CNIDUS

As intimated above, things began to decline in the 3rd century but the profusion of large Byzantine churches betrays a certain will to survive. However, Cnidus was very exposed and when the seas became insecure it was the first to suffer. It has the privilege of harbouring the **earliest attestation of Islamic presence in Asia Minor**. The graffiti, found in 1969 and dated to AD 717, asking for God's protection, have been identified in the church in the Doric stoa, which was turned into a mosque when the Arab army, mainly made up of people from the Middle East and north Africa, settled here. They were on their way to Byzantium, where their siege failed. In 1095 Cnidus was in Seljuk hands. Later it came under the rule of the Menteşe dynasty until it fell to the Ottomans and was set up as a pirate base in the glorious tradition of Alanya and Scalanova (now Kuşadası), to name but two examples of the genre. The town of Cnidus itself was too exposed and settlement retreated to the heights, away from the sea.

THE LORYMA (BOZBURUN) PENINSULA & THE RHODIAN PERAEA

The **Loryma or Bozburun Peninsula**, facing Rhodes (*map A, 8*), lies at the north end of a busy sea lane. The same was true in medieval times, when a ship loaded with broken glass ready for recycling foundered on the south coast near Serçe Limanı; a painstaking excavation enables us today to see what was fashionable in the mid-11th century. Some of the vessels can be seen in the Bodrum Museum of Underwater Archaeology. This waterway was equally important in Hellenistic times, when Rhodes was flexing her muscles and aiming to exert control over navigation and trade in this area, among the conflicting interests of the successors of Alexander the Great.

Already in Classical times Rhodian cities owned land on the mainland, the territory known as the **Rhodian Peraea**, 'Rhodian land on the other side'. Its extent grew steadily, peaking in the period between 188 and 167 BC, when the land south of the Meander was in Rhodian hands. Rhodes' power was brought to an end when Rome asserted its control. Administratively, the Peraea fell into two categories: the Colonised Peraea (the Cnidian Peninsula, although excluding Cnidus itself, which was a free city) and the Incorporated Peraea. The latter was not vassal land: its status was equal to that of the motherland. Roughly speaking the Incorporated Peraea included the land from Psyscus (Marmaris), providing access to the Anatolian interior, down to Loryma, as well as the enclave of Daedala in the Gulf of Fethiye (among its remains are some rock-cut tombs and an acropolis, but they have not yet been studied) and further south the island of Megisti (Kastellorizo), opposite modern Kaş (*map B, 7*).

Recent excavations and survey work have shown that much of the Incorporated Peraea was used for **military** purposes. **Loryma**, the settlement right at the tip of the Bozburun peninsula, at the head of a deep gulf, goes back to the Archaic Period. It offered shelter to the Athenian fleet at the time of the Peloponnesian War. With time it acquired defences, one inland acting as a refuge, and in the 3rd–2nd century BC the harbour was fortified with a structure 324m long, 30m wide and 2.45m thick on the tip of the west peninsula. With nine square towers and two round towers suitable for archers and small torsion artillery, as well as five posterns, it was a good **garrison fort** poised for active defence. In the same area, at sea level, twelve **shipsheds** embedded in the rock have been identified. Their style is the same as those on Alimia, the island west of Rhodes. Placed on an incline, these sheds could be used by light, fast warships and by patrol boats. The presence of an **arsenal** is hinted at by the designation of the bay as *oplothiki*, the ancient Greek word for arsenal. Other coastal defences and installations identified in incorporated Peraea suggest a network of strategic harbours.

The **commercial** aspect of Rhodian involvement on the mainland has also come under scrutiny, yielding exciting discoveries. In antiquity as well as today, **Rhodian wine** was highly thought of. The Athenian statesman and orator Aeschines was already singing its praises in 370 BC; it probably sweetened his exile. The wine was transported in amphorae of a known style with stamped handles, guaranteeing that the grapes were from Rhodes.

Recent research in the area of Hisarönü and Turgut in the northern part of the peninsula, a land less rugged than the south and favourable to cultivation, has focused attention on the gridded settlement of **Bybassos**, whose defences date from the Archaic Period and which covered an extensive area. Though its harbour is now silted up, quays and moles and large storage facilities have been identified, as well as a busy potters' quarter with many kilns, an installation seemingly too large for strictly local use. This has led some German archaeologists to take a closer look at the Rhodian stamped transport amphorae, which have a wide distribution from the Black Sea down to Babylon and from the Persian Gulf to the Mediterranean. They may not all have been filled in Rhodes, suggesting that perhaps not all Rhodian wine in antiquity was absolutely DOC. Other sites of this sort, but on a smaller scale, have been identified in the Incorporated Peraea.

However, the work of understanding what went on on this peninsula is still in its infancy. The political structure is not yet clear. In antiquity it was more densely settled than the Cnidian peninsula and the small centres may have been united in a league. The remains at **Kastabos** (east of Hisarönü at Pazarlık), on the ridge of the Evren Dağı at 275m above sea level, which include ruins of a large temple of 11m by 23m with large marble columns on a massive platform, a theatre with a capacity of 5,000 and a processional way—this is what Spratt saw in 1860—could have been the meeting place of such a league or alternatively the Temple of Hemithea, a healing deity who had a local cult and to whom, as we know from sources, there was a temple in this vicinity. The complex, whose name is not Greek, grew up before the arrival of the Rhodians and represents a form of healing unconnected with Asclepian practice, pointing to a strong **survival of the indigenous element** which possibly characterised the development of the peninsula. While Asclepius had a more 'hands-on' approach, Hemithea stood over the sleeping sick; hers seems more a sort of faith healing than medicine. We are hampered in our quest by the scarcity of excavations (although modern geophysical-based research can do wonders) as well as by a general lack of interest on the part of the ancient Lycians in the life of their northern neighbours. Written records are scarce.

Settlement on the peninsula, mainly on the heights or by the coast, peaked in late antiquity, as the remains of large churches show. By then overexploitation and deforestation (shipbuilding and kilns) had taken its toll, leading to erosion and eventual abandonment. The Byzantine comeback in the 13th century was short and the Menteşes who took over from them have left next to no legacy here.

CAUNUS & DALYAN

Hovering between land and water, neither fully Carian nor fully Lycian, backed by high mountains to the northeast reaching well over 2000m and thereby protected from the cold winds, the large Caunus enclave (*map A, 8*) has been a specially protected area since 1990. The aim is to stabilise a mixed environment while at the same time allowing its commercial exploitation.

Mixed environments were places of choice for settlement in antiquity as they provided diverse sources of livelihood. In Caunus' case a non-exhaustive list would include: fishing and fowling in the marshes; fishing with traps slung across the sluggish river; and harvesting rare crops such as *Liquidambar orientalis* (Storax), which grows in swamps and whose leaves were used in antiquity as incense. The climate here is also perfect for figs, both fresh and dried. In the past dried figs were an important commodity, being used for medicinal purposes and as an alternative source of sugar. They also travelled well. Add to all these advantages Caunus' convenient access to the sea, overlooked by some higher land, and the stage seems set for a prosperous settlement. Yet this was not to be. While the evidence of persistent occupation is certainly not lacking (and will be discussed below), it consistently went together with a reputation for **ill health**, suggesting a malaria-ridden environment. A city where 'the dead walk the streets' (to quote the 4th-century BC cytharist Stratonicus, as related by Strabo; *14,2,3*) and whose people (according to Dio Chrysostom, writing in the first century of our era; *32.92*) deserved their misfortunes and should be wiped out by fever 'because they were stupid', would not seem destined for success.

Today many things have changed. For a start, due to poor drainage, Caunus is no longer by the sea, which is about 5km away and the river Dalyan, the ancient Calbis, has changed course many times, moving eastwards. It has in the process silted up the inlet that was Caunus' older harbour, north of the acropolis. The new harbour to the west (the Sülüklü Göl), the centre of Caunus' commercial life until late antiquity, is now a shallow lake suitable only for leeches (as its Turkish name indicates). Yet after a long period of abandonment, Caunus is now alive again. This is an astonishing reversal of fortunes since Freya Stark visited in the 1950s: she found it deserted apart from a lighthouse and observed a few turtles courting, though at Dalyan she recorded a flourishing fishing industry producing salt mullet and a sort of red caviar. Malaria, credited with wiping the settlement off the face of the earth in the 15th century, has been eradicated—though mosquitoes, presumably not infected, can still be a problem.

In line with its special status in the **Köyceğiz-Dalyan Environmental Protection Area**, 461km square in size, no industrial development is allowed beyond agriculture, forestry, tourism and fish farming. The need to maintain a balanced ecosystem has been recognised, with saline water from marine transgression and fresh water input from springs and melting snows, enabling some 700 types of plant and 180 species of bird to thrive. However, just one look at a map makes the extent of the agricultural exploitation apparent, especially around Lake Köyceğiz, as well as the building of houses on agricultural land despite planning restrictions. That brings its own pollution, with fertilisers and pesticides that will inevitably leech into the water system. South, around Caunus itself, agriculture is far less present: fisheries and tourism are the mainstays of the economy.

Since the days of Freya Stark, Caunus has developed into a **prime tourist location** aided by three large, beautiful sandy beaches, perennial sunshine, the proximity of Dalaman Airport and also by the *Caretta caretta* turtle, a sort of mascot of the place, which should be experienced, by sharing its environment, but not seen (*see below*). The massive human presence here will inevitably take its toll, as nothing much is done to limit the damage. This is always the case with **conflicting interests**. The rules are there but the interests of the local people who want to maximise profits, and those of the authorities in charge of protection, are not aligned. It is all very well to restrict tourist accommodation to the town of Dalyan, but is there a cap on the number of pensiyons operating? One would hope so, since waste water is treated and then returned to the lagoon. Is there a cap on the number of licensed boats plying their trade on the lake and on the river? Their number has gone up since this has become a protected area; the erosion of the banks and the damage caused by unprotected propellers, which slice up any form of life in the water, have increased. Besides, many tourist boats come from Marmaris and are licensed there. Boat operators flout the rules when they advertise 'Feed the turtles!' cruises, since such practice is not legal according to Turkish animal protection laws. There is still plenty of room for improvement.

A SHORT HISTORY OF CAUNUS

Finds dating from the Archaic period have not so far been matched by evidence of a settlement; quite where the finds came from is not clear. Apart from a foundation legend related by Ovid in his *Metamorphoses* (*9, 431ff*) in which he mentions a Caunus, grandson of Apollo, who fled Caria and the incestuous advances of his sister, we are left with what the Caunians themselves believed, namely that they came from Crete. Herodotus, however, did not agree with them and saw them as Anatolians. By the time the Persians invaded Lycia and Caria in 540 BC, the place was developed enough to offer resistance: no one else could do likewise apart from Xanthus. For about 100 years the Caunians played a careful game, not joining in the ill-fated Ionian revolt which culminated in the crushing Persian victory at Lade off Miletus (494 BC) but signing up to the Delian League when fortunes turned and Persian expansionism was apparently checked. Appearances were deceptive though, and by 387 BC Caunus was back in Persian hands, incorporated into the satrapy of Caria. Fortunes varied in the troubled times brought about by Alexander

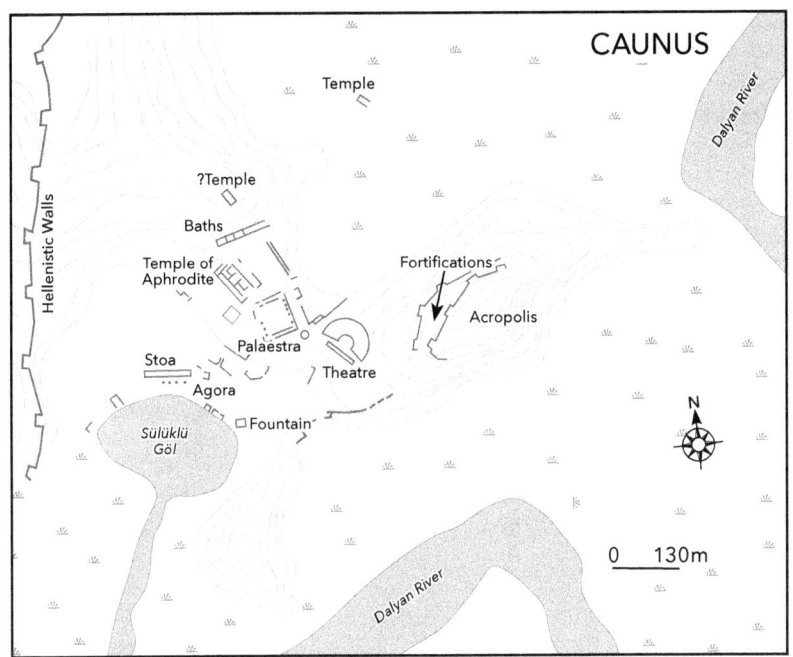

the Great and his successors. Perhaps the nadir came when they were sold for 200 talents by Rhodes to the Ptolemies of Egypt in the early 2nd century BC. By then the long shadow of Rome was extending across Asia Minor; after a short period of independence, Caunus was incorporated into the newly-formed Province of Asia. It must have had a prosperous harbour for the Romans to bother. Perhaps they were attracted by the flourishing slave market and the *Sal caunitis* (*see below*). Beyond this, the story is a blur. There is a church, pointing to a Byzantine development, and a number of inscriptions in Greek, one of which enabled the identification of the site in the mid-19th century. Archaeological exploration came much later. The site is now being investigated by Turkish and German teams.

EXPLORING CAUNUS

The best way to approach Caunus (*open daily April–Oct 9–8, Nov–March 9–5; charge*) is via a short boat trip from Dalyan. Boat trips will vary in scope: some include a visit to the necropolis with its stunning rock tombs, some will get as far as the sea. Be sure you know what you are getting. The boat will take you to a small quay, from where a path leads you to the entrance booth. In the distance, to the right, is the **acropolis**, 152m above sea level. The wall circuit, with towers at the summit, (the Herakleion) spans the Archaic to Byzantine periods, with repairs and restorations. It may have originally served as a refuge and later as a garrison fort.

The slope to the north of it was terraced in the Archaic period. It is supposed that the original **settlement** was connected to the harbour below. When it silted up in antiquity, the settlement occupied the slope to the northeast of the Sülüklü Göl, again set out on terraces, roughly in the 4th century BC. It was enclosed, according to some, by a short wall roughly following the line of the ridge running behind the theatre and the later Roman baths. The wall on the Persikon, a height closing the harbour to its south, may have formed part of the scheme, though it is not clearly dated. Not much later, the **wall circuit** was greatly enlarged to take in all the heights to the north and enclose a very large area. The wall can be followed on the ground. A number of towers and posterns have been identified. According to McNicoll, it was built with minimal expenditure, with no provisions for torsion artillery. It was possibly commissioned by Mausolus, who would have wanted to keep the Rhodians in check.

In the **Hellenistic/Roman town**, built on terraces cut into the rock, a number of features have been identified. The area has been much spoliated for local use over the centuries. The 94m long **stoa** (dated to the 3rd century BC and which buried the temple of Aphrodite Euploia), where statue bases seem to provide evidence for bronze statues, closed the **agora** (where the slave market was held) at the north end; up the slope, excavations have revealed that what was to become the Temple of Artemis was originally a chamber cut in the virgin rock. In that respect it resembles the beginnings of Didyma and of the Temple of Apollo at the Letoön. Finds have confirmed an Anatolian cult of the mother goddess. To the east end of the terrace is a cult area dedicated to Apollo (1st century BC), which two centuries earlier had been sacred to the mythical founder of the city, Caunus. Indeed his image was found here, a 3.5m tall baitylos (a small obelisk, also used as the symbol of the king on the coinage) housed in a round building with an altar, on which the portico was later built. The **Temple of Apollo** on the east side was a simple structure in antis, surrounded by a portico. Later a Byzantine church was built into the southeast corner of the portico. Further up the slope the **Roman baths**, which were still standing to their full height in the 1950s, led on to the palaestra area, in the middle of which stand the remains of a 5th-century basilica built with spolia. From the palaestra to the theatre, do not miss the mystery **measuring platform**, a circular structure with a maximum diameter of 16m. It consists of three concentric steps built in stone with no evidence of any superstructure. A number of fine lines appear to divide it into 16 equal parts and thus could be related to the positioning of some sort of measuring instrument. Alternatively, an obelisk found in pieces nearby could have been mounted on it. Vitruvius' wind measurement machine has been mentioned by the excavators. The **theatre** cut into the slope, possibly constructed in the Hellenistic period and enlarged later, could seat 5,000.

THE ROCK TOMBS

In their prime position, the impressive rock tombs are best explored from the river. Most sport an Ionic temple in antis; other details showing a clear Greek influence, either directly or mediated via Caria, suggest the presence of itinerant workers; those that imitate wooden structures are earlier and point to a Lycian connection. The most elaborate tombs are also the most inaccessible and therefore the most difficult to service. A closer examination has identified traces of the tools used (pick, hammer, toothed chisel), remains of stucco mouldings and traces of paint as well as strategically placed holes for scaffolding or footrests; the beginning of work would have been done hanging from ropes secured from above. Most are unfinished, left incomplete at various stages; the premature death of the patron may have been the cause. Generally speaking the practice of rock-tomb burial appears to have dwindled in the 3rd century BC. In the 1980s a pristine rock tomb dated to the late 4th century BC, on the Thracian coast of the Sea of Marmara at Tekirdağ, shows what might have been. It yielded a bed, a couple of stools, a footstool, a marble table, metal and clay vessels and weapons hanging on the walls: the setup of a funerary banquet reflecting the status of the deceased.

ON THE BEACH
Caunus has a number of heavenly beaches, long sandbars stretching seemingly forever, among which the **İztuzu beach** (4.5km) is the most popular; it is estimated to receive some 5,000 sun devotees in the summer. The beaches are as much of an attraction as the archaeology, if not more. But they do not belong just to the tourists. For much longer they have been a nesting site for **two species of turtle** (*Caretta caretta* and *Chelonia mydas*), one of 17 recognised and protected spots in Turkey. This has imposed a number of restrictions. Access is barred from May to October from 8pm to 8am, which is when the females come ashore to lay their eggs. Towels and other sunbathing equipment are not allowed close to the water. Strong lights at night and excessive noise that would disorient the hatchlings, are also banned, together with showers entailing the use of polluting creams and soaps. The policy appears to have been a success as the number of turtles has increased. This success is mainly due to the single-mindedness and amazing energy of **June Haimoff** (locally known as Kaptan June), an English lady now living in Dalyan, who has been relentlessly campaigning to preserve the habitat for its wildlife. She successfully fended off projects such as a 1,800 room hotel by bringing the world's attention to the problem and eventually managed to persuade the Turkish government to grant protected status to the area. She is also the founder of the **hospital for injured turtles** on İztuzu beach. Her work has inspired a whole young generation of Turks. It is even quoted in school texts. Let us hope that future generations will continue her work.

While you are at İztuzu beach you can visit the **ancient salt pans** located at the south end, at the foot of a cliff to maximise evaporation. Temperatures here are said to reach 60°C in August; the strong southwesterly winds do the rest. The pans are not much different from modern salt pans: 18cm deep, they are about 4m in diameter and are made of lined mortared limestone rubble. Forty-eight pans have been identified, and four channels with sluices to fill them up in the winter. Archaeologists are looking for more. Salt was big business in Caunus in Roman times, if not before. There was a flourishing **salted fish industry** and its garum, a fish-based sauce said to taste like *nuoc mam* and capable of hiding any other unwelcome flavours, was very popular. Both trades used lots of salt in the manufacturing process. Pliny (*31, 99*) waxes lyrical about *Sal caunitis*, a gift of Poseidon to mankind. Mixed with resin and honey it is, according to him, the perfect remedy for eye diseases and boils.

LAKE KÖYCEĞIZ

To the north of Dalyan, Lake Köyceğiz (Köyceğiz Gölü; *map A, 6*) will appeal to birdwatchers (cormorants, ibis etc.) and the health-conscious alike. Hot sulphur springs and mud baths at Sultaniye are a timely reminder that the whole area described in this chapter sits on faults. Indeed there are also mud baths in Ekincik. At Sultaniye, with its indoor and outdoor facilities, the miracle mud promises the perfect complexion. The lake itself (measuring 6km by 26km and just 25m deep) is fed by its own springs and the snowmelt from the surrounding high mountains. Its drainage is poor and being barely at sea level, it suffers from marine transgression, hence the **strong salinity**. A lot of work has gone in in the area to make it agriculturally productive: mainly citrus, olives and flowers are grown. Back in 1837, when Charles Fellows (*p. 26*) was here, the area was of interest for more than its wildlife, being the power centre of the local *derebey*. Something more than a wealthy landowner (*ağa*), he had his own army and his own fleet (ten men-of-war cruising on the lake). The difficulty of communications in those days meant that the sultan in distant Istanbul had to rely on delegates. When reforms made power more centralised, local governors became Istanbul appointees, with the result that not only the army and the fleet disappeared, but also the *derebey*'s fine dwelling that Fellows lovingly drew, a three-storey edifice of stone and wood with porticoes and verandas.

PRACTICAL INFORMATION

GETTING THERE AND AROUND

Dalaman Airport (*map A, 8*) has wide-ranging international connections. The airport has a bus service from Marmaris *otogar* stopping at Köyceğiz, Ortaca (for Caunus) and Dalaman town.

By bus: Most destinations can be reached by bus from the **Dalaman otogar**, located well outside town to the north; a minibus service run by the municipality is planned, linking the centre of town to the *otogar* and the airport. **Marmaris** *otogar* is by Route 400 on the east edge of town. **Cnidus** is served by bus from Marmaris, but it is a long way.

By boat: A number of locations (including the Bozburun Peninsula) can be visited by boat on day trips from Marmaris. For more on boat trips, see 'What to do' below.

Tourist information: You will find this at your hotel and at information kiosks, though these seem to be rarer now, with the spread of the internet. For **Marmaris** go to the kale (*open Mon–Fri 8–5*).

WHERE TO STAY

The area is well equipped with accommodation: Dalyan offers plenty of choice. For something a little different, try the **Palamubuku Hotel** (*palamutbukunet.com; T: 90 533 383*

95 16) with its own beach on Cnidus' south coast west of Datça; or for a quiet inland retreat the **Triopia Otel** (*triopiaotel.com; T: 90 536 222 04 04*), where you forego the beach for beautiful countryside, though you can still see the sea. The **Kaya Guesthouse** (*kayaguesthouse.com; T: 90 532 176 46 24*), in an old renovated stone building between Datça and Reşadiye, is an excellent alternative.

The old town in Muğla is well worth exploring. Spend a night at the **Turcer Hotel** in Kütüphane Sk in a maze of alleyways.

Marmaris also makes a good base. There is plenty of choice of places to stay, especially at the west end of the gulf. However, Marmaris itself is pretty modern, so once you have seen the castle there is not much left to detain you and the concentration of hotels ensures that organised trips will call here.

WHAT TO EAT

Food will be a mixture of fast food, traditional Turkish food and something in between, with extensive offers of vegetarian and vegan lunches.

The best bet is to go for fish. There are numerous references to *palamut* (bonito) in place names but it may by now be overfished and you might not find it available on menus. **Olta balık** in **Akyaka** is one of a number of good places in the area and its *mezes* are unsurpassed.

WHAT TO DO

There are a lot of **boat trips** on offer; these often combine visiting some ruins and having a refreshing swim (or more than one). You can spend the rest of the time sunbathing on deck. Operators have gone to a great lengths to stand out in a crowded market. Do not be lured by the promise of a pizza: this is not pizza country; rather choose a trip that will stop at a good *lokanta* with traditional healthy Turkish fare.

The **Marmaris Spring Festival** is held annually in May, with competitions, street performances and concerts. In June–July there is a **cinema festival**. But Marmaris's heart is in its marina, which in around mid-May hosts the **yacht festival**, where you can keep up to date with all the latest innovations.

LYCIA

Heading east from Dalyan on Route 400, one enters Lycia. The River Indus (now the Dalaman Çay; *map B, 5*) has been a recognised border ever since the time of Herodotus.

Defining Lycia, however, is still an ongoing process. Tourist literature likes to identify it with the whole of the Tekke Peninsula, in other words equating it to the entirety of the limestone mass which rises to over 3000m with Fethiye to the west and Antalya to the east, bounded by the sea to the south and in the north by an undefined border that dissolves into the Anatolian Plateau. This is a very large area, not all of which shows the characteristic markers—be they tombs, inscriptions or settlements—that can be said to be typically Lycian. A better definition of Lycia is given by the map prepared by Thomas Marksteiner, a leading researcher in the field. It shows a line starting at the Dalaman Çay, taking in the whole of the Xanthus river valley and then dropping quite precipitously south and meeting the sea on the west side of Cape Gelidonya (*map B, 8*). North of this line, a Lycian presence is scarce or non-existent, at least according to the current state of research. With a coastline prone to silting, a very rugged wild terrain (where in the course of his three-month survey in 1842 Captain Spratt (*p. 31*) came across a brown bear, adding it to the already long list of wild animals including leopards, wolves and jackals), a troubled history entailing destruction and reconstruction (often on the same spot, the only one available), and the imponderables of geology (earthquakes, a sinking coastline with marine transgression and the development of marshes), the prehistory of the land still holds many secrets.

After a general presentation of the physical aspects of the area, this chapter will cover the whole of the Tekke Peninsula including the west side of the gulf of Antalya, a liminal area between Lycia and Pamphylia.

The peninsula is basically quite a poor, hard land with very little alluvium suitable for cultivation (what there is is restricted mainly to the valley of the Xanthus, the Eşen Çay, and a coastal plain east of Finike). Arable land is to be found in the north, and more so since lakes have been drained in modern times. In the past, **water** was a constant problem: either because there was not enough of it or else there was far too much, during fearful storms such as those described by Texier (*p. 32*) and Fellows (*p. 26*). **Timber** suitable for shipbuilding (cypress and cedar) provided a steady resource though the ages; trunks could be driven down the rivers in the right season. The forests were extensively exploited in antiquity but as late as the 8th century AD there was still enough timber left for the Arabs; deforestation and erosion followed, though log driving could still be observed in the 19th century. The broken nature of the terrain encouraged **political and social fragmentation**. Pliny the Elder counted as many as 36 cities, and according to some sources there were even more. But they were small: habitation was mainly concentrated by the coast, retreating to the interior when and if necessary. This coastline, where the Aegean meets the Mediterranean, where a good north wind would ensure a secure passage to Alexandria and where an anticlockwise current facilitated coastal navigation from Egypt, Syria and Palestine to Greece, was also full of danger as it was so exposed. The many wrecks here bear witness to this.

Land communications have always been bad. The coastal road dates only from after WWII. The routes marked on the Patara *Stadiasmus* (*p. 83*) are thought to have been little more than tracks. Archaeology and historical sources seem to disappear in medieval times. According to Ibn Battuta (*p. 22*), the interior (the area around Cibyra; *see p. 61*) was flourishing in the 14th century, but when Charles Fellows visited in 1838–40, he found just a scattering of nomads and gypsies in the countryside while the few, small cities inland were full of Greeks and Armenians. It was apparently the renewed interest of the Europeans in the commercial possibly of the coast (by developing for instance Antiphellos, now Kaş) that drove the Ottoman authorities to the sea. Now with the tourist boom of the Turquoise Coast their interest remains firmly there.

FETHİYE & ITS GULF

Fethiye (*map B, 7*), a city of c. 150,000 inhabitants, lies in the eastern part of the ancient Glaucus Sinus, a gulf named in homage to its gleaming waters. Today, with its lovely climate and perfect sea, it is a choice tourist destination for Turks and foreigners alike and it has grown and grown. Itself a recent foundation, Fethiye developed to the east of the site of ancient Telmessus, a city whose history is partially known and whose remains were still substantial in the 19th century. At the time the area was settled by Greeks and it is their interest in trading and shipping that encouraged the Turks to move the administrative centre from Düğer, inland near Tlos, down to the coast. The new town, then called Makri (after the island closing the harbour, which has the same name), became an outlet for chromium production, exporting 150 tons in the 1950s; later, after the destructive 1957 earthquake, the town was rebuilt and renamed Fethiye in memory of Yüzbaşı Fethi Bey, an Ottoman pilot who died in an accident in 1914. Unfortunately, ancient Telmessus served as a quarry during the rebuilding. Debris was piled into the harbour to make a new esplanade and worked stone was used in modern buildings. Earlier on Fellows's (*p. 26*) 'perfect theatre' had been dismantled and the stones taken to Istanbul to build the barracks at Üsküdar. The chromium industry is now largely a thing of the past since tourism has taken over.

TELMESSUS

Telmessus, though it hovers between Caria and Lycia, does have a Lycian name (Telebehi), from a mid-5th-century BC list of cities that paid tribute to the Delian League, an Athenian-led confederation intended to fight off the Persians. It also has a very prominent Lycian tomb by the Belediye. Over a hundred years ago this tomb was standing in the sea, two thirds of its plinth under water. Now it is on dry land. The crested arched lid and the articulations, imitating wood, are typically Lycian and Lycian-language inscriptions have been found. On the other hand, Telmessus is separated from Lycia in that same tribute list. We are on surer ground in thinking of the city as having an **Anatolian background**, in spite of the tall mountains barring access to the north. Its development through the centuries mirrors very much what happened on the Lycian coastline, especially in the interplay between the mainland and the islands. The area has now been extensively studied and surveyed. Moreover, thanks to tourism, there are many boat trips to islands where time has stood still and the ruins are still there to show it.

Telmessus, the place name, has an Anatolian ring to it. It is possible that the original population was a mix of Anatolian settlers and Cretan immigrants. The chosen spot, deep at the south end of the gulf and protected at the entrance by the island of Makri, was ideal. It was a good enough spot to tempt the forces of the Lycian League led by Perikles, the dynast from Limyra (*p. 102*), to capture it in the 4th century BC. But his hegemony was soon brought to an end by Alexander the Great. Telmessus was then briefly ruled by the Ptolemies, coming into the hands of Pergamon after the peace of Apamea in 188 BC. The political map of Asia Minor was redrawn at this time, to suit the interests of the up-and-coming Roman Republic, which was on good terms with the Attalids of Pergamon. The latter went on to found the new city of Antalya, to which Telmessus could provide useful backdoor access. This suggests the presence of a land connection via the Karabel Pass (1300m) and on along today's Route 350. Since the Attalids did not control Caria, they had little choice.

In due course Telmessus became part of the Roman **Province of Asia**. As a harbour, Telmessus found the 7th-century Arab incursions particularly challenging. It is possible that the fortifications above the harbour were begun by Anastasius II in the 8th century (*see below*) and in gratitude, the town adopted the name of **Anastasiopolis**. In the end they proved an insufficient deterrent, though when the Arab threat abated and the Byzantines reasserted their control over the coast, a number of **opportunistic settlements** sprang up on the mainland and on the islands. Some have left impressive remains that can be visited, the visit combined with a good swim. They all show roughly the same layout and are all tightly packed settlements with narrow roads and no public amenities except what space is afforded by church atria. They are strictly devoted to trade, and the storage of water and merchandise takes priority. Sites are undefended as they could only prosper if the sea was safe. This is the sort of shift that can be observed much further east, where Arykanda becomes the dense, packed and austere Arif (*p. 106*); Some sites show occupation from late antiquity to the 6th/7th century, followed by a revival in the 12th century and not much beyond that date, as the land came under Turkish rule.

VESTIGES OF ANCIENT TELMESSUS

Telmessus itself came into the hands of the Turks in the 13th century; they called it Günlük (hence the Günlükbaşı suburb in Fethiye); first it was in the hands of the Menteşe then it fell to the Ottomans in 1420. It was always an important military harbour and also served commercial interests (wood, wheat, wine, flour, linen, dates). After a fire it was rebuilt orthogonally, in 1885, and by the end of the 19th century, with its mixed Christian and Muslim population, it had become a 'Little Smyrna'.

The **Fethiye Museum** (*open Tues–Sun 8–5; charge*) has a certain amount of Lycian material though most of it (such as the trilingual stele and the rather crude image of the Mother Goddess) appears to have come from Xanthus further south. It does very little to complete our knowledge of Telmessus. The material has no specific provenance; it has just turned up in official and unofficial excavations.

This leaves us with the **descriptions of travellers**. The '**Tomb of Helen**' that E.D. Clarke drew in 1824, a very large monument with a squat monolithic lid in the Carian style and the typical wings (an old print shows three such monuments close together), has disappeared without trace. As for the 'perfect' **theatre** described by Fellows (*p. 26*), Charles Texier (*p. 32*) made a fine drawing of it and of its scena with five doors. It measured 76.5m across and had been tentatively dated to the 1st century BC. The site has been excavated and what is left of it can be seen by the main coastal road, with some rock tombs in the background. Of a second theatre up the slope, dated to the 2nd century AD, only a depression in the rock remains. More rock-cut **tombs** can can be admired at the other end of town, just above the bus station. Among them is the **Tomb of Amyntas**, where Texier carved his name on the lintel and noticed in the process traces of red paint. The tomb is a standard temple tomb, Ionic in style, with remains of three acroteria on the pediment. At about the same level is the **castle on the acropolis**, built in a mix of styles. It has been suggested by Clive Foss that Anastasius II fortified the hill above the harbour (the style is in keeping and this emperor is known to have been keen on coastal defences) using whatever he could lay his hands on, which would account for the Hellenistic spolia. He is thought to have built the castle as well as a harbour wall, now almost completely obliterated. The Byzantine Comneni completed the work in the 11th–12th century, in their last attempt to control the sea. The enclosed area is very small but it is a good vantage point and from the sea it would have looked impressive, encircling the crest of the hill with its double skin. Built of stone, bricks and spolia, it had a number of square and round towers.

Telmessus is destined to remain something of a mystery, however, because research has been quite sparing and much has thus been lost. By tradition it was a great place for **divination**, with or without the assistance of snakes, which were supposed to come from Snake Island, one of the old names for Makri. There is a long list of ancient authors, inlcuding Pliny the Elder, Arrian and Cicero, to back this up. It seems that the local women and children were endowed with prophetic vision. This gift seems to have been lost over time. Even the snakes have gone; you can plan a picnic and a day out on Makri without cause for alarm.

BYZANTINE SETTLEMENTS

Examples of these can be visited on the west side of the gulf at **Lydae**, where a Hellenistic city grew into a large settlement in late antique times; at **Tersane Ada** ('Dockyard Island'), which preserves various photogenic remains, and especially south of Telmessus at **Gemiler Adası** (variously also called St Nicholas Island or Lebissos or Perdikonisi because of the partridges). It is now a national park (**Ölüdeniz Milli Parkı**; *charge*) and has interesting remains intermixed with survivals of a later reoccupation in the 19th–20th century, when the island accommodated about 7,000 people, mainly Greeks. They left with the advent of the Turkish Republic in 1923. The large churches date from the 19th century but there are a number of mid-Byzantine chapels, some with traces of painting.

Due south of Telmessus is the village of **Kayaköy** (*map B, 8*), abandoned in the early 1920s and now deserted. It has been resurrected as a tourist attraction, a destination you can now reach by quad bike, on horseback and in a myriad other inventive ways for a day 'full of adrenalin'. While you are there, take some time to meditate over the futility of simplistic solutions like population exchanges.

THE INTERIOR NORTH OF FETHİYE

Going north, one encounters very rugged and wild terrain. Beyond Üzümlü (Cadyanda) the Lycian influence wanes. Looking at a physical map one can see that the two main lines of communication, the Xanthus and Arycandus valleys, enclose a massif, the ancient Massicytus, with the Ak Dağı reaching 3024m; beyond is valuable arable land better accessed from the north (and, to some extent, from Telmessus and Antalya) than from the south. Here are the remains of four cities, which at some point were united in a **Tetrapolis**: Oenoanda, Bubon, Balboura and Cibyra spread out in the long transition to the Anatolian Plateau. They mark the Hellenistic enthusiasm for urbanism which Rome later reinforced, creating a secure administrative network to control local populations and bring them securely into the imperial fold. Like other urban settlements (e.g. Sagalassos, Kremna; see *Blue Guide Aegean Turkey*), they were abandoned when the central power, either Rome or Byzantium, failed.

The area has been extensively and thoroughly surveyed but not much excavated and while the settlements present themselves to us in their Roman garb, there is evidence of much earlier occupation from the 4th millennium BC (e.g. Çaltılar Hüyük and the tumuli with painted chambers at Elmalı). It remains difficult to make connections, however: the possibility of an early seasonal occupation has been put forward. A number of **Lycian rock-cut tombs** in the area have been identified and studied and dated to the 4th century BC. They are classed as Lycian because they imitate wooden structures, which is a typical trait of Lycian funerary architecture. So far **no Lycian settlement** has been found to go with them. It has been suggested that Perikles, the dynast of Limyra who signed himself King of Lycia, may have brought this region under Lycian control and that these could be the tombs of his governors. After the failed Satrap's Revolt in 366 BC, Lycia was incorporated into Caria under Mausolus. Ethnically, moreover, this northern land belongs to the Kabalians and the Mylians—mentioned by Herodotus (7,77; 7,92) and by Strabo with plenty of ambiguities—and more generally speaking to the Pisidians.

CADYANDA

Cadyanda (in Lycian Kadavañti; *map B, 7; open daily 15 June–2 Oct 9–7, 3 Oct–14 June 8–5; charge*) still belongs to the coast since, from the 969m plateau among the pine trees, there is a good view of Telmessus. Fellows (*p. 26*) first described it and identified it from an inscription. Its name means 'rich in grain', which does not quite tally with its present name (Üzümlü), 'rich in grapes'. It is reached from Üzümlü village by a steep path. The walk takes a couple of hours (it might make sense to take a taxi) and you should set aside about an hour and a half for the visit. There is a well-marked visitor trail on the site and you are advised to keep to it because of the unguarded cisterns.

Located on a natural route between Caunus and Araxa (a Lycian city in the Xanthus valley, known from sources and with some fine tombs), Cadyanda's elevated position also suggests a very early occupation, though this remains unproven. Coins dated to the 5th century BC and some limited Hellenistic remains lead on to the Roman period, which is the evidence one sees when strolling around in the pine overgrowth. Cadyanda seems to have been abandoned in the 7th century AD, by which time it was too close to the sea and the roving Arabs.

The city was enclosed by a **wall** revealing repeated repairs. The best section is to the southwest, with finely joined polygonal blocks. It consisted of two skins with a rubble filling, was backed by regularly placed buttresses, and the top was capped by slabs providing a wall walk. It stands in places to 6m. Inside, starting from the north, are the ruins of a temple close to four intercommunicating **cisterns** (of which the site has plenty more since there was no aqueduct because of the difficult topography). The **stadium**, or rather running track, 900m long and 9m wide, where two different athletic festivals were held according to an inscription, is opposite. Remains of **baths** and of an **agora** flanked by a **stoa** have been identified further south. The **theatre** is Hellenistic in shape, the arc it describes greater than a semicircle. The vaulted **tombs** are outside the walls. Cadyanda, according to some, is vastly overgrown and difficult to reach but you are richly rewarded, especially if there are few visitors (which is usually the case). The place is peaceful, at rest with itself. It is a town that once was and has now died, and nature is taking its course.

OENOANDA

Situated on a commanding spur 300m above the surrounding plain and 1300m above sea level, in an environment suitable for cultivation and stock breeding (though the sources of its prosperity in antiquity are still not fully explained), Oenoanda (*map B, 7*) is in a well defended position that might have attracted early settlement were it not for the lack of water. Just as in the past, Oenoanda today is for the determined. To reach it you have to be ready to face a 1.5km hike from the village of İncealiler to the east; a path will lead you roughly to the Esplanade (*see below*). The other side is steeper. The site itself is very overgrown. İncealiler is 5.5 km east of the Karabel Pass on Route 330 on a secondary road south.

Some would like to find **Hittite roots** here, drawing a parallel with Wiyanawanda, which crops up in Hittite tablets, and therefore some allusion to wine production (the name means 'wine land'). Opinions are divided on the matter. The site is at the top of the Xanthus valley, overlooking the river where it runs east–west. This suggests a possible defensive settlement (one of a chain), developed by Eumenes II of Pergamon to cover the road from Telmessus to Antalya. Alternatively it could have been a colony of Termessus (*p. 120*), as an inscription in the bouleuterion appears to indicate. Lycia is also present here, with the inscription on the **Licinia Flavilla tomb** on the south slope west of the aqueduct, which lists twelve generations of Lycian ancestry. The style of the remains is mainly Roman, showing Roman involvement in the building or rebuilding of structures in the early 1st century AD. A resettlement of Italian veterans has been suggested. Whatever its history, it is certain that Oenoanda flourished during the Empire, declining in late antiquity when a new, smaller circuit of walls was built. This can be traced on the west side of the site and it included a fort which was lined with small rooms on the north and east sides. After a brief Byzantine revival, the site collapsed in the 7th–8th century. There is a bishop of Oenoanda in Church documents from the 12th century but he may well have been living in Byzantium, away from his flock, assuming anyone was still here.

The earliest survival is the **Hellenistic wall**, which can be followed for 65m in the area to the south, where a saddle connects the spur to the hill beyond. The style of masonry is reminiscent of that of Eumenes II in Pergamon, with two walls built with well-fitting stones filled with rubble (emplecton). A gate and two towers, one round the other pentagonal, have been identified. The **round tower** controlled the gate and the higher hill to the south, while the **pentagonal tower**, rising to three storeys, was equipped with a top floor suitable for siege engines. The wall, which survives in places to its original height, had a wall walk c. 2m wide. Traces of the defences on the west side that Spratt (*p. 31*) documented are now lost. The **acropolis**, 400m to the northeast, has some cisterns showing how the water supply was originally organised.

OENOANDA'S MAIN CLAIM TO FAME

Perhaps the very seclusion of Roman Oenoanda, altogether prosperous but high up and remote, inspired lofty thoughts in its inhabitants. This was certainly so for a certain Diogenes, who having 'reached the sunset of life' around the first half of the 2nd century AD decided to share his thoughts on the great questions of existence with his peers, that is those of them who could read. He wanted his message to be permanent and accessible and at that time there was no better place than the Hellenistic agora, also known as the Esplanade.

He therefore set up a stone **inscription** whose estimated size has continued to grow since the first fragments were identified in the 1880s. The latest estimate is 260m square and 25,000 words. Little did Diogenes know that in late antique times the Esplanade would be cut off from the city by a defensive wall. The inscription was dismantled and used as spolia—and since then the quest to piece it together again has been part of the attraction of surveying in and around Oenoanda. Fragments of the inscription have been identified in a well 4km away.

Diogenes was a **follower of Epicurus**, the 3rd-century BC philosopher who preached *ataraxia*, i.e. freedom from fear, as the main goal in life, together with the avoidance of pain. He identified fear of the gods as the main obstacle to human happiness. He did not deny their existence but placed them outside the human sphere. The gods had not created the world and had no interest in running it; they did not wish to be disturbed to mete out punishment to malefactors. They were confined to a life of perfect serenity in some other place; however, they had to be worshipped, as the act of doing so inspired peaceful thoughts in the human mind. Besides religion and theology, Epicurus' teaching covered other branches of knowledge such as physics, epistemology and ethics. All of this was made available to the people of Oenoanda.

EXPLORING OENOANDA

Approaching from İncealiler, one arrives at the **Esplanade**, a modern name to indicate this open space. Here was Oenoanda's claim to fame (*see box above*), the original **Hellenistic agora** bordered by stoas with Corinthian fluted columns on three sides set at an angle as in Assos (*see Blue Guide Aegean Turkey*) and with the same topography and layout. It was cut off from the town by the late antique wall that one can see in the distance, beyond the bases for statues of notable citizens. Note to the right the **Doric temple**, reused as a bastion when the wall was built. Beyond is the **theatre**, with a Greek cavea and a Roman scena on substructures partly cut into the natural limestone slope.

The rest of the site shows that from the 1st century AD onwards the city was provided with all the customary Roman amenities. There was a **second agora** with its **colonnaded street**, a couple of **baths** and a **palaestra**. The monumental architectural style, with monolithic columns and coffered ceilings, suggests an abundance of funds. Oenoanda was a place where euergetism apparently worked very well, beginning with Opramoas (*p. 109*), who financed the baths after the AD 141 earthquake.

The **church** towards the south, with a nave and two aisles, was built with spolia. Apart from the lack of a main temple, two other buildings not yet located pose a conundrum, since to judge by the inscriptions, Oenoanda was keen on athletic and music festivals. There must have been a stadium somewhere. There was also a 'boukonisterion', a structure whose function is uncertain although it appears to have been related to sport. Again, it is known from an inscription and boukonisterion is a term only attested here.

To the extreme south is the **aqueduct**, which could supply Oenoanda with c. 1000 cubic metres of water a day. It is dated to the 1st century AD and is probably linked to the building of the baths. To allow the aqueduct through, the Hellenistic wall was dismantled and sophisticated solutions (including perforated stone blocks 2m long) were used to deal with the question of pressure. The water came from about 5km away via a pipeline provided with silt traps.

BALBOURA

Taking the road north to Gölhisar, the ruins of Balboura are on a side road to the left, marked just short of Altınyayla (*map B, 5*); the location is called Çölkayığı, literally meaning 'ship in the desert'.

Situated at 1500m above sea level, with the highest known Lycian acropolis (although thought to be of Pisidian foundation), Balboura is surrounded by marginal land only suitable for pasture. It has been surveyed since T.A.B. Spratt (*p. 31*) discovered it and identified it from an inscription in the mid-19th century. Cores show that the climate has deteriorated. It may have been a more welcoming place 2,000 years ago; wine presses have been found. An **acropolis** to the north (Asar Tepe) had houses on terraces facing south. The site was chosen for its strategic value. Various early lines of wall have been identified. It is thought that at some point, from around the 3rd century AD onwards, the walled acropolis served as a refuge. The Roman conquest broke up the Tetrapolis of Oenoanda, Bubon, Balboura and Cibyra and Balboura was remodelled in the Roman style.

Balboura was situated close to the Dirimli Pass (1580m), controlling access to Cibyra (*see below*). Roman interest in it may have been related to road building and communications. In the Roman town, the **civic centre** (not excavated) lay to the southeast and is originally Flavian (1st century AD), with baths, a nymphaeum and an aqueduct, and later a couple of churches huddled around a paved agora with a triple gate, much plainer than that at Ariassos in Pamphylia (described in a succeeding chapter). In the agora itself, statue bases set in two exedrae show a desire to be a part of the Roman imperial apparatus, as local worthies (Meleager, a magnate and Onisimos, a city slave) erected bronze honorific statues, an expensive undertaking, more costly than marble. The Temple of Nemesis is part of the same impetus. This area of town had its own **wall circuit** in the 4th–5th century. A **couple of theatres** cut into the rock on the acropolis slope are small and appear unfinished. They may have hosted the **local music and sport festival** (the Antoniana Meleagria) with wrestling and the deadly *pankration*, a combination of boxing and wrestling where no holds were barred (bar biting and gouging out one's opponent's eyes), as well as civic assemblies.

The demise of Balboura is poorly documented. Decline set in around the 7th/8th century. Seljuk pottery dated to the 12th century appears to be, by its shape, more appropriate to nomads. Ottoman records show no permanent settlement in the area. On the whole, Balboura's Romanness never went very deep. While the elite played in turn at being Hellenised, Roman and even Lycian, the inscriptions show a persistence of local names. It was a thin veneer.

BUBON

The third city of the Tetrapolis has recently achieved fame but for the wrong reasons. Bubon lies in the area of the Yapraklı Dam, c. 1.6km south of the village of İbecik (*map B, 5*) at Dikmen. It was first identified by Captain Spratt, who reported a theatre, many buildings on terraces and a form of fortification at the top of the hill.

Despite a shortage of evidence from official excavations, we know of Bubon through numerous inscriptions. The city benefited from a donation from Opramoas (*p. 109*) but the sum of 2,000 denarii was paltry compared to other donations of his. At the time of Commodus (r. 180–92), Bubon was officially praised for successfully suppressing banditry. Such marks of imperial favour, publicised in the theatre, were possibly instrumental in helping Bubon to reach the top rank in the Lycian League (three votes, the highest category). Beyond that we know nothing.

Illicit excavations, on the other hand, have been rife and they included the plundering of the Sebasteion, the locus of imperial worship. This happened in the 1960s and at the time a sudden availability of Greek/Roman bronzes was commented upon in relevant circles in the US: artefacts seemed to be flooding the market. The archaeologist George Bean (*p. 22*) had noted and publicised the looting c. 1966. Salvage excavations in 1967 unearthed a bronze torso (now in Burdur Museum). According to Jale İnan, who excavated the Sebasteion in the 1990s, a cast of the torso fits a head which is now at the Metropolitan Museum in New York. She also discovered a number of statue bases *in situ* in the Sebasteion, with dates ranging from Nero (r. 54–68) to Gallienus (r. 260–8) and was the instigator of a campaign to recover what was looted in the 1960s. At the time of writing the matter still remained unresolved.

CIBYRA

In *Epistle VI*, Horace comes up with a throwaway phrase: *Cibyriatica negotia*, which makes it clear that in his day (late 1st century BC), business was the vocation of Cibyra (*map B, 5*) and its region. Situated at the centre of a large **agricultural plain** which produced oil, wine, wheat and wood, Cibyra also boasted iron works and local mines (which inspired Captain Spratt (*p. 31*) to dub it 'the Birmingham of Asia'). More importantly still, it was situated on the **road to Phrygia**. Small wonder that when the Romans broke up the Tetrapolis of which Cibyra was the head (we do not know much about their reasons for doing this apart from the fact that the Romans found Cibyra troublesome), Cibyra was incorporated into the Province of Asia. The other three members of the Tetrapolis were assigned to Lycia. So much for the first two centuries of the current era when Cibyra flourishes; however we are still in the dark as to its history before and after this date.

CIBYRA'S EARLY BEGINNINGS AND DEVELOPMENT

As a commercial node linking Lycia and Phrygia, Cibyra may well have been settled from early times, but possibly not in the precise spot where the town is now. Attention has been turning to a lake nearby, with a rocky island in the middle. Spratt has left a good description of it, which of course shows its state in the mid-19th century. The steep rocky island (Göl Ada, 10km east of Cibyra) had the ruins of a large defended town on it and there was a causeway linking it to the shore. The lake was full of reeds and provided excellent fishing. In Spratt's time there were three Turkish families living on the island and there was a caravansaray on the shore. The island no longer exists; at the beginning of the 20th century the fortifications were demolished and a couple of hamlets were brought together to form today's village of **Gölhisar**, where in spite of the name there is no lake (*göl*) and no fortress (*hisar*). It is possible that the earliest settlement was indeed on the island and that later, in late Hellenistic times, the Pisidians moving west founded present Cibyra.

In 189 BC the Roman consul Gn. Manlius Vulso certainly found something in Cibyra that he was able to tax mercilessly (*Livy 38,14,3*). According to Strabo (*14,6,31*) it was a truly cosmopolitan place, where one could could hear Greek, Pisidian, Lydian and Solymian spoken in the streets. Cibyra flourished during the first two centuries of Roman rule. Even earthquakes caused no lasting problem as Rome more than once stepped in to aid with repairs; the town renamed itself Caesarea Cibyra as a mark of respect to the distant benefactor. According to Pliny, Cibyra had a vast territory. This was a time of large estates in the hands of elite senatorial families, including the sister of Marcus Aurelius. *Negotiatores* (businessmen) also frequently appear in the inscriptions, as do priests of the Imperial cult, who would have organised the gladiatorial games.

Cibyra remained undefended until late antiquity but trouble began with the Goths and the Isaurians (4th and 5th centuries), after which came plagues and later the Arab invasions. Cibyra shrunk back within its fortified agora and by the 6th–7th century it was no more. A bishop of Cibyra is attested in the 10th century. According to some he had retreated to Göl Ada, a well-defended position, but we shall never know. In 1332/3, when Ibn Battuta (*p. 22*) came this way, he found a Türkmen chief settled on the island, with little control of the land around. This was lawless territory, a land of brigands, neither under the control of the Seljuks nor of anyone else. The Türkmen chief offered Ibn Battuta an armed escort to see him safely to Denizli. Eventually, squeezed between the Karamanlids, the Ottomans and the brigands, the local emir sold his territory to the Ottomans for 80 gold coins. A religious disagreement (the locals were Alevi and the Ottomans were Sunni) prompted the transfer of populations mentioned above and the obliteration of the island.

CIBYRA TODAY

Cibyra is destined for great things, becoming a big tourist centre. And though it is located in an improbable place, a long way from the beach, hopes are high. It could easily be that by the time you get here, there will be a ticket booth. It could even be calling itself a World Heritage Site: so far Cibyra is on the 'tentative list', but it is a UNESCO hopeful. At the time of writing, however, entry was still free and there were no set opening times. But bearing in mind that the remains are scattered and there is a lot of scrub around, you will need to take care.

The site is approached from the east through the **necropolis**, where Cibyra's main pastime is well attested: gladiatorial games and animal hunts featuring a variety of beasts (from bears to ostriches). Some stunning reliefs can be admired in the museum at Burdur (*map B, 6*). Beyond that is the city proper, on a slope rising west. It has only been partially explored thus far, so that we have highlights of the city but no overarching structure. At its top end, the city stands 100m above the surrounding plain. A **triumphal arch**, Doric in style, leads to the fine **stadium**, which doubled up as an area for gladiatorial games. The stadium was 197m long and could accommodate 10,000 spectators. The eastern side, built up against the hill, originally had 21 rows of seats; the western side was lower. A vaulted ruin to the west is possibly a 6th-century martyrium. The centre of the city is higher up. The **agora** had cisterns beneath the paving. It had a **colonnaded street** leading into it from the south, but the relationship is not clear. The agora was Cibyra's last redoubt in the 6th–7th century. At the summit on the ridge is a fine **theatre** built in local limestone and marble: it measures 81m in diameter. It is Hellenistic in style and is dated to c. 100 BC. It was probably enlarged later by adding an extra tier of seats at the top. Close to it is a 3rd-century bouleuterion or odeion in large limestone blocks, 45m in diameter. It was covered, had windows and apparently even a heating system. Its cavea sits on a natural slope. The remains next to it belong to a Roman **bath**. Beyond the theatre are the remains of a church, one of the two identified, both early Byzantine. More notably, this was also probably the **potters' quarter**. No kiln has so far been identified but there are plenty of wasters and a lot of misfired pottery. It seems that Cybira was producing fine ware for everyday use at the table. There is no coarse ware for the kitchen. It exported little but also imported little. Production continued into the 6th century. The town's water supply is still a bit of a mystery.

THE UPPER XANTHUS VALLEY

The site of Xanthus itself, with the Letoön and Patara, is described below (*p. 68*). Exploring the heart of Lycia beyond these sites is best done by private transport. Settlements tend to be on high ground away from the river since the Eşen Çay (the modern name for the Xanthus river) meanders, changes course and floods when the Taurus snows melt. The vantage point beside the river, affording control without the risks involved in proximity, was Xanthus and it made its fortune. But Tlos, Pinara and Sidyma all sought out vantage points as well.

TLOS

Tlos (*map B, 7; open daytime; charge*) lies just east of the village of Düğer, north of the Saklıkent Milli Parkı. As you approach, you can see the great attraction of the site: a huge rock with an impressive escarpment and defended all around. In times past it provided the **acropolis** for the settlement, which spread out to the east. From the acropolis one has a commanding view of the Eşen Çay valley, of the sea, of Mt Cragus and of the Taurus mountains. To the north was the Karabel Pass leading to Cibyra (*see above*) and traces of a paved road have been found. The summit was still an attraction in the 19th century, when it was the summer residence of the local *ağa*. Fellows (*p. 26*) spent three happy days there entertained by the *ağa*'s brother, oblivious of course that the full name of the *ağa* was Ali Kanlı Ağa ('Bloody Ali'). The antiquarian took an interest in the rock-cut tombs on the sides of the limestone acropolis and especially the 'Bellerophon Tomb', noticing traces of paint (now lost) on the horse's wings. The Lycian tombs (mimicking wooden architecture) suggest that this was the seat of a dynast and according to some, Tlos goes back to the time of the Hittites, assuming that the Lycian name of the settlement (Tlawa) is correctly reflected in the Hittite Dalawa, mentioned as a settlement in the Lykka land.

There is little left of Lycian Tlos apart from the tombs. Coins confirm that it was part of the Lycian League. Persian occupation (which is presumed, given the history of the area) left nothing; the Hellenism that followed may, according to an inscription, have seen the erection of an early Ptolemaion (an honorific monument for an Egyptian ruler).

Today's Tlos is Roman and Ottoman. The city appears to have followed the usual trajectory. Roman expansion, which brought a wealth of civic amenities, a cosmopolitan community with a Jewish element in the 1st century AD (they had

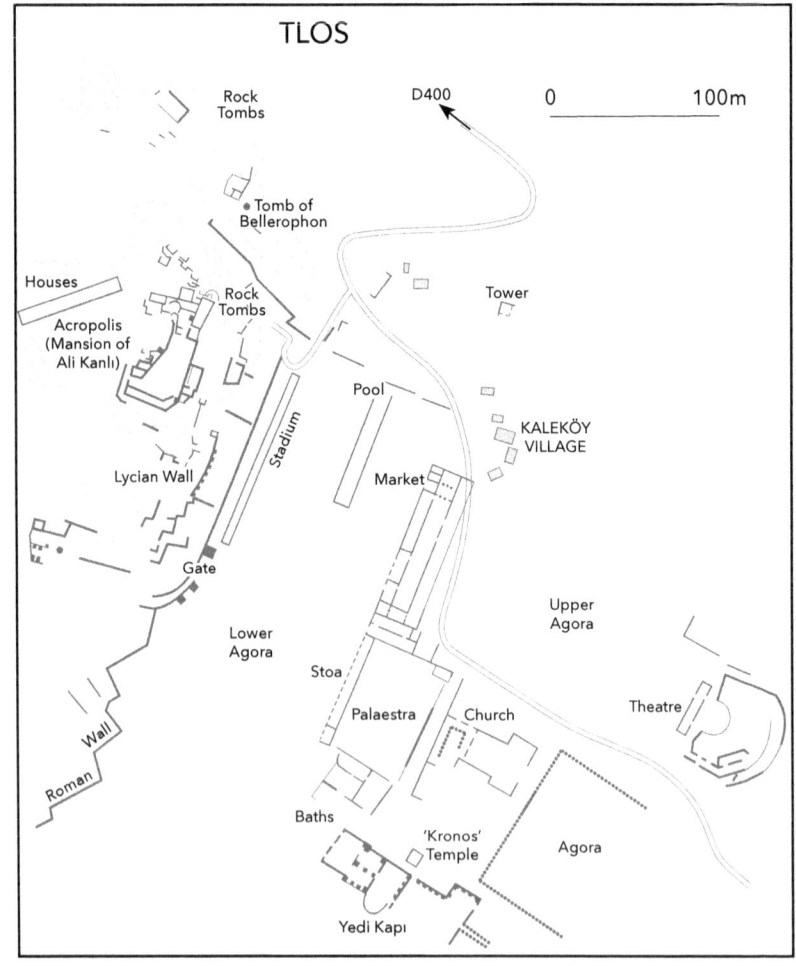

their own magistrates), and then contraction and the building of a defensive wall at the foot of the acropolis (look out for the incorporated sarcophagi and column drums). Its walls enabled Tlos to hold out in the Dark Ages, after which it was no more. Christianity is attested by a large early Byzantine church and a bishop in the 12th century.

EXPLORING TLOS

The terrain is rough and security measures are scarce; it is important to tread carefully. **Ali Kanlı's mansion** (*see above*) has almost obliterated any pre-existing structures on the acropolis, but being built with spolia, it has a few inscriptions built into it among the stone blocks and the bricks. Part of the building was rock-cut and one can still see the beam holes for the upper floor. A porch was built at the south end. From there you have a great view of the city below. The rock-cut steps are believed to be ancient and related to a temple which no longer survives. The stables were on the north side. They are just above the '**Bellerophon Tomb**', which lies beyond the defensive wall to the north. A trail leads to it and there is a ladder leading up to it for closer inspection. It is still always known as the Bellerophon Tomb, but though the horse appears to have wings, the rider is in Persian attire. A very damaged figure is thought to represent the chimaera, also part of the Bellerophon legend, but it takes some imagination to make it out.

The **lower town** has a number of monumental buildings but information is still rather contradictory and confused; the area of settlement is believed to be to the south and east. Tlos was keen on sports, as the stadium and the palaestra clearly show. The **stadium** could seat 3,500 people. The **market building** to the southeast is thought to have been two storeys high. To the south of it the **palaestra** adjoined the **baths** with the **Yedi Kapı**, its seven arches possibly the remains of an exedra. Between the baths and the early Byzantine **church**, a platform with two Corinthian columns is said to have been a **temple to Kronos**. In between these buildings three agoras are mooted. The **theatre** to the east was originally Hellenistic, until it suffered in an earthquake. In its present state it is 2nd-century Roman, paid for by the munificence of Opramoas (*p. 109*), who gave 60,000 denarii, as opposed to the mere 2,000 he contributed to Bubon. The new theatre had seats for dignitaries in polished limestone with carved lion's claws: Freya Stark saw them in the 1950s.

PINARA

Pinara (*map B, 7*) is to the west of Route 400, reached by following signs to Minare. It overlooks the plain and blends beautifully into the slopes of Mt Cragus.

Originally built on an elevated platform to the west (later the higher town and acropolis), it expanded east, creating a substantial lower town. In between, a steep cliff face is full of rock-cut **tombs**, Fellows's 'dwelling places for the eagles' (one does wonder at past health and safety rules). It is here and at the so-called Royal Tomb that the **Lycian heritage** of Pinara can be seen. Unfortunately many tombs have been used as dwellings or animal pens and the friezes are now blackened. However the Lycian style can be seen in the architecture, imitating wooden structrues, and in the

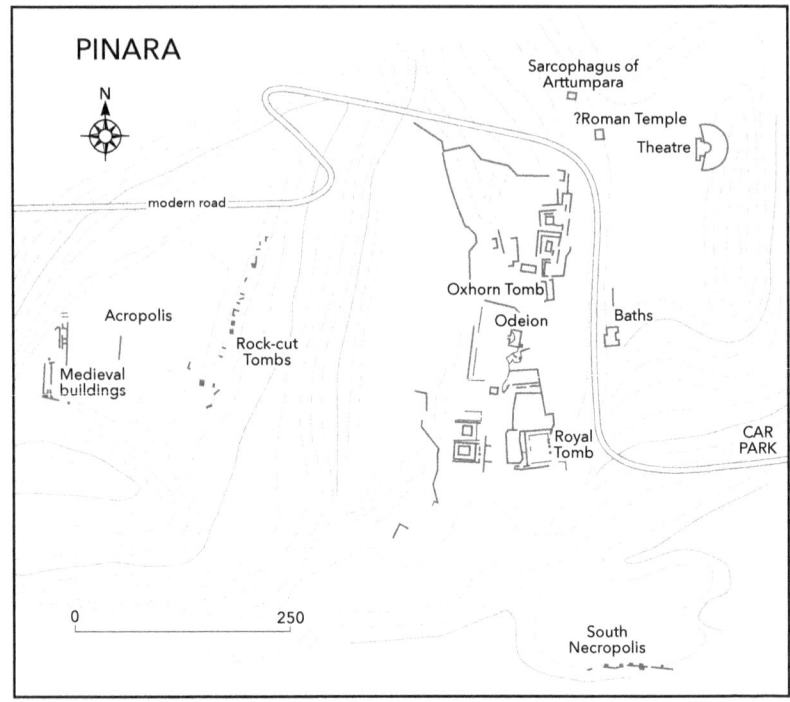

ogival lids with ox horns at the top. It is very possible, therefore, that Pinara goes back to the 5th/4th century BC, at which time it would have been a Xanthian colony. Its territory may have stretched to the coast, where it had its own **harbour**. Pinara belonged to the Lycian League, in which it had three votes.

When Alexander the Great took Pinara, it had no defences. After the interlude of the diadochoi, it came under the rule of Pergamon and then of Rome. It was at this time that the city was redeveloped to the east, with its lower town apparently on a grid and with the usual amenities: **theatre**, **temple**, **odeion**, **market-place** and in due course a **defensive wall**. According to his *vita*, St Nicholas of Sion (a historical figure not to be confused with St Nicholas of Myra, from whom Santa Claus is derived) was appointed bishop here and built a beautiful church to the Mother of God, which has not been located. By then Pinara had already shrunk, possibly retreating back within the confines of its acropolis. It was abandoned in the 9th century.

Pinara has not yet been thoroughly excavated legally. On the other hand its geological woes have attracted seismologists and the like. Located in a critical quake zone and crossed by two faults, it has suffered three known quakes: in AD 141, 240 and 1851. The lower town is separated from the acropolis by a normal fault and from the hill to the east where the theatre is, by a thrust fault. There are various spots where earthquake damage can be seen in the lower town. These include shifted and rotated blocks at both ends of the theatre and tilted seating blocks; cracked lintels in door and window frames; collapsed columns with axial fracturing; walls not collapsed but sinuously deformed; rotated building structures and more besides. Researches have also investigated the Lycian **sarcophagus of Arttumpara**, right at the north of town (*see plan*), which has shifted on its plinth. They concluded that the movement was not due to quake damage but to looting with explosives: some of the older locals do remember hearing a loud bang sometime in the late 1970s.

SIDYMA

Sidyma (*map B, 7*) lies on the north edge of the Cragus massif, at a point that was later to take on a historical significance. In European documents it is here that the first mention of Turkey as a state is made. The **Sandak Dağı** jutting into the Mediterranean, the 'Caput Turquiae' of a 14th-century portulan, was then the recognised border between the Emperor and the Sultan.

Sidyma today is somewhat lost in the wilderness, which adds to its charm. The road is poor but passable with care and local people are pleased to see you. You first reach Dodurga on Route 400, 6km south of Eşen before Gölbent. The modern village has been built among the ruins: the mosque is on the site of the baths, for example, and reuses columns form the Doric stoa of the Roman agora. The arched chambers with apsidal ends and painted stucco decorations that Charles Fellows (*p. 26*) saw in the 1840s are no longer there. Little is known about the site's early history.

The name itself, ending in 'ima', suggests an old settlement of Anatolian origin. Its harbour was called Kalabatia. From the coins we know that the town was a member of the Lycian League and there is one pillar tomb, a typical Lycian trait. At the same time, a number of the sarcophagus tombs are Carian in style. The remains are generally Roman and Byzantine. As a sideline the town also offered an oracle of Apollo. The site has not been officially excavated and a number of monuments that were noted earlier on seem now to be lost or hidden in the undergrowth.

The steep **acropolis** (820m above sea level) to the north, accessed by rock-cut steps, is occupied by mid-Byzantine defences with round towers. The town, 300m lower, is to the southeast. A number of civic buildings beyond those already mentioned have been identified by inscriptions and spolia: a **sebasteion**, a **theatre** and an early Byzantine basilica with a nave and two aisles; you can indulge in a spolia safari by looking at the modern village houses. The **necropolis** to the east of the village has some interesting monuments. Tombs do not recycle easily and they remain scattered among fields and gardens. One in particular, planned as a temple in antis, has an interesting coffered ceiling, a single slab still in place with female heads and flowers that were originally painted.

Sidyma has left no mark on history apart from a single bright moment when the future emperor Marcian, then a simple soldier and feeling unwell, happened to pass through. Here he had a premonition of his imperial destiny. A huge eagle was seen spreading its wings over him while he was asleep. When Charles Fellows visited, he noted bears and wolves, so it was a wild area then, making Marcian's prophetic eagle a not unlikely occurrence. Certainly Marcian did not forget the kind locals who had looked after him in his illness and rewarded them with important positions in

Lycia. On the whole, Sidyma seems to have had staying power. It was fairly remote and had no need of a defensive wall in the late antique period; it still had a bishop in the 8th century.

THE LOWER XANTHUS VALLEY

The Eşen Çay (the modern name for the ancient Xanthus) forms the western rim of the Ak Dağları massif. Rising to 3024m, the massif stretches to the sea, blocking communications by land while, in the hinterland of Kaş, Tuzle Tepe (1366m) is barely 5km from the sea. Land links have always been problematic here: today's land route is very recent. The route north was also difficult, only passable via Finike and the valley of the Arycandus (the modern Akçay). The Demre Çay, which gave Myra an advantage in antiquity, mainly runs parallel to the coast, affording limited but vital access inland. The surest means of communication was therefore by sea and it is this fact that afforded the Xanthus river valley, all 60km of it running north–south, its importance in antiquity. It was also broad, in places as wide as 5km, affording the possibility of agriculture in an area that was otherwise short of alluvial soils.

THE CITY OF XANTHUS

The city of Xanthus (*map B, 7; open daily April–Oct 8.30–6.30, Nov–March 8.30–5; charge*), a UNESCO World Heritage Site perched high on a rocky plateau overlooking the river but untouched by its turbulence, with a view of the sea and its own harbour at Patara (*p. 78*) and the Letoön (*p. 76*) on its doorstep, figures prominently in antique historical accounts as a key site of Lycia.

Finds yielded by excavations suggest that it had a lifespan of 1,500 years; and yet after many years of excavation there is little to see. The tourist industry is not well served here. This is not the fault of the French excavators, who have spent 60 years meticulously piecing together Xanthus' past. The problem is caused by the use and relentless reuse of spolia, by earthquakes and by the exposed nature of the site. In addition, the present environment does not help. Pictures in the brochures never show this but Xanthus stands on the edge of an expanding agricultural area, with a profusion of plastic-covered greenhouses, and is crossed by a modern tarmac road. It overlooks an ugly modern concrete bridge. If you want to get an idea of the river as it was in antiquity, you have to look upstream—that is, until that area too is colonised by polytunnels. The same applies to the Letoön; Patara has fared slightly better. Xanthus is therefore no Ephesus, where you can get the feeling of walking in the past, with its remains still standing at good height beside you; nor a Troy, where the lack of sizeable ruins is made up for by history, poetry and the Homeric spirit; nor is it an Arykanda (*p. 105*), lost in the wilderness. No amount of re-erecting of columns will change that. The best way to enjoy time in Xanthus is to make yourself at home with its history. Then the stones will make more sense.

HISTORY OF XANTHUS

First, a few words about the **topography** (*for a plan, see overleaf*). Xanthus sits on a plateau, roughly square in shape (600m by 700m), with its highest point to the north (130m). It is edged to the west by a cliff reaching down to the river; by a steep slope to the south and a more gentle valley to the east. Communications were to the north (Tlos) and east (Phellos, near modern Kaş); the river could be forded here and was navigable for small boats; indeed, in the 19th century it was still used to send firewood and salt fish from the interior to the coast and then on to Rhodes. The name of the river (*Xanthe* in Greek and *Sirbis* in Lycian, both meaning 'yellow' or 'fair') is a reference to the amount of mud it funnelled downstream. No harbour was afforded by the river delta because of extensive marshes. Patara was by the coast to the east, where a water inlet, now a swamp blocked by sand dunes, provided a safe anchorage. On the plateau, two heights are noteworthy: to the extreme west, the so called Lycian acropolis (68m above sea level), well defined by cliffs; and to the north, the so-called Greek or Hellenistic acropolis (though no acropolis has been found there), which is 60m higher. In antiquity Xanthus was closer to the sea since the present coastal plain was under water.

The **earliest finds** come from the southeast corner of this roughly square area. They are the animal reliefs now in Antalya museum, but without a context they cannot be attributed with any certainty to a palace, gate or tomb. They are monumental in style and provide evidence, according to some, of neo-Hittite or Phrygian occupation dating to the 8th/7th century BC, which would be in line with a Hittite text where Awarna has been identified as Xanthus. If that is so, Xanthus was a place of consequence well before the Persians took an interest in it. Quite how important it was is not clear, since the earliest finds on the Lycian acropolis, dating to the 8th century BC, suggest contacts with the Aegean islands and Ionia and, at the time, no great wealth.

According to Herodotus (*1,176*) the conquering Persians besieged Xanthus in 540 BC, coming up from the river valley, and when the inhabitants realised they could not win they committed mass suicide, setting fire to the acropolis (by which we understand the Lycian acropolis). The layer of ash beneath the 6th-century BC level is evidence of the Persian destruction. The town was re-established by 80 Xanthian families, who had happened to be away at the time of the siege. There followed a time of rule by dynasts, local strongmen with Persian backing, until Xanthus was swallowed up by the Carian Hecatomnids. It was never a polis, it was an indigenous town with indigenous institutions and monuments. Hellenisation came much later, towards the end of the Hellenistic period. It had been thought that the refounded town, going by its Lycian name of Arñna, was limited to the Lycian acropolis, and a couple of Oriental-style cult edifices have been identified there, showing Eastern links and suggesting a cult of Artemis in its earliest form, as at Ephesus. However, recent excavations have also identified a number of dwellings outside the acropolis, which allow us to make sense of the extensive Classical-style defensive wall which encloses the whole site and shows evidence of subsequent rebuildings and repairs. The presence of tombs *intra muros* shows the **indigenous character** of the city. Even well into the Hellenistic period there was no clear distinction between the city of the living and the city of the dead.

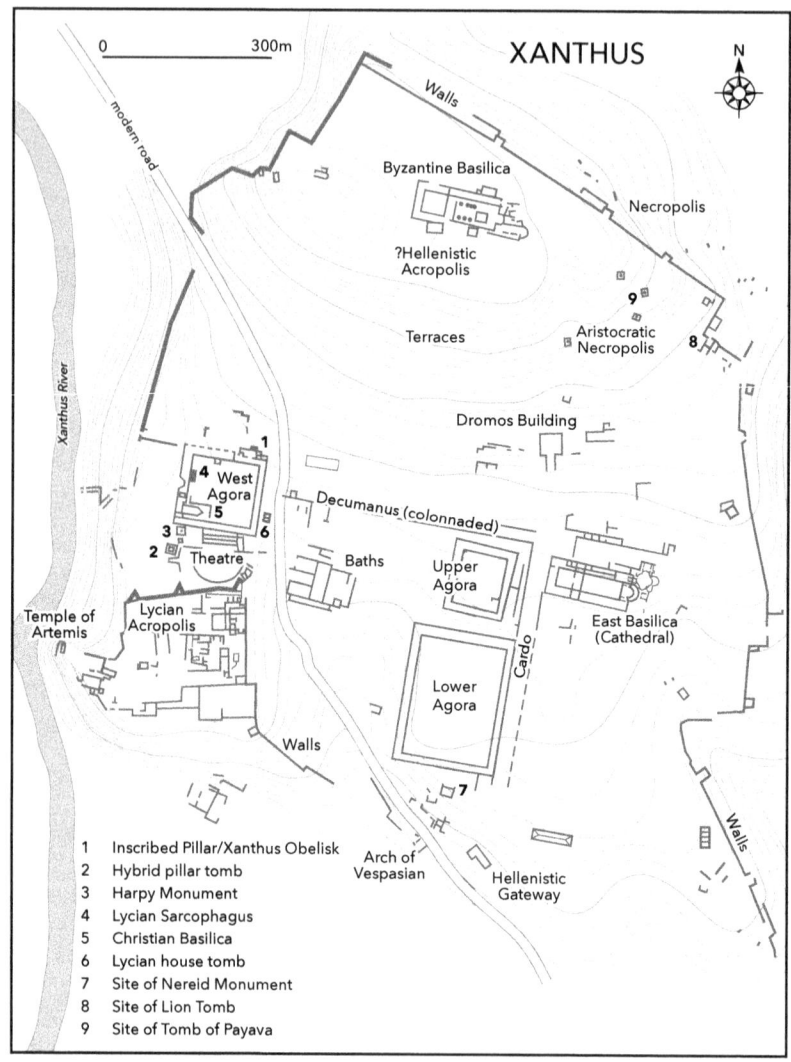

1 Inscribed Pillar/Xanthus Obelisk
2 Hybrid pillar tomb
3 Harpy Monument
4 Lycian Sarcophagus
5 Christian Basilica
6 Lycian house tomb
7 Site of Nereid Monument
8 Site of Lion Tomb
9 Site of Tomb of Payava

The **Lycian acropolis** at Xanthus acted as a refuge; it had a river access route cut into the rock and was fortified with a monumental wall with corner towers. The **city wall** was extensive (2km). Remains of it cannot readily be seen because of relentless rebuilding. Evidence has been found in the northern part of the circuit near the gate. Here, on a stump of square, Classical tower in polygonal masonry, a round Hellenistic structure was built in ashlars. The extent and pattern of Classical urbanism is not well understood. The so-called **Dromos Building**, a building in polygonal masonry that was not a dwelling, has not yet been investigated. As it is situated in a very central position in town, just north of the crossing point of two axial thoroughfares, the later Roman cardo and decumanus, it may have been of considerable importance. Hellenistic Xanthus remains a bit of a mystery, perhaps because this was the time when the Letoön expanded, and thus the centre of interest was there. Xanthus may not have been the leading city in Lycia at this time, but was in charge of the sanctuary, the focal point of the Lycian League (*p. 80*).

After it surrendered to Alexander the Great in 334 BC (a move foretold by a miraculous event, a bronze tablet inscribed with Archaic characters welling up in a spring and predicting the defeat of the Persians), Xanthus changed hands from the Seleucids to the Ptolemies, and then to the Rhodians, becoming a **free city** in 167 BC. In the turbulent times at the end of the Roman Republic, Xanthus was sucked into the rivalry between Antony, Octavian and Brutus. It suffered heavily at the hands of the latter (apparently another mass suicide). There are several buildings from the time of the early Empire, suggesting that the incorporation into the **Province of Asia** brought some benefits, although the capital was moved to Patara. A few remains from that period have been identified, such as the **Arch of Vespasian**, set up by the governor Sextus M. Priscus in AD 68–70 and still standing. Other buildings attested by inscriptions, for example the gerousia, have not been located. The **aqueduct** tapped springs from 9.5km away near Çayköy, where a purpose-built catchment basin has been identified. From there a canal brought it to the North Gate over four bridges; the estimated flow was about 5000 to 7000 cubic metres a day, which was probably not sufficient for the population. The masonry is Roman. The theatre was rebuilt in its present form, possibly on an earlier one. Hadrian, the emperor who built so much elsewhere, left little here, He was more occupied with the Letoön.

It was in the **late Empire** that Xanthus enjoyed a true building boom, which in great part destroyed what had been built before. In turn these buildings were scavenged by the Byzantines (*see below*). By now the town was on a **grid** extending to the east. A **cardo**, running due north from the Arch of Vespasian, met the paved **decumanus** coming in from the west at a perfect right angle. A **dipylon** (or possibly a tripylon) marked the spot. A wide **colonnaded street**, with shops on the northern side, ran west to the so-called West Agora. This agora, next to the theatre, had a portico and occupies the space that the Obelisk refers to as an 'agora', though its function is not clear (*see below*). To the west of it was a large **civic basilica** with three aisles and an apse at the end. At the intersection of the two main streets, by the dipylon, two new large open spaces were laid out, known as Upper and Lower Agoras. The **Upper Agora** had a civic basilica on the east side (as in Cremna and Smyrna) with cisterns in its substructures supplying a fountain at the south end; it was divided internally into three aisles, the westernmost of which was a portico. This grand building has been compared to the markets at Alinda and Aigai (*see Blue Guide Aegean Turkey*); it shows that in the Roman period, Xanthus' centre shifted to the east. A number of baths went up. Archaeologists working on the lower levels of the above-mentioned Upper Agora have identified late Hellenistic domestic buildings. It seems that in the late Empire the city walls were somewhat neglected.

Xanthus' fortunes did not abate in the **early Byzantine** period. Earthquakes and a change in religion prompted a new spate of recycling of the city's building material.

But to judge by its houses and churches, Xanthus did well in late antiquity. On the **Lycian Acropolis** large, two-storey peristyle houses with mythological mosaics overlay the Classical layer (with no trace of intermediate Hellenistic occupation). In terms of style and luxury the buildings have been compared to the terrace houses of Ephesus. A number of fine churches were also built, of which five have been identified. Of these, the very large **East Basilica** (74m by 29m), next to the Upper Agora, stands out. It had a large atrium, a narthex and a nave and two aisles, with an *opus sectile* floor, marble capitals, mosaics on the vaulted ceilings, a *synthronon* with a bishop's cathedra at the east end, and possibly a gallery. Syrian influence has been detected in the decorative plan. The baptistery was in the northeast corner and had a marble-faced pool. To the north, on the **Hellenistic Acropolis**, an area that has been so far neglected but may have been occupied in Hellenistic times, a grand church with an atrium carved out of the rock went up on the terraced slopes facing south. It is thought to have been a pilgrimage centre.

An earthquake in the early 6th-century, followed by the Persians and finally the Arabs, necessitated some precautionary measures. The city walls were repaired and the Lycian Acropolis was refortified. In the process the peristyle houses were demolished and the theatre lost part of its upper tier. The prow-shaped towers at the north end of the walls are typically Byzantine.

The demise of Xanthus is poorly documented. Churches dwindled into chapels; the East Basilica was given up and its tetraconch baptistery was modified to become a church in around the 11th century; it still had frescoes and a newly-carved templon; it has been compared to the harbour chapel at Side. Times were hard and coins are rare finds indeed. It is thought that by the 11th/12th century Xanthus was deserted.

Its rebirth was the work of 19th-century explorers. First Captain Francis Beaufort (*p. 23*), busy charting the coasts of Lycia, sent reports of the ruins back home. Then the antiquarian Charles Fellows (*p. 26*) explored Lycia systematically, making notes, drawings and copies of inscriptions. Xanthus was his favourite city; he even played cricket here. Once the agreement of the sultan had been secured, Fellows was instrumental in the transport of Lycian antiquities to Britain. In Xanthus today there are a number of pedestals whose upper parts are in the British Museum in London.

EXPLORING XANTHUS

Coming from the car park and taking the theatre as your reference point, you will be able to explore, get a feel for the site and admire the Lycian tombs that are still standing in what was once the heart of the city. They go a long way to show how different this was from a Greek city, from which death was banished to outside the civic boundaries, even in the case of heroes. The **theatre** itself has been much modified and rebuilt, including transformation into an arena for gladiatorial combats, which entailed removing some of the lower seats and building a safety wall. Part of the upper tier was lost later, as mentioned in the History section above. With your back to the theatre you can see, beyond the agora, the so-called **Xanthus Obelisk** or **Inscribed Pillar [1]**, in fact a tomb resting on a two-step platform. A pedestal on top of it was originally a chamber made of decorated slabs (now in Istanbul Archaeology Museum) and with a cover (now in the British Museum). The pillar itself, a monolith shattered by an earthquake, is inscribed on the four sides in Greek (an epigram), in Lycian A (dealing with matters political, eulogising the deceased and legitimising a change in the line of succession) and in Lycian B (poorly understood), dealing with matters religious. It can be dated roughly to the late 5th century BC. The reliefs, with representations of the dynast, enclosed a space sufficient for a couple of cremations, possibly of the dynast himself, whose name is not clearly readable, and the nephew of another dynast. The remains also suggest that there was a seated statue on top.

To the west of the theatre, next to a **hybrid tomb [2]** (a pillar tomb surmounted by a sarcophagus, Lycian-style, and dated to the 3rd century BC; the pillar is a reuse), is the **Harpy Monument [3]**. This is in fact a misnomer due to an incorrect interpretation of the reliefs, originally thought to represent the Greek myth of the Sirens bearing away the souls of the dead. It is now believed to reveal Persian influence but the name has nevertheless stuck. The reliefs (originals in the British Museum, copies *in situ*) enclose a space at the top of a very tall pillar standing on a monolithic base 4m by 4m and 1.5m high. The pillar is 5.5m tall and weighs ten tons. The square bosses (on all sides but the east) were for lifting it. The pillar is partly hollowed at the top end so that, combined with the marble panels, the height of the chamber is about 2m. The chamber was entered via a small aperture on the south side that could be closed with a stele. It is dated to the 5th century BC and it was apparently made for the dynast Kybernis. It was closed with a capstone in the shape of an inverted pyramid. The monument stood in a very prominent position, both in Lycian and Roman times, and was respected. Its high visibility, enhanced by the paint on the reliefs, means that it could be seen both from the theatre and from the agora. Later tombs, believed to be Hellenistic, are known in the area. In the first half of the 5th century AD the Harpy Monument was taken over by a hermit, possibly a stylite, which accounts for the crosses and religious paintings on the inner surface of the panels.

On the way to the **colonnaded decumanus**, note the **house tomb [6]** next to the road, built of stone which completely imitates woodwork. The Byzantine **East Basilica** (its fine mosaics now covered) is just after the end of the decumanus.

The location of the so-called **Nereid Monument [7]**, originally the Ionic Trophy Monument, is due south beyond the end of the cardo. Today there is nothing more than some tumbled-down blocks since the monument itself is in the British Museum. When Fellows discovered it, it was inhabited by gypsies. At the time its small, temple-like structure was hailed as evidence of Greek presence in Lycia, but though the Greek influence is undeniable (the temple shape and the Ionic style), it is more of a fusion of East and West. One just has to compare the three female figures right at the front, with their light clothing fluttering in the breeze and revealing the bodies beneath, with the heavy garments of the women in the Parthenon frieze or the stiff caryatids of the Erechtheion. Comparisons have been drawn with the Amazons from the temple at Bassae, but those are reliefs, while these Nereids (or whatever they represent) are carved in the round. The reliefs on the side of the building are Oriental in style and theme, concentrating on city sieges and court life. The monument is thought to have belonged to the dynast Erbinna (Arbinas) and to represent his ascent after death to a mythical heaven, sharing his destiny with heroes.

Continuing east you can roughly follow the line of the wall to the **Lion Tomb [8]**, dated to the 7th–6th century BC. The relief showing a lion attacking a bull is in the British Museum. Further on is the site of the **Tomb of Payava [9]**, also in the British Museum. Dated to the 4th century BC, it had two grave chambers, a lot of stone representations of wooden elements and a lid like an upturned ship's keel, all truly Lycian. You can see a modern granite replica of it, complete with grieving maidens, in Nunhead Cemetery in London, south of the Thames. It was built in the mid-19th century for John Allan, a shipowner, by his son, who had been impressed by the newly-opened Lycian Gallery at the British Museum displaying Charles Fellows's acquisitions.

Beyond the wall to the north, the post-Hellenistic necropolis was used for burials of ordinary townsfolk.

A LYCIAN WAY OF DEATH

We know little about the day-to-day life of the Lycians but we can be certain that they attached a great importance to the disposal of their mortal remains. Tombs made of stone have well survived the injuries of time. While dwelling houses may have had a large timber component, which does not last, and while settlements were rebuilt over and over again, the tombs, even within settlements, were respected and on the whole they were made of unwieldy material, ill-suited to reuse for other purposes.

An **Early Bronze Age village** in the Lycian hinterland, in the Elmalı region, retains evidence of both its houses of the living (*megara*: consisting of one room, possibly with a porch, and a superstructure in wattle and daub—which does leave evidence if a fire hardens the clay) and its houses of the dead (*pithoi*). Some graves are within the residential area while some are outside, arranged in an orderly way suggesting a necropolis. *Pithoi*, varying in size depending on whether they had to accommodate the remains of an adult or a child, had a grave marker. Analysis of the bones suggests a violent society: fractures to the radius are typical of a defensive reaction to aggression, and such fractures are frequently found. Whether those inhumed were Lycians or not we do not know. There is a big time lag between this cemetery and the next expression of care for the dead in the land that we call Lycia.

Lycian tombs have been studied and catalogued according to type. The earliest is the tumulus tomb. The prototype is the **Kizilbel Tumulus**, also in the Elmalı region, which consists of a mortuary chamber built in stone with a paved floor and covered by a gable roof, also in stone. The structure was then buried in a tumulus made of stone and a limited amount of earth. The remains of a tall male, a rider who possibly died of a bone infection, were found inside. The chamber was lavishly painted, on the walls, ceiling and part of the floor by the stone bed. The style of the painting is Assyrian, as are the themes of the banquet and the stag hunt, but on the other hand there are also references to

Greek mythology. So Kizilbel is an Archaic tomb, hovering between East and West. Tumuli are not very frequent in Lycia but they have been identified as far south as Phellos (near modern Kaş). The location of the Kizilbel Tumulus, enjoying high visibility on a tall ridge affording a very good views, is typically Lycian. The dead wanted to enjoy a beautiful panorama and to be seen from a distance. This feature is common to other types of Lycian tombs.

A stand-alone building such as the **Nereid Monument** was perched on a ridge, from which its podium eventually fell; so was the **Trysa Heroön** (now in the Kunsthistorisches Museum in Vienna). References to **timber construction**, with round and square beams protruding, are frequent in the stand-alone tombs, shaped like houses sometimes of more than one storey. The rock-cut tombs, hewn out of the cliff face with façades resembling houses or temples, have commanded much atttention (e.g. Myra). **Sarcophagi** are frequent in Lycian necropoleis and here again there is a typically Lycian type: very tall, sometimes resting on a high podium, all the better to be seen. Their crested lids, shaped like an upturned keel (according to some, another reference to carpentry), with or without ox horns, are also typically Lycian.

Last but not least is the **pillar tomb**. There are not many examples of this but those that exist are in prime locations (in the case of Xanthus in the centre of town) and respected by later building developments. Pillar tombs are tall monoliths with a grave chamber at the top made of four slabs and covered with an imposing roof.

A number of these tombs, especially the grandest, were the burial places of local rulers, the dynasts. Their deeds, beliefs and aspirations are immortalised in friezes (211m long in the case of the Trysa Heroön) or in lengthy inscriptions (the Pillar Tomb in Xanthus).

The reason for the survival of so many tombs is the fact that, although they can be robbed (and indeed they have been robbed repeatedly), they do not make good spolia. We can therefore appreciate the creativity and ingenuity of the Lycian stone workers in monuments like the sarcophagus in Cyaneae, which is cut out of an outcrop of rock, the lid and base cut from a single block and the entrance from an opening in the lid, or in the transformation of the lifting bosses into decorative elements.

According to inscriptions, the tomb had an afterlife itself; generally speaking tombs were for the immediate family, though there are instances of jointly owned tombs, shared by brothers for example. The integrity of the tomb had to be protected according to the wishes of the deceased, who made the necessary financial provisions for this. Violators were cursed (or possibly more effectively fined if they could be caught); whistleblowers were rewarded. The responsibility lay with the relatives or with the city authorities, implying possibly a civic archive of tomb management.

THE LETOÖN

Three kilometres south of Xanthus, on the other side of the river, is the Letoön (*open daily April–Oct 9–8, Nov–March 8–5; charge*), the emodiment of why there are no shrines or temples in Xanthus itself. It has become clear that the cult at the Letoön is very ancient and well precedes both the Greek influence and Roman annexation. It is thought that at Xanthus the dynastic tombs in the centre of town may have provided a quasi-religious focus for reflection when debating and adjudicating civic affairs.

The site is barely above sea level, with a high water table that has proved challenging for excavators; it is regularly flooded and visits can be difficult in wet weather. Nature has profited from this and there is a growing population of frogs and turtles, the latter sunbathing on emerging column drums and making appealing subjects for pictures.

The Letoön, which can now be admired in its Roman imperial magnificence, stems from humble beginnings around a spring. This was located to the south, roughly in front of the later Temple of Leto. Structures dating to the Archaic Period have been identified beneath the temple; the offerings confirm a **cult of the mother goddess**, later assimilated to Leto, and of water nymphs. The status of the nymphs is not clear: they may have been helpers rather than co-deities. It is possibly at this spring that Alexander The Great received intimations of his future success against the Persians.

The **trilingual stele** in Lycian, Greek and Aramaic, now in Fethiye Museum, marks the takeover of the Letoön by the Hecatomnids in the mid-4th century BC. In it Pyxodaros makes the boast that he was the satrap of all of Lycia, though in reality he only controlled part of it. The Hellenistic redevelopment of the site entailed the construction of the **theatre** to the north. Built c. 100 BC, this large structure (74m in diameter, with its cavea partly cut into the rock) only acquired a scena much later. Its original purpose may have been to act as an assembly point for the Lycian League (*p. 80*) administered by Xanthus; the theatre may have acted as a meeting point for social, political and religious concerns.

The **three Hellenistic temples**, well aligned in the south of the site, became the focus of the cult of the sacred spring while the nymphs were relegated to a grotto, later obliterated by the Hadrianic **Nymphaeum**. Ovid's description (*Metamorphoses VI*) of the trials and tribulations of the pregnant Leto, hounded by a jealous Hera, now comes to life. After giving birth to twins on the island of Delos, she brought them here to wash them in the Xanthus. Rebuffed by the local shepherds, she found assistance from the wolves, which is how the locals (then known as Trmmli) came to be called Lycians, from the Greek word for wolf (*lykos*). From the scant remains of the three temples, one can see that they respected structural elements of the earlier cult. They may be the work of Erbinna (of the Nereid Monument; *p. 73*), who was certainly an admirer of things Greek.

The Roman imperial cult was introduced by Claudius in the 1st century AD. This entailed replacing the Hellenistic rooms to the north with vaulted structures. On its north side, the complex faced an agora, identified by the space south of the car park. A **double portico** (Ionic inside and Doric without) graced the north end of the new building, in which a number of rooms were devoted to the imperial cult, as testified by

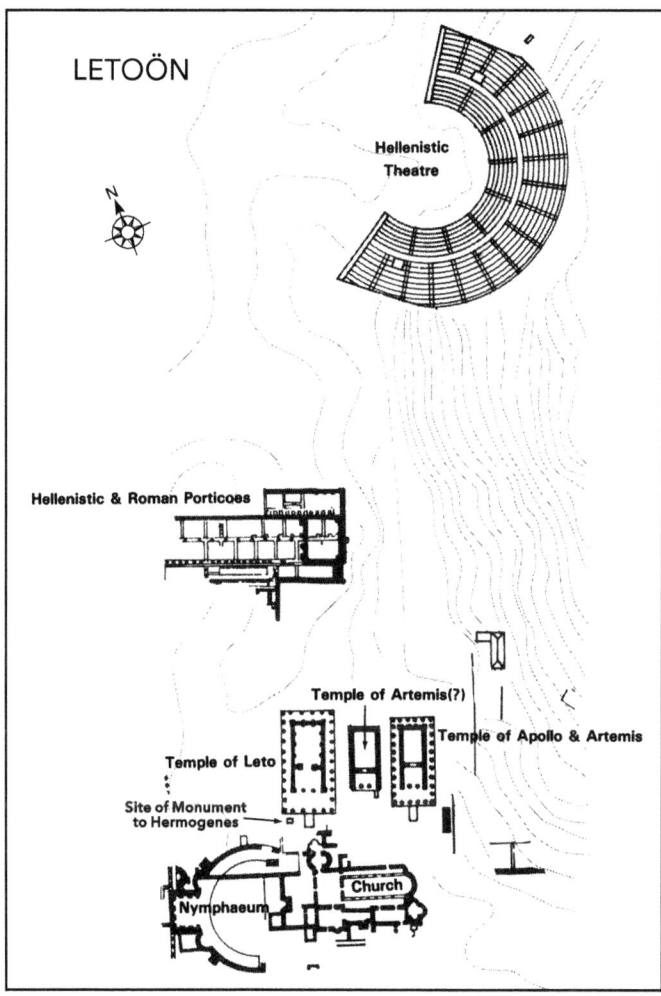

the statue bases such as the one for Gaius Caesar, who died in Limyra (p. 105). Hadrian redeveloped the south end of the site with his massive **Nymphaeum**, connected to the structures to the north by a west portico which had a propylon where the sacred way between the Nymphaeum and the Temple of Leto led to the east.

Decline appears to have set in quite early, around a hundred years later. The site was damaged and there are traces of fire. Can blame for this be laid at the feet of the Goths, perhaps? The site was afterwards neglected and silt was allowed to accumulate, which was particularly bad for the Nymphaeum. The **Christian basilica** east of it, 20m by 30m, was built with spolia mainly from the temples. It may have belonged to a monastery since there are traces of industrial activity (glassmaking) and in the surrounding area are a number of tombs, the majority of them belonging to men. The church was in a way quite luxurious, with mosaics, marble and a synthronon, but it only lasted 100 years. It may have been the Persians who were responsible for its destruction, which was followed by abandonment. Over time the environmental deterioration, with the coastline receding and the water surges of the river and the gushing spring, made this a perfect spot for the spread of malaria.

PYDNAE

Variously known as Pydnae or Kydna, this is a garrison fort/citadel intended to protect the coast and stop sudden seaborne attacks. Originally its situation would have been by the sea, commanding a good view from its height (30m). Now it is 1km inland, surrounded by marshes. The masonry is in the same bossed polygonal style that can be seen on the Lycian Acropolis at Xanthus: it is Hellenistic. It has been suggested that Ptolemy II (283–246 BC) willed it, to ensure supplies of wood for Egypt; there does not seem to be another reason for additional defences at the time.

Pydna is situated to the west of the Xanthus River, overlooking the next watercourse, the Özlem Çay. It is not far from Gavurağılı and is on the Lycian Way. It is rather overgrown but that only adds to the experience: a real ruin in its natural state. You will need good shoes for scrambling about.

The structure is roughly pentagonal with towers and salients. The towers, mainly on the south side, where the danger came from, rose to three storeys and had slit windows for archers. According to J.P. Adam, the fort appears to have been built at minimal expense. Its walls are rather narrow (1m to 1.2m, though they did have a paved wall walk) and construction is directly on the rock, with no foundations. The inner structure of the towers was all of wood; the roofs were tiled. Three posterns suggest a passive defence. The main gate is on the north side. Note the cracked lintel, one metre thick and weighing three tons. The crack may have been the work of an earthquake. Unable to repair it, the Byzantines, who built a three-aisled church against the east wall, blocked this original entrance and opened a new gate not far from it to the east. They are also responsible for the crenellations.

PATARA

Patara (*map B, 7; open daily April–Oct 8–7, Nov–March 8–5; charge*) has a seemingly endless, perfect sandy beach that rightly tempts many tourists. It is also a recognised nesting site of the *Caretta caretta* turtle (*p. 49*), so there are restrictions on use and development. Until recently, the inland village of Gelemiş had remained small-scale, but things are changing. Fortunately, Gelemiş does not threaten the archaeology. It is well out of the way to the north; the site of the old city of Patara is between the beach and the village. Here archaeologists have been at work for many years, trying make sense of the remains, some of which are quite conspicuous. The topography, however, has changed dramatically since antiquity. The beach did not exist and Patara was a city with one of the best harbours on the south coast. So before looking at the history and archaeology of Patara, it makes sense to concentrate on the topography.

SEEING THE ANCIENT ENVIRONMENT

If you stand on top of Kurşunlu Tepe (65m above sea level; *see plan on p. 82*), just at the back of the theatre—a scramble but well worth it—and look just over 500m to the northeast (where a Neronian lighthouse used to stand), you will be looking along the line of the coast in antiquity. From there going north, a body of water wider to start with and then narrowing, continued for 1.6km. That was the **harbour of Patara**, the reason why the city developed here and prospered until the environment changed. Now the entire area is marshy or choked with undecayed vegetation. The two pear-shaped depressions you can see in the distance (Tekerlek Gölü and Ak Göl) are the remains of the marshes, barely 5m deep; the original harbour would have been deeper. Today's marshes are fed by springs, some of which deliver more than fresh water (sulphur for instance). The alluviation of the Eşen Çay together with wind-borne sand have caused the coastal progradation and have gradually blocked the harbour. As a result, the marshes are now just above sea level. The archaeologists' work has been quite different from the traditional combination of trowel and brush. Radar and geophysics have been liberally applied and some encouraging results have been obtained. Unfortunately the two lakes have proved very difficult for scuba divers to investigate. The bottom is covered in a layer of horrible jelly 30 to 200cm thick and visibility is close to zero.

It was not just the harbour that made Patara's fortune; the site also had some heights: **Kurşunlu Tepe**, mentioned above, and, opposite it to the north, **Tepecik** (36.5m above sea level), and **Doğucasarı Tepe** further to the east and higher. The **earliest signs of occupation** come from these sites, including a 10m deep cistern on Kurşunlu Tepe, partly dug in the rock and partly built, which is not fully explained. They show that Patara had a much longer life than that suggested by its present Roman and Byzantine remains.

A BRIEF HISTORY OF PATARA

In the 2nd millennium BC, the Lukky (as the Hittites called the Lycians) had a reputation as a sea people: after all, they invaded Cyprus in the 14th century BC. The Yalburt Stele (found in the Konya area) mentions a Pttara, where the Hittite king Tudalya IV sacrificed before embarking home after a campaign in the southwest of Asia Minor. Other references point to the Ugarit fleet sheltering in a Lycian harbour. These combined references all point to Patara as a **working harbour** at that time, the anchorage of the main Lycian town, Xanthus. In addition, Early Bronze Age pottery has been found on Tepecik. Classical finds on the hill at Doğucasarı hint at a possible seat of a dynast occupying the acropolis of a settlement situated around the harbour. So far the evidence is patchy, partly due to lack of investigation and the difficulty of the site.

From Herodotus (*1,182*) we learn of another side to Patara, as a **divination centre**, the location of a famous oracle of Apollo. No temple to Apollo has been located, though it would conveniently support the hypothesis and also corroborate its status as a store for the archives of the Lycian League (*see box below*), housed in the temple when Patara became the capital of Lycia under the Romans. It is difficult to believe that this could have been a rural temple, as has been suggested. There is quite a large area of Patara for archaeologists to investigate, taking into account the extent of the **Hellenistic wall** that has been traced from behind the theatre all the way to Doğucasarı and from there to Tepecik and down to the harbour. The best-preserved remains are in the two last-mentioned localities.

THE LYCIAN LEAGUE

There is much talk of the Lycian League as a model of democracy, especially since the discovery of the bouleuterion at Patara. Here the League would hold its assemblies, while the papers were kept in the Temple of Apollo (also in Patara but not yet located). But this was in Roman times, when Patara was the capital of Lycia and the League had ceased to have any political power. Rome would not have tolerated the presence of an indigenous power centre.

Originally, but it is uncertain quite from when, the League was an organisation linking Lycian towns and cities, some of them—Xanthus, Tlos, Myra, Olympus, Patara and Pinara—more important than others, having three votes each. The others had fewer votes, some only a fraction of a vote. The League could impose fines, mint coins (with a *triskele*, believed to be the symbol of the sun and therefore related to a god of light, Apollo), convene an assembly every year to elect a Lyciarch and other federal officers; it could also settle disputes between cities and it controlled communal land.

Although Strabo (*14,3,3*) maintains that the strength of the League ensured the political stability of Lycia during the troubled times at the end of the 1st century BC, this does not really appear to be backed up by facts. When Brutus wanted to destroy Xanthus, the League did nothing to prevent it and this is not the only such instance. Rome did not suppress the League. Lycians were still able to come together but they did so for other purposes, namely for festivals, fun and games, celebrating being Lycian but always with a big Roman brother in charge of politics.

The new breed of Lycians, as fostered by Rome, is well represented in the Letoön in a monument located near the portico (its site is marked on the plan on p. 77). It celebrates **Hermogenes, son of Apollonios**, a citizen of Xanthus, of Rome, and of many other places where he had excelled in running competitions. His list of victories is very long. It also shows that he travelled a lot. The monument with which the League honoured him was quite substantial: 3.6m long and about 1m tall, it was composed of four inscribed pedestals with two bronze statues at each end. One of them faced visitors as they entered. Hermogenes was given a life appointment as organiser of the games in Lycia and it is significant that the nomination had to came from the Roman emperor. By the 1st century AD the Lycian League was not sufficiently independent even to handle this—but one supposes that it was expected to defray the cost of the monument.

After surrendering to Alexander the Great, Patara was ruled by the **Ptolemies** and by the **Seleucids**, getting dragged into the disturbances that marked the end of the Roman Republic. Unlike Xanthus, it managed to avoid destruction and from then on it went from strength to strength, overshadowing Xanthus itself and becoming the **seat of the governor of Lycia**. A lot of buildings went up and the harbour prospered. It had a long life, managing to deal efficiently with the twin dangers of the degrading environment and external aggression. By the early Byzantine period a **double wall** with well-spaced rectangular towers, and another some 10m away, went up (the Roman town had been unwalled). The new defences excluded a number of churches, the theatre, the stadium and the gymnasium; the bouleuterion and the Baths of Nero were filled in and became bastions. The agora, assuming it occupied the space north of the theatre, was abandoned. By the **inner harbour** just next to Tepecik, the harbour stoa was incorporated into the walls while still gracing the seafront. As always the walls were built with spolia—but carefully, in no great hurry, intended to protect but also to impress, just as at Side. In the late Byzantine period things seem to have taken a turn for the worse, but still Patara did not give up. In the 10th century it was a **naval base** of the Byzantine Empire, which accounts for the works undertaken to keep the harbour going.

The Byzantine chronology is still not fully understood, although to quote from the 9th-century biography of St Nicholas of Sion, 'Patara, once one of Lycia's most famous cities, is now a village'. Decline had set in. The town had been militarised and further **reduced in size** to the west side of the inner harbour; the defensive wall was now 4.4m thick and double in the south portion. A temple became a corner bastion. Dwellings were densely packed. The peninsula, with additional defences, was the Byzantine **kastron**, with a domed church in the middle.

The **Seljuks** conquered Patara in 1211; it was destroyed in an attack from Cyprus and was later abandoned. However it was functioning as a harbour as late as 1478/9 when Cem Sultan, the unfortunate younger brother of Beyazıt II, signed a treaty here.

EXPLORING PATARA

Patara is a very exposed site, making it safer to visit it in the late afternoon, when the sun is less harsh. You enter the site at the **Arch of Modestus** (*see overleaf for a plan*), a fine ashlar construction of the 2nd-century AD commemorating Mettius Modestus, the governor of Lycia and Pamphylia, and erected by the citizens of Patara, 'the metropolis of the Lycian nation' (to quote the inscription on the north side). Ten metres high and 19m wide, it had six consoles for as many statues of the governor and his family. The **aqueduct**—indispensable for operating the four baths so far identified—ran along the top of it. It came in from the east and ran along a channel for over 20km, reaching in turn three distribution reservoirs located to the east of town, from where the aqueduct branched out west and southwest to the harbour and to the residential quarters. Investigation of the aqueduct has been delayed because the ruins of one of the distribution reservoirs was used a radio telegraph station at the time of the Ottoman Empire and was thus off limits to archaeologists. Judging by the inscriptions, the aqueduct dates to the 1st century AD, with later repairs. It may have been preceded by a Hellenistic one.

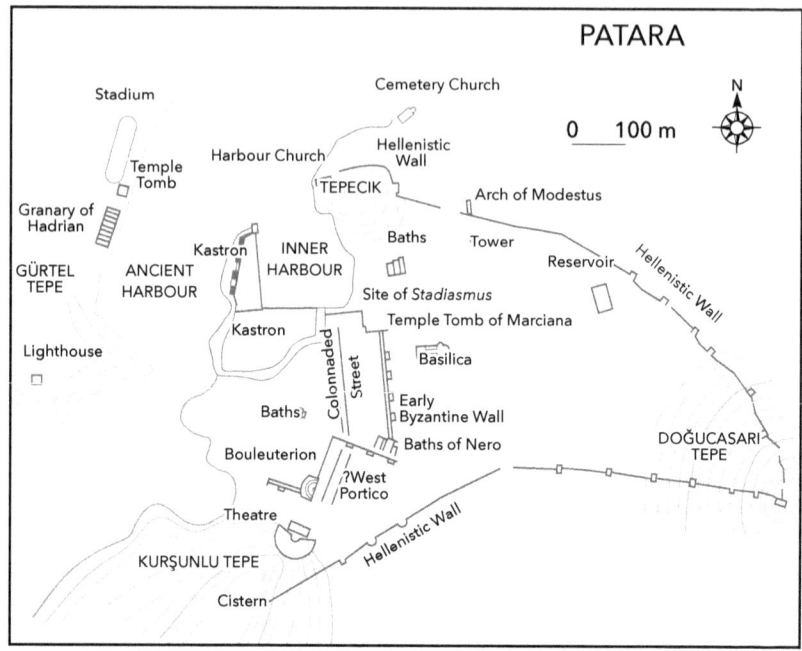

Past the remains of baths and the 1st-century AD **temple-tomb of Marciana**, a much-missed infant (she was only four years old when she died), you arrive at the **colonnaded street**, which ran due south. This paved street, 12.60m wide and with shops to the west, still cuts a very good figure today. According to some, it connected the inner harbour with the agora, and although the location of the agora has not been proven, evidence of a large portico at the south end of the street lends support to the hypothesis

The newly restored **bouleuterion** marks the southernmost end of the early Byzantine wall, of which it became a bastion. With its blindingly white stonework, the building now looks strangely modern. Its latest restoration, willed by the Grand National Assembly of Turkey, has not been a success, turning it into a cross between Lego and fantasyland. It has modern windows and doors but no roof and the walls are artistically jagged. What would the Lycian League delegates who used to meet here make of it, not to mention the Lyciarch (the elected chairman), whose seat has survived?

The **theatre**, on the lower slopes of Kurşunlu Tepe, has not been 'improved' and is much better. It is well preserved, mainly because it was buried under tons of sand. In the 18th century Texier (*p. 32*) saw its two-storey scena still standing. Eighty-four metres wide, it is a Roman structure, possibly on a Hellenistic antecedent. Note the row of high-backed seats halfway up; the ambulatory at the top had a temple in the middle. In late antique times a protective wall for animal combats was erected around the orchestra.

Beyond these highlights, little is known about the Roman city, which may have been gridded. Eight temples are known but private housing remains elusive. The stoa that was financed by Opramoas (*p. 109*) may be the one at the south end of the inner harbour, later incorporated in the early Byzantine wall. The line of this wall is well known. You can see it clearly by the assembly building. It then turns right, taking in the baths, and ran due north to the harbour. A spectacular find was made in this area in 1993. Inscribed blocks belonging to a monument looking a bit like a Lycian funerary pillar had been built into the wall. Fifty-nine such blocks have been identified, resulting in a structure 7m high. This is the **Patara *Stadiasmus***, a list of distances between cities, the local equivalent of the Milion in Constantinople and its predecessor the Miliarium Aureum in Rome. These monuments were the material expression of Roman dominance: the Empire could organise space. On the *Stadiasmus*, places as far away as Cibyra are indicated. This does not mean that the Romans criss-crossed Lycia with roads: there are no milestones to suggest that. There is evidence for a 1st-century AD 'coastal' road east of Patara, which hugged the 700m contour line and connected Patara to Cyaneae and Myra, with side roads leading down to seaside settlements. On the whole, however, the *Stadiasmus* was the starting point of a network of trackways, not highways. It is possible that Rome improved the existing tracks and psychologically their interventions were quite effective. The *Stadiasmus* showed the gratitude of the Lycians for peace and stability and the end of banditry and was dedicated to the emperor Claudius, whose statue may have topped the pillar. Alas, the work was apparently unfinished.

On the west side of the main harbour inlet is Gürtel Tepe, which has not been fully explored. It is best approached from the beach. Here stood a **lighthouse**, Neronian in date according to the inscription. It was built on a podium 20m by 20m and based on the blocks strewn round about, may have been over 8m tall. Further on, the Hadrianic **granary** (65m by 32m) may or may not have been a granary. It is similar in structure to that at Andriake (*p. 98*), but there are doubts. Granaries—and there good examples around the Roman Empire—were built for storage and to combat vermin. This calls for good ventilation, normally insured by a suspended floor (*suspensura*). The windows here are large, however, contrary to the known *horrea*, where they are small to discourage infestation. No facilities for loading and unloading have been identified. It is also difficult to see what wheat could have been stored here. Lycia was no breadbasket of the Empire. It is doubtful that its meagre agriculture could have fed even its own population. One is reminded of the inscription stating that Opramoas sent grain to Xanthus to feed the children. Storage structures in Tlos and in Xanthus suggest a risk of famine, a recurrent theme in Asia Minor. The case of the Patara 'granary' remains open.

Beyond the Corinthian style temple-tomb, the remains of a **stadium** have been identified. The slope of Gürtel Tepe is thought to have been residential in antiquity, with buildings laid out on terraces. However, the area is now under a thick cover of sand and still awaits investigation. Moreover, the system of communications between the two parts of town across the top end of the harbour is not fully understood.

KAŞ

You will note that going east from Patara, after Kaş, Route 400 takes a turn inland, giving up the coast as too difficult to negotiate. In effect it behaves as the Roman road did, and rejoins the coast to Myra. It is an established fact that in this region, in the past as now, the sea was the highway. If that has now fostered a yacht and sailing culture, so be it. It has also preserved the coastal environment, which can be enjoyed by tourists thanks to the many boat trips on offer.

ANCIENT KAŞ (ANTIPHELLOS)

Kaş (*map B, 7*), with its twin marinas on either side of the Çukurbağ Peninsula (which is still waiting for the promised canal at its base to ease communications), is now the operating centre of a successful tourist industry. It has lost some of its sleepy charm in the process. This was once a quiet fishing village, propelled to the status of regional administrative centre in the 19th century by the Ottomans, who moved operations from Kasaba in the interior to here. At the time the area lived from fishing, sponge diving and the exploitation of timber resources. T.A.B. Spratt (*p. 31*) still saw timber being transported from the interior on mule back, sawn into manageable planks and taken to Kastellorizo (the island opposite the harbour, now belonging to Greece) and then to Egypt.

Kaş has a past when it was **Hebesos**, to give it its Lycian name; the Greeks called it **Antiphellos**, the harbour of the city of Phellos 5km inland (*see below*). Its fortunes varied. It did best under the Romans, when the sea was safe. Pliny praised its sponges (5, 131). Today there is not much left of its past. The settlement was at the base of the peninsula, possibly to the east of the **theatre**. The latter is rather small, with seating for 4,000, but it makes up for it with a very fine view. Just over a half circle in circumference, its shape is Hellenistic. There was apparently no scena (though this could have been made of wood), but in any case, the sea would have made an excellent backdrop. The present restoration of the orchestra is modern. Apart from the theatre, the 450m long remains of the **sea wall** and of the Hellenistic temple that have been identified on the way back to town between Necipbey Cd and the ancient piers that Spratt saw in the harbour and which have now vanished, the rest of what Kaş has to offer consists of **tombs**. The local limestone is apparently easily worked. There are rock-cut Lycian-style tombs north of the theatre facing east; among them the **Doric tomb** (a single room cut out of the rock with a relief showing women performing a ritual dance) has been tentatively dated to the early Hellenistic period. The monument has been little studied and has been damaged by recent reuse. More tombs are on the east cliff. You can admire them even at night, when they are lit up. The **Lion Tomb**, also called the King's Tomb, at the top of Uzunçarşı, a pretty cobbled street off Cumhuriyet Meydanı in the centre of town, is very remarkable and shows what can be done with lifting bosses. Rather than cutting them off or leaving them in place, ugly as they are, you can use your ingenuity to make snarling lions out of them. The tomb is typically Lycian with its upturned keel lid and tall pedestal cut out of the living rock and containing another burial. The **Lycian inscription** on the side of the lower chamber is still poorly understood. The tomb is dated to the 4th century BC.

ANCIENT PHELLOS
As for Phellos ('Stony Place'), the ancient city of which this was the harbour, its site is disputed. Some would like to identify it with the ruins north of the village of **Çukurbağ**, high up at 750m in the hinterland of Kaş, 5km northeast. This could be the Lycian Vehinda, which appears on coins. Here there is a recognisable acropolis, as well as defensive walls and tombs, all in Lycian style and which you can explore if you want a day out. Alternatively Phellos could be **Sebeda**, west of Bayındır in the cove south of Kaş. Take your pick: you will have to approach Sebeda by sea.

EAST OF CAPE ULUBURUN: APERLAE, SIMENA & CYANEAE

The rest of the coast was accessible only by sea in antiquity and to understand the archaeology you need to think along those lines. If you take a boat trip from Kaş—and there are many to chose from—for a lovely day out on the water, once you have left Kastellorizo behind and negotiated your way around some smaller islands, you get to **Uluburun**, a well defined cape with razor sharp unforgiving rocks pointing due south, where a famous Mycenaean wreck was excavated after it came to grief over 3,500 years ago (*see Blue Guide Aegean Turkey*). Here the coastline turns east and is very busy with islands and peninsulas, coves and harbours. The area is geologically unstable because it sits on an east–west fault that has caused some areas to sink (e.g. the mainland at Aperlae) and others to rise (e.g. the long peninsula known as Sıcakyarımadası); **sunken settlements** are a feature of this stretch of coast and a delight to boat owners, who will show you walls, streets and steps. Unfortunately swimming in these areas is now forbidden, but you can see quite a lot from the deck. Excavating is also off limits here; however, by intense surveying, both in the water and on land, the history of this extraordinary corner of the world has been pieced together.

GEOGRAPHY AND HISTORY
The main sites are **Aperlae** (*map B, 7*), deep in a west-facing cove defined by the Sıcakyarımadası; and the inlet of **Üçağız** (the literal translation of the Greek Tristomo, meaning three openings) a complex harbour 3km long and 500m wide, closed by the long island of Kekova, whose name is believed to be a reference to the abundance of partridges at some point in its history. The **three openings** are to the north (leading to Kale), to the east (between Kekova island and the mainland) and to the south between Kekova and Sıcakyarımadası). In this area, which is favoured by nature up to a point, there are clear signs of an intense economic development well into the 6th century AD, in spite of the **lack of water**, **poor communications** and the **unpredictable weather**: the limestone massif looming large on the northern horizon can cause sudden squalls and violent storms.

In the period which is best understood because of the lack of excavations, that is the late antique/early Byzantine period, a fundamental **synergy** linked the coastal settlement to the prosperous interior in spite of the bad communications. The interior had agricultural products and timber, all of which needed to reach markets. One was close by: the people of the coast had no room and no water to grow food; timber though had a more distant market. The small harbours supplied the local transport hubs to where logs could be loaded on bigger ships and on to Egypt.

As long as the sea was safe it was a win-win situation, but first the Persians and then the Arabs created havoc. Defences went up and settlements contracted. When the Byzantines lost control of the coast to the Arabs after the battle of Phoenix, not only the coast declined but also the hinterland. The population melted inland for safety. The environment degraded, ports were not maintained, subsidence and silting created marshes.

APERLAE & ITS SYMPOLITY

Aperlae (*map B, 7*) was, in Roman times, the leader of a sympolity with Simena, Apollonia and Isinda, three small nearby towns. This is as much as we know about the civic status of Aperlae and for that matter of the other towns; all combined, they had one vote in the Lycian League (*p. 80*). We know the situation in the 3rd century AD; before then, things are a bit more obscure. Aperlae is a remarkable and unique settlement. Its remains, a small settlement and a small harbour, have shed light on a neglected area of archaeology, **small-scale coastal navigation**, which in antiquity would have been the norm in mountainous regions such as Lycia. This activity is difficult to investigate: the infrastructure may well have been flimsy, possibly just of wood, and the settlements themselves may have been prosperous but not necessarily wealthy enough to erect large structures that can survive the passing of time.

Aperlae is an exception: it was a small harbour devoted to cabotage, successful enough to leave substantial remains, and yet abandoned and never occupied again; in addition, it was remote enough to discourage pillaging on a large scale. It first came to the attention of archaeologists in the 1970s, through the work of two American amateur archaeologists and keen sailors, Robert and Cynthia Carter, who surveyed it meticulously with the permission of the Turkish authorities and published their findings. Later intensive surveys followed. The site has not been excavated and its early beginnings are therefore shrouded in mystery. It may or may not be a Lycian foundation, there is no evidence either way.

Aperlae sits in Asar Bay, at the west side of the isthmus that connects the mainland to the long peninsula known as Sıcakyarımadası. This is certainly a protected space but as a harbour it is not very good. It is cramped and would have been even narrower in antiquity, before the mainland started sinking; the prevailing winds are from the south so it can be difficult to get out; only the land breeze in the morning will help. Small as it was, it would have been sufficient for small boats with a limited range. It is thought that boats from Aperlae would have called with their cargoes at the larger ports of Andriake or Patara. In times of need, there remained the possibility of crossing the isthmus (1.5km) and putting to water in the Üçağız inlet to the east. However, there is no archaeological evidence for this; the hypothesis remains unproven.

Judging by the style, Aperlae's defensive walls (*see below*) are Hellenistic with Roman alterations. The original walling may have been the work of the Ptolemies, who were always interested in good sources of timber. There is little else Hellenistic to see; Aperlae boomed from the time of the Empire to late antiquity, when the sea was safe and there was huge demand for the **purple dye** used by the Romans and others before and after them for prestige articles of clothing. Evidence for the processing of the *Murex trunculus* mollusc is here to see: the *vivaria*, huge shell middens (1600m square), west of the city in the ravine on either side of the Roman bridge; more shells dumped in the sea; or the crushed murex shells mixed in the Roman mortar. Only the *opercula* are missing: they were used to make some sort of incense. Aperlae's fate was linked to the safety of the sea. When that broke down, Aperlae folded. First the Persians came and then the Arabs. The battle of Yarmouk, where the Caliph defeated the Byzantine emperor in 636, showed how serious the danger was on land; the battle of Finike in 655 showed that the Arabs were also masters of the sea. Aperlae and other places along the south coast never recovered. The 10th–11th-century Byzantine 'reconquest' did little for Aperlae.

EXPLORING APERLAE

Aperlae is accessible on foot along the Lycian Way, on a trail coming from Apollonia. Otherwise you visit by boat, either your own or by joining one of the many boat trips on offer. Part of the site is underwater because of the sinking of the coastline (*see above*), but swimming and snorkelling are not allowed. The ruins are set on the hill overlooking the cove.

The most visible remains here are the **defensive walls** in good ashlar, Hellenistic in style. They have been built to accommodate the lie of the land. To the west they face a ravine and a steep slope; there is just one tower. The highest point (a possible acropolis) is to the north while the east section, facing a gentle slope and more exposed to enemy incursions, has four towers. The **main gate** was in the southeast corner. The south stretch of the defences was removed in Roman times, leaving the harbour completely undefended: the town gradually descended to the sea. Other stretches of walls, which you can see coming down to the harbour to east and west, are dated to the 6th/7th century, when apparently Aperlae was in the hands of pirates, or at any rate in a difficult situation; they are built of rubble. Extra walls on the **acropolis** date to that time. Inside these walls, **buildings** and **cisterns** have been identified but not excavated. The area is very overgrown. The rest of Aperlae is by the sea and beneath the water. By the sea are the remains of two **baths** (east and west).

The **underwater remains** are laid out on an orthogonal grid to a maximum depth of 6m. They are Roman in date. It is thought that the Hellenistic harbour installations were very minimal and built of wood. A sinuous **sea wall**, late antique in date and made of spolia, has been identified; it ran the whole length of underwater Aperlae. A **jetty**, 22m by 6m and with a tower at its base, is now 60m from the present coastline. The sea wall was apparently wrecked in an earthquake, possibly in 529. Three **vivaria** (to keep the *Murex trunculus* in good health until processing) have been identified. They are made of Roman bricks and hydraulic mortar and have a tiled floor on a bed of cobbles. Further industrial installations are to the west. Out of the total of five **churches**, two are underwater. Such expressions of piety may be related to a budding **pilgrim trade** since the town seems too small to have supported so many large churches, all roughly early Byzantine. There is noticeably no effective mole to protect boats from the large waves created by the south wind. There is no recognised boatyard or repair yard or assembly point, unless it was in the open space just south of the baths next to the church. There are apparently no buildings there. A freshwater spring, now in the sea, is by baths.

KEKOVA ISLAND

Today, a boat trip will take you from Aperlae to Kale (ancient Simena). On the way there will be a stop on the coast of Kekova, an island with no water. In spite of that, its proximity to Andriake (only 7km from the easternmost point) has encouraged intermittent settlement. There are two main foci: Tersane to the northwest and Karaloz, in a cove on the south coast to the east. Snorkelling and swimming are not allowed in these areas, a prohibition that must be taken seriously.

It is normally **Tersane** (the submerged city, *batık kent*) which is visited by tourist boats. The settlement consisted of about 50 dwellings, partly built, partly cut in the rock. This hardly constitutes a city, but there is also, on dry land, a Byzantine basilica with a nave and two aisles and with traces of mosaics and large windows in the apse. In the water one can see streets, steps and the foundations of houses, some quite large and some with apsidal rooms, which is a late antique trait. A number of cisterns have been identified. No trace of a necropolis has been found on the island, suggesting that the dead were taken to the opposite shore.

SIMENA

Simena (*map B, 7*), in the Üçağız inlet, sits on the tip of a long east–west limestone peninsula, a good position for controlling traffic. A small Lycian polis and possibly the seat of a dynast, it developed during Hellenistic times when it was walled; later it prospered under the Romans. The ancient town and a number of Lycian tombs are now partly under water. A Doric stoa, a small compact bath house (now built over) from the time of the emperor Titus, and traces of terracing with streets and steps as well as houses have been identified. The early Byzantine church, over 20m long, was still standing in the 19th century when Turkish settlers moved into the area. The site was used as a quarry and a mosque, now abandoned, was built over part of it.

The best attraction of Simena is inside the **castle**, which once belonged to the Knights Hospitallers and may have been used at times as a refuge. There is not much left of the original; the usual restoration works have added crenellations and a fluttering Turkish flag. The rock-cut **theatre**, originally a bouleuterion, is a jewel. Barely large enough to accommodate 300 people, it looks out over the best view you can imagine. One does not need a scena in a situation such as this and it looks as though it never had one. Since the ascent is a bit of a scramble, it is advisable to choose your time of day carefully.

APOLLONIA, ISINDA AND TEIMIOUSSA

The other two members of the sympolity, Isinda and Apollonia, may be worth a visit if you have your own transport or are walking that stretch of the Lycian Way. **Apollonia**, southeast of Kılınç (north and west of Aperlae), has an occupation span from 500 BC to AD 600 but it has not yet been investigated. The ruins, on a summit called Boğazcık, are wild and extremely evocative. You will see stretches of walls believed to be Byzantine, a small theatre, a well-preserved Byzantine chapel, remains of a bath and a great many tombs. Watch out for the vaulted cisterns: they can be a hazard.

Isinda, which has been identified from an inscription, is a short walk west of the village of Belenli (exiting the Kaş–Finike road at Ağullu). It is quite a strange choice for the alliance, as the other three cities are rather close together and similar, while Isinda appears to be in a different ecological zone and communication may have been difficult, with the Kırandağ in the way. The ramparts are well preserved; around is the usual spread of Lycian tombs, two with Lycian inscriptions.

The ancient settlement of **Teimioussa**, of which the Tristomo (Uçağız) inlet was the harbour, is to the east on a poorly-signed path off the main road. The site has not been investigated; it is wild and very fetching, with tombs and ruins.

CYANEAE

Another site linked to the Üçağız inlet is Cyaneae (*map B, 7*), less than 6km to the north, connected in antiquity to the harbour by a rock-cut road. Cyaneae has been intensely surveyed but not excavated. Only the theatre has been cleared. It can be reached from Route 400 by taking a marked side road at Yavu to your left going east. The road is a dirt track and is acceptable for the first couple of kilometres, then there is a sign to your left and the road deteriorates: it is advisable to walk to the end of it (about 1km). It leads to the theatre set against the hill. The town is c. 100m to the east and stretches to the north.

Sitting at the centre of a rocky and poorly watered territory that does not reach the coast, this was the Lycian Turaxssi, possibly the seat of an **oracle of Apollo Thyrxeus**. It developed as the main polis between Antiphellos (modern Kaş) and Myra, probably exploiting the **timber resources** of its territory, stands of cypress, sandalwood and tall cedar, ideal for shipbuilding. This was all processed in the inlet of Tristomo (Uçağız), an international trade centre. The town, on a rocky plateau, 729m at the highest point, was probably the seat of a dynast in the 5th–4th century BC, whose residence was c. 200m east of the theatre in the walled **citadel**. In Hellenistic times the town expanded and was defended; stretches of wall with gates can be seen. The present ruins date mostly from Roman and Byzantine times. Cyaneae was a very packed settlement, mainly of small dwellings. In the centre, an empty space has been recognised as the **agora**; it sits on Hellenistic substructures; a **bouleuterion, baths, library, market** and other civic amenities (including a temple to Eleuthera) have been identified. The Byzantines added three **churches** using spolia, which were eventually replaced by chapels. Scattered around in the town are a number of **Lycian sarcophagi**. Out of town the **theatre**, 50m in diameter, is originally Hellenistic, remodelled in Roman times. Its scena was partially cut in the rock. In front of it, the remains of a large Christian basilica (one of three, the others are northeast of the acropolis and in the necropolis further north and out of town) may occupy the site of a pagan temple.

The **history** of Cyaneae is one of prosperity followed by contraction. There was still a bishop in the 12th century but he may not have lived here. Certainly the city must have declined after the 10th century, about the last time the Byzantines tried to control this stretch of coast. Cyaneae's **territory**, which appears to have been densely settled, also declined about that date. Eventually nomads took over.

Getting around must be done with great care. The site is overgrown and there are many bottle-shaped cisterns lurking. These were the principal source of water. The main attraction are the sarcophagi, of which there are plenty, with worked bosses and tall pedestals; they have proved very resilient—though they all have a hole cut in them somewhere, the work of tomb robbers. The necropolis has some rock-cut tombs, one of which, in the shape of a house-tomb with apparent square beams and a single Ionic column dividing the front opening, has a sarcophagus on the roof; it comes with burial instructions. The sarcophagus was for the owner (Perpenenis) and his wife; the rest of the family were to occupy the tomb.

BETWEEN TWO RIVERS: THE DEMRE ÇAY & THE AKÇAY

Before joining the coast at Demre (*map B, 7*), Route 400 loops its way through the interior through another mountainous region. Traces of the past are lost between the modern urban sprawl and the greenhouses. But there is a past here, sometimes abruptly coming to an end as at Sura, or still going strong, as it is in Demre, or ancient Myra, which has reinvented itself as a world centre for Santa Claus, in direct competition with Lapland.

The interior, however rugged, also comes into play. It is noticeable how the Demre Çay river takes an east–west course to skirt around the Alaca Dağ, whose highest peak rises to 2338m, 15km from the coast. Even so, the valley offered refuge when things got tough on the coast, as the development at Dereağzı shows. Further east, the valley of the Akçay, the ancient Arycandus, offers a route north between the Alaca Dağ and Kızlar Sivrisi Tepe (3086m). According to T.A.B. Spratt (*p. 31*), the Arycandus was used by the people of Elmalı, well into the interior, as a connection to the sea.

SURA

Four kilometres west of Demre, signed from Route 400 by the usual brown sign pointing to a footpath, Sura (*map B, 7*) is living proof of the vitality of the coast in antiquity. We have already seen a profusion of small harbours, evidence of commercial nous; this is a different site, tapping another source of income. In antiquity Sura was celebrated for its **fish oracle**, courtesy of Apollo Sourios. On the strength of it, Sura (a Lycian name), which was never a city, survived well into the 9th century AD, as testified by the remains of its churches. Sura is still not well understood and has neither been excavated nor intensively surveyed. It therefore comes with the aura of a pristine site (though cut in half by the modern road) and you will be rewarded for your exertions with fine views and some impressive Lycian tombs.

The **acropolis** of Sura sits on a plateau overlooking a ravine from where in antiquity water flowed into the sea. It is now marshy. The Temple of Apollo is down this declivity, not easy to reach. The plateau had a **wall circuit** with towers and a free-standing **observation tower**, 11m by 7m. It has not been precisely dated: it could be Hellenistic, reused and repaired during the Byzantine period. Within the enceinte, a building of unusual shape on the highest point remains unexplained. Partly cut in the rock, it has a **cellular structure**: it looks more military than residential. In its latest phase it shows Byzantine occupation. On the slopes, traces of terracing have been recognised as well as oil presses. But Sura's main focus was down the ravine to the west at the **Temple of Apollo Sourios**, which in antiquity could be reached by steps from the plateau (traces of the path are still visible). The Doric temple (13m by 7m with columns in antis and surviving to a good height having been over time buried in the alluvium) was originally situated facing a whirlpool: this was the **Fountain of Apollo**, where karstic springs formed a small stream that reached the sea now 1.5km away. According to Pliny (*32,17*), some of these springs were sulphurous. The flow of the springs was operated by priests, who possibly tampered with it in order to create more or less turbulence, and interpreted the twists and turns of the fish coming up to feed. They were offered cooked meat on a spit. Plutarch takes the phenomenon very seriously in his treaty on the intelligence of animals (*23*) and compares it to the observation of the flight of birds, another standard practice in antiquity. We do not know much about Apollo Sourios, and it does not help that the inscription inside the temple refers to Apollo Sozon, another manifestation of Apollo, which has its origins in Phrygia in central Anatolia; however, another inscription in the temple suggests that Ptolemy X, the Egyptian king exiled in Myra in 88 BC, may have come here for divine inspiration. If so, he was misled, since he mounted an expedition to Cyprus, where he died.

Sura's history remains to be deciphered and its archaeology to be conducted. According to Hellenkemper, judging by the inscription and the number of Lycian tombs in the vicinity, some of them very complex, the acropolis may once have been the seat of a local dynast. The Byzantine churches down by the temple and up on the acropolis testify to a lasting occupation, with large early Byzantine structures later shrinking to chapels. They may reflect the triumph of Christianity stamping out a pagan cult or the taking over of a pilgrimage trade. There was still life down by the spring in the 19th century, when the cove was called Vromo Limiona and the Greek Orthodox Church rebuilt a chapel inside the ruined Byzantine church.

DEMRE & ANCIENT MYRA

Taking the Myra area as a whole, which includes Demre (today's name for ancient Myra) as well as its former harbour at Andriake and two more sites to the immediate east (Stamira and Issium), one can make a powerful case for this having been a key area in Mediterranean navigational history, at least from Hellenistic times. The development of the interior along the valley of the Myros river (now the Demre Çay) is also relevant, as the interaction between coast and valley was a fundamental element of the region's continuing prosperity into late antiquity and beyond. It will be dealt with separately.

The landscape today has changed quite a bit. Andriake is now landlocked, no longer a harbour, and Myra's acropolis is a full 3km from the coast. The Beymelek lagoon, closed by a sandbar, suggests dunes and sands blown in, while excavations have shown that, in the case of Myra, the remains lay under several metres of alluvium. The theatre itself, now fully excavated, was unearthed from a 5m thick blanket of hillwash.

EXPLORING ANCIENT MYRA

Myra is an ancient site, although little remains to show for it. Its Lycian name was Muri and it was a dynastic seat. The Hellenistic fortifications intended to protect the sea and land approach from east and west (*see below*) show that it was already a significant place at that time. However, the Lycian inscriptions, the tombs which the Byzantines used as wine cellars and the 5th-century BC walls on the acropolis could push back the date of occupation to Archaic/Classical times. Until excavations are conducted we will know no more. Everything is now a vast expanse of greenhouses.

Myra was well situated, with a good harbour in a natural sea inlet and good interior communications via the valley. It was an important member of the Lycian League (*p. 80*), with maximum voting rights. It minted its own coins, was an administrative centre and in due course made a seamless transition into the Roman world. It was by then a busy trading town connected to Limyra to the east by a ferry service. It was a stopping point for travellers on their way to and from the Levant.

The **acropolis**, with the theatre on its south slope, was walled. The **town** below, on the flat alluvial plain of the Demre river, well protected by cliffs (where the rock tombs are) and further north by the river gorge, was exposed to the east, where the lie of the land was more gentle. It had a defensive circuit of Hellenistic date, to which the Romans paid no attention until the emperor Marcian restored and enlarged it in the mid-5th century. Known monuments are scarce. There are ruins of two baths and of a civic basilica. Traces of an **aqueduct** cut in the rock have been identified; it was 25km long. Coins showing an Artemis very much in the style of the Ephesian Artemis (*see Blue Guide Aegean Turkey*), with all sorts of appendages on her body, more connected to the Anatolian cult of the mother goddess than to Apollo's beautiful sister, have not been matched by a known temple. However, there must have been one, as a temple to Artemis Eleutheria was restored by Opramoas (*p. 109*) in AD 141 following an earthquake. A **Roman road** has been identified beneath Alakent Cd., possibly connecting the theatre with the town to the south and with the agora, which according to sources had a gilded statue of Tyche in its centre.

The sarcophagi, in imported marbles from Attica and Pamphylia, as well as the wealth of the necropoleis, suggest a rich city. **Christianity** came early to Myra. St Paul came past in AD 60, though he did not preach here. He was a prisoner at the time, on his way to Rome to stand trial, and was soon to be shipwrecked off Malta. The legend of St Nicholas (the precursor of Father Christmas) dates to the 4th century. The saint (*see box below*) gave Myra a publicity scoop that lasted centuries, with some ups and downs, but which is still going strong today: St Nicholas' basilica is a favourite destination for Russian newlyweds.

Myra's apogee came at the time of Theodosius II (408–450). It was already a metropolis but now it became the **capital of the Roman province of Lycia**. The **productive hinterland** was also booming and the **harbour** was busy with commercial and international passenger shipping. This prosperity lasted into the early 7th century, when Myra with its riches became an obvious target for **Arab raiders**. From this time onwards the history of Myra is the history of the church of St Nicholas. The town itself almost ceased to exist. The port at Andriake went out of use and a new harbour opened (*see below*). Eventually there were **two settlements**: one on the walled acropolis with its own church (Kastron) and another around St Nicholas' basilica, which was also walled. Outside these perimeters the place was either deserted or occupied by Arabs and Türkmen. In the mid-10th century, Emperor Constantine Porphyrogenitus could well wax lyrical about 'thrice blessed' Myra, but he was in Byzantium and could not see the devastation. After the Battle of Manzikert (1071), the basilica was deserted and safety was sought on the acropolis. In 1362 Myra was attacked from Cyprus and the population enslaved; the site was abandoned. There was still a bishop of Myra in the 14th century. Where he resided is not clear. Myra disappears from Orthodox Church records in the 15th century.

When Freya Stark (*p. 32*) visited in the 1950s, she painted a dismal picture of the place, which was then inhabited by Turks from Epirus, some 200 of them. She observed the silting of the gorges on either side of town, the buried columns with just their tops poking above the surface, the theatre three quarters submerged, and she noticed that the sculptures which Texier (*p. 32*) had seen earlier were no longer there. The basilica of St Nicholas, over time covered by some 5m of alluvium, was in a pit full of brambles. This was possibly the result of restorations initiated in 1863 by the Czar of Russia, who had bought the property but was unable to complete the work since the Ottoman Porte put an end to his activities. It is thought that while work was in progress the Russians appropriated some of the bones of the saint, who is one of the most venerated in the Russian Orthodox Church (*see box below*).

WHICH ST NICHOLAS?

St Nicholas looms large in Demre/Myra. This town, which has so little to show of its past, has developed a flourishing tourist industry based on the basilica of **St Nicholas of Myra** and the saint's identification with Father Christmas (Santa Claus). By some miraculous twisting of the evidence, St Nicholas has become part of the heritage of Turkey.

The trouble is that while there certainly is a church in Myra that is associated with the cult of St Nicholas, there is no historical evidence that such a figure ever existed. He is said to have lived in the 4th century, to have been born in Patara and, as Bishop of Myra, to have performed miracles and have become the patron saint of merchants, scholars, the unjustly imprisoned, travellers, sailors, children and impecunious young ladies in need of a dowry; he can also find lost property, part the waters, feed the starving... The list is long and growing. Over time some of the aspects of his miraculous activity, such as the bestowing of secret gifts or a particular fondness for children, have resulted in an assimilation with Father Christmas, who also secretly and anonymously gives presents (though St Nicholas never went down a chimney; according to his legend, he crept through a bedroom window to leave bags of gold for three poor girls who needed money to marry).

In the 6th century St Nicholas was a popular saint in Lycia, at the time when Myra was in decline while the interior still prospered. The fleshing out of his elusive persona appears to have started around the 8th century and from there, within a hundred years, the cult spread to Byzantium, where there were 25 churches dedicated to him.

This transition from legend to reality made liberal use of another St Nicholas, the historical **St Nicholas of Sion** (his monastery was at Karabel, some 20km inland from Demre), who was famed for his miracles. These feats were of a different sort from those listed above. It is possible that in the interior, paganism was not completely dead; thus we find St Nicholas busy with exorcisms, purifying wells and fighting demons, as well as feeding the poor. He is in any case a historically documented figure of the 6th century. We know that he was bishop of Pinara; the Sion Monastery has been identified and shown to be quite well endowed. The **Sion Treasure**, now in large part at the Dumbarton Oaks Institute in Georgetown (USA), was recovered in obscure circumstances east of Limyra in the early 1960s and is proven from the inscriptions to have belonged to the Sion Monastery. It contained some 60 pieces, mainly church silver furnishings, plates, lamps, candelabra and altar coverings, all squashed and possibly ready for melting.

By the end of the first millennium, pilgrimage was well established at Myra. It was centred around the extramural church and the tomb of St Nicholas that it supposedly housed. The action of the sailors who stole the saint's bones and took them to Bari in southern Italy on 9th May 1087 may have been prompted by private initiative (it is too late fathom their motives) or may equally have been something more complex, such as a state-sponsored enterprise. Possessing **venerable relics** in those days was prestigious, a source of civic pride (as Venice well knew when it took the bones of St Mark from Alexandria and then housed them in a magnificent basilica). In the late 11th century, **Bari** stood at a crossroads. The Byzantines had just lost it and the new power, the Normans, were looking for legitimacy; moreover, they were the rivals of Venice in terms of trade with the Levant and securing the relics of a venerated saint would have been just the publicity coup they needed. It is noticeable that at this time the Benedictines were able to move into a purpose-built new abbey in the centre of town. The land, donated by the Normans, just happened to be the newly-conquered Byzantine kastron, the citadel. So there was room there for dwellings, for the abbot's palace, a hospital and of course a church, on top of a holy tomb. The only thing missing were relics, and Myra supplied them. Such an arrangement must have received the blessing the pope, Victor III, himself a Benedictine.

Every now and then the Turkish press announces that the **tomb of St Nicholas** has been located in the sprawling church at Myra (the identification being based on a supernatural, heavenly aroma emanating from a mysterious, miraculous substance). But archaeologists still hoping for a sensational find here must not forget that relics of St Nicholas are held today in Bari, Venice, Russia and Rome and that there is a finite number of bones in the human body.

ST NICHOLAS' BASILICA

The basilica (*generally open daily April–Oct 8–7, Nov–March 8–5; charge; check times on religious holidays*) is presently in the centre of the city of Demre. It is well signposted and cannot be missed. Originally it was intended to be outside the city, connected to it by a kilometre-long portico, built according to legend by a general of Constantine's whom St Nicholas saved from execution. This means that we must hypothesise an earlier building, since the earliest extant remains date to the 6th century, when Justinian built or rebuilt a basilica with piers, possibly after the earthquake of 529. At that point the basilica was already a renowned pilgrimage centre. It has been suggested that the pagan spring festivities (the Rosalia) had been re-adapted here for a Christian cult. Whatever the shape of the cult, which included a night-long service and attracted large donations, it is certain that the Arabs or the Persians (or both), who sacked the place in the 630s, had heard rumours of a rich treasury.

The later phase of the church had a dome, lost in 19th-century restorations. After more Arab incursions (they were now based in Crete), a new church dating to the 8th–9th century was built to a completely new plan: a **cross-domed basilica** of the style that was current in Greece and Asia Minor. At the east end was a central apse with three windows and a synthronon; at the west a narthex and exonarthex; and there was an extra aisle on the south side. This is the church that you see today. However, bear in mind that the superstructure has been completely rebuilt and does not fit the standing columns. Later interventions added to the structure (it is indeed a sprawling church), improved the flooring, added frescoes and increased the number of graves, as it was standard practice to seek burial close to a saintly figure. All the known graves appear to have been looted, a great loss to our knowledge of this site. In Amorium, for example (*see Blue Guide Central Anatolia*), the pristine tombs found at a church of contemporary date have revealed prestigious burials of persons in full regalia of silk and gold.

The **tomb of St Nicholas** remains elusive. According to popular lore, when the Italian sailors came for his holy bones in the 11th century (*see box above*), they asked one of the local people where the tomb was; in those long-ago days its location was common knowledge. Sometime during the Dark Ages, between the 6th and the 8th centuries, the church was walled with rubble faced with spolia from the city's Hellenistic defences. The circuit had gates and massive towers. After that the history of the church is patchy. Pilgrims still arrived. In 1340 they found the town destroyed; the only life was in the basilica.

The modern quest for St Nicholas and his basilica started around the 1820s but when Charles Fellows (*p. 26*) visited in the 1840s, he found a single priest, living in the monastery that had been built on top of the church, which was by then buried.

MYRA'S THEATRE AND NECROPOLEIS

To complete a visit to Myra you should not miss the **theatre**, to the north on the edge of modern Demre. Originally it would have been outside the city's walled circuit and just beneath the acropolis. In local limestone it had a seating capacity of c. 14,000; Opramoas (*p. 109*) financed the restoration after the AD 141 earthquake. The cavea rests on the rockface while the sides are built up. It had provisions for a *velarium* and in the restoration of AD 141, the orchestra became an arena. You can go hunting for **graffiti** here. There is one to Tyche, the goddess of the fortune of the city, more or less at the centre of the diazoma near one of the steps leading to the upper seats. The scena (which was buried under 5m of alluvium) is remarkably well preserved, especially the reliefs with theatre masks; among the remains are granite columns.

Two **necropoleis** testify to a long and wealthy Lycian past. The first one, on the cliff face northwest of the theatre, presents a riot of Lycian tombs of all sorts. Traces of colour and Lycian inscriptions have been identified. The **painted tomb** is in a different necropolis along the valley of the Demre Çay, an area with other rock-cut tombs and free-standing monuments. It was made famous by Charles Fellows (*p. 26*), who brought the Lycians to life with his description of the funeral banquet scene with the man dressed in purple drapery reclining on a yellow couch with red designs opposite his wife arrayed in a purple dress, red mantle and yellow veil. Fellows was here in summer, the wrong time of year in those days, because of malaria. Everyone except for the lone Orthodox priest had gone to the upland *yaylas*.

ANCIENT ISSIUM

Developments further east at Yukarı Beymelek, above the Beymelek lagoon, which have been identified with ancient Issium, show a definitive interest in the area both to prevent mountain people from raiding the Myra Valley while keeping an eye on the sea and collect tax and dues.

The site of Issium can be reached by private transport, taking the unconventional sign inland to Issium (the sign, to 'İsion Kalesi', is on a wooden board fixed to a construction looking like a little tiled house with a window, at Yukarı Beymelek, roughly opposite a mosque, on the D400 as it skirts the north shore of the lagoon, c. 8km from the centre of Myra). Follow the road (İskele Cd.), paved with faded red and white bricks, to the end (about 10mins). Then you can see the towers of Issium. Going further means an uncomfortable scramble. The defences here, on the very edge of the Massycitus mountains (Akdağ) and built on a slope, would have had a sweeping view all around. According to McNicoll, the fort consisted of two tall towers linked by a curtain wall. Its slender build suggests it could resist only small-scale attacks. The height of the four-storey towers, estimated at 25m, indicates Issium's role as an observation post controlling the mountains to the north and the sea. It is dated to the Hellenistic period and if the name Issium has anything to do with Isis, it may be the work of the Ptolemies, who controlled the area in the late 3rd century BC.

There are good remains on site, especially of the towers. The northern one has cisterns, one inside and one outside, so take care. Note the slits that may have been used for catapults. The curtain wall has not survived as well.

ANDRIAKE, THE ANCIENT HARBOUR OF MYRA

NB: There were at least two harbours serving Myra: Andriake (or Andriace) to the west of the promontory (*described here*) and Taşdibi to the east (*described on p. 99*).

The site of Andriake/Andriace (*open daily 8.30–7; charge*) is at the end of the Çayağzı Yolu by the modern stadium to the west of Demre town centre. There was an early road connection between Myra and Andriake, as shown by the necropoleis flanking it. The former harbour is now completely landlocked. What is left is a marsh, a nature reserve to the delight of birdwatchers.

It is possible that Andriake is older than Myra. Certainly its favourable position by a sea inlet, providing a safe harbour like that at Patara (*p. 78*) and access to **fresh water** (though there are also salty and sulphurous springs in the area), with an **elevation** right on the coast to control the surroundings, may have attracted settlement from early times. The ruins overlooking the present marina (walls and towers) are said to be Hellenistic. Bronze Age pottery has been occasionally found in the area but it remains impossible at the moment to connect Andriake with Bronze Age wrecks like the one off Uluburun, which is Mycenaean.

Andriake has not yet been thoroughly investigated and it could prove difficult anyway because of the marshy terrain. Present remains show that it flourished until the late antique period, rivalling Patara, though it was never a polis. It is in the first two centuries of the present era that the urban structure was organised, possibly on a gridded plan. It included **baths**, an **agora** (called the plakoma; *see below*), a customs building and a **synagogue** (with a provisional date of around the 5th century AD) identified by the finding of a menorah, graffiti and inscriptions. The quay was graced with a number of **bronze statues**, the earliest honouring Tiberius. The harbour may have been protected by a chain.

By the 6th century it was deemed more convenient to transfer activities to the north side of the harbour, where a **walled Byzantine compound** with wide streets, elegant houses, an industrial-sized watermill (which is inundated and could be earlier), two churches and a necropolis have been identified. Residential districts sprawled on terraces outside the defences. A large Byzantine house with small barred windows below (storage level) and a grand first floor with large panoramic openings

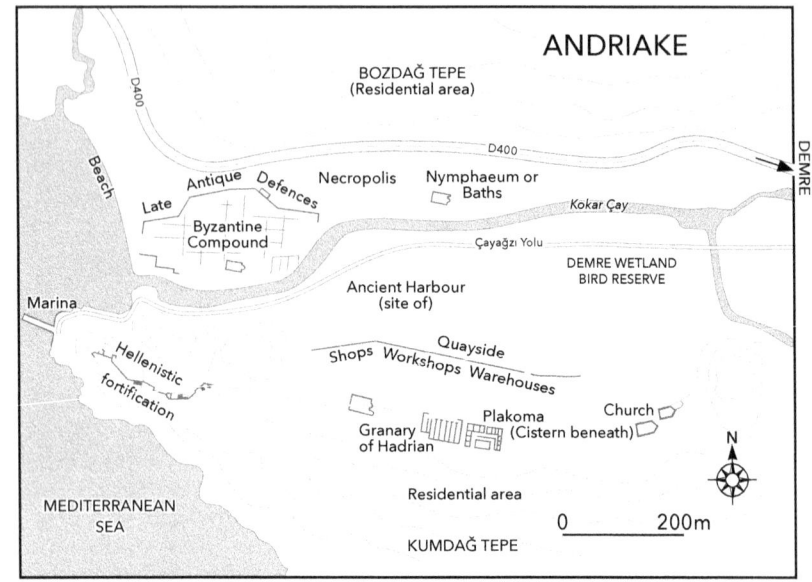

to enjoy the view, shows the taste of the new elite, now abandoning the inward-looking Roman peristyle house and happy to build outside the town.

Andriake appears to have waned even earlier that Myra, around the 6th century. The reason for this was probably due to the **deterioration of the harbour**, which started silting up, while the air became foul and unhealthy. After 655 there is no evidence of any attempt to rehabilitate the damaged structures. Andriake is not mentioned in medieval portulans and there are no coins beyond the 7th century. The replacement harbour, active for pilgrims and trade from around the 10th century, was 3.5km away to the east at Taşdibi (*see below*).

EXPLORING ANDRIAKE

Andriake is not fully equipped for visitors, certainly less so than Patara, but it is catching up fast. Its life span has been shorter and its remains are less impressive. It was never a city; it belonged to Myra. Its archaeology is difficult. On the other hand, the site has a clearly-signed path and is wheelchair friendly. Its main attraction is the **granary** (although in its identification as such, the same reservations apply as for that at Patara; *p. 83*). Built by order of Hadrian, the eight-room structure, possibly once fronted by a porch, was probably a store in a more general sense; as the inscription at the front says, these were horrea, a generic term for storerooms, not necessarily implying grain. Measuring 63m by 32m, it had a pitched roof covering three rooms on either side. Holes have been identified for a wooden structure to cover the middle. The roof was tiled. Now fully restored and rebuilt, it is open as a museum (*open daily 1 April–1 Oct 8.30–7, 31 Oct–14 April 8–5.30; on the first day of religious holidays closed until noon; charge*) with very interesting Lycian artefacts.

The next stop must be the massive vaulted **underground cistern** in beautiful ashlars in the **plakoma**, the extensive agora (40m by 30m), a paved square as the name indicates. The cistern is on the south side while the other three sides had shops in the porticoes. A wooden walkway allows you to get a good close-up view of this monumental structure: it is really impressive. This area had gone out of use by the 6th century AD. A huge murex shell midden, for the mollusc that produces **purple dye**, shows that this was the centre of operations about that time. The cistern would have come in handy because the process of dyeing, one step further than producing the dye itself, requires a lot of water. We can be sure that no dyeing took place at Aperlae (*p. 86*); there just is not enough water to spare. Additionally, since purple dye processing is a smelly job, it is normally carried out away from habitation and in positions with favourable winds; one can conclude therefore that at the time when this area was given over to dyeing, the nearby granary had fallen out of use and this part of town was no longer residential. According to the investigators, the **ecological damage** caused by such intense exploitation (six million molluscs are estimated to have been processed here and by the end these were mainly juveniles) may have a direct correlation with the present scarcity of murex in the surrounding waters.

TAŞDİBİ (STAMIRA)

When trade and pilgrimage picked up in the 10th century, by which time Andriake had fallen out of use, Myra revitalised the harbour at Taşdibi to the east, between Taşdibi and Sülüklü beaches (it is very probable that the sailors from Bari landed here when they came for the bones of St Nicholas; *p. 93*). Taşdibi can be reached by driving due south to the sea from the centre of Demre and taking Kömürlük Cd to the west. It will lead you to Taşdibi plaj. The site is a small promontory which now has a modern harbour on its south side. There is not much there left to see; the passage of time has been unkind to Taşdibi. However, a quick look from the top of the promontory, with views of Myra's kastron, of Kekova island to the west and of Cape Gelidonya to the east, explain the Hellenistic remains, possibly a tower. At the time of the Byzantines' last effort to control maritime trade in the region, the Byzantine 'reconquest' of the 10th century, which first began to totter with the defeat at Manzikert (1071) and finally foundered just 100 years later after another defeat at Myriokephalon, this harbour was known as Stamira.

The 35m-long **rock-cut landing stage**, identified on the east side of the promontory where the water is deep and where operations would have been well protected from the west winds and gales, dates from this period, unless it is Hellenistic. In about 1225 the Seljuks built a tower (*manar*) on the promontory, which explains why the location appears in medieval sources as 'Torre di Stalimure'. Scanty remains of the structure, which was still use in Ottoman times until it was pounded by a tsunami in 1741, suggest that it was circular, built on a platform, quite thick walled (1.2m) and c. 25m tall. The interior was of wood. In its heyday the manar would have been part of a chain controlling the coast. The term 'manar' is Arabic for 'guiding light', suggesting that it may have acted as a lighthouse.

DEREAĞZI & THE INTERIOR

Dereağzı is a site up the Myra Valley, where the Karadere and the Kasabadere meet to form the Demre Çay (the ancient Myros), in an excellent strategic position controlling access both ways from a height (380m) on the fringes of the Kasaba Plateau. It has been identified with Mastaura in Lycia. To get there, head north from Myra in the direction of Dirgenler (*map B, 7*). The road runs along the valley of the Demre. After c. 20km, having crossed the river and entered another valley, you should enquire about the footpath which accesses the ruins from the north (c. 400m). From the top you can overlook the Taurus Mountains, the Kasaba Plateau and the Myra Gorge.

The triangular spur was already recognised as a **defensive position** by the Lycians; a fort in polygonal masonry has been identified at the south end and a number of early 5th–4th-century BC rock tombs and sarcophagi are dotted around. South of the citadel, traces of a theatre and a possible Lycian settlement suggest a lower town. The site was reoccupied from late antiquity up to the 12th century, when life had become difficult on the coast and in the plain. The defences, with rectangular, pentagonal and triangular towers, enclosed buildings and cisterns and a church. Outside the walls to the south, a watch-tower occupied the highest point. As times became more challenging and the countryside was left to the Türkmen, the Byzantine city in the fort huddled around the church and sought security, both physical and spiritual, behind ever stronger defences. It eventually went out of use and the area was reoccupied by the Ottomans, purely for strategic reasons.

The **church down in the plain** to the northeast, about 1km away and now lost among the greenhouses, is yet another poorly understood development; it is dated to the 9th–10th century and with its complex design and building material that came all the way from the Marmara region, it is thought that it was not a local project but enjoyed imperial patronage. It may have been a monastery or a pilgrimage centre or possibly even a cathedral: it certainly signalled growth when everything else was in decline. The impressive remains of the domed basilica have been extensively studied. Its plan shows an inscribed cross with a dome and barrel vaults extending to the exterior walls, galleries, narthex, exonarthex and towers.

ARNEAI

To the north, on the Kasaba–Arykanda road near Çağman (*map B, 7*), are the remains of Arneai (local name Ernez), a very isolated development rarely mentioned in antiquity, but connected to Myra, possibly because of the timber trade. The city is abundantly identified by its inscriptions and by the evident survival of the name. Its antiquity is proved by an inscription in the Lycian language, but it was never important, even though in Byzantine times its bishop ranked ninth under the Metropolitan of Myra. Arneai was the head of a sympolity of which we know very little. The very rare coins of Arneai are mid-3rd century. The inscriptions reveal a close association with Myra, whose territory was adjacent to the south.

The extant ruins are mostly Byzantine. The ring of **walls** still stands for most of its length, with towers and at least two gates, but the greater part was repaired in medieval times. In the interior are **two churches** and some unrecognisable remains of buildings; the public buildings mentioned in the inscriptions, notably a gymnasium and a public guest house, are not now discernible. From earlier times there survive a few **tombs** of Lycian type, some parts of the **city wall**, and numerous **inscriptions** of the Roman period, mostly built into the late wall; one of them is an ex-voto to a local deity, Tobaloas.

BACK TO THE COAST

From Myra, the only way east is along the coast. Here the rock has been recently blasted and is still raw. The road crosses an empty landscape, devoid of even a single greenhouse. Make the most of the drive and take a break at the Mağralı beach, one of the few accessible on this stretch, pristinely clean (take your rubbish away with you).

FİNİKE

As soon as you reach Finike (*map B, 7*), you are back into the world. This has always been a harbour and it is now launching into tourism; it makes a useful base for getting around. There is little to see of its past: scraps of a Hellenistic wall and the remains of a small castle above the harbour (Hellenistic with Byzantine repairs) which acted as a refuge in the Dark Ages.

The coast here has offered good anchorage since time immemorial; this would have been the very last landfall on the way to Cyprus, the Levant and Egypt. It was the harbour of Limyra (*see below*) and as Limyra declined in late antiquity, Finike grew in importance. In due course it became the point where Christianity met Islam, with momentous consequences such as when in 655 the Arabs destroyed the Byzantine fleet here and gained control of the coast. It became for the Arabs the access point to the riches of the interior, namely cypress wood, which was scarce in Alexandria. Finike was still going strong in the late 12th century but under another name. In the sources it appears as 'Portus Pisanorum', at a time when pirates from Pisa roamed the seas and sought revenge in 1182 for the massacre of the Latins, in other words the Roman Catholics (mainly Italians) of Byzantium. The area was wholly lost after the Seljuks crushed the Byzantines at Myriokephalon. Later on, under the Ottomans, it gained importance as a landfall on the journey from Egypt to Istanbul. There seems to have been no Roman presence here, though they are credited with building the road into the interior along the Arycandus Valley, as shown by a milestone from the time of Diocletian.

LIMYRA

To do justice to Limyra (from Finike on the way north to Elmalı, take the right turn at the brown sign; stop at the theatre; *bear in mind that parts of the site are not open to the public; otherwise the site is accessible*), one has to think about its geology and hydrology. The site extends from the acropolis (316m) c. 800m northeast of the theatre, along the slopes at the foot of the Toçak Dağı, a spur of the Bey Dağları, to the lower town, the flat area to the south where eventually the Byzantine city developed and Limyra drowned.

Research has shown that the slope originally faced marshes that turned into a freshwater lake, later silted up. On this the lower town was eventually built. The mixed environment was attractive and there is evidence of early settlement going back to the Neolithic. According to some, Limyra can be identified with the Hittite Zumarri, meaning 'water-rich'. And indeed Limyra is water-rich; in the end there was just too much of it. Work by Austrian archaeologists, geologists and hydrographers have concluded that Limyra is a drowned city, drowned in a surplus of water as the karstic structure of the Toçak Dağı was altered by earthquakes and subsidence, causing the numerous springs to change course and affecting the water table of the Byzantine city. The efforts made by the Byzantines to deal with this problem, i.e. dumping gravel to raise the ground level, simply compounded the problem. Another aspect of the archaeology of Limyra is that while the slope has lost part of its archaeological remains through severe erosion, the lower town has been continuously inhabited at least since Hellenistic times and building material has been recycled *ad infinitum*. Roman and Hellenistic Limyra has been reconstructed by studying spolia.

A SHORT HISTORY OF LIMYRA

Limyra makes a grand entry into history with **Perikles** (b. 435 BC, r. 380–362 BC), a Lycian who admired things Greek as his name shows, and was a minor satrap at the time when Lycia was in the hands of the Persians. He had an impressive career that included defeating Xanthus and conquering part or all of Lycia. Certainly someone (or he himself, Mausolus-style) thought his achievements were worth remembering, which would explain his heroön (*see below*) The **acropolis** had been walled in the 5th century BC and contained aristocratic dwellings in the style of the Lycian acropolis at Xanthus. As the defences extended south, the ground was terraced and more houses went up. They were cut in the rock and built up, perhaps in mud brick. They had fireplaces; the roofs were not tiled, they were probably covered with straw and clay. The first evidence of occupation of the **lower town** is Hellenistic, with the Ptolemaion (*see below*), and archaeologists have been able, in adverse circumstances, to detect a grid pattern. Hellenistic Limyra, represented by inscriptions and tombs, fed the spolia mill. Roman Limyra's fate was the same: we are left with a **theatre**, the stump of a funerary monument (*see below*) and a couple of baths. The 65.5m diameter theatre is late Hellenistic, with substantial repairs of AD 141 after an earthquake (Opramoas again; *p. 109*); it became an arena in the 3rd century and the scena, of which not much remains, is Severan. It was apparently later connected by a **colonnaded street** with granite columns to the lower town. The other monument that is certainly Roman is the cenotaph of Gaius Caesar (*see below*).

The Byzantine period is more visible, also because the town drowned and settlement came to an end between the 8th and 10th centuries. Apart from the **church**, possibly a monastery, immediately south of the acropolis, this phase can be seen mainly in the

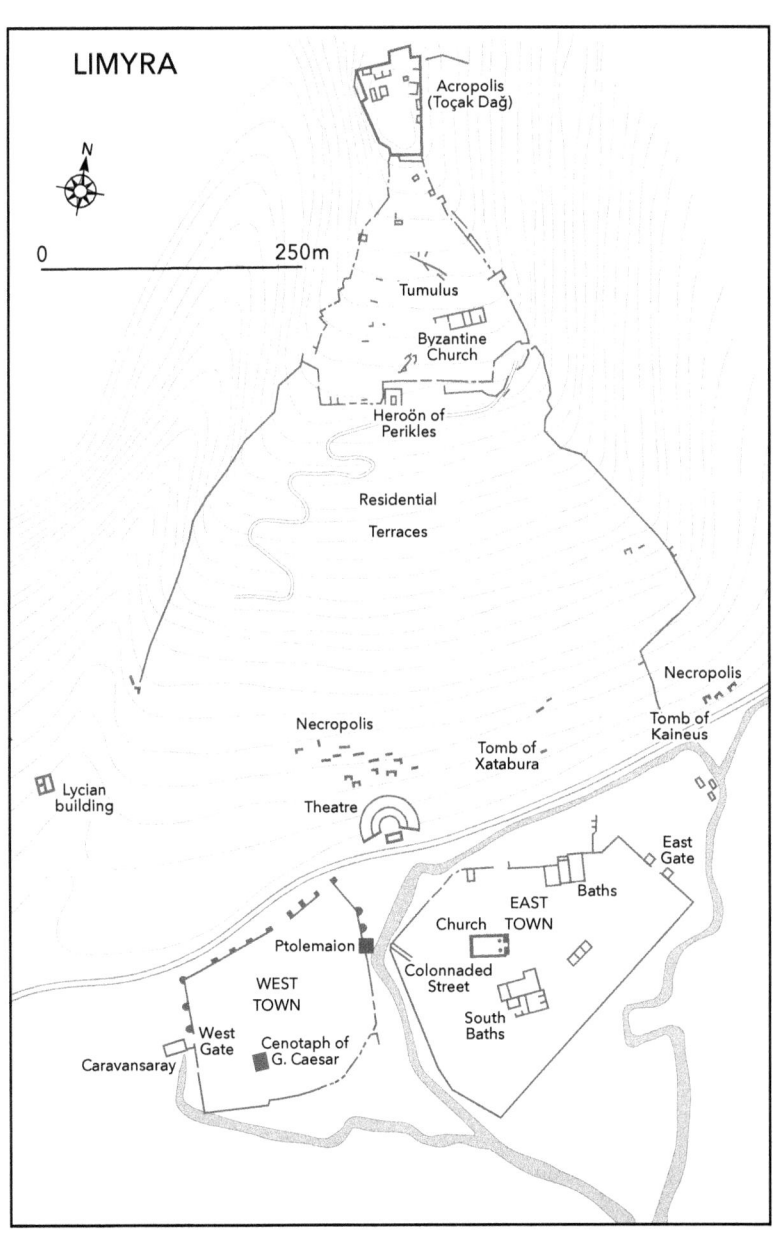

lower town, where the late antique and Byzantine developments show that Limyra was still doing well. The new religion left its mark, with a few churches with frescoes, polychrome glass mosaics and *opus sectile* floors. The **cathedral** was a grandiose 40m by 23m, built on top of a temple. The Ptolemaion had a smaller basilica church built partly on it, with marble capitals and a marble screen.

Things became difficult in the 5th–6th century and defences went up in the lower town, enclosing two separate urban conglomerations referred to today as the **West Town** and **East Town**. A river ran between the two and had to be accommodated. In the process, the old monuments were cannibalised. Both enclosures had smart, impressive gates and the west city received an overhaul of its **defences** (perhaps to fend off the Arabs), with the addition of closely-spaced towers on its north and west side. The settlement disregarded the Hellenistic grid and was tightly packed with narrow streets. As the water level began to rise, the East Town was abandoned first and eventually life ceased at Limyra around the 8th–10th century. When Spratt (*p. 31*) travelled there, the water had been put to a good use to power a water mill, operated by nomads living in thatched huts.

HIGHLIGHTS OF LIMYRA

The best bits of Limyra exist either in fragments in the Archaeological Museum in Antalya and in the dig house stores, or in the minds of the archaeologists and architects who have reconstructed the appearance of the complete buildings.

The **Heroön of Perikles** is the oldest monument in Limyra. It is situated high up on the slope, 300m below the acropolis, partly cut into a cliff and south of a wall defining the original Lycian settlement. In that sense it resembles the Nereid Monument at Xanthus, on the edge of the site with high visibility and intended to impress visitors. It was found to contain a *kline* (couch) and evidence of other furniture. Like the Nereid Monument, it was shaped like a Ionic temple on a high podium, with an ornamentation that is a fusion of Greek and Persian influences, but the mix is not as good. Its caryatids have none of the grace of the so-called Nereids. Their heads, covered with veils, and their long twisted tresses, impart an Anatolian look to them. The acroteria (four in the corners and two on the ridge) have more movement. They associate Perikles' memory with god-like heroes, giving him a divine right to rule. The friezes on the east and west walls of the cella show processions that could be either military, or depicitons of the departure for the hunt, both things with which a ruler of the time would want to be associated. It was the location of a hero cult up until the time of the Romans. One gets the impression that while the concept expresses adherence to Greek artistic canons, the execution was local.

The **Ptolemaion** is down in the West Town. Dated by style to the time of Ptolemy II Philadelphus (c. 3rd century BC), it has had a difficult life, ignominiously ended by being incorporated into the Byzantine wall. Over 1,000 fragments belonging to the monument have been identified, many of them built into the wall or dumped in the river or strewn across the terraces. According to an inscription from Xanthus, there was a cult of the Ptolemaic family in Lycia at some point: this may be an expression of it, to celebrate the military or other successes of the dynasty. The Ptolemaion basically consisted of a square base, 14m by 14m (height unknown), with an Ionic tholos on top, its conical roof surmounted by a massive acroterion. At the four corners of the base, four pairs of lions roared. There is evidence in the decoration for the use of metalware, which of course is no longer with us. The reliefs appear to have had military overtones. A few larger-than-lifesize statues, now in Antalya Archaeological Museum, have been identified as belonging to the decorative scheme. Whatever the style was, the Ptolemaion was certainly very heavy. Built as it was in an area with a problematic water table, it may have been unstable and have come to grief before it was dismantled and its constituent parts put to other use.

Near the Ptolemaion is the **cenotaph of Gaius Caesar**, who died here in AD 4 on his way back from the East, where he had been seriously wounded in battle. He was a nephew of Augustus, the son of his only child Julia. He had been adopted by Augustus and was groomed for succession. Of the monument erected here to commemorate is memory, only the core in *opus caementicium* remains in place. It was built on a paved surface that was later threatened when water started encroaching. Levels were raised but by then the cenotaph had become no more than a source of spolia. It has been reconstructed as a plinth on a socle surmounted by a cube-shaped temple. The ornamentation, bonded to the core with bronze clamps, included marble facing and marble pilasters decorated with scrolls and tendrils. On the pedestal, a frieze celebrated Gaius' military achievements. The roof may have been pyramidal. A good comparison for the monument is the Tomb of Theron at Agrigento (Sicily), dated to the 1st century BC. The quality of the workmanship is very good, comparing well with the Ara Pacis in Rome, though executed by artists from Asia Minor and not from Rome.

Last but not least are the **necropoleis** (east and west), which are very extensive and include a lot of fine Lycian tombs, some with friezes while others replicate wood structures in stone. Among them is the **Tomb of Kaineus**, 150m east of the theatre: over time a spring opened in it, again showing the difficulties of water management in Limyra.

ARYKANDA

Arykanda (*map B, 7; open daily 15 April–2 Oct 8.30–7.30, 3 Oct–14 April 8.30–530; charge; closed till noon on religious holidays; if there is no one at the ticket booth, just go in*) sprawls on the east slope overlooking Route 635 from Finike to Korkuteli. Stop at the brown sign for refreshments and prepare for some scrambling. The site is vast. It is on a slope ranging from 912m in altitude at the acropolis to the north (with an observation tower right at the top) down to 600m in the south, where the approach route is. The site, which has been known for some time, has recently been taken in hand and presented to the public. Still, is it a bit remote and requires some physical effort. The words 'We had the site to ourselves' recur frequently in write-ups and this in fact is the major attraction of Arykanda, which is in the wild and looks just as an abandoned city should look, deserted, atmospheric and overgrown, but not too much so, so that one can still get around. There are warnings about snakes and scorpions, so watch out. You can drive on an unmade road up to the ticket booth where there is a small car park. At this point you are directly below the theatre. That should help you find your way around since there are no signs.

Arykanda was **Lydian city**, with a name-ending that sounds properly Anatolian. It may have Lycian roots—and indeed there are coins here of Perikles of Lymira—but there are no Lycian inscriptions. The local strongman could have been a Luwian; after all, we are on the edge of Lycia. He probably lived in a keep, high up where unspecified occupation is attested from the Bronze Age. Arykanda expanded to its present size (500m north–south and 1500m east–west) in Hellenistic times, followed by Roman reworkings. The Byzantine transition was short-lived. However, towards the end, the inhabitants decamped to the safety of Arif (*see below*)

Arykanda was wealthy, a wealth that was presumably based on **timber**, hewn from the beautiful stands of cedar and cypress that grow on the slopes of the Akdağ immediately to the east, and that were so beloved of the Egyptians, who indeed left evidence of their presence with images of Isis and Serapis. The inhabitants had a reputation for being extravagant and profligate. They certainly built themselves a fine town, with luxurious houses partly built on terraces and partly cut in the rock and with all the required civic amenities. It was not gridded. The list of deities worshipped here is eclectic and wide-ranging: it included gods and goddesses that one would expect, such as Apollo, Ares, Athena and Artemis (but worshipped under four different guises), as well as Mithras and some complete outsiders, like Somondeus, a mountain god, presumably local. **Water** was stored in cisterns and also supplied by an aqueduct from the springs of the Beydağı.

When life became more difficult, with the demise of the coast under Persian and Arab pressure, the Arykandans **retreated to Arif**, on a small promontory (245m by 105m) a few hundred metres to the south on the other side of the modern road. This was all that Arykanda was not. It was small and compact, not luxurious, planned and strictly functional. In addition to the steep slopes, it was defended with towers and walls; inside the enceinte, housing was closely packed and tall, apparently up to three storeys. A couple of baths have been identified but no aqueduct, only cisterns. There were no civic buildings, nor open spaces; safety was in religious observance and there were as many as seven churches. Arif is a single-period site, showing that austerity did not work for the Arykandans who went to live there (about one thousand of them). The site had a short life and was soon abandoned.

Arykanda meanwhile still lay on the slope, protected by its remoteness and bad communications. Even Arif did not use it as a source of spolia; people helped themselves instead to material from the necropoleis lower down. Indeed, Arykanda has survived well, in spite of an earthquake or two. Buildings have been covered by landslips; which make the ancient limestone look quite new after excavation, and robbers have been discouraged by the logistics of removing spoils and then getting them down to the coast (though the columns of the agora have disappeared).

EXPLORING ARYKANDA

Arykanda is best enjoyed by taking time to get around, examining the ruins but also absorbing the view, feeling the surroundings and enjoying the scenery, complete with snow-capped mountains. After the **Heroön of Naltepe**, which has been reconstructed as a small Corinthian temple-tomb, you will come across a large **bath-gymnasium** complex, the largest in Lycia, with arches still standing. Past the remains of a **Christian basilica** and the Trajanic **Sebasteion**, the **latrines** and the **nymphaeum**, you will see the **prytaneion** and the **agora**. This had a temple of Tyche in the middle and you can see the remains of shops on three sides. To the north was the **odeion**, built by order of Hadrian. Entered through a triple portal to the south, it was very ornate, with seats clad in coloured marble. The **theatre**, further uphill, describes an arc larger than a semicircle. It was badly damaged in the earthquake of AD 141 but beyond that time it has done very well. The well-preserved scena is Roman. The **stadium**, long (106m) and narrow (17m), had to accommodate the slope in its design; it really looks more like a running track than a fully-fledged stadium. It only has seats on the north side and is Hellenistic in date. On the same level to the west, another **agora with shops** has been excavated. Behind it a **temple of Helios** and a **bouleuterion** that stood at the end of a 137m long **stoa** have been identified. The slope below was residential, with beautiful villas. To the east and west of the settlement are the **necropoleis**, with elaborate temple-tombs, barrel-vaulted tombs and sacrophagi.

A SIDE TRIP TO IDEBESSUS

Idebessus (*map B, 7*) is accessed south of Arykanda taking the east turn at Yalnız and driving on about 10km at Karacaören/Kozağacı; ask to be shown the forest path. The town, at an altitude of c. 1000m, is on a road in between the Kızlar Sivrisi Tepe (3030m) and Tahtalıdağı (2375m), allowing people from the coast to reach Antalya without negotiating the tricky coastline (described in the next chapter). The town has only recently been surveyed and has good remains because of its remoteness—though it was not remote enough for Arab raiders, after whose visit it was transformed into a Byzantine kastron. Idebessus appears to span a period from the Hellenistic to some time after the final demise of the Byzantines. Its name features in the Patara *Stadiasmus* (*p. 83*), though its Lycian character (it belonged to the League (*p. 80*) in Roman times as a member of a sympolity) is somehow obscured by strong Pisidian elements. There is no obvious Lycian architecture and there are no Lycian inscriptions. But this was a small town and excavations may tell a different story. It seems that its heyday came when it was in Roman hands, in the 2nd–3rd century.

The site is overgrown, so visiting has to be done with care. The city had an **acropolis** to the south, walled with towers. Three **churches** have been identified, one on the acropolis, a large one outside it to the north, and one to the south. The **theatre**, possibly Hellenistic and rather small (600–700 people), is also outside the acropolis; it could have been a meeting place since there is no trace of a scena. A **bath-gymnasium** fed by a water channel has been identified, Otherwise the rest is **tombs**, plenty of them. Some are monumental, on a podium with an exedra, while the numerous sarcophagi show by their ornamentation that there was some wealth here.

RHODIAPOLIS

On the way to Rhodiapolis, you might be tempted by **Corydalla** at Hacıveliler, a suburb of Kumluca (*map B, 8*). But the Sion treasure (*p. 94*) is no longer here, and neither is Corydalla itself, where Spratt (*p. 31*) saw some beautiful remains including a theatre, some 40m in diameter, but of which only the depression on the southwest face of the hill is now left. Corydalla was stripped to build Kumluca in the 1950s.

Rhodiapolis, a little further to the north, is signposted from Kumluca. It would have suffered the same fate as Corydalla had the government not intervened to save it and turn it into a tourist attraction. Remote monitoring with cameras and sensors was installed, reducing the number of fires, illegal excavations and stone robbing, and archaeologists moved in. The town that you see today is the Roman town, which is being restored somewhat enthusiastically, making for a lot of rebuilding with blindingly white new stone, a profusion of scaffolding and a loss of any feeling of walking in the past. With all the cranes and bulldozers, it feels more like walking around a building site. But when the restoration work is completed and has had a chance to age, it will look very good.

Little if anything is known of Rhodiapolis' pre-Roman past; it has not been fully investigated. Geometric sherds have been identified out of context, suggesting a 700 BC occupation, and the name itself, Rhodiapolis, hints to a connection with the Rhodians, who were active in antiquity along the coast. The site, on a hill overlooking the expanse to the south and with good control of the north approach and a Hellenistic observation tower, can be deemed strategic, providing early warning of trouble. However, because of its geology the site is not well equipped with springs and wells. Early Rhodiapolis had to make do with cisterns, either built or cut in the rock, until it got an aqueduct. Rhodiapolis certainly had a **Lycian past**, as shown by the Lycian graves going back to 300 BC and possibly earlier. A 5th-century BC coin bears the city's Lycian name: Wedrei. Unfortunately we do not have Lycian buildings or remains to go with it. The earliest buildings are late Hellenistic and incorporate some spolia. Indeed, inscriptions testify to the presence in Rhodiapolis of Greek-style institutions in the 2nd–1st centuries BC. Rhodiapolis' claim to fame is **Opramoas**, a 2nd-century AD Lyciarch, a powerful member of the Lycian League (*p. 80*) at a time when it had ceased to be politically relevant under Roman rule but remained an expression of the social bonding of the Lycians. The city had a Byzantine phase, in which the Roman buildings were recycled either as masonry or in lime kilns (one such was found in the agora, which at the time when it was operational must obviously have fallen out of use). It shows retrenchment; and ultimately Rhodiapolis was reduced to a **kastron** to the west of the theatre on the highest point. There is no evidence of occupation after the 11th century. When Spratt (*p. 31*) visited in 1842, he could appreciate the defensive position of the settlement, a height surrounded by cliffs where the necropoleis were. The theatre was buried but recognisable and he could make out three churches, the fortified height to the west (the Byzantine kastron) and the aqueduct coming in from the west. Now there is more (*see below*).

OPRAMOAS, THE MAN WITH DEEP POCKETS

The name of Opramoas crops up quite frequently in descriptions of Lycia, especially in the context of public buildings, frequently theatres damaged by earthquake. Most of the time this means the disaster of AD 141, which occurred during Opramoas' lifetime. But he also paid for gifts for games, to endow civic buildings in general, and even for dowries for girls from poor families, for the funerals of indigent citizens and for primary schooling for Xanthus' children and food for the poor.

Euergetism, as giving in this context is called in the Roman world, was a way to stamp one's mark on the landscape and gain imperial favour. But it requires a lot of money. Opramoas made donations to about 30 Lycian cities, ranging from 200,000 denarii for repairs to various structures after AD 141 down to 7000 denarii to Choma, a city in the interior, for a new stoa and a temple to Augustus. The estimated total of his largesse is around two billion denarii. This was at a time when 50 denarii would meet the needs of an ordinary citizen for one year. We are told that Opramoas was very rich and that he held public office in the League and in religious matters. He was a landowner and had shipping interests, though the sea is a bit far from Rhodiapolis. The source of his wealth—enormous for a relatively insignificant place like this—remains a mystery. It is easier to explain Herodes Atticus, another *euergetes* from about the same period, who funded a number of projects in and outside Greece. He was from a long aristocratic lineage that could claim descent from the mythical Athenian kings, was a Roman senator, was wealthy in his own right and had married money.

What was Opraomas' motivation, beyond pleasing the new Roman masters? That he did so can be seen quite clearly in his tomb, a rather unattractive cube with steps and four columns in front, in the immediate space below the theatre. It was built with 55 huge ashlar blocks and no mortar and covered with a tiled roof. On the sides it bore copies of letters from the emperor and from grateful municipalities, recipients of Opramoas' generosity. This monument, said to be equally popular with epigraphists and with treasure hunters, has not fared very well. Already under the Byzantines it was used in the kastron, for the wall and part of the paving. Over time it collapsed and suffered damage; pits were dug here and there. The inscriptions eroded. The plan of the excavators was to put it together again for the public to admire, but that seems to have been unsuccessful. According to news in 2017, the pieces had been put together in the wrong order. The front, totally robbed apart from the door frame, had been entirely rebuilt of bright new limestone ashlar in a somewhat botched style. At the time of writing, the unfinished project had been covered with plastic and was awaiting completion.

EXPLORING RHODIAPOLIS

According to the excavators, Rhodiapolis was a planned city. It is difficult to see how this can have been so, since very little if anything meets at right angles and from their own plan one cannot detect any grid. The topography is just too compelling, so compelling that Rhodiapolis quickly ran out of space to expand. It was, however, planned in a different sense: huge **underground cisterns** were part of the buildings' architecture and of the structure of the terraces. They are all similar, vaulted and built to the same plan: water was taken seriously here. The south-facing **theatre** (which would offer a fine view were it not for the greenhouses), barely 40m across and now heavily restored, reveals a Hellenistic origin by its shape. It is accessed from the north and, from the west, by a fine flight of steps. It sits partly on a natural slope with a built east wing. It had the required slots to fit a *velarium*. Eventually parts of the theatre were used for the Byzantine tower on the north side of the kastron. The stage building, 8m wide and 16m long, is Roman. Beyond is the **core of the town**. Here **two stoas**, a two storey-one to the east and a single-storey one to the west, meet at an acute angle; they had mosaic floors. They focus attention on the central monument, the **mausoleum of Opramoas**. Next to it to the east, a large building has been identified as a meeting hall. The **kastron** with a basilica church, the bishop's residence and large cisterns, is to the northwest of the theatre. The rest of the site is taken up by official building and private houses built on terraces. Among them a **round temple** (or is it a macellum?), an **Asclepieion** as the inscription shows, large baths, the **agora** at the back of the double-storey stoa with cisterns below ground, and a **nymphaeum** have been identified.

A SIDE TRIP TO GAGAI

The ancient town of Gagai (*map B, 8*), signposted off Route 400, may deserve some attention because of its past reputation. It was the home of the *Lapis gagates*, a form of lignite resembling jet, though none can any longer be found anywhere in the area. It must be hidden under the greenhouses. In antiquity it was prized for its medicinal properties and was lauded by writers from Pliny (*36,19*) to Galen. Apparently it could keep away snakes, help diagnose epilepsy, cure bowel disorders and calm hysterical women (it is not clear how the remedies were administered). It also doubled up as jewellery. However, it did not bring much luck to the city of Gagai, a possible Rhodian foundation first mentioned in the early Hellenistic period. The town, which may have survived into medieval times, has been mercilessly plundered. The theatre is now no more than a depression. Gone are the lovely seats with dolphin-shaped armrests and the city walls that Spratt (*p. 31*) saw.

PRACTICAL INFORMATION

GETTING THERE AND AROUND

The Lycian peninsula is between Dalaman and Antalya airports, both of which have good international connections. Dalaman airport has a bus service from Fethiye.

Lycia is served by three good roads: on the coast, in the interior and one linking the two through Elmalı. There will be buses and *dolmuş* along them. This does mean, though, that you will need to make sure there is time both to get to your destination by bus and to get back.

The **bus stations** are either in the centre of town (Kaş and Demre) or on the edge close to Route 400 (Finike, Kumluca and Kemer). Fethiye *otogar* is also in the centre of town, by İnönü Blvd. Some sites, like Arykanda and Xanthus, which are not far from the main road, can be reached on foot if you ask the driver to stop at the right place. But you will need to plan your return. Other sites are not so amenable, such as Patara, which is 5km from the nearest main transport route.

A number of locations (including Fethiye) can be visited by boat on day trips. For the Üçağız area, the best way to get around (unless you are walking the Lycian Way) is also by boat. Playing hide and seek with the various island, peninsulas and inlets of the busy geography here is fun and it makes a great day out.

Inland places like Cibyra will require private transport or joining an organised tour.

TOURIST INFORMATION

You will find this at your hotel and at information kiosks, though these seem to become ever rarer with the spread of the internet. For **Fethiye** go by the sea near the ancient theatre.

WHERE TO STAY

The area is well equipped with accommodation: **Fethiye** offers plenty of choice. This is the land of small *pensyions*, basically because the space is so constrained between the mountains and the sea. At **Simena** a good place to stay is the Teras Paradise Guest House (*T: 90 536 493 71 61*) just south of the castle, with a wonderful view of Kekova and a semi-submerged Lycian tomb; it is worth the extra outlay. In **Demre** a stay with Salih Topuz's family at the Kent Pansiyon on İlkokul Cd., north of town (*kentpansiyon.com; T: 90 242 871 20 42 salihtopuz@hotmail.com*), is receeommended, for a warm welcome and full immersion.

If you do not feel you have to be by the sea, Hoyran Wedre Köy Evleri in **Hoyran** village, south of Route 400 c. 3km from the coast, is a good choice; you will enjoy the quiet countryside and the breakfast spread (*hoyran. com, T: 90 242 875 11 25*). And if you happen to be in the interior, at **Elmalı** for example, spend a quiet night at the Tuba Otel at Hükümet Cd. 62 (*T: 90 242 618 55 00*).

WHAT TO EAT

When in **Fethiye**, combine exploring and having a good meal: try the **Ada Restaurant** on the Şövalye Adası/Fethiye Adası, which you can reach by water taxi from the shore. The menu is not extensive but what there is, such as grilled octopus or sea bass, is very good. The view and the atmosphere are fantastic. Otherwise, you will find a choice of eateries along the coast. They cater for tourists and the fare offered will reflect that. But if you are in **Elmalı** at the Tuba Otel, cross the road and turn left to **Şişci Ömerin Yeri**, which has been going since 1966 (the original Ömer, the şişci or 'man with the spit' (as in şiş kebap), has probably been succeeded by a descendant) and have a *piyaz*, a hearty bean salad with peppers and tomatoes, much beloved in Turkey. With it have freshly baked bread; if you do not know how to ask, point to the grill where it is being baked non-stop. After exploring **Arykanda**, visit the little *lokanta* by the waterfall next to the main road. While enjoying a well-deserved cool ayran and a *gözleme*, have a look at the imaginative kitchen arrangement and at the old copper samovar.

WHAT TO DO

Apart from antiquities, there are also natural phenomena. In the **Saklıkent Milli Parkı** (Saklıkent Hidden City National Park; *open daily 8–8; canyon only open May–Oct; charge*) is a canyon created by the relentless erosion of the Dargaz Çay, an affluent of the Eşen Çay (the ancient Xanthus river). The canyon is 300m deep and 16km long and very narrow. Part of it is passable on gangways or along the river bed and there are plenty of fine waterfalls. The park is well equipped for tourists looking for a day out and for specialists looking for adventure. The owners, who who discovered this natural wonder not long ago when they were looking for a suitable spot for a trout farm, boast of serving 3,500 meals a day (you will not be alone here).

For walkers, Fethiye is the starting point of the **Lycian Way**. From here there is only 540km to go, so put your boots on.

Towards the end of October, the **Kekova Yürük Food Festival** is held, centred in the village of Kapaklı, between Demre and Simena. You will be able to sample food from a nomadic culture with various sorts of cheeses, *pekmez* (a sort of syrup) and olives and enjoy a get-together with the local community.

WESTERN PAMPHYLIA

Pamphylia comprises one huge gulf, giving it plenty of coastline and a small plain, a resource that is exceedingly precious here, where flat land is at a premium. The precise borders of Pamphylia are unclear and there seems to be nothing that can be said to be typically Pamphylian in terms of style (such as the sarcophagus shape that is so unmistakably Lycian, for example). The language, a pre-Dorian Arcadian, may point to the origin of the colonisers but it is little represented and not fully understood. The remains, some of which are quite impressive, are mainly Roman, examples of urban imperial architecture, and as such are not distinctive. The name of the region itself does not help. Pamphylia, meaning 'all the tribes', points less to a single ethnicity than to a melting pot. In this region the vast gulf of Antalya takes centre stage, stretching from Cape Gelidonya in the west (*map B, 8*) to Alanya in the east (*map C, 7*), which in itself provides an arbitrary border with Cilicia (there are other proposed break-off points; the question is not settled). Nevertheless, the essence of Pamphylia is a single long coastline, with Antalya, the shining jewel, at its centre.

The plain at the foot of the Taurus Mountains that protects Pamphylia from the bitingly cold north winds has been created over geological time by the reworking of limestone-rich waters. This has produced an expanse of travertine into which rivers flowing from the north have cut their beds, sometimes disappearing underground. In antiquity the land was agriculturally productive (grain, oil, cattle and sheep) but at times yields were insufficient to feed a growing population. This was a land of big cities, contrasting markedly with Lycia and its abundance of small settlements. The largest and the most enduring such city was Antalya (the ancient Attaleia), positioned at the top of the gulf and blessed with a deep harbour where there was no danger of silting. Another coastal approach was Side, situated on a narrow peninsula that could be cut off and defended. Otherwise the other cities, e.g. Perge, Sillyum and Aspendos, were in retreat from the coast and in the case of Perge and Aspendos, connected to it by a river navigable by small craft.

Pamphylia was a land of traders and appears to have been under continuous economic expansion up to the 6th century AD. Trading was based on a secure Mediterranean. When that failed and pressure from inland increased, the situation deteriorated—with the notable exception of Antalya, which was able to withstand all obstacles. This chapter explores the west coast of the gulf. The area between Antalya and Side, including the hinterland, is covered in the chapters that follow.

OLYMPUS, THE CHIMAERA & PHASELIS

At Cape Gelidonya (or Kırlangıç Burnu, both names a reference to the migrating swallows that like to make a stopover here in spite of the lack of water), spare a thought for the ancient mariners who came to grief here, leaving us fine shipwrecks. Recently, scuba divers have identified a spread of sarcophagi on the sea floor confirming that this was truly a dangerous place. Going north the area is one big national park (Olympus Beydağları Milli Parkı), with peaks rising over 2000m, leaving just a narrow strip of coastline where the modern road runs. This has always been a treacherous coast: rocky, full of cliffs, subject to the vagaries of the wind and in antiquity impassable. Communication was basically by sea. This did not quite suit the purposes of Alexander the Great when he wanted to move a whole army out of Lycia and up to the cities of Pamphylia; even that great man had to resort to taking his army inland when the beaches proved impassable because of the threatening sea.

OLYMPUS

The town of Olympus (*map B, 8*), in Turkish Olimpos, on the Akçay, offers a refuge and fresh water on this inhospitable coast. The river mouth is closed by a sand bar in the summer, when the river is at its lowest. You will be rewarded here with a good swim. Before setting out to explore, it is important to understand the development of Olympus. In the sources, the original Olympus, a prominent member of the Lycian League (*p. 80*), was up on the mountains to the west and this was its harbour. So we need to consider the original Olympus first.

A SHORT HISTORY OF OLYMPUS
According to Classical sources and to an inscription, Olympus left the Lycian League in the early 1st century BC and came under the rule of a certain **Zeniketes**, one of the many pirates that swarmed around the Mediterranean until Pompey put a halt to their raiding in 67 BC. Zeniketes turned his inland town into a fortress, and when he was attacked by the Roman army led by Publius Servilius Vatia Isauricus in 78 BC, he set fire to his house and perished with all his family. The town, described by Cicero as an 'ancient city with all kinds of ornaments' (*Against Verres 2,1,56*), went into decline; it probably did not help that it was despoiled by Verres when he was an official in the newly-established province. This Olympus has not yet been identified with any degree of certainty. There are various possibilities based on a description by Strabo stating that from it one could see Lycia, Pamphylia and the Milyas further north, hence suggesting a very elevated location. The population moved to Korikos, 4km east by the coast, which is where the **new Olympus** developed from a small harbour settlement into the city that you see now. It had no agricultural hinterland and was cut off from the interior by a forbidding topography of cliffs and canyons. In the days when the sea was safe, being so close to it was a blessing, but this turned into a nightmare when the Arabs took to the water, only abating slightly when the Caliphate moved from Damascus to the more remote Baghdad in the second half of the 8th century. Altogether the town appears undefended.

It has been suggested that towards the end of the 7th century Olympus was the seat of a religious community, and the number of churches seems to support this. By the 9th century, this stretch of coast was deserted. Later, the Crusaders took an interest in it, or perhaps the Genoese roaming the seas and looking for landfall at

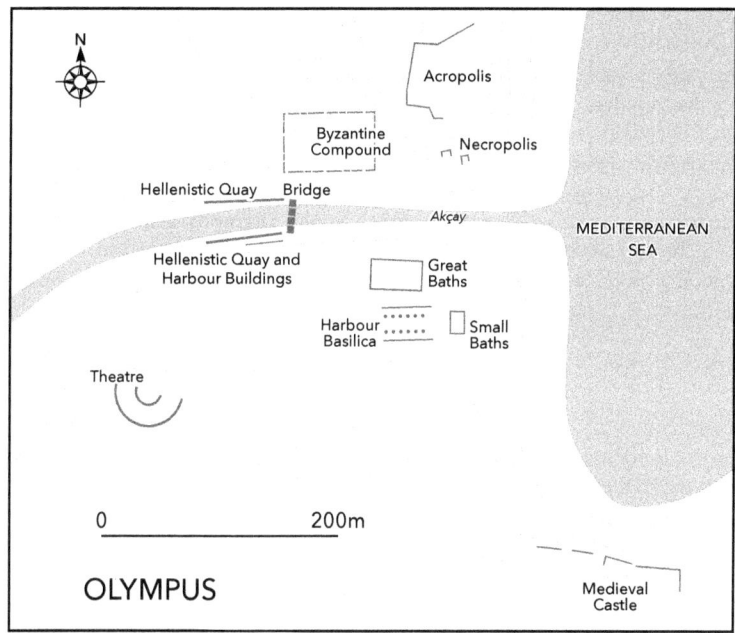

Ceneviz Tepesi, the promontory at the south end of the sand bar. The Venetians were doing likewise 7km to the south, which is why Çavus Limanı was called 'Porto Veneziano'. Both settlements collapsed when the Ottomans took control. In the 18th century the Yürüks occupied the area, which proved a convenient kışla in which to spend the winter. At some point a watermill was installed and in the theatre a lime kiln went up.

EXPLORING OLYMPUS

You can reach Olympus (*open daily; charge*) by a short walk along the beach south from Çıralı, or come by car along a signposted sideroad off Route 400. The town is divided in two by the stream. Bear in mind that the site is quite overgrown in places.

The **Hellenistic quays**, with big polygonal blocks reinforcing the river bank, were connected by a bridge with three arches 18m wide, of which the abutments remain. To the north is the **acropolis**, which together with the heights to the south (Ceneviz Tepe) guarded the entrance. Among the remains to the north, note the compound built by the early Byzantines, in which a **fine Roman portal** shows that the Christian centre was built into the temenos of a pagan temple. Two churches were identified inside, belonging to different periods. They were both quite large and decorated with frescoes; one had imported granite columns, mosaic floors and marble revetments. An enigmatic building is further north, with mosaics with Christian motifs and images. It has been interpreted as the **bishop's palace**. Altogether six churches have been identified, suggesting by their size and style a booming economy in the late antique period followed by contraction in mid-Byzantine times. The **Roman town** is more visible south of the river, with **baths** and a **theatre** badly damaged, possibly in the earthquake of AD 141.

The **necropoleis** are on both sides of the river to the west: with their plastered vaulted chambers, they are not Lycian. Nor are the two tombs just south of the acropolis, with a poetic inscription and the well-preserved carving of a boat.

From Tekirova, south of Olympus, the **Sea to Sky Olympos Teleferik** will whisk you to the top of the Tahtalı Dağları (2375m). From there you can indulge in paragliding all the way to the sea, or simply have a meal at the strangely-named Shakespeare Restaurant.

THE CHIMAERA

Twenty minutes' drive from Çıralı, and after an undemanding walk of half an hour, you come to the eternal fire of the Chimaera, the Yanartaş or burning stone (*charge*), mentioned in the written sources from as early as the 4th century BC. Of late it has been revamped for tourist purposes and legend has been added to legend. The latest (dating from 2012) extols it as the original Olympic Flame, a claim which was not very popular with the Greek officials at the Olympic Games.

The Chimaera is a **spontaneous perennial flame** issuing from the ground at an altitude of 270m in a clearing c. 20m by 30m on the wooded hillside. It has been visited by many travellers, who have left a variety of accounts. According to Methodius, the martyr-bishop of Olympus, the fire did not consume the flesh and bushes grew quite happily in its vicinity. Going by the statements of a 13th-century Arab geographer, its flame could be seen from Antalya, almost 60km away. Well-to-do Turks whom T.A.B. Spratt (*p. 31*) encountered when he visited in 1842 thought that some of its by-products, such as soot and the sulphur-rich water at the bottom of the pit, had **healing properties** and they happily daubed it on their skin and eyes.

The size of the Chimaera varies from a full bonfire (Beaufort, 1811; *p. 23*) to a few flames that need to be kindled with a match. The smell is a mix of iodine, coal, gas, benzine and petrol. It seems agreed now that methane seeps from the ground and ignites when it comes into contact with the air. It is the source of the **methane** (around 150 tons a year are needed to keep the flames going) that still intrigues geologists. The local geology is very complex. There is a lot of chromium in the rock (apparently one can see the veins of it on the cliff face) and the area was prospected for oil in the 1960s. Meanwhile, tourists flock to see the Chimaera, to enjoy the views and to roast marshmallows, while more poetically the Turks remember the legend of the burning love of Sarı Kız for the lord of the Taurus Mountains. The site itself is more than the flame. It has not been excavated or surveyed so the whereabouts of the **Temple of Hephaistos** remain problematical, though there is some worked stone that could have belonged to it. There are a couple of Christian buildings (a three-aisled basilica and a chapel), perhaps built to stamp out pagan influence. The cobbled road coming up from the coast suggests a pilgrimage route. The fires are obviously more impressive at sunset, but it can be cold and windy up on the rocks.

PHASELIS

Phaselis (*map B, 8; open daily summer 9–7, winter 9–5.30; charge*) is signposted from Route 400 between Tekirova and Çamyuva. You can drive to the small museum northwest of the town, where you can park and buy your ticket. You may find the admission charge quite steep, but here you are getting more than ruins, you are getting fine beaches as well, all in a cool pine cover.

HISTORY OF PHASELIS

A harbour in an otherwise harbourless coast (the next one north is Antalya), Phaselis developed early thanks to its **favourable topography**: a 75m high elevation to the north, provided with a **spring** to feed the later aqueduct, and a rocky **acropolis** to the south, well protected by its steep sides. In between was a marshy expanse that has shrunk over time, allowing urban development. The line of the coast offered **three harbours**: a shallow one to the north with a breakwater (un-dated but believed to be Hellenistic or earlier) now submerged between two natural reefs; a small central harbour now partially silted up but which would have been easy to defend; and a south harbour large enough for commercial purposes and sheltered from the southeasterly winds. It is believed that this last one was developed first, possibly serving the defended north settlement.

We know little of **early Phaselis** but we can fall back on historical sources that show that it existed as as a harbour city and also that it enjoyed a rather unflattering reputation. The environment was not to everyone's liking; people in antiquity complained about the hot, oppressive climate, the unhealthy air and strange odours (*Livy 37,23,1*). The inhabitants themselves, if we are to believe Demosthenes, were 'unscrupulous scoundrels' (*Oration 35*) and the Athenian musician Stratonicus thought they were rascals only surpassed by the people of Side. Cicero, fulminating against Verres, put in a good word for them but he called Phaselis a Lycian town inhabited by Greeks, betraying poor local knowledge. This is not a Lycian town, there is nothing Lycian anywhere here. So who first settled? Hellenkemper proposes the Phoenicians with a later Rhodian input. Phaselis was already of some consequence in the 6th century BC, when it was the only city on the south coast to join forces with eight others to set up a sanctuary in the Egyptian delta near Naucratis, an important trading harbour. Later it took to the arts when one of its sons, Theodactes, a prolific playwright who lived most of his life in Athens, won first prize in the Mausolus funeral competition in the 4th century BC.

In the 1st century BC it succumbed to the easy gains of **piracy** and in 48 BC when Pompey put in here after the battle of Pharsalus, 'little Phaselis' was deserted, at least according to Lucan's *Pharsalia*. Things improved after the Roman conquest. All public land was confiscated but the Mediterranean was now safe and trade flourished. Phaselis was remodelled in the Roman style and possibly also received a visit from the emperor Hadrian himself.

The **Roman and Byzantine town** developed by the sea in the area between the central and the south harbours and the acropolis. Here one can see how successful Phaselis was as a commercial and military settlement, roughly until the 10th century

118 BLUE GUIDE MEDITERRANEAN TURKEY

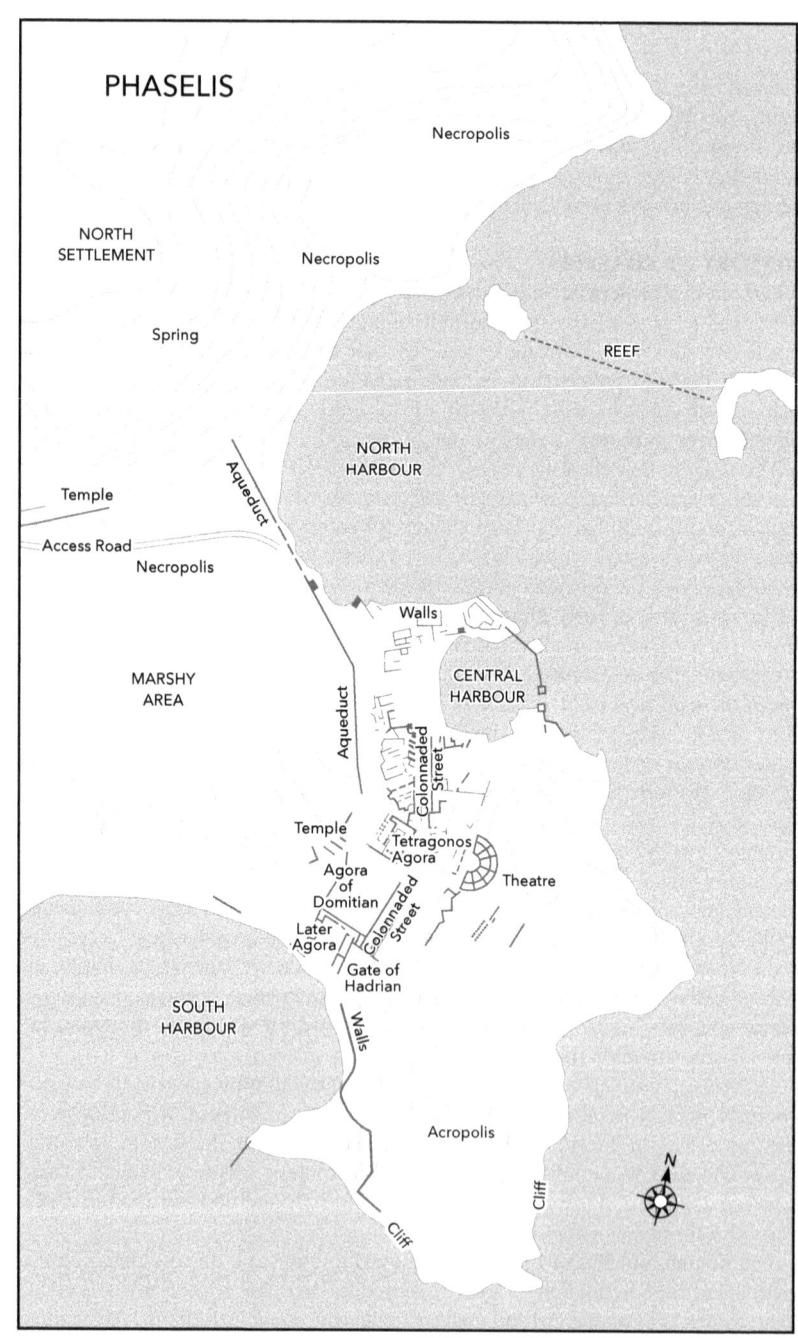

when, according to a reused inscription, spolia from Phaselis were used to build Antalya's second, outer wall. The main business of Phaselis was trade, whether timber, dates or the 'Rhodinum Phaselide', a special unguent mentioned by Pliny (13,5) as a cure for many ailments.

Phaselis flourished into late antiquity and early **Byzantine times**. The cathedral in the civic centre, on the isthmus north of the acropolis, was large and luxurious and had a bishop's palace next to it. The town at this time remained largely undefended. Disruption came from the Arabs in the 7th century. The reaction of the Byzantines when they returned, in the 8th century, was retrenchment. The town shrunk back to the acropolis and to its harbours on either side. The defences were strengthened. The theatre on the acropolis slope was included in the defences and was built up inside. On the isthmus, private buildings encroached on the public space while public buildings were given over to industrial use, as the slag shows. The harbours remained important: their quays were renovated and the defences strengthened. The rest was abandoned.

EXPLORING PHASELIS

Phaselis has not been stripped bare like Rhodiapolis (p. 108), which is to its advantage. There is shade here and as a visitor you will be able to enjoy, as at Arykanda (p. 105), a feeling of discovery among the uncontrolled growth.

You enter the site from the north, with the marsh to your right and the north settlement to the left. This, from the style of the defences, is Hellenistic or possibly earlier. The spring feeding the **aqueduct** (430m) is here on the south slope. There are a number of its arches and ashlar piers extant, some of them in the sea. At the aqueduct's south end a distribution system was in place, feeding a fountain and baths whose recycled water cleaned the nearby latrines.

The small **central harbour** is immediately to your left by the beach. Its already small opening was further reduced by a stretch of city wall carried on moles and protected by two bastions. It may have had a chain; this was Byzantine work (and a reuse of earlier defences), when they brought their military fleet here for winter shelter and repairs.

From here you enter the civic centre, with a couple of **agoras** to your right and the theatre (see below) to the left. The space between them is occupied by a **colonnaded street** in two misaligned segments to accommodate one of the agoras. The **Gate of Hadrian** is at the south end, with its inscription on the architrave confirming that it was erected on the occasion of his visit in AD 131. It is still unexcavated and more evocative than the one in Antalya. You see it at its original level, with no modern building in sight and it is followed by a long stretch of the original paved road. Imagine a single-arched structure with Corinthian capitals and a coffered ceiling and add, in your mind, the noise of screeching carts and vendors advertising their wares; it is better than the hum of steady urban motor traffic.

The early Roman **theatre** is rather small, with capacity for some 1,500 spectators, resting on a slope with a corridor at the top end. It was built in the local conglomerate with a limestone facing. The scena, with five doors and decorative niches, does not seem to have a proscenium, though this may have been of wood. The theatre later became a Byzantine kastron. It went out of use and houses were built within it at the same time that the area was walled, adding to the natural defences of the cliffs.

The **south harbour**, perhaps the earliest, in use when Phaselis functioned as an emporium, may have been defended by an extension of the wall on top of earlier Hellenistic structures.

WEST & NORTH OF ANTALYA

Three sites west of Antalya should retain your attention. Two of them are lost in the woods: you need to be prepared to walk and scramble.

TREBENNA

Trebenna (*map B, 8*) is on the south edge of the Güllük Dağı Termessos Milli Parkı, west of Antalya. Coming from the south, make for Geyikbayırı via Hacısekililer and Çağlarca. When you arrive in Geyikbayırı, you will need directions. The site is 2.5km away, hidden in the forest.

Trebenna may have been politically Lycian (it belonged to the Lycian League; *p. 80*) but more precisely it stood on the edge of three worlds, where Lycia, Pisidia and Pamphylia met. It had its heyday in the 3rd century AD, when it minted coins and built a number of impressive tombs. It was a small town but with its complement of civic buildings: baths, a meeting house, sebasteion and Byzantine basilica. It does not appear in the sources; our knowledge comes from inscriptions and from the coinage. It retreated within its defended acropolis in the mid–late Byzantine period. The settlement of some 40 houses was clustered around a middle-sized church and may have lasted until medieval times, one of the few in Lycia and Pamphylia to do so. The bishopric lasted much longer: there was still a bishop of Trebenna in 1958. It has not been excavated.

Trebenna's *raison d'être* may be the same as that of Termessus (*see below*): Antalya's connection with the Aegean via the upper reaches of the Tekke Peninsula. In the case of the Evdir Han (*also described below*), connections were also important, but in a different direction: north towards the Seljuk heartland.

TERMESSUS

Map B, 6; open 15 April–2Oct 9–7, 3 Oct–14 April 8–5; charge; the ticket booth closes 2hrs earlier than the site; you will need to set aside at least 2hrs for your visit. The site is very large and exploring it involves a lot of clambering around. You will need good shoes as well as food, water and suncream.

Termessus, in the Güllük Dağı Milli Parkı, is these days definitely on the tourist circuit, visited by organised trips from Antalya. Alternatively you can reach it by public transport, by *dolmuş* going from Antalya in the Denizli direction. Ask the driver to drop you at the brown sign for Termessus. In the summer there will be taxis there, waiting to drive you to the site, 9km away. If you find their proposed fare excessive, be prepared to refuse it. The drivers depend on visitor custom and you may be able to come to an arrangement. The driver will drop you at the car park at the north end of the site. Remember to arrange a pick-up time.

If you have your own transport you will be able to drive on the very same road that led to the city in ancient times. This, obviously, was not designed with cars in mind, so you will need to be patient and drive slowly. After the ticket booth you still have a good 20mins of scrambling ahead of you before reaching the ruins.

HISTORY OF TERMESSUS

Termessus, like Trebenna, was positioned on the edge of Pamphylia, Lycia and Pisidia, though in antiquity it was generally considered a Pisidian city. The locals called themselves **Solymians**, a reference to the ancient name of the Güllük Dağ, Mount Solymus. They spoke a Pisidian dialect which Strabo calls Solymian, and though we know little of it, it is found in inscriptions. The early history of the Solymians is also little known and lost in legend, but like true Pisidians they were warlike right from the start. According to Homer (*Iliad Book VI*), Bellerophon subdued the 'warlike Solymi' after first dispatching the Chimaera (identified by some with the eternal fire at Çıralı; *p. 116*). If these Solymi are the same people, they had recovered by 333 BC, when Termessus makes its entry into history. Arrian, in Book 1 of his *Anabasis of Alexander*, gives a faithful description of the topography the site which this particular branch of Pisidians had chosen to settle in. There was such an abundance of ridges, cliffs, steep ascents and precipitous heights that the great commander gave up and decided to go to Phrygia via Sagalassos, which he did unproblematically. Thus the combination of fierce fighters living in an eagle's nest paid off. It is not quite clear how the people survived at over 1000m of altitude with no arable land in sight, but they did. Their geographical position probably helped, since they controlled access to the upper part of Lycia, where it melts into the Anatolian plateau. The collection of tolls and dues, as well as a spot of banditry, may also have been part of the story.

The foundation of Antalya (Attaleia) by **Attalus II** of Pergamon, to give himself a window on the Mediterranean, also plays its part. The land route across Lycia went from Telmessus (*p. 53*) steadily east and as Antalya grew, Termessus grew out of the collection of tolls and dues. Attalus certainly showed the town his favour with the bequest of a stoa, an act which in those days was interpreted as a tangible mark of royal favour. At the time Termessus, faithful to its reputation as a place of fierce warriors, kept on fighting the Lycians and afterwards pulled off a master stroke by taking the right side in the Mithridatic wars, putting them on the right side of the Romans. As **friends and allies of Rome** they could set their conditions and maintain a qualified independence within the Empire. Their territory was quite large, stretching to Ariassos, Perge, Attaleia and down to Phaselis, according to Hellenkemper an area some 800km square.

The Termessians kept their own laws and collected their own customs duties. They would not be encumbered with Roman soldiers except by order of the Senate and their coins (minting had started in 100 BC) dispensed with any reference to the emperor, either in words or images. Termessus continued to prosper as one can see from the remains, which are mainly Roman. An intriguing survival is the colonnaded street, which comes from nowhere and leads nowhere and shows no connection to the heart of the city where the stoas and theatre are. Was it a gift from the Romans to the Termessians, perhaps? Any self-respecting Roman town had such a street, after all. The Termessians may perhaps have had greater appreciation for the aqueduct, of which a few arches remain, certainly a better way of distributing water than cisterns.

Christianity is attested by graffiti in some of the tombs, but no church has yet been identified. The end of Termessus is badly documented; by the late Empire there is evidence of famine (inscriptions) or at least of gratitude for assistance. In the early Byzantine period, spolia were used to erect walls to protect the centre around the agora. It would have been a safe, remote spot to survive in, but it seems that by the 5th century, Termessus was no more. Perhaps there were no more tolls and dues to be collected as trade patterns changed, and nor was there anyone left to raid. Or perhaps the town simply suffered from one earthquake too many. In the 19th century the **Ottomans** re-occupied Termessus as a strategic location.

EXPLORING TERMESSUS

Although the existence of this eagle's nest of a city has been known for some time (Charles Fellows, T.A.B. Spratt and Karol Lanckoroński all explored it in the first half of the 19th century), little work has been done because of the altitude and the difficult access. The site is quite overgrown; you need to be careful. Termessus sits in a hidden valley between high cliffs in a rugged landscape. In its urban development the topography had the upper hand. Where the natural defences were lacking the Termessians built **city walls** and you can see a stretch of those after walking up from the car park along the so-called **King Street** (the ancient paved entrance way) with a lookout tower to the right. The road goes through the remains of the **gate** that effectively barred access from the plain and doubled up as an inexpensive **oracle** (no need to trek all the way to Delphi). An inscription on the east wall gives the list of the standard responses to any throw of a variable number of astragali (a sheep's ankle bone that was used like a die in antiquity). There was a similar oracle in the agora at Cremna (*see Blue Guide Central Anatolia*) but this was not only a Pisidian phenomenon, the practice was widespread around the Mediterranean. The advice given was rather non-committal ('Think it over', 'Consult with friends'), but couched in verse to make it more appealing.

Nearby are the **remaining arches of the Roman aqueduct** supplementing the cisterns, of which a number are dotted around and covered with grates for safety. Going towards the centre of town, on the left the walls of the **bath-gymnasium** are two storeys high in places. It is an impressive, well preserved building with extant doors and window frames and the curvature of the roof. Just think that there is more of it buried. To the right are the remains of the **colonnaded street**, which has not yet been investigated so it may be longer than the 120m identified so far. About 9m wide, it had shops on the west side and quite a lot of honorific statues, about 100 going by the recovered bases. Despite this, it is peripheral to the centre of town and remains a bit of a puzzle.

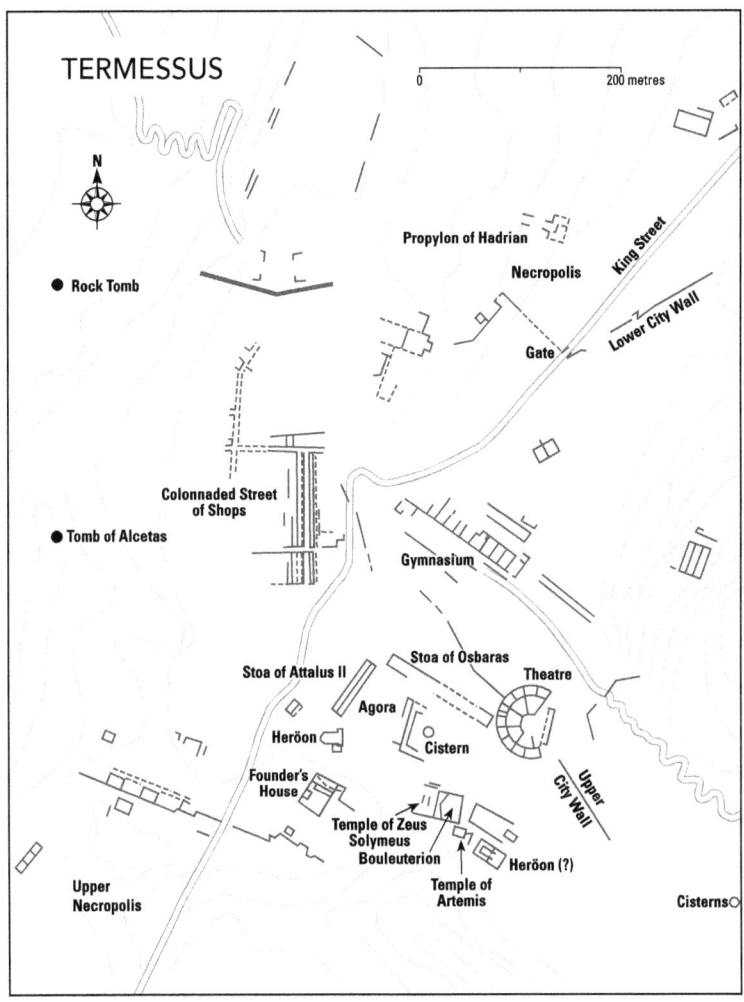

Follow the sign to the heart of the city, the trapezoidal **agora**. It was enclosed with **three stoas** including, to the west, the one funded by Attalus II (*see above*). To the north was a Roman successor, some two hundred years later but in the same style with two storeys, the gift of a wealthy local, Osbaras. There was a third stoa to the southwest. You cannot miss the huge water **cistern** to the northeast.

Facing a tall cliff, the **theatre** is still in good shape. It has not been precisely dated. It could be Hellenistic with later reworking to extend the cavea for the stage building. The façade of the Roman scena was quite luxurious, with marble and stucco decoration. It could accommodate over 4,000 people. The views from the theatre are stunning and must have made it difficult for the spectators to concentrate on whatever was going on on stage. The **bouleuterion** (or an odeion) is dated by its style, with beautiful drafted ashlars, to the 1st century BC. It survives to the upper floor, to a total height of 10m. It was roofed over—not a minor enterprise—with a span measuring 24.5m. When George Bean (*p. 22*) visited in the 1960s, he found evidence of marble veneer and inscriptions with the letters picked out in red.

The presence of at least six **temples** is attested. They have not fared well: they lie in a heap. It seems that Artemis was a popular deity. She had two temples. One, shared with a dedication to Hadrian, was at the entrance to the city. Of this only the stepped podium and the entrance (**Propylon of Hadrian**) still stand. The other **Temple of Artemis**, by the southwestern corner of the bouleuterion, was funded by a local lady by the name of Aurelia Amasta and by her husband. One of the other temples identified might have been the earthly abode of **Zeus Solymeus**, apparently the chief deity of the city. Termessians also worshipped Mars and Asclepius and Hygieia, for whose temple they procured granite columns from somewhere.

Necropoleis are well in view all around the site, with richly decorated sarcophagi and rock-cut tombs, some featuring that Lycian trait of imitating wood wherever the terrain is at all suitable. The **tomb of Alcetas**, halfway up the middle of the west slope, is a particular favourite. Alcetas (according to Diodorus Siculus, *Book 18*) was an early Hellenistic figure at the time when the diadochoi were vying for portions of Alexander the Great's conquests. He had featured prominently in Alexander's Indian expedition and was supported by the Termessians in his bid for power. He was opposed by Antigonus I Monophthalmus, the Macedonian general with one eye. When he was beaten by him, he took refuge in Termessus. Antigonus followed him and demanded his surrender. After some dithering the elders consented, for the general good but against the wishes of the young people of the city. Alcetas, preferring death to captivity, killed himself. His body was handed over to Antigonus who subjected it to great indignities. The young people of Termessus recovered it and eventually buried him in this beautiful tomb—at least, it was beautiful in its original form, before treasure hunters and earthquakes intervened. The tomb itself is partly carved in the rock and partly built. The mounted soldier in relief, wearing a mantle fluttering in the wind and holding a spear, is riding without a saddle, about to rein in his galloping horse. According to some, there are similarities with heroic representations of Alexander the Great. Otherwise there is not much to go on to support the identification with Alcetas. There are other military elements about, such as the carving of a shield and a sword, so perhaps the hero was really buried in the sarcophagus nearby.

EVDİR HANI

Evdir Hanı (*map B, 6*) is a Seljuk han at Düzlerçamı. It is on the eastern edge of the village, reached by taking the signed turn on Route 330. The structure, measuring 66m by 52m, was built by Izzedin Keykavus around 1214, when the Seljuks were masters of the south coast and were keen to foster trade from Konya to the Levant, via Antalya. This would have been the first stop when leaving Antalya to go north. It takes the form of an enclosed courtyard with vaulted corridors on three sides and an enclosed room on the fourth, possibly for the animals. It was built with limestone ashlars on a rubble core. The entranceway is the usual feast of muqarnas and is quite impressive considering the state of the rest of building, which has been neglected for a long time. The masonry does not contain spolia, yet there are a number of sarcophagi in the area, suggesting that this crucial access point to the interior had a Roman presence earlier on. It may be the site of Eudocias, of which the necropolis appears to have survived as well as the cisterns, providing evidence of an irrigation and water distribution system of Roman date. Its building stone was reused in the 19th century in Antalya.

North of the Evdir Hanı, signposted from Antalya on Route 650 in the Yağca district, is the **Karain Cave** (Karain Mağarası; *open 9–7, closes at 5pm in winter; charge*), a cave complex now aspiring to UNESCO's seal of approval. Access is demanding (457 steps) and there is no shade, so perhaps it is best not to visit on a hot summer day. The cave is located on the slopes of the Sam Dağı and overlooks the travertine expanse 100m below. It is thought that in prehistoric times there was a lake here and there is a claim to continuous occupation from very early days: this was a good defensive position and the cave also offered excellent air-conditioning, warmer than the surroundings in winter and cooler in summer. Most of the finds are in the Archaeological Museum in Antalya and in the Museum of Civilisations in Ankara.

ANTALYA

The Pamphylian Plain is a series of thick travertine terraces built by the relentless work of the waters flowing in abundance from the Taurus mountains to the north. The depth of the rock is said to be 40m in Antalya, reaching 340m at the north end. While some rivers cut through the rock, forming majestic canyons and impressive waterfalls, others disappear underground, resurfacing as springs. The travertine meanwhile decays and turns into terra rossa, a soil with good drainage, favourable to agriculture. The high mountains afford protection from the cold north winds at the same time as supplying timber and providing summer pastures.

At the south end of the plain, where the travertine has weakened and formed a cove—today just large enough for a yacht marina but in the past sufficient for a harbour—sits Antalya (*map B, 8*), the queen of the Mediterranean. This is the best site on the coast as far as harbours are concerned. The next one would have been Side to the east (*described in the following chapter*), though over time its harbour suffered from silting because of the currents and wind-blown sand. Antalya had none of these problems: the cove is deep, untroubled by river outlets bringing silt, or by winds forming noxious dunes. It comes therefore as a surprise that such a good spot was apparently overlooked until the 2nd century BC, when the Pergamene king Attalus II Philadelphus (160–139 BC) decided to found a city here and to name it after himself, Attaleia. The full history of the site before this time is probably buried under the concrete that has engulfed this stretch of coast, but there are some pointers.

Recent finds in a necropolis 8km east of the centre, at the former Doğu Garajı bus depot, are dated to the 4th century BC. George Bean (*p. 22*) in the 1960s suggested that the various ruins he could see by the shore, also 8km east from the centre in the district of Lara, just beyond the point where the Düden river reaches the sea in a spectacular waterfall, belonged to the Hellenistic **polis of Magydos**, which lingered long enough to have a bishop in the 6th century. West of town the same scenario applies to **Olbia**, which is attested in the ancient sources from the 4th century BC and could be identified with the fortress described by Strabo (*14,4,1*) on the banks of the Arapsu. They probably became casualties of Attaleia, when whatever community it was that huddled around the harbour became the recipient of royal favour. And for lack of more information, it is with Attaleia that the history of Antalya starts. Excavations have been non-existent and there are no reports of any pre-Hellenistic finds in a meaningful context during urban redevelopment.

HISTORY OF ANTALYA

Back in the 6th century BC, Pamphylia was in the hands Croesus, King of Lydia, as an outlet to the Mediterranean. Later it came under the Persians, who exercised various degrees of control. With Alexander the Great, the Persians were ousted and after his death Pamphylia came into the hands of his successors. It was not until the Treaty of Apamea in 188 BC that Pamphylia became a possession of the Pergamenes.

The Romans, who had defeated the Seleucids at Magnesia, rewarded their faithful allies, the Pergamenes, with access to the Mediterranean. And so Attaleia was born, a creature of Pergamon. The kingdom could now access the Mediterranean on a direct inland route (taking about five days, quicker than the sea route), south to Telmessus (*map B, 7*), a Pergamene enclave, and across to Termessus (eight days). However, the relationship between Termessus and the new foundation of Attaleia is not clear, just as the question of Greek colonists is unclear, if one agrees with Bean's suggestion that the Pamphylian language was an ancient Greek dialect from Arcadia, preceding the arrival of the Dorians, and mixed with some Cypriot. If so, this would suggest a very early Greek presence in the region.

We have little evidence of early Attaleia apart from its walls (*see below*), nor indeed do we know much about its Roman period, when it was a place of the same stature as the other older Pamphylian cities (Aspendos, Perge, Syllion and Side), though we can conclude that, as a latecomer, it must have had a smaller territory. After the troubled times of the 1st century BC, when **piracy** flourished and Zeniketes of Olympus (*p. 114*) roamed the seas, Attaleia settled into almost 300 years of **Pax Romana** and weathered all events afterwards, those same events that caused the decline and fall of the other Pamphylian cities. The same has been true right up to the present day. As a result—and unlike in, say, Perge (*described in the following chapter*)—there is not much of a Roman town to look at. **Development was continuous and obviously destructive**, but paradoxically this is a sure mark of success. Those cities in which we can 'walk in the past' are cities that have failed. Antalya was never one of them. One can assume that it once had the full complement of Roman amenities. Some of them have been identified and the mere fact that Constantine found statues here worthy of display in his new capital's Hippodrome suggests some opulence. **Early Christianity** is poorly attested since St Paul only came this way in order to sail to Antioch (*Acts 14, 24*); however, the Church of the Virgin (*see below*), a project possibly sponsored by Justinian, would have been grand enough for a bishop, so perhaps we may assume one.

Later, as the other cities atrophied, Antalya held her own against the **Arab threat** (from the 7th century), though ultimately it became their base for raids to the north as far as Amorium, Konya and Nicaea. Retaken by the Byzantines, Antalya became the **base of the imperial fleet** and the capital of the military district. After the Battle of Manzikert (1071), Byzantium lost control of the south coast and Türkmen soon began infiltrating the countryside. This marked the end of things for the hinterland, where cities died and the disappearance of the old place names marks discontinuity. Antalya still held out, supplied by the sea. At some point in the 12th century both harbour and town were in the hands of the Venetians, who built the long stairway connecting the two. You can still climb the 44 steps, starting near the İskele Cami by the harbour. Antalya's fortunes returned with the arrival of the **Seljuks of Rum**, when after settling in Konya, they looked both north and south. Sinop (on the Black Sea) fell to them in 1214 but Antalya was harder to subdue and did not surrender. It was taken by force in 1216, after being besieged by land and sea. Now the Seljuk sultan could style himself 'Lord of Two Seas'. Despite this, though, the Seljuk imprint on Antalya is almost invisible. They rebuilt the wall—and one can tell the difference

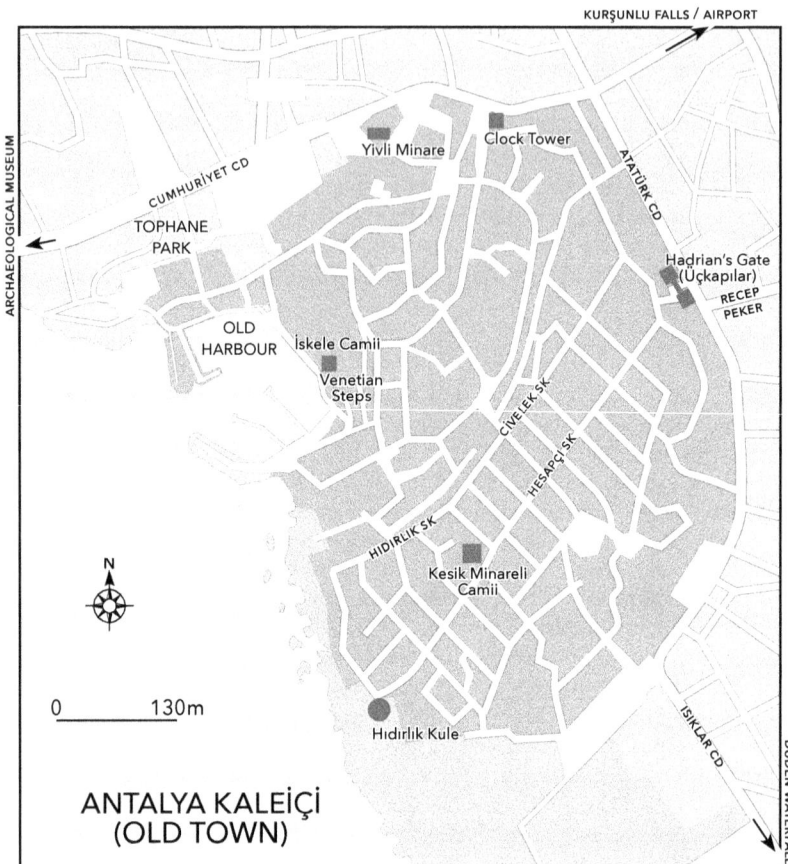

ANTALYA KALEİÇİ (OLD TOWN)

in the inferior quality of the work—but otherwise there is little but tiles, which are attributed to their residence, though its location is unknown.

Through all this, Antalya went on as usual, a commercial centre for goods and slaves, exacting tolls, and through its maritime traffic gaining intelligence of the situation in the Mediterranean, especially along the Cilician coast. For a brief time it was in the hands of one Aldobrandini, an adventurer of uncertain ancestry, possibly from Pisa, who was acting on behalf of the Latin Empire in Byzantium, but the city soon returned to the Seljuks who set about protecting the Muslim population.

According to sources, the new arrangements included **internal walls** with ditches and towers, and **separate quarters** for different religions. The traveller Ibn Battuta (*p. 22*) lists separate quarters for Christians, Greeks, Jews and Armenians. The ruler, his Mamluk slaves and the Muslim population occupied a citadel said to have been to the north of the walled area. When the city walls were pulled down in 1913, Roberto Paribeni (*p. 30*) observed four separate walled areas, including one around the harbour for traders, a wedge to the north (a possible Seljuk area, going by the stray finds), and the old town (Greek and Roman) in two blocks to the south. Around the harbour, the traders who were non-Muslim were locked in from the outside on Fridays and at night.

With the arrival of the Mongols, the Sultanate of Rum repaired to Alanya, wishing to put the Taurus Mountains between them and the newcomers. The **Emir of Antalya**, Tekke Oğlu Osman Bey, adopted a drastic solution. In 1402 he wrote to Venice asking for protection, vowing to cede Antalya to the *Signoria* and to become a Christian himself. But the *Serenissima* was otherwise busy and did not take up the offer. In 1415 the Ottoman sultan Mehmet I took Antalya and sent the emir in gilded exile to İstanoz in Lycia, near today's Korkuteli. The Ottoman period was uneventful on the whole, although when the Ottomans conquered Egypt, the trans-Mediterranean trade that had so enriched Antalya took a shorter route, with goods delivered directly to Istanbul. Antalya partially lost its key position as the interface between land and sea transport, though trade still remained a mainstay of the economy, together with weaving and spinning. The town expanded beyond the walls, in part also because of refugees form the Caucasus and the Balkans. In 1920 it had a population of 20,000. Today it is well over one million. The great infrastructure works of the 1970s and the tourism boom of the south coast have destroyed and buried the past.

EXPLORING ANTALYA

With such a colourful and busy history it is not surprising that so little of Antalya's past has survived. But there are ways to make sense of what little is left. The most rewarding area to see is **Kaleiçi**, the old town, formerly walled. The **wall circuit**, endlessly built and rebuilt from the 2nd century BC by the ruling power of the day, and under restoration as late as 1813, when the local emir rebelled against the Ottomans, was demolished in 1913. The city was bursting at the seams by then and priorities were different: one of the reasons quoted for the demolition was that the inhabitants of Kaleiçi needed more fresh air. A few stretches of wall still stand and, of course, there is the plan that Lanckoroński (*p. 28*) made in the late 19th century. The line of the walls can be traced in the modern Cumhuriyet Cd. and Atatürk Cd., which run down to the coast and along the harbour. This was roughly the Hellenistic outline, which changed little until the Byzantines added a second wall with a berm and ditch cut in the rock, turning the town into a veritable kastron in the early 12th century. There is evidence for five **gates** and some 40 **towers**, not evenly spaced as one might expect from so many rebuildings. There is nothing left of the internal walls, though it seems that the Seljuk emirs contributed, as was the custom of their time, to keep the Sultan happy, describing themselves in the dedicatory inscriptions as 'Weak slaves of the Sultan'. Of the wall towers a few have survived, such as the **Clock Tower**, which acquired its present appearance in 1894, when clock towers were all the rage in the Ottoman Empire and became part of the cityscape from Gjirokastër in Albania to Erzurum, an efficient way of making sure that the populace would be able to prostrate themselves in prayer at the right time. Spolia in the fabric of the Clock Tower include parts of marble theatre seats, suggesting a nearby location for that building.

Down by the east side of the harbour stands another tower, which in its day would have marked the south edge of the Roman town. The so-called **Hıdırlık Kule** was in fact not originally a tower but a mausoleum, in style dated to the second half of the 1st century AD. It can be compared to the Tomba degli Orazi e Curiazi at Albano Laziale, south of Rome. Originally it would have been outside the walls but was incorporated at a later date because of its sheer size and solidity. Over 13m tall, comprising a square base with a round top, it was clearly not part of the defensive circuit as it was not linked to it and there was no access to it from the top of the wall. Inside, it has an arrangement suitable for a mausoleum, with chamber tombs. The top part is missing. A cuboid supporting a monument, possibly a quadriga, has been suggested. The twelve moulded fasces on either side of the entrance to the east suggest someone of high rank, possibly a senator or a provincial governor.

Of all the gates, the best extant example is **Hadrian's Gate** (*see box*), locally known as Üçkapılar, a reference to the three (*üç*) openings. This triple-arched structure, now restored to its full glory, would have made any emperor proud. According to the inscription on the architrave (or, more accurately, since its metal letters are missing, to the arrangement of the holes to fasten them), it was built before AD 121 and rededicated on the occasion of Hadrian's visit in AD 130. In the 6th century it was renovated and replastered. A new road surface was built, using granite columns for a new threshold, in which ruts 1.17m apart showed the gauge of the transport vehicles. Later, when security demanded it, two arches were blocked up. When Lanckoroński (*p. 28*) recorded it, the gate was well buried and missing its columns. Now it looks magnificent.

HADRIAN: THE RESTLESS EMPEROR

The name of Hadrian frequently crops up in connection with a gate, storage building or wall, monuments built by his order: one would like to think that he saw the completed structures. Like many emperors, including his predecessor Trajan, Hadrian had the building bug. He liked the idea of stamping a Roman presence on the landscape with something majestic and beautiful, suggesting the Romans' ability to tame nature as well as people. He also suffered from another bug, the travel bug. Trajan travelled a great deal as well, but this was on the course of military duty; he had to be on hand when conflicts flared up. Hadrian instead was busy consolidating the Empire—in fact even slimming it down a bit, shedding unmanageable territories such as Mesopotamia and parts of Dacia for the sake of keeping the rest secure. His successor, Antoninus Pius, never left Rome.

Looking back at the life of Hadrian, one can see that he ruled for 20 years and was travelling (and therefore with no fixed abode) for twelve of them. How did this all happen? Travelling in those days, even for emperors was long and cumbersome and meant being away form the centre of things, i.e. Rome. Hadrian solved this conundrum by having a travelling government. His retinue must have been vast. It included a military escort, officials, staff, the emperor's private household, slaves to serve everyone's needs and a variety of specialists including architects and builders as well as artists for decorative stonework. The logistics must have been a nightmare.

Hadrian was born into an upper-class, cosmopolitan milieu in Spain in the colony of Italica. His father was a Roman senator and his mother came from Cadiz, an ancient Phoenician colony. His wet nurse was Germana, a barbarian from the north. By the age of five he had already been in Greece, Smyrna and Ephesus, following his father on his official postings. From the age of 14, when he embarked on his military career, he began visiting the provinces and acquainted himself with the frontier systems *in situ*. He followed Trajan to the East—in fact there is virtually no province of the Empire which he did not either visit or where he did not leave his mark in stone. It was during his travels that he met the love of his life, Antinous, at Claudiopolis in Bithynia, today's Bolu, 50km east of Istanbul.

Restlessly inquisitive (to quote Tertullian), he explored all curiosities, inspecting everything for himself, whether it was the site of a border wall or earthquake damage. He was aware of the psychological effect his presence would have on the garrisons and the sick soldiers he visited, and kept an eye on his popularity ratings. He knew too that the bestowing of Roman benefactions would always go down well (though in the case of the new aqueduct at Alexandra Troas, which cost as much as the tribute of 500 cities, his largesse did raise some eyebrows). Though his restlessness did attract criticism, it does not appear to have troubled him. He did not particularly like Rome, a sprawling, stifling, corrupt and corrupting city. As for his villa in Tivoli, it was more a collection of nomads' pavilions in stone than a traditional Roman villa. He much preferred Greece, where he felt at home. His nickname was Graeculus and he grew a beard to complete the image. On the whole, however, Hadrian did not truly belong to anywhere, and yet at the same time he was nowhere a foreigner.

Very little is left of the **old harbour walls** at Antalya. There is, however, a print by Cornelis de Bruyn dated 1714 (in which the town appears as Sattalia) which shows the walls up to the crenellations and a couple of towers. It also shows the arrangements of the piers intended to narrow the entrance to the harbour, which could then hold 15 galleys. At the end of the piers are stumps, the remains of the two towers (8m by 8m in travertine) that protected the harbour. One may have been a lighthouse. They are now completely submerged. The narrow entrance, just over a hundred metres, was guarded in the 15th century by an iron chain, pieces of which were offered to the pope as a trophy in 1472 and which were for some time draped over the entrance to the sacristy of St Peter's in Rome. A new chain was in place in 1521.

Looking inside the circuit of walls, it has been suggested that the main thoroughfare was today's **Hesapçı Sk**, running from the Hıdırlık Kule to Hadrian's Gate with the town laid out on either side. There is evidence (remains, inscriptions and other sources) for 16 **churches**, one of which is of particular importance as it has been thoroughly examined and partially excavated, allowing us to fit another tessera into Antalya's mosaic. The Şehzade Korkut Camii or **Kesik Minareli**, halfway along Hesapçı Sk, was originally a church dedicated to the Panaghia, built in the Roman agora with Roman spolia, including remains of a 2nd-century AD temple. The large church may have been willed by higher powers in Byzantium, perhaps Justinian himself. It went through at least three phases, being regularly repaired and improved after any setback. In that it shows the vitality of the community, which was able to ensure the survival of one big monument through all sorts of adversities. Unlike most late antique and Byzantine churches, it did not shrink to the size of a chapel when danger threatened. It began as a cross-in-square structure with a nave and two aisles, galleries, a clerestory and arcades covered in marble and mosaics, possibly at some point acquiring a dome (instead of the original wooden tower), as the reinforced piers suggest. It was 37m long including the narthex. To the west of the narthex a cruciform martyrion was later added. The church maintained these dimensions through various repairs and renovations. It was transformed into a mosque early in the 13th century and acquired a minaret in 1361 but when Peter I of Cyprus took Antalya in the same year, it was converted back into a church The name of the mosque refers to a later event of the Ottoman period, when Beyazıt II sent his son Korkut here as governor. It is not clear how long the mosque remained in use. In 1896, both mosque and minaret caught fire and the minaret lost its upper section. When M.H. Ballance surveyed and recorded the building in the early 1950s, it was known as Cumanin Camii or Cami Kabir but was out of use and in ruins. At the time of writing it was being restored, the minaret had been rebuilt and it was to reopen as a mosque.

Another landmark minaret in Antalya is the **Yivli Minare**, a slim construction near the mosque of the same name. It was originally a victory *manar*, dated by inscription to the first quarter of the 13th century, one of a number built by the Seljuks to celebrate their victories. In an eastern style from Iran, which at the time was run by a different branch of the Seljuks, it had a stone core covered by bricks forming eight vertical torus mouldings. When Alaeddin Keykubad I turned the nearby church into a mosque belonging to a külliye, the manar became its minaret.

To this meagre list of historic vestiges we can add an **aqueduct**, of which a few arches could be seen in the early 20th century, outside the walls in the north part of town. Judging by the accumulation of sinter, it probably entered the town at the tower of Julia Sancta, next to Hadrian's Gate, and went on to baths and nymphaea (though there is no hard evidence of these buildings). Equally missing is the colonnaded street, without which no town could call itself a Roman city. Recent building works a few hundred metres outside Hadrian's Gate have revealed a **necropolis** (pre-Roman according to local information) and the building plans have been altered so that the tombs can be displayed *in situ*. Nothing is published yet; the past remains deeply buried. The more recent past, that of the traditional Turkish house with bay windows spanning the width of the narrow streets, can still be experienced in Kaleiçi in the pedestrian thoroughfares. The interior of the houses and the plentiful woodwork were recorded by Lanckoroński (*p. 28*) during his stay in the 1880s.

The new **Antalya Archaeological Museum** (*open daily 8.30–7; check for opening times on religious holidays; charge*) is about 40mins walk to the west beyond Tophane Park along Konyaaltı Cd. Alternatively, you can take the Heritage Tram from Üçkapılar (Hadrian's Gate) to the end of the line, but you may find in the end that going on foot is quicker, as there seems to be a lot of waiting involved. The museum is certainly very large but unfortunately somewhat disappointing. It houses an accumulation of material from the whole region but Antalya itself is very poorly represented and not explained at all. Among the displays is the statue of Plancia Magna (*p. 144*) from Perge.

PRACTICAL INFORMATION

GETTING THERE AND AROUND

Antalya airport is to the east of the city. There is a shuttle from the airport to the *otogar* (Bus 600) on the west edge of town. Minibuses will take you to the edge of the old town. Take the one marked Üçkapılar and alight when you see Hadrian's Gate. The airport is also connected to the city by tram (**Antray**), for which you can buy a ticket at the stop outside the domestic terminal (have some coins with you). If you get off at Hizmet Paşa, Hadrian's Gate will be within easy reach, even with luggage. Ask for Üçkapılar.

The modern town is unremarkable; the **old town** is almost certainly where you will want to be for your stay. However, it is much pedestrianised: if you have a car, note that driving is restricted and parking can be challenging.

From the *otogar* you will be able to take a coach to a large number of destinations.

WHERE TO STAY

The old town of Antalya seems to be equally divided between souvenir shops, hotels and eateries. Try the **Özkavak Hotel** on Civelek Sk, between Hadrian's Gate and the Clock Tower (*ozkavakboutiquehotel.com.tr; T: 90 533 322 94 33*). It looks a bit old-fashioned inside but the shower is excellent and the garden is a lovely place for breakfast. Alternatively, the **Minyon Boutique Hotel** (*minyonhotel.com; T: 90 242 247 11 47*) has all the charm of an old house, with Ottoman-style fireplaces with the characteristic hood. Most hotels offer a swimming pool but they tend to be miniature, offering a space to sunbathe by but not really for a swim.

WHERE TO EAT

The old town of Antalya is well stocked with places to eat, many of them catering to foreign visitors. If you feel like something truly local, however, be bold and explore beyond its borders. For fish, try **Doğu Garajı Balık Evi** on 1343 Sk (get to the end of Recep Peker Cd, continue 100m along Değirmenönü Cd and turn left). On exiting Hadrian's Gate, you will find Recep Peker Cd roughly in front of you, a bit to the right). Along the same Recep Peker Cd, **Toprakana Gözleme** is a great experience. The *gözleme* comes with all sorts of fillings (potatoes, cheese, spinach, meat and mixed) and is made right in front of you by a lovely Anatolian lady, who by the looks of it keeps the place going single-handed. When she is done with your *gözleme*, she will bake batches of *bazlama*, yet another addition to the family of Turkish flat breads. Nice on its own, the *bazlama* tastes even better with cheese or a knob of melting butter. Other possibilities include stuffed vine leaves, *mantı* (the Turkish version of ravioli) and *katmer* (an alternative to *baklava*).

WHAT TO DO

For a swim spend a day out at **Topçam Plajı** (*charge*), out of town to the west beyond the Archaeological Museum. It is a fine sandy beach with pine trees. People come with their BBQs.

Antalya also offers the chance to spend a day out in a green setting by a **spectacular waterfall**. You have choice. The **Kurşunlu Şelalesi** (*open daily 8–6; charge*) is off Route 685, clearly signposted c. 10km northeast of Antalya. The **Düden Çay** river offers a number of small waterfalls in a park in the Düden Başı Mahalle, north of town (*open daily; summer 9–7.30, winter 9–6; bus 54 or 78*); take a picnic with you. The water is recycled from the local plant, meaning it is clean. At the very end of its course, the Düden Çay reaches the sea and jumps off the cliffs. The waterfall is located on the east side of town and you can also see the sight from a boat or by swimming off Lara beach.

THE PISIDIA HERITAGE TRAIL

To cover a few sites north of Antalya, this chapter follows a section of the Pisidia Heritage Trail, a project devised by the British Institute of Ankara to promote awareness of ancient sites among both the people that live in their vicinity and the wider visiting public. The proposed trail of 350km stretches from Sagalassos in the north to Selge in the east and links ten archaeological sites. It aims at providing a route, guides and a guidebook, information on accommodation and campsites. At the time of writing, orientation signs had been set up and a website and e-guide were due to be launched. For updates, see the British Institute website (*biaa.ac.uk*).

ARIASSOS, DÖŞEME BOĞAZI & SIA

Ariassos (*map B, 6*) is signposted west from Route 650 at Dağbeli, 51km north of Antalya. It is always accessible and there is no entrance fee.

At an altitude of 1000m, it controls a pass linking Pamphylia and Pisidia. The road runs along the bottom of the valley; a number of public buildings stood on either side, while the slopes were terraced for residences, public buildings and necropoleis, mainly to the south and east. The site has been extensively surveyed but not excavated. From the sources (Artemidorus of Ephesus names it in his list of 13 Pisidian cities in 100 BC) as well as from stray finds, we know that it existed in Hellenistic times; it was then walled and minted coins. By 189 BC, after a spell under the Seleucids, it was under the rule of the Kingdom of Pergamon and when the last ruler bequeathed it to the Romans, it was incorporated in the province of Galatia and later joined to Pamphylia. It had a Christian history as a bishopric but no more news of it surfaces after the middle of the 5th century. Its situation on a main road had perhaps by that time become a liability. The ruins were first examined by Karol Lanckoroński (*p. 28*) in his extensive survey. He mistook it for Kretopolis, a Cretan settlement. The correct identification was made later, by a French epigraphist in the 1890s. Altogether, the history of Ariassos is still to be written.

The site is well spread out and mainly in ruins. Take your bearings from the lone standing monument, the **triple arch**, a 3rd-century monumental gate which originally had an upper part with an inscription, now fallen, and two consoles for imperial busts. Built with a rubble core faced by ashlars, it occupied a narrow point of the valley and marked the **north entry** to the town. Hellenistic **city walls** showing later repairs, with towers and bastions, have been plotted from here running north and west for 1250m. The gate, rather plain in style, was complemented by a number of statues, of which only the bases remain. The **main road** ran to the southwest; a number of public buildings have been identified alongside it, among them three Christian basilicas, one of which was positioned as if to obscure the arch. The **forum** has been identified and further west, cisterns and an outline of the **theatre** on the north slope. A **nymphaeum** in mortared rubble and ashlar facing, remains of which survive, roughly closed Ariassos's high street. Beyond it is the south necropolis.

Ariassos at first made do with **cisterns** and local **springs** but in Roman times it had its own gravity **aqueduct**. This brought water from 3km away in terracotta pipes, with occasional basins to trap silt and control the flow. Approaching the town it ran into a tunnel, now filled with rock and debris. The provision of piped water was important for the **gymnasium** and the **baths**, which have been identified. The west slope was mainly residential. It is thought that the original **Hellenistic settlement** was up this slope, not far from the **bouleuterion**, which was of the traditional type, built in large ashlars and with twelve rows of seats.

The **necropoleis** have been thoroughly investigated. They contain rock-cut tombs, sarcophagi and built tombs. An impressive mausoleum, with a 9m by 9m podium with a vaulted chamber within and tomb building above, suggests that someone at some point did want to make a bid for fame and renown. Altogether, however, the impression that one gets from Ariassos (though this may well change if the place is ever excavated) is of either poverty or a different use of resources, or simply isolation.

DÖŞEME BOĞAZI

Döşeme Boğazı (*map B, 6*) means 'paved passage' in Turkish, and that is exactly what you will see at the Döşeme Pass, 2km north of Kovanlık, from where it is signposted. Here is a long stretch of the **Via Sebaste**, exactly as it was in the past—and it is a long past, stretching from Hellenistic to Ottoman times. Throughout the ages everyone came through here, on a road that linked Side to Aspendos and then divided at Laodiceia (modern Denizli; *map B, 5*) to reach Ephesus or Pergamon. It was built by the Romans, negotiating the topography and connecting important places in their newly-formed province of Asia. It is possible that earlier on it was just a track, though early Hellenistic lookout structures suggest a strategic interest that goes beyond simple commercial use. The Romans made it into a **metalled road**, 6m wide and suitable for wheeled transport. A milestone from the time of Augustus, dated 6 BC, survives to prove it; they resurfaced it a number of times. A *mansio*, or staging post, went up and there are impressive remains of it: a large building with a courtyard, intended for the use of people on official business. It was possible to rest, eat and change mounts there and in this way news and instructions could travel fast. By the 4th–6th century there may have been a **small city** here; the remains of several churches point in that direction. It was not only officials who travelled this road, however, but also ordinary people going about their day-to-day business. They too would have neeed to be fed and accommodated somewhere. The road remained in use well into the later 19th century, as testified by travellers' accounts. In 1890 the Ottomans decided to build a new road and placed it to the west. The Via Sebaste remained in use but only by local shepherds taking their flocks to the mountains in summer. The road and the surrounding area remained unchanged and completely forgotten about.

SIA

Sia is near Karaot (*map B, 6*), to the east of Route 650 at Dağbeli, 13km north of

Döşeme Boğazı. Dubbed the best-kept secret in Turkey, it is indeed difficult to find. At Karaot ask for directions, mentioning 'Taştandam Ören Yeri', the 'archaeological site'. The small city is on a slope in the middle of a pine forest. It has been surveyed but not excavated. Sia (the name comes from an inscription in which the citizens of Sia express their gratitude to the emperor) may have begun as a Hellenistic settlement. The well preserved **walls** with eight towers, some standing to the second floor (and you can see the sea from there), and three gates date from that period. Sia appears to have flourished in the 3rd century when it acquired a complement of Roman civic buildings including (going by the scattering of round bricks from the *sospensura*) a bath house. The **agora** was a compact, neat affair about 20m by 30m in size but big enough to accommodate a dedication to the emperor, a small temple and a number of statues, possibly of local worthies. The inscriptions on the statue bases (all that remains) are illegible. The **necropolis** at the foot of the slope has a number of complex tombs with sarcophagi and built structures showing some wealth. Interestingly Sia has a largish **church**, certainly not a chapel, which has been dated to the 4th century. This suggests that when the new religion appeared here, there was no room in the agora, which was small anyway and already full, so the church had to be built on the periphery, as is the case with a number of early churches. The flat area below in the necropolis was all that was available. The church, possibly next to the tomb of some local Christian martyr, went up there and the pagan necropolis became a Christian cemetery.

MELLI & PEDNELISSOS

To this day **Melli**, to the east of Kocaaliler (*map B, 6*; ask there for directions), off Route 685 north of the Karacaören Dam, remains a mystery. It is, as Stephen Mitchell put it, a small but perfectly formed Pisidian city with a life span stretching from the 3rd–2nd century BC to the end of the 7th century. The end could have come with the Persian invasion followed by repeated Arab raids. The area was resettled by the Ottomans.

Melli has all the appurtenances of urban life: a rock-cut **theatre** (small), partly attached to the rear wall of the **market building**; an **agora** (small); a number of dwellings, in one of which Apollo Claros (whose oracle was quite a way away to the west; *see Blue Guide Aegean Turkey*) was venerated. The **necropolis** suggests some wealth, with sarcophagi and built tombs. A fragmentary bronze head, found in the area by illegal excavators and dated stylistically to the 2nd century AD, poses the same questions as the Bubon bronzes (*p. 61*). There is also evidence for five **churches**, suggesting a good survival into late antiquity and beyond. Unfortunately, none of the inscriptions provides a name for this city, a settlement that does not appear in any historical sources. Attempts at linking it with Mylias, the region to the west, on the ground of a perceived assonance, are misguided and misleading. We may have to conclude that this is one of the many small Hellenistic cities set up between the mountain and the plain, part of a plan to control space.

PEDNELISSOS

For Pednelissos (*map B, 6*) you will need to get around the dams in an easterly direction towards Kozan. The site is 1km east of Serik near the village of Hasgebe, in a locality known as Bodrumkaya. It is set on the west and south slopes of the towering rock that gave it its modern name.

The site has been known for over 100 years and was then correctly identified as Pednelissos on the basis of the ancient sources—Polybius (*5,72*) and Strabo (*14,667*) among others—and by the coinage. Even so, little is known about its history. The location has a good view over Pamphylia as far as Sillyon (*p. 147*). From the remains and the sources (which dry up around the 5th–7th century), a development can be charted from Hellenistic to early Byzantine times. Preservation is uneven since the lower town was used until recently for agricultural purposes.

The settlement is at the top of a valley, well defended by nature with a ridge linking three hills to the east. The town is spread out on the west and south slopes. It was defended from the beginning. The gap between two high points on the ridge to the east was made safe with a **wall** of rough stones, still standing quite high, and a possible observation tower went up on the westernmost hill. The area was accessed by a flight of stairs cut in the rock, beginning at the **agora**. The centre of the lower town, which was also defended with a wall and towers, is dated to the 2nd century BC. In the paved agora, built on a terrace, stands one of the best preserved buildings of Pednelissos: the **market building**, which compares well with those at Alinda (*map A, 6; see Blue Guide Aegean Turkey*) and Aigai (*map A, 1; see Blue Guide Aegean Turkey*). It may look tidy and orderly, but on closer inspection there is evidence of a lot of reuse and alteration. Without excavation it is difficult to date it, although it appears to be Hellenistic, with later developments. The upper part would have opened onto the agora with a **stoa**, as at Aigai. The three-aisled **basilica** in the southeast corner of the agora, measuring 31m by 18m, is thought to be early Roman and Doric in style, at least judging by the remains. **Three temples** have been identified. The most important one was outside the south city wall, standing in its own temenos. A relief cut in a monolith suggests that it was dedicated to **Apollo Sideton**, who is identified as the same Apollo as appears on the coins of Side and later of Pednelissos, showing contacts between the two cities. A number of holes on the surface would have supported bronze attachments. The relief has been dated to c. 320 BC; it has a Greek appearance but it is thought that the workmanship was local.

The demise of Pednelissos is obscure. **Five churches** have been identified, showing a sustained Christian presence. It is thought that decline started around the 7th century and that this settlement, of difficult access but also with marginal agriculture, lingered on to the 12th century.

SELGE

Situated on the fringes of Pisidia, Selge, near the village of Zerk (now Altınkaya; *map B, 6*), is reached after a challenging drive. The town itself is at an altitude of over

1000m and overlooked by high peaks, for example the Bozburun Dağı (2504m). Selge controlled one of the access routes to Pisidia and according to the sources, it had a thriving economy in spite of an unfavourable environment: the altitude and the need to irrigate did not stop the Selgians from making a name for themselves for their olives and olive oil, as well as for wine and good pastures. In addition, they drew on their large territory for medicinal plants. One of these was the root of the iris, from which an oil, excellent for massages, was extracted. Another was *Styrax* which produced a resin used in the perfume trade and as an antiseptic, antirheumatic and good for clearing the lungs. Pliny, Strabo and Galen all had a good word to say for the *Selgiticum*.

The **history of Selge** is still quite obscure, in part because the settlement, though known since the mid-19th century, has not been fully excavated. Certainly what one sees today is the Roman Selge, but there is incontrovertible historical evidence that it was already a fully-fledged polis by the time Alexander the Great appeared. Its coinage goes back to the to the 5th century BC, when it apparently had connections with the cities on the Pamphylian plain. The old name of Selge, as it appears on coins, remains to be explained: 'Estlegiys' is very similar to Aspendos' old name of 'Estwediiys'. Both are old local names and have no Greek root; they are both probably Anatolian.

By the time of **Alexander the Great**, Selge was a community with civic institutions. We know this since it made overtures of friendship while the Macedonian army was busy besieging Termessus. The Selgians may have felt vulnerable in their mountain stronghold. They were eventually able to weather the Hellenistic period, getting into trouble only once but successfully repulsing the Seleucids in the early 2nd century BC, while at the same time—going by the inscriptions—feuding with their neighbours, Sagalassos, Pednelissos and Aspendos. Like many other places in the area, the Selgians showed an interest in things Greek and invented for themselves an improbable Greek ancestry. Later, after a short stint as part of Galatia, Selge was incorporated into the **Roman Empire** and underwent the usual rebuilding to give it the appearance of a Roman city. Never mind that it was remote; its new guise was evidence that *romanitas* reached anywhere. Its coinage continued into the 3rd century AD.

The transition to **Christianity** left a number of churches (some with mosaics) built into temples and public buildings, but troubled times were not far away and the Hellenistic walls that had been deemed superfluous went back into commission. The city shrank, the churches turned into chapels. The marauding **Goths** got here in 399 but they came in vain. Selge was then, so the historian Zosimus tells us, 'a small town' and was able to repel them. Nevertheless, this was only staving off the inevitable and the Selgians eventually dispersed. Even though times were troubled on the coast, Selge proved too remote to act as a refuge The town was abandoned and only rediscovered in the mid-19th century.

EXPLORING SELGE

Selge today is at a crossroads. Whereas up until recently it was used as a quarry for ready-made building stone, the modern village is now in an archaeological

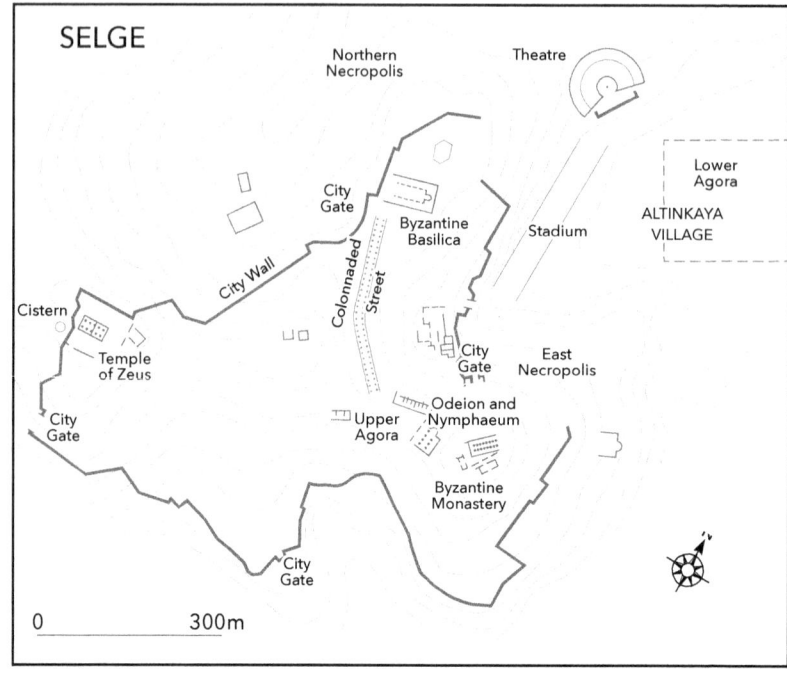

conservation area and a national park. This imposes restrictions on land use by the locals, meaning also that they are not allowed to build extensions to their houses. These changes have been resisted because they impose constraints without any compensating benefit. The tourism that figures so prominently in the economy of the ancient cities on the plain is here subdued, because although there are plenty of ruins, in the eyes of most visitors they are just heaps of stones. Buses come to the theatre, the town's only immediately recognisable feature, and then return to the beach after the visitors have taken a few pictures. It is not surprising that the local community would like to see an expansion of the tourist trade, with some accompanying infrastructure and an appropriate presentation of the site. They would also like a share of the revenue. At the time of writing, nothing very much was happening. Selge certainly looks as it should, like a long-deserted town. But contemporary economic imperatives are different.

To get your bearings, start your visit at the **theatre**. Partly cut in the rock and partly built of the local conglomerate, which flakes easily, it could accommodate c. 10,000 people. A number of details are known about the scena, now collapsed after being struck by lightning. It had two tiers of columns (Ionic and Corinthian) and a number of niches. Southwest of the theatre ran the **stadium** (edged on the east side by the modern road, otherwise grassed over). It was 27m wide but apparently too short to host a full stadium race. Other places with a difficult topography, such as Arykanda, had the same problem. It is a fact though, that the victory **inscriptions** on the stadium only refer to citizens of Selge, suggesting a restricted use for it. It is known that in its heyday Selge hosted an important festival every four years, for which a full-size stadium would have been required, but this has not been located. Both stadium and theatre were outside the Hellenistic walls, which took in the area following the contours for a length of 3.2km. Along this course in the 1960s, Bean (*p. 22*) identified a number of towers spaced every 90m.

From the top of the theatre, looking to the southwest, you can make out the three hills on which Selge was built, to east, west and north. The one to the west was the Kesbedion, the religious centre of the city, where the only marble monument, a **Temple of Zeus**, was to be found. The area had its own defences. The **two aqueducts** serving the city, one from Bozburun Dağı and the other from the west, arrived here; they were carried on arches across the marshes and then, gaining height on the Kesbedion, filled a tall distribution tower. The aqueducts supplemented the **cisterns**. On the high point to the east, remains of a **Byzantine monastery** have been identified, possibly reusing an earlier structure, a Byzantine basilica, built close to an earlier podium temple.

In the hollow in the middle was the heart of the city, centred on the **colonnaded street**, a paved way 230m long with limestone Ionic columns and shops on either side. It led (with a kink in the middle; topography again) to a small temple to an imperial figure. The **upper agora** (the large lower agora is now occupied by the modern village to the northeast), furnished with a couple of **stoas**, was surrounded by a **nymphaeum**, an **odeion**, a **Temple of Tyche** and, on the north edge, a large building on three stories which Laurence Cavalier has identified as a **Hellenistic market** and storage space. Other buildings can be surmised from the accounts of early travellers such as Lanckoroński (*p. 28*), who reported vaulted structures, probably baths.

The **necropoleis** extended north and east of the town, where there were also a couple more churches.

PERGE

The provincial municipality declared 2018 the 'Year of Perge', the aim being to increase tourism from the 60,000 or so visitors it receives now, to the hundreds of thousands, even to the million mark. This may have been a little premature, since the requisite infrastructure was not yet in place. What is certain, though, is that one should hasten to visit Perge, before it is swallowed up by Antalya.

Advertised as being located 19km from Antalya, Perge (*map B, 6; open daily, summer 9–5, winter 8.30–5.30; charge*) is in fact on the very northeast edge of the city, near the village of Aksu, an island of rough land among a sea of buildings, greenhouses, factories, the site of the Antalya 2016 Expo and the airport (6km to the south). All this makes things a little difficult. Visual pollution is a serious threat: how is one supposed to appreciate the antiquities in such an incongruous setting? Secondly, there is the archaeology. Perge is more than just what is inside the walls and on the acropolis. To try and understand the development of the city, one needs to look at a much wider area. Unfortunately Perge has not only been robbed in the past, but illicit settlements have sprung up comparatively recently on what are clearly archaeologically sensitive zones, the one to the immediate east of the acropolis for example. It now has a school, a mosque, houses and a cemetery and obviously those things are not going to move. The ticket office and car park are also in sensitive areas. Agriculture is another factor to consider, as tractors go deep and disturb antiquities, while irrigation brings other problems. Meanwhile, however, Perge is there and it awaits you.

A SHORT HISTORY OF PERGE

Perge has a number of foundation legends, most of them involving the diaspora after the Trojan War and, as a sideline, a Hittite past based on an unproven identification with Parha, a city in the kingdom of Tarhuntassa, from a tablet found at Boğazköy dated to the 13th century BC. There is nothing more solid. By the time it appears in history, Perge is fully clothed (albeit with no walls): it is a city. A 4th-century BC geographer mentions a city located 10km up the Kaistros (today's Aksu), which was then navigable for small boats and provided with a **sea harbour** at Magydos (*p. 126*), to which it was linked by a road used in winter and in the spring, when the river would have been too full. This fits Perge perfectly. The village of Solak on the Aksu, 4km east of Perge, is at the end of an ancient road marked by tombs on either side. A number of Roman spolia are built into its houses, but no quays or moles have been located so far (this was a geophysical survey and there were no excavations). It has been interpreted as Perge's **river harbour**.

When Alexander the Great came past in 333 BC, Perge was unwalled and wisely decided to befriend him, offering guides for his travels inland. After being contested for a time by the warring diadochoi, Perge ended up in the lap of Eumenes II, King of Pergamon. The settlement was expanded and took on a true Greek character. The first coins, a sure sign of economic prosperity, date from the 2nd century BC and bear the image of **Artemis Pergaia**. Greek learning also took hold. A local mathematician and geometer, **Apollonius**, studied in Alexandria and wrote several treatises including one on the properties of the sections of the cone, codifying the concepts of circle, hyperbole, parabola and ellipse which are used in astronomy. Another notable Pergeian was **Varus the Stork**, a witty sophist so nicknamed because of his red nose and fiery temper.

Contacts with the Romans, in the shape of the grasping governor **Verres**, were not so positive. He ransacked the Temple of Artemis Pergaia and was later castigated by Cicero in one of his famous orations. Formally part of the Roman Empire under Claudius, Perge settled down to become the Roman city one sees now. **Christianity** came a couple of decades later, when St Paul and St Barnabas preached here. The new religion put down firm roots, judging by the number of churches and basilicas, and the local bishop participated in the councils of Nicaea and Ephesus.

Perge was a **metropolis** at the time of the emperor Tacitus (275–6), showing that it had a military role in those difficult times, when the **Goths** and later the **Isaurians** were threatening. Justinian in due course (by then Perge was the ecclesiastical metropolis of Pamphylia) intervened to stem the decline but the Arab invasions were the final blow. The city was abandoned and people either fled to the mountains or repaired to the acropolis and in the 9th century, the bishop found safety in nearby Sillyon.

On the whole, one could say that Perge was doomed by Antalya's rise, which concentrated Byzantine resources there, as well as by the proximity of the mountain region with its troublesome inhabitants.

EXPLORING PERGE

You will probably need about three hours and plenty of sun cream, as the site is large and unshaded. For a plan of the site, see overleaf. You will be coming in from the south, having the theatre and the stadium outside the walls, before the ticket booth to your left.

The **theatre** against the slope of the west hill, the Koca Belen, is not precisely dated. The shape is over a semicircle but there have been many reworkings. It had an estimated capacity of 14,000. A gallery at the top of the cavea was a place for patrons to socialise or find shelter. At an unspecified date the orchestra was modified for gladiatorial games and for wild animal shows. The scena, with its baroque friezes and statues with mythological scenes of giants and centaurs engaged in mortal combat, is from the mid-2nd century AD. It recently collapsed because of the vibrations from lorry traffic along the road, carelessly built close to the back of it and has been partially reconstructed in Antalya Museum. From the road you can see the remains of a monumental **nymphaeum** with five niches.

The **stadium** is a free-standing building on arched substructures, 34m wide and 234m long with a rounded end at the north and capacity for 12,000 spectators. At some point it was divided in half, for unknown reasons. The south end is now destroyed. A reconstruction is planned, using the limestone and breccia blocks now lying around. This would have been the prime location of Perge's games, such as the Asyleia Augustea celebrating the right of asylum, a coveted honour linked to the temple of the local manifestation of Artemis.

This brings us to **Artemis Pergaia** and her magnificent temple, so much praised by Strabo (*14,4,2*) and which is supposed to have been large, on an eminence, but which has not been located. The eminences which could be its potential site are two hills on either side of the city (Koca Belen to the west and İyilik Belen to the east), as well as the acropolis to the north. The two hills have provided no evidence of large buildings; on the acropolis an inscription of a Paolina Artemisia, priestess of Artemis, has been found in a Byzantine cistern associated with a column structure. The problem, however, is that the acropolis is not outside the city, where according to Strabo and other authors the temple stood. The quest continues. Anything depicting this particular Artemis as she appears on the Pergeian coins, with stars and a crescent moon, perhaps a bust or just a lump suggesting a **meteorite** in the style of Pessinus, would be a very good clue. The temple was maintained by the town with the help of the Plancii family and prospered in Roman times, even though the new rulers tried hard to curb the cult.

THE PLANCII FAMILY

The Plancii are very present in Perge, beginning with Plancia Magna. Her benefactions are attested in various inscriptions and while her role as priestess of Artemis has sent everyone looking for the temple, which remains so far elusive.

Plancia Magna was a second-generation immigrant belonging to a family that had made its fortunes in Asia Minor. Her family tree can be traced through a number of inscriptions. In Rome the Plancii appear already interested in the cult of Diana (the Roman version of Artemis), to whom they dedicated a temple, and in Asia Minor they continued to build temples to the goddess. Plancia Magna was the daughter of Plancius Varus, who had risen to senatorial rank, implying that he had money. However, the family fortunes appear to have started more humbly, in trade and business. The Plancii possibly moved from Atina in the Latium hinterland, 160km southeast of Rome, at the end of the Republic, when the province of Asia came into being. We find Plancii with large estates in Galatia and Bithynia. We also find them in Selge and they left one inscription in Antalya. The transition from business to administration would have been eased by injections of cash, benefactions to the community and useful connections. At the height of their power, c. 2nd century, the Plancii were deemed worthy of a public statue, in bronze (and thus with very little chance of survival).

While normally only the statue base and dedication survive, in the case of Plancia Magna we have the statue itself, in stone (in Antalya Museum) and one can see how powerful women, in this case one who was not an imperial wife with divine status, were represented. If we consider that Plutarch in his *Moralia* (*138–146*; 1st century AD) writes that 'a good wife ought to be most conspicuous when she is with her husband and stay at home when he is not there', then it seems clear that Plancia Magna would have failed the test, since she is conspicuous without any husband in sight. But how far can she go, how assertive does she look? For a start she is heavily draped, but one can imagine the body of a matron. But this contrasts with the youthful, almost childlike, expression of the face. She appears defenceless and wrapped in modesty, which is curious since one would think that a woman of her power, abilities, financial standing and stature in the city would have been older and bear on her face the marks of a life lived to the full. Emperors are not portrayed like 15-year-olds with plump cheeks and a demure attitude, so why should females be?

The **city walls** are an impressive feature of Perge. They must have been built between Alexander's visit in 333 BC (when there were no walls) and 189 BC when, according to Livy (*38,37*), Gnaeus Manlius Vulso, the Roman consul, found a Seleucid garrison here. The layout of the walled city is small and compact, with the high ground east and west no longer included. Whether the acropolis was walled or not is open to debate. Lanckoroński (*p. 28*) in the late 19th century saw some stumps there but the question has not been settled.

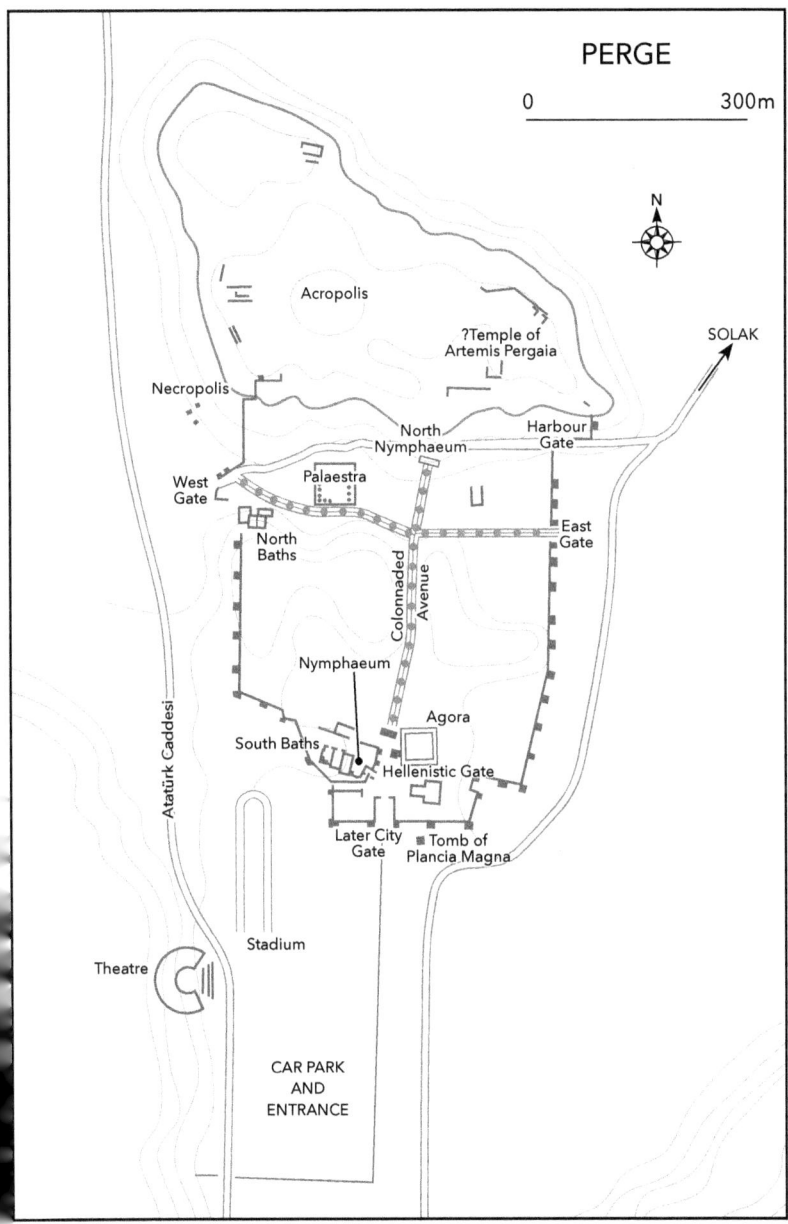

Built in solid limestone in well-cut bossed ashlars, the Hellenistic city wall had some 40 **towers**, three or four storeys high and closely spaced, and few sally ports suggesting, according to McNicoll, a passive defence which would have subjected any attacker to a concentrated artillery onslaught from the towers and from the top of the wall. Three **gates** have been identified, to the west, east and south. The first two are guarded by two towers and last one has the extra security feature of a killing ground, oval in shape, between the two round towers. One is reminded of the Mindos Gate at Halicarnassus (*covered in Blue Guide Aegean Turkey*) and the main gate at Side (*see p. 160*). Inside the circuit, the town was laid out on a grid, the only Pamphylian town so organised; the state of Antalya in this respect is not clear. The wall extension to the south is late Roman and dictated by necessity.

In about AD 120 the Roman authorities decided that the town could dispense with walls and the public area of the city was extended by pulling down the Hellenistic defences. It was a matter of prestige; the Plancii paid for it and were not modest about their contribution. The oval **Hellenistic Gate** was remodelled, retaining the round towers and closing the space to the north with a triple arch dedicated to Hadrian and loaded with imperial statues of Hadrian's immediate family and predecessors. A new **agora** was set up, 65m by 65m with granite columns, mosaics and frescoes and possibly a macellum in the middle. The south entrance to the town was landscaped to impress, with a liberal use of marble, both plain and coloured, which had to be brought from afar, decorating two **monumental nymphaea** to the west and several statues of worthies, founders both known and mythological, and benefactors, set up in the court in niches and on ledges by the wall; the Plancii clan figured twice. Artemis Pergaia was represented as well, in a relief among priestesses and devotees. The area has not yet been fully excavated.

The main feature of the town is certainly the **colonnaded avenue** with Ionic marble and granite columns, which runs in crooked lines roughly forming a cross, oriented on the cardinal points. It is possible that the layout reflects an earlier processional way to the elusive temple of Artemis Pergaia. The thoroughfare was unusually wide (28m) because it accommodated a central canal (*euripos*), showing that Perge had plenty of available water; indeed it had **two aqueducts**, having relied on cisterns before the Romans. One aqueduct tapped the Kurşunlu Çay close to the famous waterfalls and the other, later one was added from the Düden Çay near the Düdenbaşı waterfalls. Both have been dated to the 2nd/3rd century, when bathhouses and nymphaea went up. The north–south colonnaded street had an impressive fountain or **North Nymphaeum** at the top end (with, to the left, steps to the acropolis) and it has been suggested that, when approaching it from the south, it would have looked as if the water came directly form the acropolis, in other words from Artemis Pergaia herself, if her temple was indeed up there. Another colonnaded street ran immediately along the foot of the acropolis to the east, in the direction of the presumed river harbour (*see above*). The colonnaded street provided a communal space for citizens to socialise and shop but it also brought an opportunity to remind them of the honorable personages to whom they owed devotion: statues of these, with honorific inscriptions, crowded the place. Among them was a governor who had paved the street with marble and another praised for his public works. A praetorian prefect disgraced and executed under Constantius II had a statue set up as a late apology by the repentant emperor. Acclamations on pillars listed the honours bestowed on the city by the Roman senate.

The **acropolis** is still awaiting full investigation. Being high up, it may be the site of the earliest settlement. Cisterns, of which there are a number, are difficult to date. They were certainly reused by the population when it retreated up here for safety. Traces of **defensive walls** have been identified (denoted by a thicker contour line on the plan), possibly Archaic or Classical. The archaeology of the acropolis may in due course fill in the gaps in our knowledge of the history of Perge, which seems to have waned in the 8th century. Life resumed at some point, at least going by the account of Evliya Çelebi; *p. 25*), who visited in 1671, but his account is confused. He talks of the Castle of Teke Hisarı, a rectangular castle with no moat, situated on a mound with a fairly high hill behind. Presumably he meant the lower town and its walled enclosure, though that is not on a mound. At all events the place was by then occupied by 70 or 80 families of Türkmen—when they were not up on the *yaylas*.

SILLYON

Rising 210m above sea level in the alluvial plain of the Kaistros, Sillyon (or Syllium; there are various spellings) is on a high plateau with steep sides, with view of the sea (in antiquity 7.5km away, now15km) and of Perge. In spite of being known at least since the 1880s, when Lanckoroński (*p. 28*) planned and surveyed it, there has been very little work done here. And that adds to its charm, as it is now wild and untamed—as Sillyon itself anciently was. On the other hand, it remains poorly understood. Most of the information comes from the sources. If you decide to come this way (*map B, 6; the sight is always accessible and entry is free*), take your time as there will be a fair amount of scrambling, and remember that the site is completely exposed.

Sillyon is on a height, which would have been a favoured spot for an ancient community. The plateau was easily settled in prehistoric times, with people farming the plain below. There was a lower town to the south. Over time the plateau was levelled and the sides were made steeper by cutting them back. We cannot put a date on this but we do know that there was no lower town when Alexander the Great came through and the locals rebuffed him. Either the mix of mercenaries and natives under the command of a Persian satrap proved too much for him, or the cliffs were an effective deterrent. Sillyon began minting **coins** in the 3rd century BC. Its time in Roman hands is a blank, though Strabo mentions it as one of the cities of Pamphylia, and going by the benefactions of one Menodora, of the local Megacle family listed in an honorific inscription, there must have been money around. Menodora made donations to various projects including buildings, oil for the gymnasium and the maintenance of indigent children, and the estimated total of her benefactions was one million denarii, a considerable sum.

Sillyon became important at the time of the **Arab invasions**, when a good defensive position was worth more than beautiful civic buildings. Indeed it did not have many of those: it was known in the eyes of its contemporaries as a small, paltry city inhabited by poor people. With Perge sinking, however, Sillyon came to the fore, becoming a **Byzantine administrative centre** because of its defended position. It

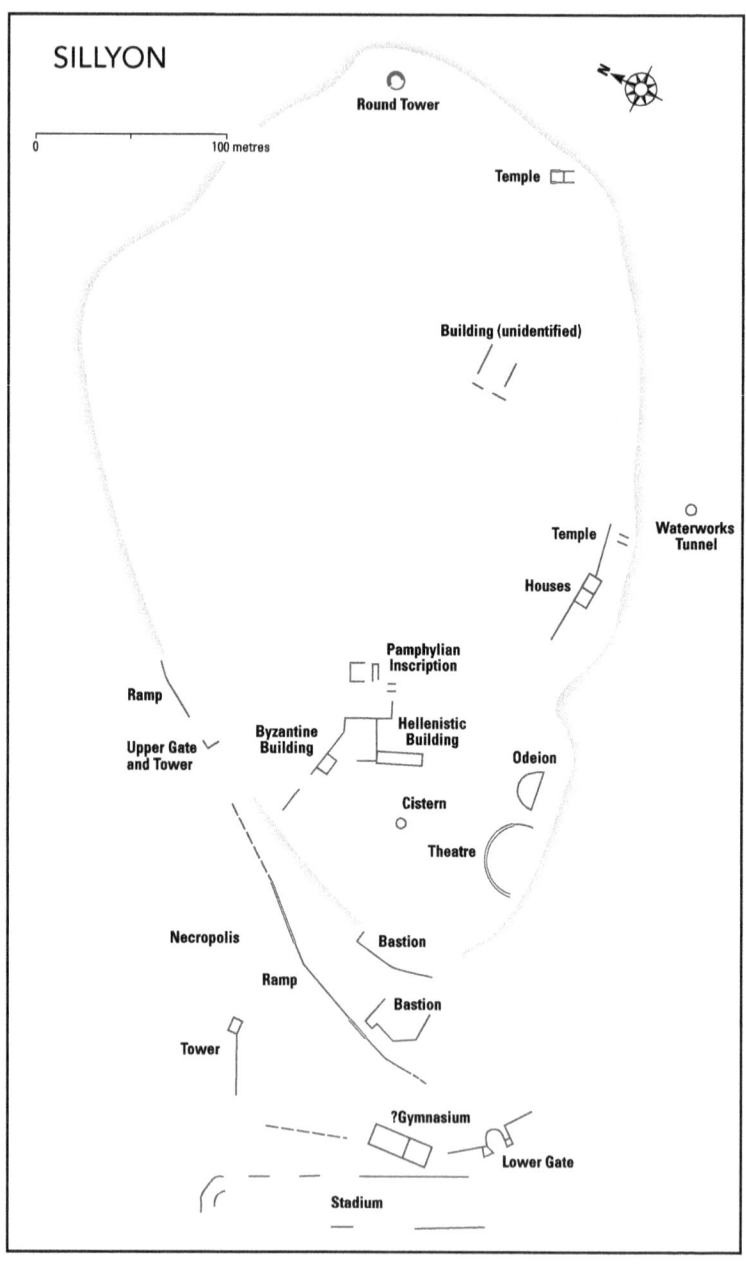

was second only to Antalya. Here was the warehouse, where taxes of all sorts were collected. In 824 the Arabs arrived, apparently by boat up the river Eurymedon (the Köprüçay). The governor at the time was a Syrian-speaker, one **John Echimos**, an eccentric character destined by prophecy (his own) to command. He managed to organise an effective defence, using all available hands including monks and nuns, and by dint of a few gifts was able to persuade the Arabs to leave. He attributed his strategy to divine inspiration and went on to become an ascetic in Bithynia and later a saint by the name of **Anthony the Younger**. Sillyon maintained the monastic tradition that had served it so well and when it became a bishopric, the bishop was a monk. It is attested up to the 14th century, but beyond that it sinks into obscurity.

EXPLORING SILLYON

The approach is from the west, via the lower town. The outline of a 174m long **stadium** can be seen, partly built against the slope and partly supported by a vaulted structure. The large building close to it has been interpreted as a gymnasium or a palace. There are **defences** with a couple of bastions and three towers, but they do not look as though they would have provided much protection; the wall is barely 60cm thick. The **lower gate** is in the same style as those at Perge and Side, with an oval killing ground. It is thought that these defences owed more to prestige than efficiency. They were not improved upon in the Roman period.

The **acropolis** is accessed from the west by two ramps, north and south. The **south ramp** is the better preserved. It was protected by towers and bastions and a free-standing west wall on the edge of a steep drop. The wall appears to have had merlons, though it is also thought that they are the remains of windows and that perhaps the 5m wide ramp was roofed (though that would have made the bastion useless for defence). On the plateau, which measures 800m by 400m (and you really have to be careful getting around because of the **unprotected cisterns**), are the remains of several buildings, mainly Byzantine.

Beyond the **upper tower** guarding the entrance, you will see remains of a **large building** standing to full height. Its ground-level construction is solid and defensive, with a single entrance and just one small window to let some light in. Above, the masonry is different: it is a single room 11m by 6m with large windows with brick arches above. The commander's palace? Next to it are a couple of small churches; one has an **inscription** built into it, 37 lines of pure Pamphylian, a form of Peloponnesian Greek with Cypriot borrowings: it is the longest Pamphylian inscription so far known.

By the south edge of the plateau are the scant remains of a **theatre**, which slid down the cliff in 1969 leaving a few rows of seats behind, while the **odeion** next to it has completely disappeared. The **residential district**, with remains of houses and of a **temple**, is along this south edge of the acropolis. This cliff is unstable.

The Turks at some stage used the so-called governor's building and built a couple of mosques. The acropolis relied on cisterns for water but there is apparently another possible source. The **tunnel** discovered below to the south, and first believed to be a tomb, is now known to have tapped a spring, now dried up. It is 27m long leading to three intercommunicating rooms, in the first of which is an inscription to an emperor. This was not a tomb. It may perhaps have been a shrine.

ASPENDOS

Aspendos or Aspendus (map B, 6; open daily 9–7; charge; ticket for the theatre and acropolis hill; the aqueduct and baths-gymnasium ruins are free) is easy to find, turning north off Route 400 in the direction of Alanya before you cross the Köprüçay, the ancient Eurymedon. The river explains why Aspendos prospered. It was navigable in antiquity and also by largish crafts, since the **bridge** the Romans built over it had a clearance 4m higher than the Seljuk construction that later took its place. You can see it on the way to Aspendos, taking a side road to the right 700m after the turning (*see p. 154*). The town is located right where the alluvial plain of the Eurymedon opens up, with a convenient height (the acropolis) barely 800m from the present bed of the river. There is no telling if the river moved, as no harbour installations have yet been found. The lower town, now mainly under cultivation, is a blank.

Aspendos is world-famous for its theatre, which has sailed almost unscathed through the centuries. As a result, archaeological research has been stymied, roads have been built, settlement has been allowed in sensitive areas and attention has been focused not on the whole city but on its one most famous feature. Excavations on the acropolis have only started recently. As a consequence, Aspendos' history comes only from the written sources, and there is not a lot to go on.

HISTORICAL OUTLINE OF ASPENDOS

Leaving out the Hittite ancestry (which is not proven) and the connection with the ubiquitous Mopsus, who is tied up with several foundation legends, it would seem likely that there was an indigenous settlement here (Aspendos is an Anatolian name) as the region was fertile, suitable for sheep rearing and horse breeding. There was also a river nearby, a defended height, a connection to the sea and a lake good for fishing, which contracted in the summer, providing a salt crop. This lake, Lake Capria (now dried up), was later praised by Strabo (*14,4,2*). Aspendos was already minting **coins** around the 5th century BC, when the first (anonymous) Aspendian enters history as the bodyguard of Epyaxa, the wife of the Persian satrap in Cilicia according to Xenophon (*Anabasis 1,2,13*). Aspendos, which on its earlier coins went under the name of Estwedys, had been—and still was—in the hands of the **Persians**, but contested by the Athenians, who beat the Persians soundly in a naval battle at the mouth of the Eurymedon in the mid-5th century BC. Their general, Cimon, completed his triumph with a second victory on land, which he achieved by the cunning stratagem of infiltrating the enemy camp with his own soldiers disguised as Persian stragglers looking for their compatriots. The result was good for Cimon and the **Athenians**, but less so for the Aspendians, who found themselves enrolled in the Athenian-dominated Delian League (and possibly did their best not to pay their yearly dues). Worse was to come a short while later, when in 398 BC at the end of their mortal combat with Sparta, the Athenians sent their commander Thrasiboulos to Aspendos to raise some money. The locals decided to pay provided he left with his army but he broke the compact, allowing his men to devastate the countryside, and was murdered in his tent. When **Alexander the Great** came through in 333 bc, the place was again in Persian hands. There were parleys and the two sides came to an agreement—or so Alexander thought as he continued to Side and then to Sillyum. He was quickly back with his army when he heard that Aspendos was being fortified. He took up quarters in the deserted town and dictated his own terms: horses, a tribute of 100 talents (one talent was over 20kg of gold) and a number of distinguished citizens as hostages. On his departure, he left a governor behind him.

There is a blank after these events until Aspendos once again crops up in the hands of the **kings of Pergamon**. When the last of them bequeathed his kingdom to the Romans in 133 bc, the newly-formed province of Asia did not include the Mediterranean coast. That did not mean no **Roman** rule: Rome certainly furnished grasping governors (the infamous Verres) and overweening consuls with their armies after protection money (Manlius Vulso).

Things became more settled with the Empire. Aspendos prospered and took the shape we see now, leaving behind it very little history; at some point it it was known as **Primoupolis**. In fact, according to a passage by the 2nd-century sophist Philostratus, it was a place of sharp trading practices and greedy merchants. Apollonius of Tyana (*see Blue Guide Central Anatolia*), a philosopher who made wild and wide-ranging claims of being able to raise the dead and tell the future, found himself in Aspendos at a time when the city was facing famine because the merchants were hoarding corn. He was apparently more effective than the city fathers in finding a solution as he was able to frighten the merchants out of their wits. Thus chastened, they released their supplies and there was bread again in Aspendos.

In **Byzantine times** Aspendos maintained its importance but was never a bishopric. The Arabs in due course came up the river, the Aspendians fled and in the 13th century the city came into the hands of the **Seljuks**, who used the theatre as a sultan's residence and caravansaray. It was abandoned in the 15th century.

EXPLORING ASPENDOS: THE ENTRANCE GATES AND ACROPOLIS

As you approach from the south, you can see a 3rd-century ad **bath complex** to the right and not far from it to the southeast, the remains of a **gymnasium**. Both were built of the local stone, a weak conglomerate, so bricks were used for the vaults. Up the hill to the left are traces of walls and remains of the **South Gate**. The theatre (*described below*) is in front of you, with a car park.

The pear-shaped **acropolis** rises 30m above the surrounding plain and is about 800m long and 500 wide. Its sides are precipitous but its surface is not completely flat, as at Sillyon; it is cut by a ravine. Three gates have been identified, the best preserved is the one already mentioned to the south. Following the path after the **East Gate** and past the scanty remains of a small **Doric temple**, the ancient path broadens into a square with statue bases closed by a single archway to the north. It is intersected by an ancient sewer from the agora. The **agora** is immediately to the left, its four main features the result of a remodelling of the previous Hellenistic set-up around the late 3rd century ad. To the east is the **Basilica**, partly built on vaulted substructures to achieve the required width of 30m. It was 50m long with cisterns and general storage below (possibly grain). It was divided into three aisles, with an ample vestibule at the north end and an apse and exedra to the south.

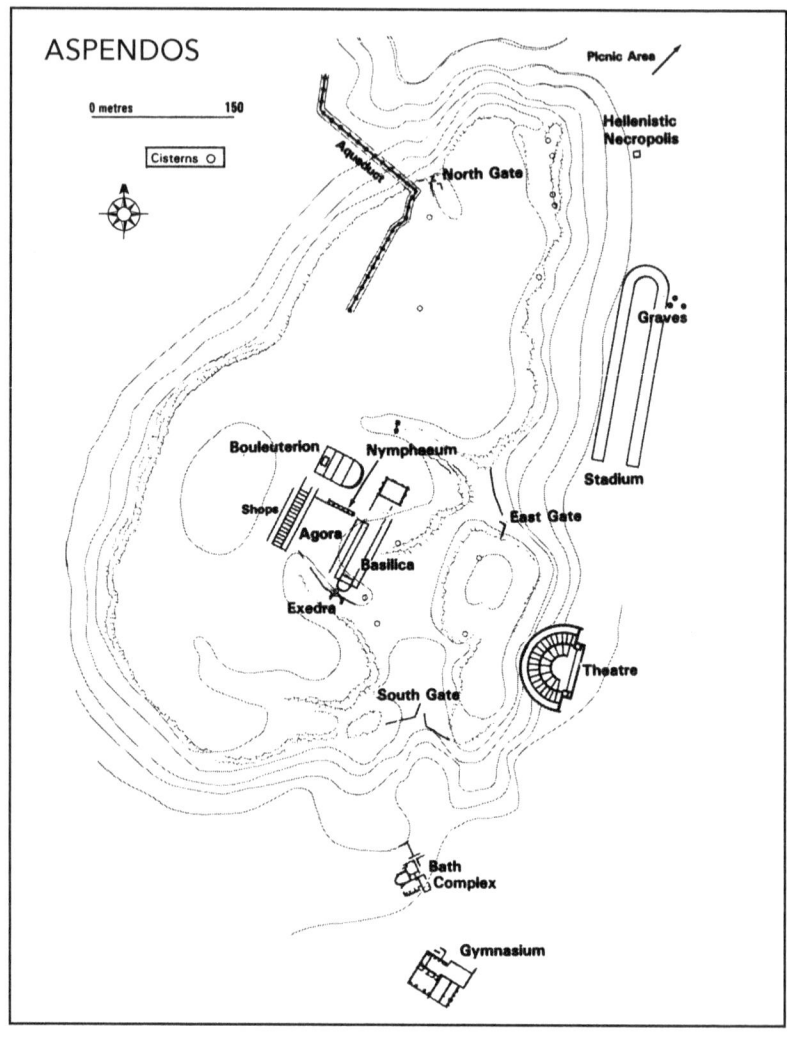

On the west side of the agora, the market building was over two storeys high, with a portico in front and 15 **shops** behind. To the north the **nymphaeum**, an Antonine rebuilding, 15m high and 32m long, was made possible by the construction of the aqueduct. Columns, statues, everything that could be removed has gone, apart from the consoles that were built into the structure. Try to imagine it though, taller and with the water cascading from a dolphin's head below the central niche and reflected in the coloured marble lining. Behind it was the **bouleuterion** or odeion (or both). It has not been excavated and not much is visible.

THE THEATRE

The theatre is Aspendos' *pièce de résistance*. It is what people come to see, either as tourists or as spectators, being in such good condition that it hosts major events every year. The building is a standard Roman theatre, partly resting against the slope to the west and partly built. It is 95m in diameter with a scena 62m long, all made of local conglomerate and, in places, marble and finer limestone. The orchestra is 24m across with a barrier. The scena, in pure baroque 2nd-century AD style, is in breccia and limestone and in the past had marble columns (probably monoliths as no stray column drums have been found) and marble statues in the niches. At the top end, a vaulted gallery offered protection from the elements or just a place where people could stretch their legs. Provisions for a *velarium* (awning) have been identified and it is thought that a wooden screen, slotted diagonally above the stage, would have been used to amplify the sound. According to an inscription, it was built by Zeno between 161 and 168 and funded by A. Curtius Crispinus Arruntiatus and A. Curtius Crispinus Auspicatus, the former having connections with Praeneste (Palestrina, in Italy). Spectacles of many kinds, from plays to *venationes* (wild animal hunts), were held here until Aspendos was abandoned. Much later the Seljuks of the Sultanate of Rum started taking an increased interest in the Mediterranean coast. Resources were scarce and it is well known that the sultans had a liking for country retreats, which they could use as bases for hunting expeditions or just as quiet places to enjoy nature. The pleasure palace of Kubadabad Saray, willed by Alaeddin Keykubad I by lake Beyşehir, is one such example. In the case of Aspendos, the pleasure palace came ready-made in the form of this theatre. Some work was carried out, to strengthen the scena building with iron clamps, for example, and three arched entrances with a porch went up at the back, as well as a buttress, which according to Scott Redford was used as a belvedere. The Seljuks appreciated a fine view: one should imagine this theatre as a Seljuk summer palace in the midst of prosperous countryside dotted with tents. The side walls of the stage, as well as the internal staircase leading to the viewing platform from the south tower and the back of the scena, were plastered and painted with the characteristic sultanic Seljuk pattern of red or black chevrons on a white background. This design is found here, in Alanya and on tiles in other places used by Seljuk sultans. Today there are only scant traces of it left, but according to Charles Fellows (*p. 26*) there was 'red and blue painted stucco everywhere' in the 1840s. The interior was also decorated with tiles (some even in the niches), some of which are now in Antalya Museum.

It was Atatürk, after a visit in the 1930s, who promoted the idea of using the theatre for modern performances. He did not quite have opera and ballet in mind, which is the mainstay of the programme at today's **Aspendos Opera and Ballet Festival**. He was a fan of wrestling, *güreş*, Turkey's national sport. Nevertheless, Aspendos' new life has been very successful, with tickets sold out well in advance and a very long season. This has created its own problems. The original theatre capacity is estimated between 7,000 and 15,000, which is far fewer than the present occupancy rate. Moreover, the use of loudspeakers elevates the sound vibration to a level that is destructive of the weak conglomerate of which most of the theatre is made. This is a structure over 2,000 years old. It should be treated as an antiquity not as a modern concert hall. The sustainability plan for Aspendos includes many excellent suggestions (new explanatory panels, bike routes, walking trails, walkways, local involvement) but unfortunately there is no provision for the protection of the theatre. Moreover, the Aspendos Arena, built 'provisionally' on Grade 3 archaeological land, is still there and shows no signs of being removed.

North of the theatre is the **stadium**, 215m long with an estimated capacity of 10,000.

THE AQUEDUCT

The accumulation of sinter at the back of the nymphaeum suggests that Aspendos' aqueduct had an active life of about 150 years. According to an inscription, it was paid for (to the tune of two million denarii) by one Tiberius Claudius Italicus in the 3rd century. It tapped two sources up in the mountains to the north, c. 17km away. The water was carried in tunnels, open channels and pipes until it came in view of the acropolis, where it had to cross marshy ground. This could not be accomplished with a Pont du Gard-style bridge since the distance, 1.7 km, was too long. The solution was an inverted syphon divided into three venter bridges separated by two towers, which are now 30m high but which may originally have been taller. The purpose of the construction was to keep the water under pressure without bursting the pipes, which here were made of stone (estimated number: 3,200), to reduce turbulence and friction with open tanks at the top of the towers, and deliver water to the nymphaeum in the agora, 14.5m lower than the springs. According to modern calculations, the system would have delivered about 5600 cubic metres of water per day, which is close to the present output of the springs.

THE EURYMEDON BRIDGE

Spanning the Köprüçay about 1km south of the theatre, this was originally a Roman bridge but what you see today is more Seljuk, as the first bridge at some point collapsed due to earthquakes or flooding. A number of studies have been conducted to reconstruct on paper the original structure. There are still Roman piers and other parts of the bridge extant. However, over time the course of the river shifted west. When the Seljuks came to rebuild it in the early 13th century, they designed a structure with a reduced clearance (the passage of ships was no longer required and there were pieces of Roman masonry obstructing the river bed) and they constructed a new ramp on the right bank. The bridge itself was narrower and kinked in the middle. Since there was no wheeled transport at that time, and things were transported by camel and mule, it was an appropriate solution.

A SIDE TRIP TO THE KARGIHAN

Turning north at Taşağıl, Route 687 follows the path of a Seljuk route between Antalya and Konya and before that of a Roman road. The Kargıhan (*map B, 6*) is dated stylistically to the time of Giyaseddin Keyhüsrev II (1236–46). It sits at the side of the road in a rural setting, 2.5 km after Beydiğin. It is in a good state of preservation and the entrance gate is not normally locked. It has some unusual features, like the separate bath building outside to the southeast of the entrance. Given how chilly it could be up here, the han has covered accommodation for everyone. People lodged at the north end, in the vaulted hall divided by a row of piers; animals in the western section, which is also vaulted but open to the elements, with feeding troughs and loading platforms. Five rooms to the east included a mosque. Service rooms and latrines occupy the south side of the courtyard, on either side of the imposing, well-preserved entrance. A number of graffiti can be seen on the plastered qibla wall of the mosque, with animals, stick figures and totemic Turkish symbols such as arrows. They cannot be dated and may belong to a secondary use of the han by Türkmen. Built in stones of various sizes and including a number of spolia (especially in the door and window frames), the han has survived well due to its remote location and has preserved its original setting.

LYRBE & THE MANAVGAT WATERFALLS

To get to Lyrbe (*map B, 6–8; free access*) from Route 400, head in the Alanya direction and follow the signs to the Manavgat Şelalesi (waterfalls; *described below*) until you see a sign to Lyrbe. It lies about 5km to the north on a good road in a pine forest. When you are there, enjoy the cool and the breeze but bear in mind that the ruins have not been repaired or consolidated and there are some cisterns about, so take care. Explored in the 1970s and again at the beginning of this century, Lyrbe is now on the tourist-bus circuit: the best time to visit is possibly lunchtime, when organised tours stop at the *lokanta*. The site is small and it quickly fills up.

Little is known about Lyrbe's origins. The name is Luwian, which would point to **Anatolian beginnings**, with a later intervention by Seleucus Nicator, one of Alexander the Great's successors. Thus it could be identified with Seleucia in Pamphylia, but equally it could be a separate Hellenistic foundation. The discovery of an inscription in Greek and Sidetan in the area next to the remains of the Roman aqueduct to Side (*see below*) does suggest **local connections with the coast**.

Lyrbe is set on a steep wooded hillside which was only accessible from the south (the approach today is from the same direction) and it has some magnificent remains which are still enjoyable even if our background knowledge remains murky. The time-span is Hellenistic to Byzantine.

The **city gate** leads straight to the **agora**, which was accessed via six gates and was originally surrounded by a Doric and Ionic portico, roughly 30m by 28m. The agora had an **odeion** with wooden benches and a **market building**, standing to the second storey on the east side; a **library** with an **exedra** to the north, a place where perhaps political debates were conducted. Many rooms had **mosaics**; two showing the Seven Sages and Orpheus charming the animals are now in Antalya Museum. The date-range for the buildings is Imperial (possibly on an earlier Hellenistic development, for example the east façade with the bossed masonry) to Byzantine (a chapel in the northwest corner). The west side of the agora is presently occupied by two galleries that are the substructures of the west portico, now lost. The rest of the town can be seen in what lies strewn around: remains of temples, a bouleuterion, baths and city walls. Due to its remote location, Lyrbe has not suffered much from stone-robbing.

Before heading to Side, make time to see the **Manavgat waterfalls** (Manavgat Şelalesi; *open daily 7.30am–10pm; charge*), a favourite place for Turkish families to go on an outing. It is cool and refreshing and while the falls are not particularly high, they are broad and magnificent and extremely noisy. The Manavgat river, the ancient Melas, short as it is, carries a tremendous amount of water, more than any other river in Asia Minor—and it shows.

SIDE

To a prospective settler, the peninsula where Side (*map B, 8; always accessible except the theatre April–Oct 9–7, Nov–March 8–5; charge*) first began must have looked like a dream location. A kilometre-long breccia tongue of land, stretching out into the sea and able to be cut off from the mainland by a single length of wall to the east. Short of an elevated plateau like Sillyon, this was probably the next best situation. Unfortunately we have very little information on Side's past which, to go by the archaeology, barely started in the Hellenistic period. A combination of factors have led to this state of affairs.

In 1812, Beaufort (*p. 23*) recognised the harbour piers, saw the ancient quay with its flagstones and beneath the water could make out the line of a mole made of sunken rocks. Later, when Lanckoroński (*p. 28*) visited, the land was empty and covered with scrub but soon other considerations got in the way. Paribeni (*p. 30*) witnessed recent damage in 1913. Inscriptions had been fed into lime kilns, the scrub was gone and the place was under the plough. Muslim refugees from Crete had been settled here by the sultan, a familiar tale at a time when the Ottomans were losing their grip on the European part of their empire. Worse was to come, from an archaeological point of view, when the coast developed as a prime tourist destination after WWII and development went unchecked. Still today the archaeologists in charge of Side complain that when developers find antiquities during building works they dump them with other ancient worked stones that are strewn around. Excavations, which have taken place since 1947, have been sparingly published. As a result, the chronology of Side is not clear and it is unlikely to get much better since the peninsula is to some extent covered with the modern buildings of the village of Selimiye.

HISTORY OF SIDE
According to Philipp Niewöhner, Side must have been settled since the **Archaic Period** and, we can add, by local people, from Anatolia. The Greek element that appears in so many foundation legends (in this case according to Strabo, who makes it a colony of Cyme) is missing in terms of evidence on the ground. The name of the place is that of the image that appears as early as the 6th /5th century BC on

coins: a pomegranate, a symbol of fertility because of its abundance of seeds. The Greek word for pomegranate is not 'side'. If there were colonisers, then they were overwhelmed by the mass of the local population and they adapted.

Greek was introduced later, in the 3rd century BC, and the local language (Sidetan, very different from Pamphylian, which is Greek-based), gradually waned. It is still not well understood. The Side that **Alexander the Great** visited in 333 BC and where he was welcomed, was technically under Persian rule. The Persians were ousted and the diadochoi came in, disputing Alexander's inheritance. Pergamon at some point is said to have controlled the Mediterranean coast but on the whole it seems that Side maintained a certain degree of independence, doing its own things, which made it a prosperous trading centre, albeit tainted by sharp practices if we are to believe Stratonicus, who famously said that the locals were the most unscrupulous people in the world. That was in the 4th century BC. By the 1st century BC, Strabo (*14, 664*) was accusing them of selling out to pirates, allowing them to trade their slaves in the local market and repairing their ships in the harbour. But they were by no means the only people in the area who were doing this. The **Romans**, who were now in control, seem to have turned a blind eye.

Side flourished and was auctioning **slaves** on its docks while acknowledging that they were free born (*Strabo 14,32*). The mountains to the north were a good source and demand was high; 2nd-century papyri from Egypt make mention of slaves from Side being sold in Egypt. The town supplemented its takings by trading oil and wheat from the plain and timber from the mountains. The archaeological record from those days, when Side was in Roman hands, shows prosperity. The first troubles came in the 4th century. The **Isaurians** made several attempts, in 353, 368, 377 and 405, but their incursions were raids, they could not mount a full siege. The **Goths** came only once, in 399, but that was enough; they attacked by sea and land, with siege engines, to which the Sidetans responded by building even taller ones. The siege left bitter memories but Side managed to shrug it all off and repaired its walls and damaged buildings. The remains, dated to the 5th and 6th centuries, show a prosperous urban life and the inscriptions testify to the continuous munificence of leading families. **Christianity** was now well implanted (alongside a Jewish community, which had two synagogues attested by inscription), with grandiose basilicas, stamping out paganism by taking over the temples. Culturally Side makes its name with Tribonian, the star of Byzantine jurists, who worked on Justinian's new code of law. Although he spent his working life in Byzantium, he was educated here. Side appears to have been a **place of learning**, as the presence of a historian of the Early Church, Philip Sidetes, a friend of John Chrysostom, testifies. He was teaching here in 405. By the 6th century Side had a bishop.

The real trouble came with the **Arab raids** in the early 7th century. Side was too exposed to sea attacks and the Battle of Finike (655) is a timely reminder that at the time, the Arabs were masters of the seas. The city shrank, cutting itself in half with a north–south wall, which could easily be built with spolia since so many buildings were in ruins. The eastern half was abandoned. Trade suffered and coins become rare. Churches became smaller, reduced to mere chapels inside the once-grand basilicas; baths were abandoned and put to other uses, as lime kilns and oil factories.

158 BLUE GUIDE MEDITERRANEAN TURKEY

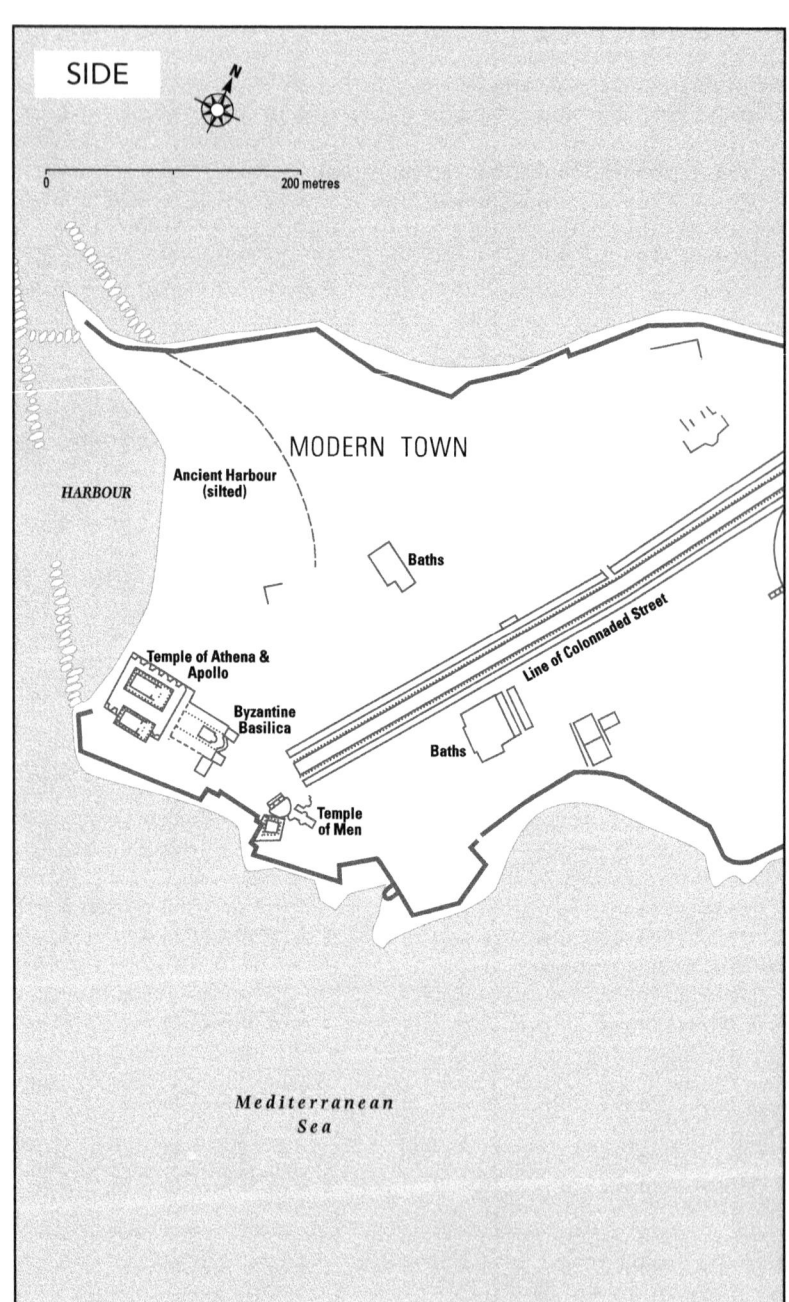

PISIDIA HERITAGE TRAIL: SIDE **159**

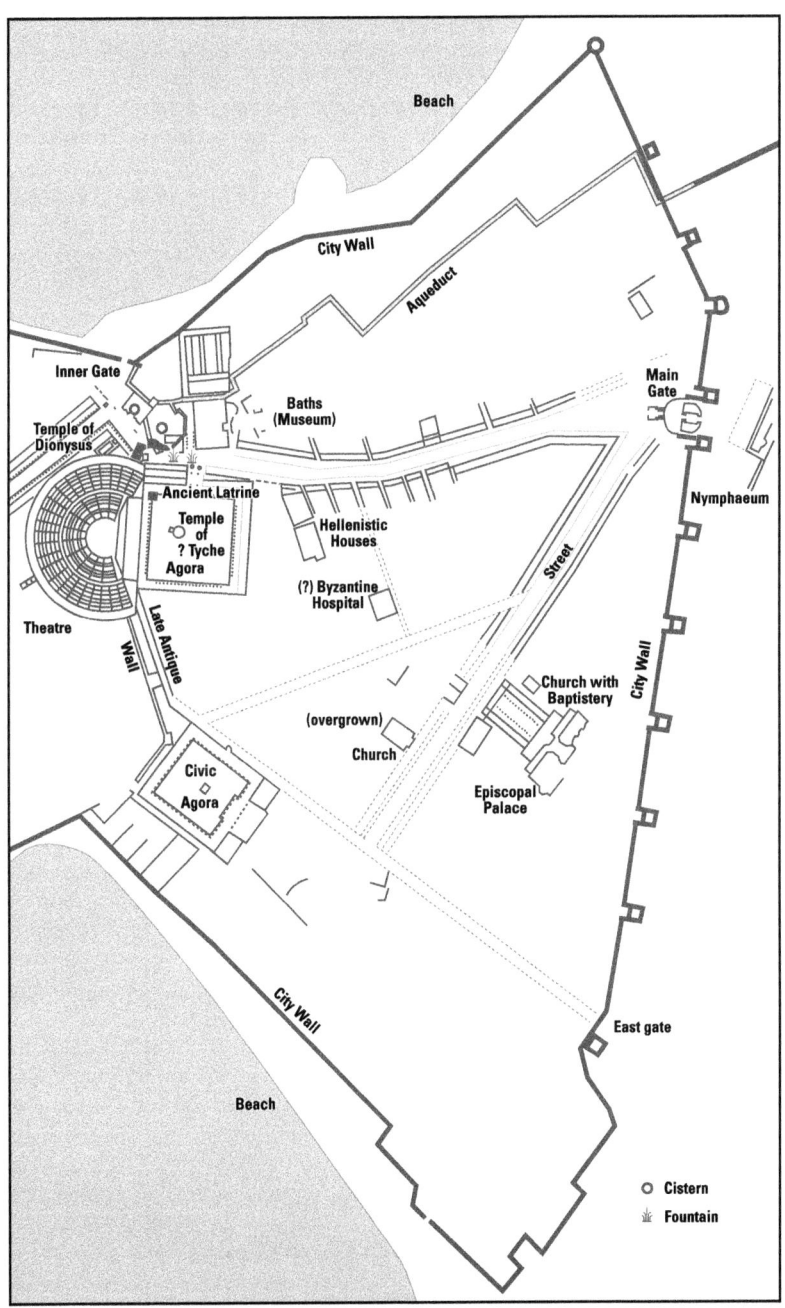

These were the Dark Ages, when the written sources dry up. By the time the sources reappear, the city is in ruins: '**Antalya the burnt**', so named by the inhabitants, who had run away to the comparative safety of Antalya behind its double wall circuit, according to the geographer Idrisi in 1118. The devastation wrought by the Arabs and the Persians disrupted trade routes and made Side unviable by disrupting its economy. There was no money to dredge the harbour, which became useless. The water supply was permanently damaged, pirates were on the loose. Running to safety was the only solution. As well as Antalya, nearby Manavgat (the Roman Manava) offered a form of safety with its Zindan Kalesi (modern name), a fastness perched high up away from the sea but still controlling a harbour and the river. In 1191 the Crusaders found Side deserted. The bishop of Side, who is attested to the 14th century, apparently lived in Byzantium from the 10th century.

EXPLORING SIDE

A visit to Side should begin with a look at the **Hellenistic city walls** that cut off the peninsula from the mainland. A stretch of them is conveniently placed next to the bus station. Built in breccia, to an original estimated of height of c. 12m with a wall walk on top and 13 rectangular towers regularly spaced, they had two gates, no posterns and a ditch, suggesting a passive form of defence. In front of the nymphaeum (*see below*) are the very scanty remains of the **Main Gate**, with two towers on either side and an internal arrangement very similar to that at Perge and Sillyon, with an oval killing ground with a narrow, constrained entrance for trapping the enemy so that they could be dispatched from the height of the walls. As in Perge, this killing ground became redundant in Roman times when Side was not threatened and the space was given over to a display of civic pride, with statues of worthy citizens, heroes and gods. The other gate (the **East Gate**), further south down the wall, was simpler.

The **Nymphaeum**, now partly reconstructed, stands as a testimony to the prosperity of the Roman period, when defensive walls could be dispensed with and water was plentiful (*see below*). Some of its statues are in the archaeological museum. It it is dated to the 2nd century AD. The Forum of Arcadius, which we know from an inscription found nearby, could have been in this area. It could be under the modern bus station.

The layout of the sea wall is known: it went all around the peninsula except for the **harbour** itself, but today only stumps are left.

Inside the town you can see a number of main axes. From the main gate to the harbour, the line of the **colonnaded street** (now Liman Cd.) is known in its entire length. The east section is tarmacked and open to car traffic beyond the arch, where it took a turn to the southwest in the direction of the temple area (*see below*). The **arch**, which was blocked up when the city shrank and has now been reopened, is far from monumental though it might have looked more imposing with its original marble cladding. There may also have been an important sculpture group on its summit.

From the main gate another colonnaded **street** ran southwest and met an axis coming from the east gate towards the theatre. This is as much as we know of the ancient city plan. There is evidence of regular Roman insulae in some parts but not of an overall gridding system. Sources point to a division of the city into four quarters (Quadriga, Altar of Zeus, Great Gate and Great Guild).

Another significant wall of Side is the **late antique cross wall**, 300m long and running north–south where the theatre is. It is made up of different sections. At the bottom, the remains of a terrace wall connected with the theatre (before the 2nd century AD). On top of that, using large spolia blocks, the Byzantines built a defence to about a height of 10m. Later the structure was topped with small spolia and tiles for a further 4.5m, obliterating the wall walk. The arch (*see above*) was blocked. The east town was cut off and access was via a narrow passage between the theatre scena and the fountain. There was another postern to the south. The wall was originally dated by an inscription to AD 330 (when Side was not on the defensive) but it appears that the inscription had been incorporated with spolia from elsewhere and the wall was in fact later, a reaction to the outrages of the 7th century.

A familiar sight of Side are the five Corinthian columns supporting a pediment and facing the blue sea at the top end of the peninsula. They show that the Sidetans liked to keep their gods close to the harbour for protection, good luck or welcome. The two main gods of Side were **Athena and Apollo** and here they had their temples, side by side in full glory, until Christianity took over. At that time, the temples, probably already ruinous, was quarried for material for the magnificent **Byzantine basilica**, facing the sea and resplendent with marble, 35m by 25m with a nave and two aisles, a polygonal apse and a synthronon. Its marble screen had a topical pomegranate decoration. The temenos of the temple was its atrium. The neo-Hittite lotus capital, dated variously to the 9th–7th century BC and which turned up during works in this area, remains unexplained. It can be admired in the garden of the museum.

Men, an Anatolian deity whose cult was centred in the city of Pisidian Antioch (*see Blue Guide Central Anatolia*) and spread as far as modern Afghanistan, is connected with the moon. The god, normally represented with two crescents growing from his shoulders (and which are thought to have been adapted into angels' wings in Christian iconography), had his temple here, suitably positioned at the end of the colonnaded street. It consisted of a semicircular cella set on a podium with columns in front. It is dated to the 3rd century AD. Another temple is just north of the theatre; because of this proximity it is believed to have been dedicated to the cult of **Dionysus**.

The **theatre** is certainly one of the best sights in Side. It may have lost its scena (three storeys high with the usual array of niches, columns, statues and reliefs), which was in due course incorporated in the new defences, but the cavea is in very good condition, only the top row of seats has been lost; it had a loggia for the governor in late antique times. Its capacity is estimated to have been 15,000. It is dated to the 2nd century AD, with alterations of a century later to accommodate combats with wild beasts and gladiatorial performances. It was made of tufa and limestone blocks and rested in part on a natural slope. Note the row of backed benches for dignitaries. It was maintained until the 5th–6th century. The two chapels built into either side of the cavea may be a memorial to the mid-3rd-century Martyrs of Side, thrown to the beasts and, according to legend, untouched by them.

The theatre was originally connected via passages in the scena to the **Commercial Agora** to the east. This brings us to an area that has not yet been concreted over and which, if it were ever excavated, may reveal some of the secrets of Side. Side had two agoras: the commercial one and another space just south of it which is believed to have been the locus of the imperial cult. Side received the neokorate several times and the emperor must have been revered somewhere. The Commercial Agora is the better known. Roughly a square, 60m by 60m, it had a monumental entrance to the north directly from the colonnaded street. Off centre a round temple, now rebuilt, may have been sacred to **Tyche**. A temple of this sort, with a conical roof, does appear on Side's coins. A stoa ran all around the agora and a marble-lined **latrine**, with seating for 24, is in the northwest corner beyond an arched passage. There are baths nearby; these as well as the aqueduct, which arrived in the city at this point, would have provided the means for continuous flushing of the latrines. The outer façade of the stoa to the north had space for statues but the agora itself was devoted to business, shops and the slave market.

The **Civic Agora** is less well understood. It was believed first to be a palaestra but there is no accompanying gymnasium. It measures 88m by 69m with a **portico** on three sides, but has no shops. It housed a number of statues of Greek and Roman gods and of a number of emperors. The Sidetans, committed traders as they were, were loth to waste any money. When the agora was refurbished at the time of the Tetrarchy, in the late 3rd century, the statues were reused, with new heads carved to fit the existing bodies. This was common practice at the time but the Sidetans appear to have been particularly good at it. You can judge for yourself from the examples in the museum.

East of the commercial agora is a large building, an amorphous shell of masonry, Byzantine in style, and now known as Side's **Hospital**. It has not been excavated and the identification is based on a passage by Procopius stating that Justinian built a hospital in Side. It is a bit thin as evidence goes; we shall see. Further to the east, not far from the line of the wall, was a large complex 210m by 125m, the religious heart of Side, fronting a colonnaded street. It contained a 60m long, three-aisled **church with a baptistery**, dated to the 5th–6th century; other structures around with vaulted rooms have been attributed to a bishop's palace set in a large garden with cisterns. The development of the area is not fully understood: it may in due course have been turned into a monastery.

A number of **cisterns** shows how water was supplied up to the late 2nd century when the aqueduct was built. A few have been identified in the area of the museum. The water for the **aqueduct** was tapped upstream from the Melas (now the Manavgat Çay), where a huge karstic spring empties into the river. The water was then conveyed via tunnels, pipes and channels over arches and bridges for 30km to Side. Some remains are still visible. Unfortunately 3km of the upper part of the works, where most of the tunnels were, is now drowned in the Oymapınar Dam. The facility was rebuilt in the late 3rd century, after the Goths' siege, by Lollianus Bryonianus, a local bureaucrat who had married money, risen to equestrian rank and appears, by the statues of him and of family in the main street, by the nymphaeum and in the theatre, to have been the chief benefactor of Side and on a grand scale. Thus were fed private homes, the fountains and the baths, of which three have been identified.

One of the baths is now the **Museum** (*open daily April–Oct 9–7, Nov–March 8–5; charge*), where you can admire the artworks that have been discovered in Side, including a couple of sphinxes from the theatre and, not far from them, the statue of a Roman emperor dated by the style of the armour to the 2nd century while the head was reworked to depict a 4th-century ruler (in the process the head became disproportionately small). While you visit, appreciate the layout of the baths, where you could progress on a circuit from cool bath (frigidarium) to steam room (sudatorium) to warm bath (caldarium) to cool bath (tepidarium), then changing room (apodyterium) and exit, without ever retracing your steps. The garden, situated on the original palaestra, is used to display the larger exhibits, among a profusion of flowers and strutting peacocks.

PRACTICAL INFORMATION

GETTING THERE AND AROUND

Antalya airport to the east of the city is your reference point. There is a shuttle (Bus 600) from the airport to the *otogar* in Antalya itself and the airport is also connected to the city by tram, for which you can buy a ticket at the stop outside the domestic terminal (have some coins with you). Practically all the sites listed here will be available to visit on organised tours. The alternative is to hire a car, which can be done at the airport. From the *otogar* on the west edge of Antalya there are coaches to a wide number of destinations.

WHERE TO STAY

Accommodation in the area is concentrated in **Side**, right at the tip of the peninsula. Here building restrictions apply because of the archaeology, so there are no big buildings but a sprawl of small rooms, with plenty of ups and downs (steps and ramps) and in a fine setting full of flowers. Try the **Leda Beach Hotel** next to the museum (*ledabeachhotel.com; T: 90 242 753 1046*), which offers an exceptional breakfast spread, or the **Yükser Pansiyon** (*yukser-pansiyon.com; T: 90 242 753 2010*), an interesting stone building with a car park in a quiet spot in Lale Sk.

WHERE TO EAT

In **Side**, the tip of the peninsula is crammed with eateries competing for space with the souvenir shops. The **Elia Restaurant** (a name inspired by olives) overlooking the harbour will serve you some fabulous fish. The restaurant is open-air, perfect for a warm summer evening.

WHAT TO DO

For the **Aspendos International Opera and Ballet Festival**, see p. 153–4.

North of Manavgat, go canoeing, rafting or hiking in the **Köprülü Canyon** (*koprulucanyon.com*) in the stunning national park of the same name.

ROUGH CILICIA

East of Side you enter Cilicia, an umbrella term for two regions that are really very different. Taking one of the proposed starting points of Cilicia, that is Alanya (*map C, 7*), the coastline stretches for well over 400km to the barrier of the Amanus Mountains, now the Nur Dağları, the 'Mountains of Light'. Over time the distinction between the west and the east portions developed and they became known respectively as **Cilicia Trachea** (from the Greek meaning 'rugged') and **Cilicia Pedias** (from the Greek meaning 'flat'). In English those regions have become Rough Cilicia and Smooth Cilicia and the traditional border between them is the Limonlu (*map D, 5*) river.

The name Cilicia is said to be related to the Assyrian *Que* and is more likely to have referred to **Smooth Cilicia** (the area covered by the next chapter) since it was here that the Assyrians had their entry point into Asia Minor. At least, that was the case in the early 2nd millennium BC, when with the blessing of the local ruler, Assyrian merchants set up a trading colony there to tap the riches of Anatolia, and also a thousand years later, when the Assyrian Empire expanded into upper Mesopotamia. Controlling the Cilician Gates, the gap between the Taurus and the Anti-Taurus, was vital in both cases. Although this was not the only entry point to the Anatolian Plateau (nor a particularly easy one, at over 1000m altitude and very narrow), the alternative, up the Göksu Valley in the hinterland of Silifke, was a long way off to the west. This much was also known to the Hittites, who gained control of the Hurrian kingdom of Kizzuwatna to access Syria. One can say therefore that Smooth Cilicia was an area of international and strategic importance, with the gateway to the Anatolian Plateau to the north and offering routes across the passes on the Amanus to the east. It so happened that this area was comparatively small, with a challenging geography, a marshy plain bisected by unruly rivers forever changing course, and backed by high mountains with deep-cut valleys. While it managed to make a living throughout prehistory and history, it was never strong enough to resist outside pressure. Its orderly aspect today, with tilled fields, booming cities and a modern network of highways, is very recent. Widespread malaria and abject poverty may now be a thing of the past—but it is a past that is not so distant.

The area covered by this chapter, **Rough Cilicia** (the Assyrian Khilakku), had a completely different historical trajectory. It had no valuable lines of communication to offer and as a result could be—and in the past was—bypassed. Alexander the Great disregarded the area entirely, proceeding in a straight line from Ankara to the Cilician Gates and east, though Rough Cilicia must have been under Persian control then. In addition, it lacked alluvial arable land by the coast or inland, which would have made it difficult to sustain a large urban population. Beyond Alanya, the coast offered no large harbours but instead a myriad small ones, which in due course encouraged the rise of piracy. On the whole, Rough Cilicia is a story of survival in adverse conditions and of neglect. The Greeks did not even try and settle there and most of the Roman activity in the area consisted in pushing the intractable locals, the Isaurians, back up the mountains. In the end it was the Isaurians who came out on top (*see box*).

YOU CALL ME PIRATE?

Cilicia and pirates are two words that often go together. But piracy was not a Cilician invention; it was as widespread in antiquity as raiding, its equivalent on land. Private entrepreneurs indulged in it as much as states. Moreover, the latter used the suppression of piracy as a handy excuse to intervene in other people's affairs. A few examples will suffice. At the height of its power, Athens raided and plundered lesser states as a way of 'encouraging' them to sign up to friendship treaties. Its definition of clearing the seas of pirates was wide and comprehensive: it was the perfect excuse for any sort of hostile action. The Romans did no less, having might on their side. In 338 BC, when they wanted to create a veteran colony at Antium, which entailed dispossessing the locals, they presented it as an anti-piratical operation. They did the same in the Balearic Islands and with the Ligurians.

In spite of these anti-piratical operations, piracy was rife in the whole breadth of the Mediterranean, but particularly well entrenched in the east, along the stretch of coast that the Romans needed in order to control access to Syria, Mesopotamia and ultimately Egypt. This, in other words, meant the Gulf of Antalya and the coast of Rough Cilicia. The latter, though poor and short of natural resources, had a particular physical makeup that was favourable to small, local, private initiatives. The rocky coast provided a myriad small coves and shelters, the sort of topography where local knowledge is indispensable. After the Ptolemies lost control of this stretch of coast, where they had developed a few small harbours to tap the inland timber resources, the locals took over and, it is said, expanded into slave raiding and other nefarious activities.

Those locals were the **Isaurians**, the perfect example in antiquity of the pirate as 'barbarian' and 'other'. They took neither to Greek niceties nor to Roman rule; they preferred the hideouts of the Taurus peaks to the protection of the emperor. They were content to carry on their business, using the small harbours and coves and keeping their families and riches inland in defended sites (there are some polygonal towers in Rough Cilicia that still await explanation), possibly often relocating. This applies to Zeniketes, who had his headquarters at Olympus (*p. 114*) and to Rough Cilicia. The coastal cities (e.g. Antalya, Side and Alanya) were complicit in providing a market, and though Rome railed about the practice, it did so only half-heartedly.

The Romans had begun to tackle the problem in the early 1st century BC, when their relentless drive east, which began with the Illyrian wars of 229–219 BC, brought them this far. After various attempts, it was Pompey the Great who brought the problem under control, mainly by turning pirates into legitimate rulers, as in the case of Tarcondimotus (*p. 231*), or by setting up colonies of ex-pirates (e.g. Adana, Epiphania and Soli). This approach bought some 200 years of peace but by AD 260, according to the *Historia Augusta* (Life of Probus), the highland was autonomous and later Rough Cilicia became known as Isauria.

On the whole the Isaurians managed to cling to their own ways longer than the other natives of the long Mediterranean coast. They remained pagan well into the 5th century and even when they enrolled in the Byzantine army they were still perceived as outsiders, as the slaughter of the Isaurians in Byzantium's hippodrome in AD 473 suggests. In the end, one of their number joined the establishment, so to speak. Tarasis Kodisa Rousombladadiotes, better known as Emperor Zeno, obtained the purple after pursuing a brilliant career as a mercenary in the Byzantine army and marrying the emperor's daughter.

APPROACHING ALANYA: ALARAHAN & ŞARAPSA HAN

As you come into Alanya from the west, you can take the route a sultan would have followed when going to or from Konya (*map C, 3*). A couple of well-preserved hans are well worth your time if you have your own transport.

First the **Alarahan** (*map C, 5*), on the banks of a stream, is reached by taking the inland turn at Okurcalar. It is about 9km. There is a convenient picnic place nearby and the building is by the road, close to a disused bridge. The han, dated by inscription to 1231, was possibly built by Sultan Alaeddin Keykubad I, after he had expanded Seljuk dominion to the sea. The style and tone of the inscription, with such honorific terms as 'Lord of the Universe, Exalted King of Kings', speaks of a victorious sultan at his apogee. He had plans for the south coast (*see below*) and wanted suitable arrangements to travel to and from Konya. The building is quite large, 35m by 45m, in finely jointed limestone ashlars, and has the standard fortress-like appearance from the outside. The layout results in a very crowded space, with a narrow corridor in the middle and passages at the sides for animals to reach their allotted stalls at the back. Apart from the central corridor, all the rest is vaulted and covered. It must have been stifling in hot weather. The outside obviously has no windows: ventilation in the presence of the usual complement of animals could be a problem. It could be that the han was not originally destined for travellers but was reserved for the sultan and his suite, which would have meant fewer people and fewer animals. Some of the rooms could have been stores or archives. The decoration is unusually abundant, with stone lighting apparatus in the shape of lions, 79 of them carved out of reused marble, and traces of red chevrons (the sultan's signature motif) on the back wall. It has been recently restored and today it houses shops and a restaurant. The central corridor is now covered.

The **Alara Kale**, roughly contemporary, is 700m up the road but at the time of writing it was closed for safety reasons and only viewable from a distance.

Alarahan would have been the Sultan's second stopping place on the way to Konya. The first one was **Şarapsa Han**, 14km east of Alarahan on Route 400, next to the road (*always accessible but not in the evening, when it is used for private functions*). It was built between 1237 and 1246 by Giyaseddin Keyhüsrev to an extraordinary and unique plan. It is a single barrel-vaulted room 70m long and 15m wide with an entrance from the north end, making it an ideal setting for banquets. It also had a mosque. The structure seems unsuitable for a han but it would have worked for a small party, with the animals and servants outside and the inner space divided by screens.

ALANYA

On reaching Alanya (*map C, 7*), you enter another world. Here you leave behind the plain of Pamphylia and come face to face with the mountains of Rough Cilicia. Alanya is built on one of them (as the main road approaches the town, it cuts through a tunnel), probably once originally an island which became connected to the mainland by a low, sandy isthmus. It may be merely 260m in height but bear in mind that 47km northeast of Alanya, the Geyik Dağları rise to over 3000m and that this mountainous landscape goes on for quite a distance; it is a land of fine stands of timber, ideal for shipbuilding.

FROM CORACESIUM TO ALANYA: THE HISTORY

Alanya certainly has a past. In an **excellent defensive position** on the rock and with some form of harbour to the east (although not very sheltered; the southerly winds can be troublesome), it was possibly occupied well before it enters the historical record in the mid-4th century BC as a throwaway remark in a list of Mediterranean harbours. The peninsula was then known as **Coracesium**, which is variously translated as 'crow's nest' or simply 'rock'. It would have been in Persian hands then, but control was loose in many parts of their empire and Coracesium may have been occupied by a local strongman. In due course, defences went up, those very same that defeated the Syrian Seleucians when they besieged it in 197 BC. Livy judged it impregnable. It eventually became part of the Seleucians' dominion and if we are to believe Strabo (*14,5,1*), a hideout of **slave-dealing pirates**, one of the many pirate bands that Pompey eventually defeated. In the uncertain days following Caesar's assassination, Coracesium found itself playing the role of lovers' gift, when Mark Antony presented it to Cleopatra. The town sailed through the **Roman era** completely unrecorded. It is quite possible that Roman development was on the mainland. In any case, Roman finds are scarce: a handful of inscriptions in nearby villages and evidence of minting from the time of Trajan. Alanya does not figure on the itinerary of 19th-century antiquarians and explorers, suggesting that there was not very much visible in the way of remains. But since it became a popular tourist destination in the 1980s, Alanya has been through a building boom and development would have cleared away anything on the rock. It must have been a substantial enough settlement, however, since it had a bishop. The position of Bishop of Coracesium is now vacant but it was filled up to 1970.

The rebirth of Coracesium came at the hand of the **Byzantines**, who gave it a new name, Kalonoros ('Beautiful Mountain'). It formed part of their plan to strengthen their presence in the Mediterranean to counteract the Persian and Arab threats. Their presence has only left a few traces, in the form of a couple of churches on the citadel. The Byzantine fortifications were later swallowed up in Seljuk work. At the same time Kalonoros (or **Candeloro**, or Skandeloro, or other variants) appears in portulans, suggesting the presence of harbour facilities available to European traders.

The Alanya we see today is the **Seljuk Alanya**. After they set up the Sultanate of Rum, the victorious Seljuks looked north and south and rapidly became masters of both the Mediterranean and the Black Sea shores (Antalya in 1207; Sinop in 1214). Alanya (1221) took a little bit longer because by then it had fallen ito the hands of Lord Kir Vard, an Armenian (*for more on the Aremian presence, see below*) who controlled other positions in the hinterland. He came to a satisfactory arrangement with the new power, took up a position in the Seljuk hierarchy as governor of Akşehir and sealed the pact by giving his daughter in marriage to the sultan.

ARMENIANS BY THE SEA

Historically, the Armenians' core land is the region immediately south of the Caucasus, more or less where the present Republic of Armenia is now. In their heyday, however, at the time of Tigranes the Great, who played his cards well in the turbulent times of the 1st century BC, they occupied a larger portion of eastern Asia Minor from the Caucasus down to Syria and—what is relevant here—stretching west into Cilicia. By AD 147, however, the Roman Province of Armenia only took in the upper reaches of the Euphrates up to the Araxes.

In 1045, King Gacik of Ani had been forced from his throne by the Byzantines. The Armenians resettled in Anatolia and started trickling through to Cilicia. At the time the Byzantines were busy regaining control of the south coast and were keen to settle the area with people who would be more friendly to them than either the Turkish nomads streaming in from Syria or the marauding Crusaders. It is for this reason that we find Armenians as far west as Antiocheia ad Cragum.

Whatever arrangement the Byzantines had in mind concerning the Armenian settlement, it was soon irrelevant, since not long after forcing the Armenians to move south, the Byzantines lost the Battle of Manzikert and plunged their empire into turmoil. The Armenians proceeded their own way. Being mountain people they eschewed the plain, preferring to settle up the valleys of the Taurus. They set up a network of inter-visible castles and strongholds to protect the civilian population and the commercial routes. Until the Mongols embraced Islam (officially in 1304), which forbade business with infidels, the two got on very well, with the Armenians supplying troops to the Mongols and ensuring that the trade routes stayed open. The Armenian king Hetum travelled all the way to Karakorum, then the Mongolian capital, to conclude the negotiations.

Soon the main port was Ayas (*pp. 216–7*), the last entry point for European traders to the East after the fall of Acre in 1291. The Armenians controlled this harbour as well as a number of important passes (notably the Cilician Gates), taking money from dues and keeping the grandees loyal. They occupied the castles and left the cities to the Greeks and the Latin merchants.

The Armenian kingdom in Cilicia lasted about 200 years. At its maximum extent it stretched north to the Taurus Mountains watershed. Westwards it reached well into the coast of Rough Cilicia and eastwards continued as far as today's Gaziantep and just north of Antioch (Antakya). It was drawn into the Muslim-Crusader conflict and ultimately consumed by it; the steady trickle of Türkmen from the East was another aggravating factor. Ultimately the Armenians were let down by their loose power structure, whereby the king was just a baron who had been crowned. The final blow came in 1375, when the Mamluks captured King Levon V and took him to Cairo. After being ransomed he died in Paris (and was buried in St-Denis). The title of King of Armenia passed to the Lusignans of Cyprus and eventually to the House of Savoy. The last King of Armenia, therefore, could be said to have been Umberto II of Italy, who died in 1983.

The Seljuks at the height of their power had ambitions for Candeloro. It could be used as a base to conquer Cyprus (only 160km away), on which the Seljuks had their sights, and the sultan had a plan to revitalise the coast.

The Seljuks' work is visible both on the rock and (through the painstaking work of Scott Redford) on the mainland (*see box overleaf*). The Hellenistic walls were repaired and rebuilt and the whole peninsula was enclosed within a circuit (*as seen on the plan on p. 172*), with towers along the line of the precipitous cliffs, and a ditch (8m wide and 4m deep) at the north end, where the lie of the land is more gentle. The east end was redesigned as shipsheds for construction and repairs (the Tersane), defended by a separate wall and a massive tower. Two defended enclosures were established to the north (Ehmedek) and west (İç Kale). The residential part of town was on the east slope overlooking the Tersane, as is shown in an early 16th-century map by the cartographer and navigator Piri Reis (though the map is not totally accurate). But first Candeloro received a new name. From now on it was to be **Ala'iyyia**, after Alaeddin (the 'n' of modern 'Alanya' is intrusive).

The Seljuk building programme required the relocation of artisans and craftsmen. Where the original beautiful Hellenistic ashlar construction could not be matched, plaster was spread onto rough mortared rubble and finely drawn lines were painted on the surface, imitating the antique style. Marble, although in short supply in the area, was nonetheless indispensable. The sultan treasured it and believed that his name engraved in marble had more power, thus his inscriptions are on (reused) marble. This superstition was also extended to projectiles, as marble ones were thought to travel further (this may account for the shortage of marble spolia). After the Battle of Kösedağ (1243), which turned the Seljuk Empire into a vassal state of the Mongols, the sultans probably spent more time on the coast as Anatolia was no longer as safe, eventually losing power to the local emirs, in this case the Karamanid dynasty. When the **Ottomans** conquered it, Alanya was insignificant. An earlier visit by the indefatigable traveller Ibn Battuta (*p. 22*) found the local emir relaxing in his garden by the shore and indulging in his opium addiction. For Beaufort (*p. 23*) in 1811, Alanya was 'desolate'. Some 1,500 people lived there, living mainly from the export of wood to Egypt.

Since the 1980s Alanya has been a mighty **tourist hub** with a population of over 200,000.

RELAXING LIKE A SULTAN

Alaeddin Keykubad I changed Alanya forever by turning it into a fortified harbour. The sultan had Cyprus in his sights, but Seljuk power did not last long. After the Battle of Kösedağ in the mid-13th century, it was largely diminished and the sultans, now vassals of the Mongols, were short of funds. This did not stop them making the most of their enforced stay on the south coast: winters were milder here and the Mongols were on the other side of the mountains. Sources mention too that the sultans were concerned with revitalising the economy, encouraging Türkmen to occupy the countryside and develop a pastoral economy, making the most of the winter pastures, the *kışla*, by the coast and moving north into the mountains in summer. The aim may have been to keep in check the unruly mountain tribes and take over the exploitation of the timber resources.

According to Ibn Battuta, mid-14th-century Alanya was mainly populated by Türkmen. Agriculture was also encouraged on a limited scale by developing orchards with figs, almonds, pomegranates and olive trees. Irrigation would add cherries, plums and apricots. Scott Redford has identified the sites of some of these orchards in the proximity of Alanya on the shores of the short rivers that gush down from the Taurus. Physical remains have included evidence of high enclosure walls (too high for deer?), tanks with a piping system, and a two-storey building affording fine views. These are the places where a sultan and his court would have lived like their 'cousins' the Great Seljuks of Persia, who had relaxed at their leisure in magnificent gardens, those *paradeisoi* of Persian miniatures. In Alanya the infrastructure was less grand but the purpose was the same: fine views, plenty of greenery, trickling water, gentle breezes, a life inspired by poetry. The pleasures would have been similar to those afforded by the Kubadabad Palace by Lake Beyşehir, west of Konya (*map C, 3*), or the Keykubadiye, another Seljuk palace recently identified on the site of a sugar factory on the outskirts of Kayseri (*map D, 2*). Hunting was another sultanic pursuit, a mark of rank. The Taurus Mountains certainly provided plenty of game, including gazelle, lynxes and leopards. These pavilions scattered on the lower slopes would have made an excellent starting point for expeditions.

Today there are various ways to get to the top of the hill at Alanya: by car, by cable car or on foot. If you choose the last option, you should start from the east side by the Red Tower (*see plan overleaf*), where the slope is gentle. Alternatively, take the cable car from the west end of the Cleopatra Beach and come down on foot on the east side.

THE RED TOWER AND TERSANE

The **Red Tower** (**Kızıl Kule**; *open April–Oct 9–7, Nov–March 8–5; combined ticket with the Tersane*) is an octagonal building incorporated into the defensive wall, over 30m tall. It looks very plain from the outside but hides a complex plan, articulated over five storeys connected with stone stairs. The roof is a terrace surrounded by crenellations. The central pier is a cistern, accessible from the fourth floor. It supplied the nearby fountain to the west and the hamam. There are no springs on the rock, which means that rainwater cisterns had to be plentiful: some 400 of them have been recorded. The Red Tower is built of rubble and limestone blocks, incorporating a few column drums, except for the top end, which is of red brick. This has given it its present name and is the result of restoration work in the 1970s. On the north façade, where the entrance is, an inscription gives the name of the Syrian builder, Abu Ali Reha el Kett. On the south face the sultan is exalted as 'Ruler of the Nations, Keeper of the Peace'. It was once thought, in view of the steepness of the hill, that the sultan had his apartments here. It has been calculated that on horseback it would have taken at least an hour to get to sea level from the top, even if the steps of the path were adjusted for horses. However, the nearby tower (now ruinous), close to the fountain and the baths, now seems more likely. It is not known where the emirs lived. Today the Red Tower houses the city's Ethnographic Museum.

From the Red Tower a path leads to the magnificent **Tersane** or **Arsenal**. Built and excavated in the rock, the structures were meant for military use by the Seljuks: they are a necessary adjunct to a military harbour, which is what Seljuk Alanya originally was. The building, of an irregular rectangular shape, had a storeroom and an office at the entrance (note the inscription in Neski, a cursive form of Arabic, above it). The five sheds vary in length from 43m to 32m and are situated at slightly different levels to minimise the necessity of cutting into the rock. Well placed away from the winter storms, they would have been suitable for ship-building and repair: they could be used all year round. The rooms are interconnected and open to the sea, with the boats resting on wooden structures. Over the years the sheds have filled up with debris and sand while erosion has affected the shape of the entrances. Going by their size, the sheds would have accommodated boats with 14 to 18 rows of oars with three men per oar. These vessels could not carry any artillery. The sheds had a long life as they were still being used by local fishermen in the very recent past.

THE WALLS

To appreciate the walls of Alanya, the best way is to walk around them and have a look: you can do this almost entirely free of charge; however, you will need a ticket for İç Kale (*open Nov–March 8–5, April–Oct 9–6.30; charge*). The walls are 6.5km long and built by a variety of hands. According to standard Seljuk custom, they were paid for by the emirs.

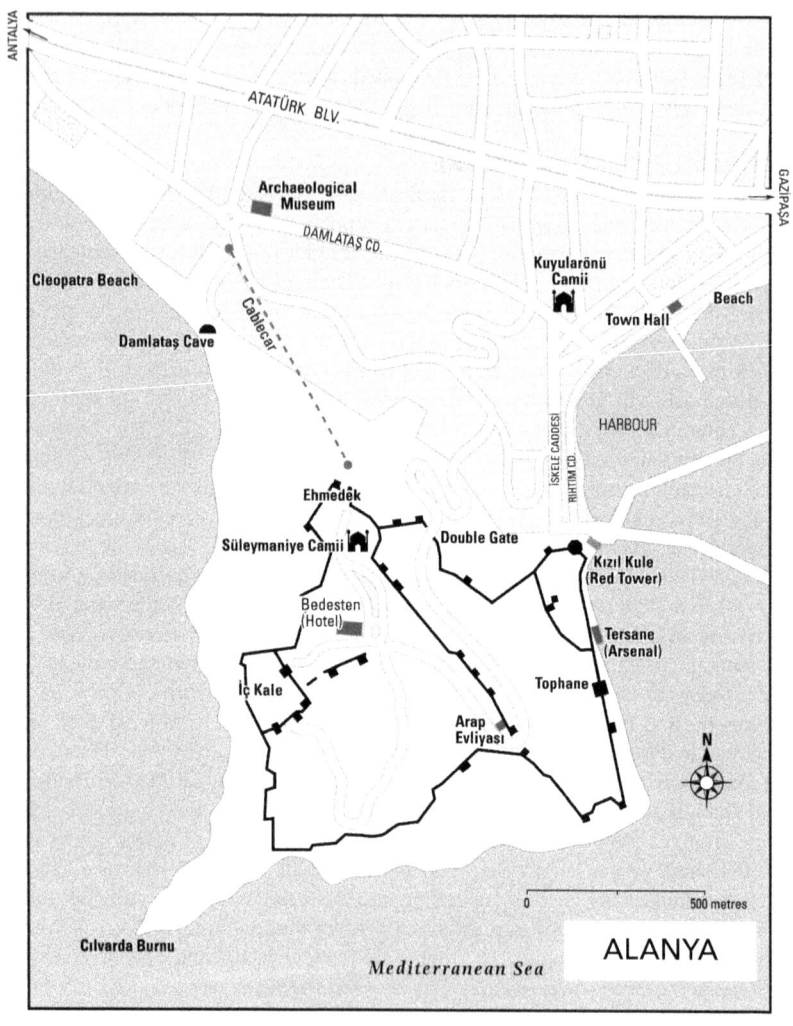

The lower part of the Hellenistic wall can be seen near the **Arap Evliyası**, where the road makes a sharp bend. Arap Evliyası is a chapel, 6m by 6m, that reuses a tower of the Hellenistic wall and was respected by the Muslim builders in Seljuk times when they made repairs. Mindful of their brief (to build a wall), however, they added crenellations to its roof. It later became a small mosque. Its style, with a flat brick dome, is of the 11th–12th century. It is thought that it got its name from a nearby tomb, possibly of an Arab saint, suggesting the presence of a Byzantine cemetery in the area.

Following the line of the wall you come to the north fortress, **Ehmedek**, which according to some means 'little Ahmed' and according to others means 'castle in the fortified area' in Chagatai, a now-extinct Turkic language. Whatever the truth, this was built as a stronghold from the beginning, with a ditch as an extra layer of defence. The Ottomans had a garrison here and the buildings were used as a treasury and prison. Immediately to the south is the heart of the settlement with the bedesten, the han and the mosque. The **bedesten**, built by the Karamanoğlu dynasty, is now a hotel. The **han**, which is Ottoman, is a courtyard building with rooms on three sides and a large vaulted extension for stables. Today's **Süleymaniye Camii** is the result of repairs and rebuilding of the original 13th-century mosque by Suleyman the Magnificent in the mid-16th century.

To the west is the **İç Kale**, the inner castle, the ultimate defence. It has an irregular rectangular shape and its own wall circuit. It is also protected by very steep cliffs to the north and west. A Seljuk bath with a heating system has been identified just outside its southeast corner. The fortress, 180m by 150m, bears evidence of Byzantine and Seljuk activity. The Byzantines built a church but there are problems with its plan (a triconch Latin cross with a cupola). This is typical of the 12th–13th century but that is a little bit too late given the history of Alanya. A series of courtyards in the southeast corner leads to a tower that could have been used by the sultan since a decoration of red chevrons on a white background, the Seljuk sultan's signature motif, have been identified. It could have been a residence or an audience room. The same decorative pattern has been used in another feature in the northwest corner between a square tower and a built cistern. There is a breach in the wall overlooking a precipitous cliff. It is popularly known as Adam Atacağı, meaning 'the place where people are thrown'. Here you need to think like a Seljuk sultan and remember how much they liked a view (and it is spectacular here) and a fresh breeze, as afforded by the theatre at Aspendos (*p. 153*), in Konya and by their belvederes: the suggestion of people being thrown from these heights is a myth. From here you can cast a look down on **Cılvarda Burnu**, a long, narrow rocky peninsula now inaccessible except from the sea. The defence walls cut it off and, for good measure, a man-made rift in the rock made land access more difficult. The peninsula housed a Byzantine monastery near the tip.

The **Archaeological Museum** (*open April–Oct 9–7, Nov–March 8–5; charge*), in the centre of Alanya near the tourist office on Damlataş Cd., behind the Cleopatra beach, has been recently renovated. Do not miss the examples of Karamanlı script, which is Turkish written in Greek letters, and the Phoenician inscription from Laertes (*see below*). The nautical hall has a full-size model of a ship laden with wine and oil amphorae and a fine mosaic from Selinus. In the garden you can see ancient stone installations once used to produce olive oil.

After the museum you have the choice of the **Cleopatra Beach** for a good swim, or the **Damlataş Cave** (*open 10–7.30; charge*), signposted at the east side of the beach. The cave is known for its spectacular stalactites and cool, steady temperature of 22–23°C, efficacious for asthma sufferers.

LAERTES, SYEDRA & IOTAPE

From Alanya the shoreline is very rugged and little settled, although it is still followed by the coast road. In the past there may just have been a coastal path and settlement was probably even scarcer: the situation is still not fully understood. There are no spectacular remains which means that archaeologists have shunned the area and only recently has a sustained programme of surveys and excavations been set up. Greek influence seems to wane here. The **scarcity of theatres** has drawn attention. Bearing in mind that theatres are cultural loci as well as places where people assemble and exchange views, one can wonder if perhaps the Ptolemies, who had several footholds here (for timber, slaves and recruiting soldiers), had little use for them and the same applies to the local chieftains who acted as intermediaries in these quests. Although the area could produce wine and oil it could not feed itself and had to import grain; overpopulation was always a risk. It remained in the past a **marginal area**, generally overlooked by the ruling powers, except perhaps the Romans at their height. Along this stretch of coast (until Silifke; *map D, 7*), one must think in terms of urbanism in a different way. There are a few places worth looking at.

LAERTES

The first stop after Alanya going east is Laertes (*map C, 7*), signposted off Route 400 from Mahmutlar in the direction of Gözüküçüklü. The road twists and turns for 8km; it is probably advisable to join a group. It is also possible to combine Laertes with a visit to the spectacular **Sapadere Canyon** (*p. 204*).

Laertes is in a beautiful spot with its ruins all scattered around. So far the site has only been surveyed. According to Strabo (15,5,2) it was a **fortress** on the mountainside with some form of harbour below. Indeed, it added a couple of watch towers to the natural defences. The settlement (identified by an inscription on a statue) appears to have been laid out on terraces. An early **Phoenician presence** can be deduced from a couple of inscriptions now in the museum in Alanya. An **agora** has been identified. It used to be associated with Diogenes Laertius (early 3rd century AD), the author of *Lives and Opinions of Ancient Philosophers*, a work weak in critical judgement and showing a tendency to overlook the general picture for the sake of minor details. He may have been born here, but there is more than one city called Laertes in the antique world. The settlement seems to have been abandoned in the 3rd century. There is no sign of any Christian presence. The main pleasure of visiting Laertes is the sense of discovery and the beautiful views—but be careful where you put your feet.

SYEDRA

The town of Syedra (*map C, 7*) is a couple of kilometres off Route 400 in the direction of Seki. It is signposted. It was a city on a height with its harbour down below, of which nothing now remains.

Syedra emerges from obscurity around the 1st century BC. An **oracular inscription** walled into the later defences appears to testify that the locals were pirates, of the sort that Pompey brought to heel. In the text they call themselves Pamphylians (the word Cilician must have had negative connotations at the time) and ask the oracle to advise them as to their actions. In answer, the oracle made the point that piracy endangered prosperity and that the Romans had taken the view that widespread safety on the seas was more important than the short-term gains of the pirates. The Syedrans seem to have been convinced and gave up their piratical ways, at least for a while—and judging by the remains, the Romans rewarded them. The town was **walled**, bisected by a **colonnaded street** with a **church** on one side and **baths** and a **gymnasium** on the other, as well as an **odeion** or council chamber, a **temple** and numerous **cisterns**. Mosaics from Syedra, especially the **leaping leopard**, can be admired in the museum at Alanya. Syedra appears to have survived to the 13th century, possibly due to its distance from the sea and the good defences which were, in due course, rebuilt.

IOTAPE

Iotape (*map C, 7*) is situated south of Syedra on the old coast road. The turning off Route 400 is about 7.5km after you leave Syedra going south. It is the perfect site as it comes with a **beautiful beach** in an appealing cove, hemmed in by the acropolis to the west. The sea is pure turquoise. If you are lucky, you will have picked a day when no one else has had the same idea.

Iotape is a **Seleucid foundation** since it bears the name of the wife and sister (or possibly daughter) of Antiochus IV Epiphanes, the last king of Commagene. The foundation is dated around AD 52. Very possibly, however, there was something here before that date; finds of Hellenistic pottery seem to suggest as much. Iotape appears to have survived to the 6th century AD, when it is listed by the geographer Hierocles. Otherwise little is known about it. Today it is known locally as Aitab.

The settlement consists of an acropolis, the **peninsula**, and an extension on the **mainland** to the east. The old coast road therefore ran across the city centre. In 1913, Paribeni (*p. 30*) saw a street with marble seats with lion's paws at the base of the isthmus that united the acropolis to the mainland. Iotape was destined to remain small because of its topography. Although it had good access to the hinterland for timber, it could not have fed a large population. Its floruit was in the 2nd century AD. Its **two aqueducts** are now lost because of terracing for banana plantations. The **acropolis**, on the small peninsula, appears to have been **walled**. Inside, it was densely settled. To the east on the opposite shore are the remains of a **bath** and of a vaulted structure, possibly an administrative building, and a Byzantine **church**. Back in the 1960s, George Bean (*p. 22*) saw some statue bases not far from the beach. They may have belonged to the **Temple of Trajan**, now identified as having been here facing the sea. Another temple was identified at the east end of the city.

The **residential area** was beyond the modern road, spread out on terraces on the hillside. Here a small church has been identified. The **necropolis** is on the hillside along the modern road to the east. It had some Hellenistic-style temple-tombs. The site is not prepared for tourists, so exercise caution when exploring.

SELINUS

The ruins of Selinus, in the modern town of Gazipaşa (*map C, 7*), are on the south side of the modern harbour, reached by taking the turning west off Route 400 (*signposted*). This is one of those rare spots in Rough Cilicia where there is alluvial soil—as you can tell by the proliferation of modern greenhouses. Because of this peculiarity, Selinus is presumed to have had a long history, although the water from the river was very hard and it glued together the pebbles on the beach. The port facilities were not of the finest and in Roman times it required an aqueduct, of which a few arches are still extant. The **ancient town** was scattered on the slope facing the south bank of the stream, now the İnceağrı Çayı. If you venture to the top of the slope (there are steps cut in the rock but also a lot of undergrowth) you can see (on a good day) as far as Cyprus. Here on the very edge of a steep cliff are the remains of a **stronghold**, continually rebuilt since its possible Hellenistic origins (as suggested by the lower ashlar courses) right up until Ottoman times, with Byzantine and Armenian interventions. It may be identified with the Castello Lombardo which features on some portulans, although it has not been investigated. The early settlement may have been around here since the river had a tendency to flooding.

Selinus flourished in **Roman** times, when it acquired the monuments we see today. In the late antique period it shrunk to a defended enclosure by the south bank of the river mouth. Here in the early 19th century, Francis Beaufort (*p. 23*) saw the remains of terraces with houses, of the defence wall and of numerous cisterns; he made a fine drawing of the castle viewed from the sea, showing that it stood on an impressive sheer cliff. Under the **Byzantines**, in their bid to take control of the coast, Selinus enjoyed a revival, as the remains of three churches attest (including a large one dedicated to Agia Tekla) and again in the 13th century, when its main monument was reworked by the **Seljuks** as a hunting lodge or pleasure pavilion. They may originally have had grander plans for Selinus but the Mongols put paid to them. There are no known Seljuk trade routes or hans further east along this coast.

EXPLORING SELINUS

Selinus is getting ready for tourists by improving the access road. In due course the ruins will be landscaped: at the moment, be prepared to cross ditches and hedges. The monuments are visible from the road to your left as you drive in.

The most important monument is **Trajan's cenotaph** at the foot of the hill. This would have been the centre of the Roman town. The agora is just a little way to the west. It is here that Trajan died, after suffering a stroke, in August 117 on his way back by ship from Antioch at the end of his failed Parthian campaign. The campaign failed because although he invaded Mesopotamia, the Romans found themselves unable to hold it and Hadrian, Trajan's successor, promptly gave it up. The cenotaph stands here in remembrance of the great emperor; in the same spirit the town for a while renamed itself **Traianopolis**. Trajan's body was taken to Antioch where it was cremated. The ashes then went to Rome and were buried in the base of his eponymous column.

The original cenotaph building was placed off-centre within a peristyle (84m by 84m), open to the river to the north. It had columns on four sides of which only one was left when Freya Stark (*p. 32*) visited. Such a structure conforms very much to the taste of the time and indeed it is dated by style rather than by inscriptions, although we know from Cassius Dio (*68,33*) that Trajan died here. What you see today is the **podium** on which the monument stood; the superstructure was lost in the Seljuk reworking. The podium contained two low, barrel-vaulted rooms (about 6m by 7m each) built in massive ashlars and separated by an equally massive wall: sturdy foundations were necessary to support the superstructure. A narrow staircase led up from the back room to the cella above, which was entered from the north. The cella was marble-paved. It had fluted marble pilasters in the corners, as Beaufort noted. It has been estimated that the Roman monument was about 13m wide and 20m tall. When the Seljuks assumed control of Selinus about a thousand years later, they reworked the monument, which was already probably ruinous. They used the marble ashlars from the superstructure, the cella, to build a wall around the podium and filled the gap with rubble. As a result the outer wall of the podium, which had been 3m thick in the Roman construction, measured 4.6m in the Seljuk building. Differences in building styles between the two skins are quite clear. The Roman podium was faced with marble reliefs while the Seljuk podium was plastered and painted with thin red lines imitating ashlar masonry. On the north façade, the medieval builders constructed an iwan, with the characteristic pointed arch, to the right of the entrance and to the left a flight of steps. They painted red chevrons around the entrance. How the upper part of the structure was arranged is not clear because any Seljuk work has been lost. It could have been a belvedere or viewing platform.

Other remains of interest in Selinus include a small **odeion** cut in the rock to the west and substantial ruins of **baths** by the river, which were fed by the aqueduct. In 1913 Paribeni (*p. 30*) saw the remains of a nymphaeum against the bath walls.

ANTIOCHIA AD CRAGUM

For Antiochia ad Cragum (*map C, 7*) you will need your own transport. It is near the village of Güneyköy, some 20km south of Gazipaşa, and indicated with a brown sign to the west, off Route 400.

Beaufort (*p. 23*) was right to survey this bit of coast in 1812, when his instructions were to search for possible hiding places of the Napoleonic fleet. There is some protected anchorage even for large vessels here, away from the strong west currents in the busy coastline, where the sea is quite deep. This was appreciated in the ancient world too, as the scatterings of Hellenistic pottery testify. The settlement lay some way away from the harbour to the east, laid out on terraces after a steep ascent, although the Hellenistic occupation has been obscured by the reworking of the ground to accommodate Roman and later developments. Moreover, in recent times, the area has found a new focus in banana plantations, hence more disturbance of the terrain.

The name of the settlement probably refers to a **Hellenistic foundation** (the name

Antiochia suggests a Seleucid ancestry; the 'Cragum' is a reference to the mountain nearby). The location looks well-suited to **piracy** and finds of wine amphorae suggest as much, since pirates in these parts are known to have traded slaves for wine. However, in Roman times the people gave up their old ways and came to appreciate the benefits of the new way of life, as the remains suggest. In the 5th century the harbour still had a role to play; the **Byzantine stronghold** (a walled enclosure protected by towers) on the promontory is telling; it was occupied as late as the 12th century by the Armenians and then by the Knights Hospitallers. The references to a **bishopric** in Antiochia may allude to this settlement, which had its necropolis on a promontory to the south. The settlement inland had been abandoned around the 7th century.

Research has focused on the harbour and the inland settlement. An underwater survey in the **harbour** has found anchors, ship ornaments and steps leading to the top of the promontory, although these remains could be difficult to date. The main research has centred on the settlement inland. The town had an **acropolis**, 300m above sea level to the south, on a hill which drops away in precipitous cliffs. A section of the **colonnaded street**, over 100m long with monolithic columns in granite from the Troad (some 700km away as the crow flies), has been identified in the middle of town. It had a monumental gate to the east and to the northeast an **imperial temple** of modest dimensions (7m by 10m) was set on concrete foundations covering a vaulted structure (according to remote sensing), which judging by its style is thought to be from the second half of the 2nd century. Elements of its decoration suggest that it functioned as a kind of inexpensive **oracle**, which worked by throwing dice and then looking up the answer on a list of possible combinations.

Antiochia has recently been in the news because of the find of an extensive **geometric mosaic** surrounding the oval pool of the baths in this area. At the time of writing the mosaic was covered so it could not yet be admired.

Work is in progress at Antiochia and there is a lot to be done. The **gymnasium** and the **basilica** are waiting to be explored and all this means working around the modern buildings that encroach on the site. It is tiring to work here, in full sun, with a lot of up- and downhill. But volunteers are numerous and enthusiastic. And at the end of the day, there is always a perfect swim to look forward to, something which is freely available to visitors as well.

THE ANAMUR HEADLAND

The modern road continues southeast relentlessly, through a rugged landscape, until it reaches a point where Cyprus is merely 72km away. This spot is the Anamur headland, on the same latitude as Tunis, towering above the sea. Immediately beyond the cape, sheltered from the biting winds that probably gave it its name, after *anemos*, the Greek word for 'wind', is Eski Anamur, ancient Anemurium (or Anemurion; *map C, 8; open 9–7; charge*), the Astalimure or Stallimuro of the portulans, signposted from Route 400. Modern Anamur is 23km northeast after a huge sprawl of greenhouses.

ESKİ ANAMUR: ANEMURIUM

Eski Anamur is mentioned in the ancient written sources as a harbour in the 4th century BC, in reference to the nearby cape, but the archaeology shows nothing pre-Roman. Apparently by the 1st century BC it eclipsed Nagidos (*see below*), which must have encouraged the Cietae and the Isaurians (both peoples of the lawless interior) to besiege it in AD 52. On top of this it was also very exposed, suffering from sea raids when the *Pax Romana* no longer held. The **Isaurian tribes** of the interior also remained a worry. Anemurium flourished in the 1st–2nd century but was in trouble with the Persians by 260. This prompted a strengthening of the defence system, which was completed in the 4th century. By then it was no longer minting coins. **Christianity** dotted the urban landscape with a few churches and there was a **bishop** (indeed there still was one in 1966, in Australia). There is evidence of some prosperity in early Byzantine times but an **earthquake** and **attacks from the sea** (the Persians first and then, repeatedly, the Arabs) proved too much. Public buildings were left unrepaired and were reused as lime kilns. The site was abandoned in the mid-7th century, though it remained a reference point for sailors. By then the settlement may have been on the headland mentioned above, which was walled. It is possible that this was the original Hellenistic settlement or its acropolis (it has not been investigated); the walling with towers and bastions looks medieval and, by the style, the settlement looks 12th century. In 1225 the emir of Alanya owned it, together with some other defended towns in Cilicia. After its destruction, the night closed on Anemurium.

REMAINS OF ANEMURIUM

The first sight that attracted visitors was at the **Necropolis** (350 tombs), up the hill right at the back of the town, 'a city within a city' to quote Beaufort (*p. 23*), who paid a visit in 1812 and noted that there were very few spolia around. Certainly compared to the battered remains of the town (building material in Anemurium, rubble faced with limestone, was not very good), one would think that the town's dead lived better than its living.

Down from the Necropolis, beyond the **aqueduct** (one of two; neither have been studied), is the town, with a number of public buildings of the Roman and Byzantine periods. Among them is the **theatre**, with a diameter of 60m, best preserved on the east side. Its cavea rested partly on the hillside and may have used the sea as a backdrop. Next is the **odeion**, measuring 31m by 20m and with a capacity of 800: it was covered and had windows. The seating was arranged in 15 rows supported by a vaulted structure. The orchestra and passages had mosaic floors. Immediately to the east is a **civic basilica**, which according to the excavator was never completed. It has an exedra to the north. There are mosaic floors on either side of the central nave but all evidence of flooring or preparation for flooring in the other areas is lacking. No tiles were found. Perhaps building work never proceeded as far as a roof.

Four churches have been identified, at least two of which had mosaic floors. The **Church of the Apostles**, outside the sea wall which protected the city on its east side, is huge: over 40m long and dated to the 5th/6th century. The **bath houses**, of

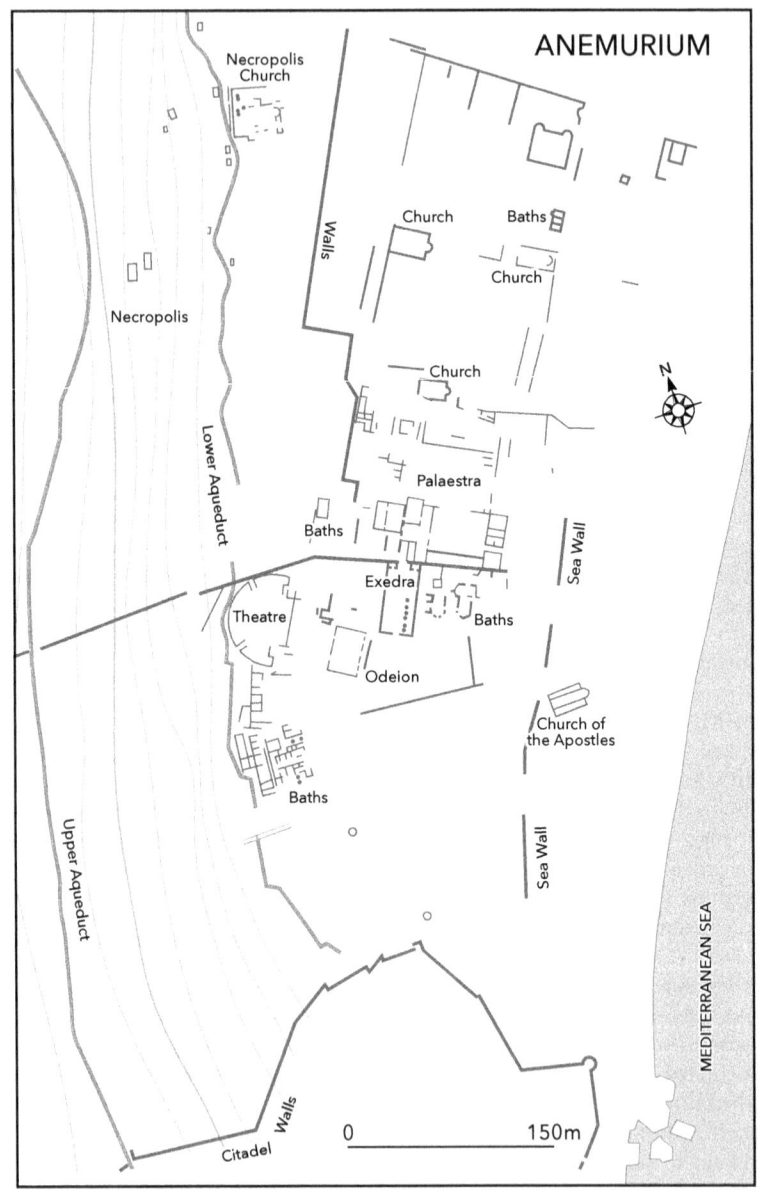

which there were at least four, also had mosaic floors and so did private buildings, including a villa right on the tip of the promontory. It therefore seems that mosaics were a local speciality: they are also found in tombs. The Anemurium school of mosaicists (if there ever was such a thing) appears to have flourished in the 2nd–3rd century when the economy was doing well and continued up to the 6th century. Apart from geometric motifs, standard Roman themes such as marine scenes and the Three Graces were favourite subjects. The quality is not particularly high: they are rather coarse compared to the finesse of the Antioch floors and indeed they show no influence from Syria or Cyprus and are closer in style to North Africa and Greece. Even so, it is regrettable that, as recently reported in the local press, they have not been protected or lifted to safety, especially since Anemurium now has its own **museum** (*open daily 8.30–5; free*) at Yalıevleri (the coastal resort district).

MAMURE KALESİ

The information about Mamure Kalesi (*open daily 8–7.30; charge*) is rather confused. Considering that it does not appear ever to have been studied or excavated, but endlessly rebuilt over the centuries, this is hardly surprising.

It is now marketed as a star tourist attraction and for this reason has been subjected to another renovation (judging by the comments in the local press, this might have been one restoration too many). PVC windows, a liberal use of modern building materials and the installation of air conditioning in the mosque do not quite accord with such a venerable building—at least, when Beaufort visited in 1812 it was venerable, albeit ruinous, and lived in by the kind local *ağa*. The patrons then were the Ottomans.

When was it first built? There is talk of the Romans but no supporting evidence. There is also talk of the Seljuks but the site is a long way from the coast which in any case they controlled for such a short time. Until proper excavations have been carried out, we must reserve judgement. It is best to visit and get an idea of the plan (and try and forget the PVC windows, the stark white stone and the perfect crenellations). Children will love it and it is situated next to a long sandy beach.

The structure, built in rough stone with spolia in the lower courses, is divided into three parts: the **inner castle** (iç kale), the **outer castle** (dış kale) and the **inner courtyard** (iç avlu), all contained within a circuit about 600m long dotted with towers and bastions. The north end facing the road had a moat. Towards the sea are cliffs. Upon entering, you are in the inner courtyard. The round bastion to the left, the twelve-sided **Başküle**, is, according to Hellenkemper, Ottoman; its platform could be used for cannons. From the inner gate you reach the outer castle with the mosque and stores. The inner castle, with a lighthouse, possibly the oldest part of the whole complex, is accessed via the gate between the two square towers.

On the other side of the road are the remains of a much overgrown **Ottoman bath**.

NAGIDOS & SOFTA KALESİ

Further down the coast beyond Eski Anamur, surrounded by greenhouses in the modern town of of Boyazı (*map C, 8*), is the acropolis of **Nagidos** (Paşabeleni Tepesi), standing defiant by the seashore by the left bank of the Bayat Deresi stream. Nagidos had an illustrious history. An early 7th-century BC Samian colony, it minted its own coins from early days and weathered the Persian occupation apparently unscathed. It went on minting coins and building defences and maintained its Greek character. Hard times came with Alexander the Great, who deprived Nagidos of part of its territory in order to give it to his veterans. It seems to have lost importance in the Roman period. The acropolis still has traces of the walls, which according to McNicoll show various techniques. **Nagidoussa**, the island 200m offshore, has Byzantine, medieval and Ottoman structures built with the spolia of Nagidos.

A little further inland, about 10km east of Anemurium and signposted from Route 400, is **Softa Kalesi**. A visit to this fortress is a good idea after experiencing Mamure Kalesi (*see above*). From its heights you can survey all the greenhouses but you can also see the sea, the territory of Nagidos, and all the way to Anemurium, as well as keep a watchful eye on the mountains to the north. It is an excellent strategic position on top of a pile of schist 140m above sea level. The Romans spotted it first. It was then called Siceae (perhaps something to do with a fig tree, from the Greek *sikia*, a fig tree?). There is no consensus as to what Softa means: theories range between philosophers and fanatics. The castle has an inner bailey (residential) and an outer (storage and cisterns), with round and square bastions and towers. The style is mixed, ranging from Armenian to Ottoman. Explore with care.

KELENDERIS & ITS HINTERLAND

Kelenderis, now Aydıncık (*map C, 8*), is just off Route 400 on the way east. It is a good place to stop and have a cool drink. There is not really very much to see, despite all the work the Turkish archaeologists have done, but this is the land of the famous **mosaic of the ship in the harbour**. The mosaic is not on view, unfortunately, but it is all over the internet and has gained widespread recognition. And though you cannot admire the mosaic, you can see the harbour, which has changed little since antiquity.

The ancient settlement sits at the deep end of a U shaped cove, which lies parallel to the highway with natural defences to the south and north. It is thought that over time the cove has filled, the land has advanced and the sea has become more shallow. It is still a very good refuge from the winds blowing from the south and southwest. The two moles closing the harbour are modern.

Kelenderis was already established at the time of the **Persians**, when they occupied Meydancık Kale (*see below*), a day's journey away in those days; it was possibly the base of one of their garrisons: the Persians would have had frequent contacts with Cyprus, which they ruled at the time. Persian-style jars have been found. The Persians were interested in Cilicia for its timber but there were also metals and textiles: Cilicia was famous for its long goat hair, *cilicium*. According to Varro (*De Re Rustica 2,32*) it was in Cilicia that the fleece of goats was first harvested. The cloth was dark, coarse, durable and water resistant, suitable for working wear as well as for making bags and sacks and a host of other purposes. It may not have had a great aesthetic appeal and was probably scratchy, hence its popularity with medieval penitents as a means of mortifying the flesh.

In the mid-5th century BC Kelenderis was minting coins. Around 280 BC it was in the hands of the Syrian **Seleucids**, being a convenient base for Cyprus, which they then controlled. It seems to have prospered at the time, as shown by lavish graves and evidence of extensive contacts to east and west. Under the **Romans** it became a recognisably Roman town and both Pliny (*5,22,92*) and Strabo (*14,5,3*) mention it, though without going into detail. Beyond that we know little. In the necropolis a 4th-century church has been identified, showing that Christianity did make an impact. According to Beaufort (*p. 23*), who was here in the early 19th century, the harbour was used by Ottoman couriers bound for Cyprus.

EXPLORING KELENDERIS
The archaeological area is by the harbour and fenced off but from either of the two modern moles you can make out the **odeion** facing the sea. To the east of it is the **acropolis**, which was walled in medieval times. Evidence shows that this followed earlier **Classical walls**. On the other side of the odeion is a **basilica**, believed to be close to what was the **agora**, and beyond a **bath**. In the waters of the harbour, a **slipway** with a pebble surface, 2.5m wide and 7m long, has been identified.

THE KELENDERIS MOSAIC
If the description above fails to bring to life the busy harbour of ancient Kelenderis, with boats carrying passengers and merchandise in and out, the famous mosaic will. It was found in town in a private dwelling, in a location which has understandably not been revealed, and formed part of a mosaic floor in a corridor. Most of the decoration is geometric but the last panel, 3m by 3m, depicts a ship sailing into harbour surrounded by a frame of lotus buds. Dated to the 5th/6th century, it is a bird's eye view of one large sailing ship and two smaller ones braving the rough seas. The town has a stoa roofed with tiles and a quay in front. At the back are the baths. A number of other buildings are shown but they have not been identified. The scene has been endlessly analysed by experts (who somewhat complicate the discussion by using a surplus of nautical terms). It may not depict Kelenderis itself as such, but it is a fair representation of a successful harbour town.

MEYDANCIK KALE

If you have your own transport, you can drive c. 10km inland from Aydıncık to visit Meydancık Kale, which is just to the south of Gülnar. This is a **natural fortress** in use since prehistory, a flat ridge 710m long and 150m wide, overlooking a rugged land short of water and of little use for agriculture. As it is cold in the winter, the castle may not have been occupied all year round but it was a strategic look-out post from which to control access to the Sipahili Valley and another point of entry to the coast from Licaonia to the north via Büyükeceli. In more recent times, that is when Kinneir (*p. 27*) visited in the early 19th century, it was a good place to hide from the Ottoman taxman, as some people from Kelenderis did.

Prehistoric occupation is attested by finds and by the post holes of Neolithic huts. According to the sources, a local petty king of Luwian extraction was chased here 'to the town of his ancestors' by the Babylonian ruler Neriglissar in 557/6 BC and everything—rampart, people and palace—went up in flames. At the time Meydancık Kale was Kirşu, the capital of the **Luwian kingdom** of Pirindu. Later the **Persians** established a presence here and this could have been the summer residence of a Persian satrap. It is then referred to as a 'fortified city'. The **Hellenistic** period is little known. It seems that the Ptolemies were here first, later ousted by the Seleucids who destroyed the place, although they possibly left a garrison here around 240–235 BC, which may account for the 5,000-piece coin hoard. In **Byzantine** times it was a handy refuge: coins have been found as well as tools linked to agriculture, but no recognisable buildings.

THE SITE

The site has been partially excavated. To the north, the entrance was fortified and reworked several times. It had a tower overlooking the access road. This was followed by a bastion showing, on the outer east side, an **Aramaean inscription**; a tower to the south housed a cistern. A ramp led visitors to a vestibule followed by a court, where they were watched from the east tower. A pillar hall with a monumental staircase to the upper levels finally granted access to the interior of the fortress via a ramp overlooked by another tower to the west. Seen from the inside, the entrance complex looked almost palatial, while the forbidding aspect of the exterior was meant as a deterrent.

Following the path, you come to the remains of **Building A**, which has been interpreted as the residence of the satrap. Its plan and scheme of ornamentation are reminiscent of the palace of Darius at Persepolis, only obviously smaller. There is the same large, central hypostyle hall, divided internally by rows of columns, and a large vestibule. The decoration, with processions of courtiers bearing gifts, is very Persian in conception and execution (no Greek influence here); the nearest parallels are in Persepolis and Pasargadae. The **tomb** to the east is particularly interesting since it has an entrance porch with the statues of two soldiers standing to attention and supporting the roof, making them altogether an early example of caryatids.

SİLİFKE & AYATEKLA

Boğsak island (*map C, 8*), before Silifke, should distract your attention from the beaches, the pansiyons and the relaxing views of the sea, prompting you to go back in time and consider survival strategies. This rocky island, 300m by 500m and just 51m above sea level, has no arable land and no trees, yet it was inhabited from the 4th to the 9th century, and with some luxury. It depended on the mainland for everything including water, but since the mainland has been built over we do not know which settlement it relied upon. This stretch of coast does not have good anchorages. On Boğsak the cliffs were cut back to provide docking facilities for small boats. The startling increase in pottery and coins in the 4th century suggests a sudden big investment. According to some, the settlers had two main lines of business, capitalising on the booming pilgrim trade to Ayatekla (*p. 187*), which enjoyed imperial patronage from the late 5th century, and at the same time servicing the general maritime trade. Although a village, Boğsak called itself a city (its name was Asteria) and judging by the buildings scattered on its northeast terraces, whether residential, utilitarian, or commercial, it had the allure of a city. Some houses built directly on the bedrock were two storeys high with tiled pitched roofs and deep cisterns cut in the rock. As many as seven churches, in limestone with timber roofs and some with marble and mosaic floors, have been identified. The island had a network of drainage channels. Boğsak developed and prospered in a busy maritime landscape as long as the sea was at peace, and other islands in the vicinity followed the same trajectory. When outside forces struck in the 7th century, Boğsak was unable to reinvent itself.

SİLİFKE

At Silifke (*map C, 8*) we meet the Göksu, the Calycadnus of antiquity. In medieval times it was known as the Seleph from the town it crossed, today's Silifke. The Holy Roman Emperor **Frederick Barbarossa**, who drowned in this river, did so '*in aqua Selephica*'. The date was May 1190, a bad time to cross since the river would have been swollen with the melting snows. Barbarossa is commemorated with a stele about 10km west of Silifke on Route 715, at a point where the road bends and overlooks the river.

The Göksu makes quite a change from the short and turbulent river courses of Rough Cilicia (though we have not quite left Rough Cilicia yet). It is long (260km) and mighty, as described by Ammianus Marcellinus the 4th-century Roman historian (*14,3,15*). It is navigable up to Silifke and affords a line of entry into the hinterland, almost to the edge of the Konya plain, as well as valuable stretches of agricultural land. In antiquity it had a major crossing point where Silifke is today, which is why there has been a stone bridge here since Roman times (*see below*). Higher up there may have been other bridges made of wood; in the dry season, however, there were a number of fording places. The Göksu delta forms a lagoon which is now an important breeding site for a large variety of birds from flamingoes to kingfishers. The loggerhead turtle has nesting sites here. However, there are problems with encroaching tourist development.

The Göksu (its Turkish name a homage to its clear, sky-blue waters) is the first of a family of mighty rivers that makes this part of Cilicia different. While the mountains are still with us at this point, they begin to recede from the sea, which is now shallower.

A SHORT HISTORY OF SİLİFKE
Today Silifke (in the 1820s, according to accounts by Laborde (*p. 28*), a miserable village with imposing remains) is a middle-sized modern agricultural town straddling the river, 14km from the delta. In antiquity it would have been closer to the sea but nevertheless it is where it is because of the felicitous combination of river and rocky spur, the site of today's Silifke Kalesi. Here was the control post of east–west traffic

and of roads leading to the interior. It is unlikely that Silifke owes its existence to Seleucus I Nicator, the founder of the Seleucid dynasty in Syria in the aftermath of the death of Alexander the Great. There was certainly something here before then. However, Seleucus Nicator nurtured the town and gave it its name, **Seleucia ad Calycadnum**. It was one of his numerous 'foundations', named after him or members of his family. He was a Greek from Macedonia and, not surprisingly, was keen on things Greek. He wanted Seleucia to be an outpost of Greek culture but he also had an eye on the unruly tribes of the interior. According to Strabo (*14,5,4*)—although he was writing 200 years later—Seleucus invited Greek colonists from nearby settlements to come with their gods and oracles. Strabo also mentions a couple of locally-born philosophers and generally, according to him, the people of Silifke looked down on both Pamphylians and Cilicians.

The **Hellenistic town** was on the slopes between the **acropolis** (Silifke Kalesi) and the right bank of the river, where today's Stone Bridge (Taş Köprü) marks the ancient crossing point. The **necropolis** was to the foot of the ridge to the south. We know nothing more about the early town: its buildings were reused as spolia by the Romans. Christianity came early and left an important mark at **Ayatekla** (*see below*). A strong **Jewish community** is attested in inscriptions.

During the time of Diocletian, Seleucia was the seat of the **Count of Isauria**, showing that it was an important military node for the preparation of the eastern campaigns against the Sassanids. By the 7th century there was an **imperial weapon factory** here. The Crusaders held the castle for a while, before losing it to the king of Cyprus in the 14th century. Silifke fell to the Ottomans in 1471.

VISITING SİLİFKE

Silifke was built around a bridge and the acropolis. There are now several bridges but the ancient one is question is the **Stone Bridge** (**Taş Köprü**), which according to an inscription was built by Vespasian in AD 77–8. It has been endlessly restored and also neglected over the centuries. In the early 20th century it had watermills built on it. What you see today is a fairly modern construction, roughly to the original design, with seven arches. About 400m due south was the Roman **theatre**, its cavea partially resting on the slope and facing east. Laborde could still see the seats; now its outline cannot even be made out in the street pattern.

About 500m away from the theatre, on İnönü Cd., are the remains of the limestone **Temple of Zeus**, an octastyle Corinthian peripteros 39m by 22m, which stood close to the eastern limit of the Roman town. It is dated stylistically to the 2nd century AD. It stood on a podium of ashlar blocks. A temple dedicated to the imperial cult is mentioned in the Life of St Thecla. It could be an earlier version of this one; it was turned at some point into a church. There is not much left of it but a solitary standing column, topped by the inevitable stork's nest. Most of the columns were reused in the vestibule of the **Reşadiye Mosque**, where you can see them now. According to old engravings, the church had a polygonal apse, large arched windows and no clerestory, in a style that could be seen in Syria in the late 5th/6th century, at the time of the building's conversion.

On the way to the acropolis, visit the astonishing **Byzantine cistern** (ask for 'Tekir

Ambar', possibly a corruption of *Tekfur Ambar*, the 'Lord's Storehouse') on Eğitim Sk. The covered, sunken structure was lined with regular-cut stone blocks; it measures about 46m by 23m and is 12m deep. The sides have a series of niches and pilasters. It originally had a tiled roof. Pipes would have distributed the water down to the town. Although the site is is presently closed, you can have a look from the outside (and if you ever get in, you need to move around carefully).

The **castle** (**Silifke Kalesi**) sits on a spur 86m above sea level. Its elongated enclosure at the top of the hill, with towers and bastions surrounded by a moat, has been repeatedly analysed by specialists in an attempt to unravel its history. At the time of writing it was being renovated (again) to promote tourism, which will mean the loss of some of the archaeological evidence. The position is unique, offering an all-round vantage point. The full sequence of its history, which may have begun in the depths of prehistory, continuing through Hellenistic, Byzantine, Arab and Crusader occupations, is still not well understood. The temple of **Athena Kanetis** (the local chief deity) may have been here.

The **circus** and **stadium** that are recorded in travellers' accounts are now lost. The same applies to the Roman town that once sprawled on the plain and very possibly across the river.

AYATEKLA

Taking the turn south off Route 715 signed to Meryemlık, one passes through the Roman necropolis, arriving at Ayatekla (*open daily summer 9–12 & 1.30–6, winter 8–5; free*) after less than 1km. The place name Meryemlık refers to the time when Seleucia was in the hands of the Armenians and they venerated the Virgin Mary here (the name Meryem is the Turkish equivalent of Mary).

Down here we are very close to the **delta of the Göksu**, with plenty of alluvial soil interrupted by a few north–south limestone ridges. The **ancient road** from the centre of town has been identified, cut in the ridge where the shrine of Ayatekla is. It has been suggested that the road was an **ancient processional way**, with the cult site of Ayatekla situated near or on an old pagan hub.

The cult was centred around **St Thecla, the first female martyr**. She is said to have been a contemporary of St Paul, who converted her, which therefore dates her to the first half of the 1st century. Historically she is attested only at the end of the 2nd century, when Tertullian inveighed against her for championing female rights. Her biography is one of the holy lives written in the mid-5th century. According to the information available she was a native of Iconium (Konya; *map C, 3*) and an early follower of St Paul's when he preached there. She broke off her engagement in order to remain a virgin, for which she was first condemned to the stake (a providential downpour saved her) and then thrown to wild beasts (who refused to touch her). The reactions of her fiancé are not recorded.

She showed the hallmark of her persona early on, performing spectacular miracles. She travelled with St Paul, spreading the gospel with him and, according to legend, eventually died here, or rather disappeared underground in the cave in which she was living (*see below*). Although fiercely opposed to the pagan religion, Thecla did nevertheless borrow from it in her quest to entice the populace away from its errors. Her image was that of a fierce virgin and she did not hesitate to call her cloister a 'parthenon', thus speaking to the subconscious of pagan women who could see in her an evolution of Athena. She could also control natural forces and tame wild beasts, giving her a kind of kinship with Artemis, mistress of the animals. Representations of her in such a guise are known. She is a long way indeed from St Paul's idea of the model woman: to use his own words, '*mulier taceat in ecclesia*' (*Corinthians 1; 14,3,4*); but perhaps what he really meant here was the church choir, in which he did not want female voices.

Thecla's cult spread around the Mediterranean to Egypt, from where it grew via the coming and going of ships in the port of Alexandria, picking up along the way a strain of the kind of asceticism that was widely practised by Christian hermits living on the fringes of the desert. The cult of Thecla at Silifke is first attested through a document unearthed in an Italian monastery, the travel report of one Egeria, a pilgrim from Gaul at the end of the 4th century who came here on her way back from Egypt and the Holy Land. There was clearly already a cult here at that time, centred on the cave in which St Thecla had died/disappeared. But what turned Seleucia ad Calycadnum from a stopover for pilgrims en route East to a major destination in its own right, was the growing importance of the town in late antiquity and the bestowal of imperial favour. The emperor in this case was **Zeno** (*p. 166*), an Isaurian who had suffered a palace coup when the usurper Basiliscus ousted him. He took refuge in Seleucia with his wife and his treasure and ultimately emerged victorious (while Basiliscus was left to starve in a cistern in Cappadocia).

There are four churches at Ayatekla, two of which are dated to the 5th century. As the site is only partially excavated, it is difficult to tell which one is Zeno's. Both show the marks of an imperial project by their size, some 80m in length, as well as by the surviving marble capitals, coloured marble, porphyry and mosaics.

WHAT TO SEE AT AYATEKLA

The area is now a wasteland, but going by Egeria's descriptions it was once full of gardens and aviaries: try to imagine it well built up, fully adapted to looking after pilgrims' spiritual and material needs, and dotted with monasteries.

There is not much left these days apart from some ruins of the aqueduct, of the baths, a few cisterns and churches. The most visible ruin is the **apse of a huge basilica**, which has been investigated. It had three aisles with 15 columns each. Not far from it is the **cave of Ayatekla**, on which a very large church was later built. It is possible to get down into the cave, in which a rectangular church, 18m by 12m, has been built, divided into two naves. The reused fluted columns could have come from the necropolis. The complex stood in a **temenos** (like a number of 5th- and 6th-century Syrian churches) measuring 180m by 60m and with its own cisterns. It had a gateway to the north flanked by towers. The wall, built in massive ashlars, may have been meant to keep the Isaurians out.

To the south is a well preserved **cistern** with a rectangular plan measuring 12m by 14m and covered with three vaults supported by columns. The outer walls are

1.7m thick. The outside is ashlar masonry and the inside is brickwork with a thick covering of hydraulic plaster.

THE GÖKSU VALLEY

Taking the road to Karaman, Route 715, which for some way follows the course of the Göksu along its deep sides, you get to the **Sertavul Geçidi** (1650m), a mountain pass or defile on the northern border of Mersin province that grants access to the interior and to Karaman (*map C, 6*). Before that, you can visit two interesting sites, Mut and Alahan.

MUT

You can see why Mut (*map C, 6*) is along this road, in cool pine-clad country. It has a Roman past but its history possibly stretches back even further. The municipality is trying hard to lay it bare for tourists.

From the sources (inscriptions and antiquary reports), Mut was known in the 1st century as **Claudiopolis** (an inscription on a sarcophagus honours the emperor Claudius, who made it a polis). Augustus had earlier made it a colony glorying in the name of Colonia Iulia Augusta Felix Ninica. After a spell in the hands of the Armenians, it became a Seljuk city around 1300.

Mut had a **theatre** and a fine building with verde antico columns (now in the Lal Paşa Camii). Traces of a colonnaded street was observed to the southeast in 1884. Inscriptions mention **temples** to Athena Polia and to Zeus, as well as a Museion. The usual suspects for causing the demise of these are the Karamanids, who rebuilt the **Byzantine castle**. In the walls of its inner and outer bailey as well as of the keep, you will find a few spolia. The ancient **acropolis**, going back to prehistoric times, may well be beneath it. Mut has an interesting mosque: while you are at the castle, enquire at the nearby tourist office about the **Dağ Camisi**. It is not a particularly beautiful building (though at the time of writing it was undergoing restoration) but it is intriguing. Situated 2km west of Mut, it is literally in the middle of nowhere: no settlement, no cemetery. Yet it is a mosque; it has a mimber. What is it doing there? The shape is square, about 10m by 10m, and it would have had a squat dome, now partially lost. It was built with spolia from Mut, as can be seen from the architrave and the fine exterior ashlars. The inside is punctuated with blind arches and ends in the remains of a dome, which may have had an oculus.

ALAHAN

Alahan (*map C, 6; open daily 8–sunset; charge*) is a complex of two churches perched on a narrow terrace 20km north of Mut, signposted opposite the Alahan *lokanta* on Route 715. From the turning there is a short drive up, with plenty of hairpin bends. The site is magnificent because the preservation is so good and the view is stupendous. However, it is not entirely clear how these churches came to be here. The site was first surveyed by a British team in 1890; later there were more surveys and limited excavations. The stratigraphy and chronology are not yet clear. This is a unique set of monuments in a very isolated spot and it is difficult to make sense of it. It could have been a monastery (but there is no communal area) or (more likely) a pilgrimage centre honouring a local saint.

The buildings are strung out along a **colonnaded walkway** connecting the two churches with other buildings (a baptistery, a bath house and tombs) in between.

The **west church** is the earlier. Dedicated to the Evangelists, it measures 37m by 16m and is partly built in the rock on its north side. As a result the narthex is misshapen. It has a fine complex portal to the west with exuberant decoration. It had a clerestory for lighting and small windows on the exposed south side. The interior was divided by two rows of ten columns. At the east end, the apse housed a synthronon. The building required massive substructures at the south end and a crypt was built inside them.

The **east church** is much better preserved, to roof level. The plan is very ambitious. It measures 23m by 15m with a wide central nave ending in an apse in which stood a synthronon, and two side aisles. Its narthex is slightly irregular in order to connect the building with the colonnaded walkway. The west façade, with three triple windows and monumental portals, is arresting. It would have been backed by a timber tower or a wooden dome on cruciform piers. This would have given it a **strong vertical dimension**, making it a **landmark** visible from a distance from the valley below.

In between the two churches stood a small **baptistery** with a cruciform font in the north aisle.

The quality of the buildings (for instance the use of stucco to imitate marble) and the modest size of the construction (though of course there are plenty of topographical constraints), as well as the fact that the baptistery and the east church appearer to be unfinished, would seem to exclude imperial involvement; moreover the pottery puts the buildings earlier than Zeno, the Isaurian emperor (*p. 166*), who would have been the obvious sponsor of such a project. It could have been the work of local architects.

UZUNCABURÇ-OLBA DIOCAESAREA

Uzuncaburç-Olba Diocaesarea (*map D, 5*), with its impressive remains, is now a standard tourist destination accessible by public transport. If you have your own transport and are driving there from Silifke, you can stop off on the way to visit a clutch of 2nd-century AD **Roman mausolea near Demircili**. They belong to the necropolis of the ancient city of Imbriogon. The town has been ploughed over but some mausolea can be seen by the road in a commanding position. There are about six of them, one standing three storeys high with a temple-like front with fine columns, a pediment and friezes, and a vaulted interior. They stand proud among the scrub. They have survived 2,000 years, which is what their owners intended.

UZUNCABURÇ-OLBA DIOCAESAREA: A BRIEF OUTLINE

Standing at 1200m, Uzuncaburç seems to have given up its original pastoral vocation for tourism, as it is now a popular destination offering fine ruins. Investigation has concentrated on surveys of the wider territory rather than excavations, but still it has not unravelled its secrets. It remains a difficult site to make sense of fully.

Situated on a rugged plateau in a karstic landscape thinly settled in antiquity, bisected by ravines and with a harsh climate, the area between the Calycadnus and the Lamas rivers (the modern Göksu and Limonlu) is referred to in the sources as an area run by priests, which has caused some to call it a temple state. However, the information we have does not compare well with other known temple states (e.g. Pessinus and Comana), which controlled rich agricultural regions. This was not a very wealthy area and it is not clear whether the territory had access to the sea. The extent of the territory has been estimated from repeated surveys of its buildings, in which the **symbols of the Teucrid dynasts** (lightning bolts, caducei swords, triskeles, shields, phallus and clubs displayed on the lintels) have been plotted. The construction techniques are also revealing; the Greek regular ashlar technique here gives way to polygonal structures using a variety of stone shapes but requiring more manpower.

The 'temple state' of Olba (a name said by some to derive from *olbos*, meaning prosperity in Greek) sits at the junction of two worlds. Strabo (*14,5,10*) gives it a Greek ancestry straight out of the *Iliad*. The local priests are said to be the descendants of Ajax, the hero of the Trojan War, son of Teucros. But the local god is Tarhunt, whose name has a distinctly Anatolian ring to it. It is therefore highly possible that this was originally a **Luwian foundation** which in due course either adopted a Greek identity or had one foisted on it. It would seem that this happened under the **Seleucids**, who assumed control of the plateau after Alexander the Great cleared Asia Minor of Persian rule. An inscription built into the temenos of the Temple of Zeus (*see below*) testifies that Seleucus I recognised the high priest of the Teucrid dynasty as a local ruler and in charge of the cult of the local deity, which over time became assimilated with Zeus Olbios.

When in 133 BC the **Romans** took over, this was the last stronghold of Seleucid power. The Romans, with their programme of urbanisation, set up a town (Olba-Ura; *see below*), while the temple site became known as Olba Diocaesarea. They respected the local cult and did not interfere with the temple apart from adding 'Diocaesarea' to the name, to remind the local population of Roman omnipotence. The priests were grateful and excavations demonstrate that to show allegiance to the distant power, they built a small Roman temple against the northeast corner of the temenos.

The **Byzantines** turned Olba's most important building, its temple, into a church, after which the city sank into obscurity. The monuments were rediscovered first by the Yūrüks, who settled in the area, and then, in the 19th century, by antiquaries.

EXPLORING UZUNCABURÇ

The site is actually two sites. There is Olba Diocaesarea at Uzuncaburç and Olba at Ura, a couple of kilometres to the southeast. The latter is a Roman town, of which Uzuncaburç was an extramural shrine and residence of the priests, the toparchs of

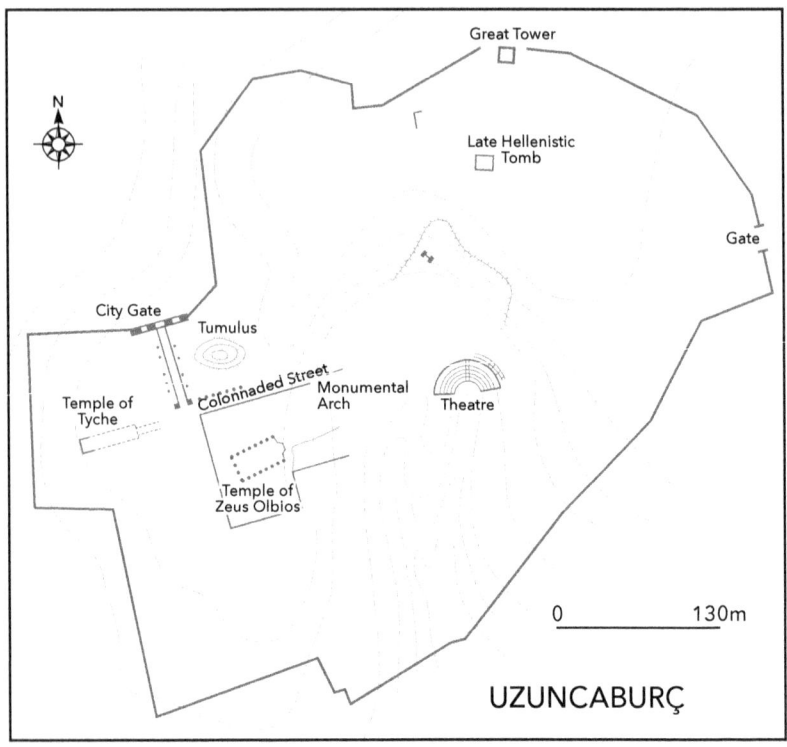

the district. The two settlements were connected by a 4km-long processional way, still in use as a track in the 1950s; the modern road runs in part along it.

Turkish archaeologists are presently working in **Olba** (**Ura**). You can climb to the acropolis and enjoy the fine views; lower down is the theatre, dated to the 2nd century, 40m in diameter, south-facing and with remains of an elaborate scena. The best remains are of the aqueduct from the Lamas (Limonlu Çay), dated to the time of Septimius Severus. The source of the water is 8km to the northeast. The impressive ruins, standing quite tall, can be seen next to the battered agora. The history of Ura is full of lacunae but we know that after a period of obscurity in late antiquity it picked up again, as the scanty evidence of three rather large churches testifies. It was then still a city.

Olba Diocaesarea/Uzuncaburç (*open 8–7; charge*) is to the west and is today the main tourist spot. Since it has not yet been excavated, we have no information about its pre-Hellenistic aspect. It is quite possible that when Seleucus built his temple he did so on top of a previous indigenous structure. Today we see a cleaned-up version of its recent past. The Yürük tents and flocks have been removed.

The site takes its Turkish name, Uzuncaburç (meaning 'a rather tall tower') from the tower that dominates it from the north (*see below*). Today we see the site as the

Byzantines left it (except that the church has reverted to a temple), when it was walled and had two gates east and west. The walls are dated c. AD 300, a time of troubles. The **monumental city gate** to the north, 32m wide and 12m high, bears an inscription of Arcadius and Honorius, the sons of emperor Theodosius, who repaired the circuit after an earthquake. A 500m long **colonnaded street** was the main east–west axis, built in the 1st century AD as part of the Roman redevelopment; in it a statue of Tiberius, now lost, had an inscription hailing him as 'founder and saviour' (perhaps more evidence of priestly gratitude?). To the south of it is the **theatre**, 48m in diameter and built in the mid-3rd century on an earlier 1st-century AD structure.

A **monumental arch** with consoles for holding statues originally had five arches; it stands to the west and led to the precinct of the **Temple of Zeus Olbios**. This was the centre of power for the priest-rulers and they they kept control of the shrine even after Augustus deposed the last of them. The temple was peripteral, measuring 40m by 21m, and stood directly on the rock with no podium. The Hellenistic temple was of the Corinthian order, a very early instance so far east, with 13m-high fluted columns that were never completed. In due course it was converted into a church, of which little can now be seen. In essence the peripteros was blocked up and the columns were chamfered to improve bonding. An apse with side chambers was added to the east. The church was basilican in plan with galleries and clerestory. Mosaics and *opus sectile* floors were laid but since the remains are wrongly aligned, they probably belong to different periods, bearing in mind also that at some point the church was turned into a mosque. The church had four corner towers in the style of northern Syrian churches of the same period, roughly 5th century.

The **Temple of Tyche** to the west, originally a show of power and money with its monolithic granite columns brought all the way from the Troad, was used as a house in the 19th century. There seems to be no trace of private houses, supporting the hypothesis that only priests were allowed to dwell here and that the populace lived in the other Olba (Ura). On the other hand, if their houses had been wooden constructions, they would have left little trace The relationship between the two settlements is still not fully understood.

The priests lived in **tall tower buildings**, of which there is a fine example to the north. The construction, six storeys high according to McNicoll, went up in the the 1st century BC. Built in fine dry ashlars with thick walls (1.2m at the base), it had an entrance to the south and a staircase to the 5th floor. The second floor had balconies and windows. It was a dwelling, an administrative centre and a refuge.

The **pyramidal tomb**, 15m high, is in a prominent spot on a summit about 1km southeast of the temple: an excellent location in terms of visibility, well adapted to keeping alive the memory of the deceased. Its pyramidal roof may have borne a statue. The structure is 5.5m square and sits on a three-stepped podium. It was entered from the south. Dated to the second half of the 1st century BC, it is similar in concept to the mausolea at Belevi and Halicarnassus, though much smaller in scale than the latter.

A SIDE TRIP TO MEZGİT KALE

The road inland from Susanoğlu on the coast goes past the village of Paslı, where a side road to the east leads to Öztürkmenli, from where **Mezgit Kale** is signed. This Roman mausoleum still stands very much in the same landscape in which it was originally built, with the difference that today irrigation allows abundant tomato crops. Apart from the two damaged sarcophagi, it is in very good condition. It is shaped like a temple, with an 8m high façade with four columns with consoles for statues; the stonework is impeccable ashlar. Dated to the 2nd/3rd century, it is locally known as the 'Tomb of the Fearless King' because of the relief of a phallus which in some cultures is a sign of great courage. There are other reliefs as well (a shield, a scorpion and a sword). Some of these symbols are Olban. Was this the mausoleum of a Roman wanting to be a local or a local wanting to be Roman?

NARLIKUYU & ENVIRONS

Narlıkuyu (*map D, 7*) on the coast, a place that likes to be associated with the pomegranate (*nar* in Turkish), is a good spot to take a break and prepare yourself for the journey to Hell and Paradise (*see below*). You can also eat some fresh fish and visit the local **museum** (*open daily Oct–mid-April 8–5; mid-April–Sept 8–7; charge*), built around the ruins of a Roman bath not far from the sea shore. The main attraction is the mosaic of the Three Graces, Euphrosyne, Aglaia and Thalia, an immortal motif that has not changed much from antiquity to Canova.

From Narlıkuyu the **Corycian Cave** (*open daily; charge*) is signposted on the other side of the road on Atatürk Cd. It is not one cave but a complex of grottoes and owes its name to the nymph Corycia, who inhabited a cave on Mount Parnassus. The name is old, perhaps bequeathed by Greeks nostalgic for the motherland. In Turkish the complex is known as Heaven (Cennet) and Hell (Cehennem). This is a very karstic region, where rivers make their way underground. One of them reaches the sea undetected in the harbour of Narlıkuyu. Over time the water has eroded the weak limestone and huge caves have formed. It is a trait of humankind to venerate outstanding natural features (caves, springs and summits). Here in Cilicia, the geology has inspired supernatural beliefs. There are several caves in this area where you should watch where you put your feet.

THE CORYCIAN CAVE: HEAVEN (CENNET)
This, situated to the north, is a large sinkhole with sheer cliffs about 250m by 30m with a depth ranging from 30m to 70m. At the bottom to the south is a deeper cave, now inaccessible, filled with the sound of the gushing river which the ancients believed connected with the Styx, the entrance to the Underworld. The place has had a long association with the divine. Pomponius Mela (*1,13*) in the 1st century AD thought it was truly venerable and sacred, the abode of the gods, however strange a choice it may seem on their part. Popular belief in the divine presence here fostered pilgrimage, perhaps to consult an oracle.

A **temple** is attested inside the cave at the east end, from the 1st century BC, as well as some construction next to the entrance of the second, deeper cave. By the 4th–5th century a **church** dedicated to the Virgin Mary was built on top of it, taking over the old cult and investing it with a distinctive anti-pagan slant, leaving the Mother of God to oppose the dark subterranean forces. Pictures by Gertrude Bell (*p. 24*) show it with three aisles separated by arcades and no roof. This was much later, at a time when it had been refashioned as a mosque for nomads. In the depression itself **remains of housing** have been noted, suggesting at some point a refuge.

Outside the cave by the edge of the cliff to the southeast, a **Hellenistic temple** was built within its temenos, from which ran the staircase to the chapel; it could still be seen in the 19th century (today's entrance to the cave is from the north). Temple and temenos were built in polygonal masonry. About 15m long, it was Doric in antis and dedicated to Hermes, quite an important deity here. It was the work of the Teucrid priests from Olba, since a list of these has been found among the spolia. It was later transformed into a **church** of the basilica type, which was much larger, 25m by 40m, incorporating some of the temenos structure; it had a nave and two aisles and galleries.

If you want to explore the cave (the entrance is from the north side of the sinkhole), wear good shoes and take a torch—and be aware that it is 450 steps down and 450 up.

THE CORYCIAN CAVE: HELL (CEHENNEM)

Situated 75m to the east of Cennet, Cehennem is deeper (128m) and inaccessible except to experienced cavers. From a smallish opening at the top it broadens to a wide sinkhole. There is no room for a rock-cut staircase. This is where Zeus first imprisoned one of the Titans (Typhon), who gave him so much trouble after he took over the governance of the world from his abusive father Cronus. He later moved him to Etna. Typhon lives on as the Devil of the early Christians and later of the Muslims.

The nearby **Dilek Mağarası** cave has no mythological associations. Its environment is known to be beneficial to asmtha sufferers.

KIZKALESİ (ANCIENT CORYCUS)

Back on the coast, Kızkalesi (*map D, 7*) is an obligatory stop for the two castles of the ancient town of Corycus. The history of this **natural harbour** goes quite a way back and it features on the portulans. Today, with its long, sandy beach, it has successfully reinvented itself as holiday destination. Corycus is first mentioned in the early 2nd century BC as a rival of Elaioussa Sebaste (*see below*), another natural harbour 4km to the northeast. Going by the funerary inscriptions it seems that some of the locals were pilots, shipowners and investors in maritime ventures, while traders handled a variety of goods from wine and oil to textiles and clothing. Later, in the 3rd century AD, it was an **imperial harbour**, housing the Syrian fleet and producing linen for sails. By then it had already been **destroyed twice**: by the Persians in AD 260 and 200 years later by the Isaurians. However, it continued to feature on many maritime charts; though a ruined city by the 10th century AD, it remained a **reference point**

for travellers to Byzantium, Cyprus or the Holy Land. To the Arabs it was Qurkus. In 1380, as the last Armenian foothold in Cilicia, it was lost to Cyprus. It was later attacked and destroyed by the Karamanids in 1448. The Ottomans followed.

We have almost no remains of this past apart form what was reused in later buildings as spolia. Corycus' pre-Hellenistic past must also be here somewhere, deeply buried and untouched.

From the sources we can gather that it was **walled** by the 1st century AD and that in Roman times it expanded east and had a **colonnaded street**, a **toll house**, a **Jewish quarter**, **baths** and **temples**. The colonnaded street was roughly along today's Route 400, where some stray column drums have been found; at one end stood a large temple dated to the end of the 2nd century. There was also a bishop but not after the 6th century; in total, twelve **churches** have been accounted for. In the literature there is also talk of **hospices**, probably for pilgrims. The water came from the valley of the Lamas (the modern Limonlu) and from a number of cisterns built and cut in the rock. At some point yet undated, as the port began to silt up, a new mole was installed and a fortification went up to ensure the safety of the harbour. This **land castle** was also intended to guard the through road from Seleucia to Tarsus and keep watch on Cyprus. Out in the sea a construction went up on a **small island** barely 400m from the coast and connected with it by a **breakwater**, part of which can still be seen. The precise dating of these two structures is controversial because of continuous repairs and improvements, but it seems that the driving force was at the beginning the Byzantine period, namely Alexius I and his admiral, the eunuch Eustachius, who wanted to rein in the ambitions of Bohemond the Crusader, Prince of Antioch, so we can possibly put the date as very late 11th century. A great part of the Hellenistic and Roman town and necropolis went into both structures.

THE LAND CASTLE

The land castle (*open daily 8–8; charge*), on a spur by the harbour, is accessible from the beach on the west side. It has never been excavated but has been surveyed repeatedly. It is square in shape with a **moat** cut in the rock all around and communicating with the sea, as Beaufort (*p. 23*) observed in 1812. The moat was crossed by a wooden bridge on the landward side to the east, where the main gate is; the entrance from the sea was to the south. It had a **double skin**, which is very much an Armenian trait, with towers and bastions on both; swampy water filled the space between them. The Armenians held Corycus until 1380. Inside, an early Byzantine **basilica** with nave and two aisles gave way in due course to a smaller church and two chapels. A few **cisterns** have been identified. Other aspects of the construction suggest work by the Lusignans of Cyprus, when they took over from the Armenians.

THE SEA CASTLE

The story is even less clear in the case of the sea castle (Kızkalesi; *open 8-8; charge*), floating ethereal and unperturbed upon the waters as if it had always been there. In its present state it is pure 21st century since it has been restored so thoroughly. There are boats which go out to it; alternatively you can rent a pedalo. It is about one quarter the size of the land castle, roughly triangular in shape, with eight bastions and towers, round and square. An Armenian inscription on the square tower (*see below*), now lost, testified to a rebuilding in 1291; apparently when it was spotted in the 19th century the local Armenians could not understand it because the language was so old-fashioned. The castle was protected all around by treacherous shoals. The original entrance was to the north, through the imposing semicircular bastion. If you are swimming, the best approach is by the **easternmost square tower**, where there is a postern. Inside are a **chapel**, **cisterns** and a lean-to **wooden porch** by the west wall and near it an open, vaulted **portico**. No Byzantine presence has been detected in surveys. It is thought that it was originally an Armenian construction.

ADAMKAYALAR

On the way east after Kızkalesi, take a detour to Adamkayalar, the 'cliff of men', signposted off the road north to Huseyinler. You will have to walk about 1km to reach the spot, which is signposted. The **rock-cut images** of men (11), women (2) and one child, carved in niches, belong to a **Roman necropolis** dated to the 2nd/3rd century. They are represented either in a martial attitude, with weapons and eagles, or in a more homely way, reclining and enjoying a meal. Unfortunately a couple of the reliefs were badly damaged in March 2019, by vandals either opposed to the representation of the human figure or simply looking for treasure in a very improbable place. One should not be deterred by this sad news; there is still plenty to see and the canyon is spectacular.

AYAŞ (ELAIOUSSA)

Elaioussa (Elaiusa, Elaeusa; *map D, 7; open access*), now Ayaş, lies on either side of Route 400, which has destroyed a fair amount of its ancient remains. On the other hand, its construction has led to a long and thorough investigation of the site by an Italian team, which has contributed substantially to the understanding of the life of small settlements on the Cilician coast.

Geologically this is a stretch of coast with a rocky promontory. Although the promontory is at times referred to in antiquity as an island, it was in fact connected by a narrow strip of land forming an isthmus. This layout created a couple of sheltered harbours, to the northeast and southwest. These are today completely silted up and under cultivation, but in the past they were very useful anchorages. Over the centuries the site has been buried under windblown sand, with dunes up to 8m; even so, stone robbing, erosion and terracing for agricultural purposes have contributed to the deterioration of the remains. Together with the two harbours, the town's ancient source of income was agriculture based on olives, as its name suggests.

A BRIEF HISTORY OF ELAIOUSSA

The **earliest evidence of settlement** is on the promontory and is dated to the end of the 2nd century BC. Elaioussa was defended by a wall closing the isthmus and by the natural cliffs all around. The area was then in the hands of the **Seleucids**, but by the 1st century BC it was minting its own coins. With Rome's sustained involvement in Asia Minor, it came into the hands of the king of Cappadocia. It is at this time that the settlement began to **expand onto the mainland** and in gratitude the king renamed it Sebaste, one of the honorific titles of Augustus. After becoming part of the **Province of Cilicia** in AD 72, Elaioussa settled down to a period of prosperity which lasted to the mid-3rd century. Its economic activity expanded to include the exploitation of the timber resources of the Taurus Mountains.

An extensive **building programme** was set in motion, encroaching on a necropolis to the north of the isthmus. The extensive necropolis which developed to the west shows an **increase in population**, which was also the reason for the **aqueduct**, which taps the Lamas (the same aqueduct that served Corycus, described above). By the end of the 2nd century, Elaioussa could style itself the 'metropolis of the coast', no mean feat. Trouble came in the second half of the 3rd century, first from the sea (the **Persians**, who also destroyed Corycus) and then mountain tribes from the north. There was a revival in the 5th and 6th centuries under the **Byzantines**. Olive oil and wine sold well and a new construction programme of Christian buildings was put in place, with the inevitable use of spolia. It appears that the people were well nourished, at least in the case of those well enough off to have a tomb and whose bones posterity has been able to analyse.

The **two 6th-century wrecks** discovered just off the coast testify to a busy trade with Syria and Egypt. However there was **unrest**, as traces of arson and vandalism show. The **Arabs**, who first came in 672, coupled with a succession of **earthquakes**, put an end to Elaioussa, whose inhabitants dwindled to a few squatters occupying the theatre and some of the tombs. Today Elaioussa has found a new lease of life as an **archaeological park**, but it is challenged by the fact that the coast road that crosses the site has recently been widened from 14m to 26m and that tourist development on the coast remains unchecked.

EXPLORING ELAIOUSSA

There is a shaded picnic ground next to the site, much patronised by local families. It is a pleasant place to relax after a visit; make sure you bring provisions with you.

Begin the tour with the **theatre**, on the mainland across the road. It was constructed by carving and smoothing the rock and modifying pre-existing structures, namely an aqueduct, as well as obliterating a residential complex with baths. Facing south, it is c. 55m in diameter and could accommodate 2,300 people. Although over a semicircle in circumference (the Greek or Hellenistic model), it is dated to the mid-2nd century AD. At an unspecified time almost all the steps were removed in a single operation (all but one used later for the reconstruction). A narrow reconstructed cuneus gives an idea of how it once looked. Prior to excavation, the cavea had been filled with earth and terraced for agriculture (lemon trees). The orchestra was originally paved with pavonazzetto marble, at least judging by a small fragment *in situ*. The scena was renovated towards the end of the 2nd century: it had five entrances, like many theatres of the time in Asia Minor. The south face of the scena had a nymphaeum and cisterns behind it. Evidence shows that the building was already deteriorating by the 3rd century, while the cisterns went out of use in the 7th century when the area was abandoned.

Southwest of the theatre was the **Roman agora**. Paved with slabs, it was square, 31m by 32m, with stoas all around, a circular building in the middle and a couple of fountains on the west side. There are fine remains of the perimeter wall in beautiful ashlars. The agora is dated to the 2nd century AD and occupied the space of a previous early Imperial building with mosaic floors. In the early Byzantine period a **basilica** was erected in this area. The new building made large use of spolia. The shape of the basilica, with two apses facing each other, is unusual; it had a nave and two aisles. The floor was a polychrome carpet in *opus sectile* with geometric motifs. Most has been preserved; at the time of writing it was being reconstructed and will be on display in due course. The baptistery was in the north aisle. The excavators believe that the two apses might have had different functions: the one to the east was for celebrating the ritual while that to the west was for displaying relics. The large number of people buried in the church suggest that it was tied to the cult of a martyr, whose name we do not know. The church was abandoned in the 7th century, when artisans used it for their workshops. It finally collapsed in an earthquake in the 13th century.

Five **baths complexes** have been identified, situated on the promontory, to the west of town and in the town. The most impressive are the Great Baths, south of the theatre and east of the agora. The building is not yet fully excavated.

The palace (*see below*) on the **isthmus** occupies the area where a polygonal defence wall stood in the 2nd–1st century BC. In the early 2nd century AD a new wall was built, as well as a stoa with marble columns about 6m deep by the north harbour. The wall with towers extended to the southern part of the promontory. A **monumental gate** marked the access to the mainland. The date of the work is thought to be around the end of the 2nd century.

The early Byzantine **palace** that followed affected the defence walls less than it did the harbour stoa. Its columns were walled up, floor levels were altered and the stoa became the palace vestibule. The palace had an unconventional plan, still incomplete because it is not fully excavated. There are huge apsidal halls on different levels, signifying a stratified society, and a unique circular portico (that can be visited) with two storeys partly cut in the rock, almost 30m across. This building stands out among the contemporary building of the town, not only by its size but also by its extravagant decoration. It was a civic building which fairly soon met a violent end: evidence of fire and wilful damage has been linked to Procopius' account of social unrest in Cilicia in the 6th century.

The only **temple** so far identified stands well outside town on a ridge to the west, overlooking the sea in a position of high visibility, a true landmark for sailors. Its dedication is unkown. It was severely damaged by an earthquake in the 7th century and later converted into a church. This was not an easy task since the temple's axis was north–south. The result was a very small chapel requiring a new entrance (*see overleaf*). The apse now faced east and was decorated with a mosaic of the Antiocheian school depicting birds and animals in an idealised setting.

Since it has no natural springs, an **aqueduct** was of prime important for Elaioussa and it had one from the 1st century AD, bringing water from the Lamas river (today's Limonlu) 10km to the east. It was channelled down the Lamas gorge and then proceeded down rock-cut waterways. Four bridges in total were required to cross as many small valleys; the aqueduct served both Elaioussa and Corycus. Its course has been plotted in full. Noticeably, when the theatre was built, the pre-existing pipes were rearranged to trace a semicircular course beneath the seats. A *castellum aquae* has been identified in the vicinity of the theatre. It is thought that a branch served the promontory. The aqueduct was still maintained and restored in the 6th century.

CONVERSIONS

When the Roman Empire evolved from a pagan state into a Christian entity, it was not only the citizens who converted to the new religion, the city's buildings underwent a conversion as well.

Christianity was only tolerated at first but when it was elevated to the status of official religion, the faithful could worship in public while attendance at the pagan temples was more than frowned upon. As early as AD 335, Constantine ordered the temple on Golgotha in Aelia Capitolina, now Jerusalem, to be destroyed and a church built in its place. In the process he found remnants of the True Cross and Christ's sepulchre. This was in a prime location at the heart of the old city. But central locations were not typical sites for early churches: when the same emperor gifted land to the Christians of Rome, he offered them a plot that was not central at all. The church of St John Lateran is barely inside the old city walls. It is not until a few decades later that we begin to see a Christian landscape developing at the heart of the city. It was Theodosius' momentous decision in 380 to make Christianity the official religion of the Empire and to increase the power of the bishops, who took over the civic administration as the old order broke down, that tipped the balance.

There are a few instances of civic basilicas turned into churches, and examples of chapels in amphitheatres—possibly commemorating martyrs but certainly taking advantage of the robust vaulted substructures—can be found from Durrës to Tarragona. However, the main targets for reuse, conversion or destruction were the temples, embodiments of the old, discredited religion with its bloody sacrifices and idol worship. They were thought to create a focus for lingering pagan sentiment and as such needed to be purified or disposed of. Temples in towns tended to be in central locations and this is precisely what worried the civic authorities, who feared that they might become a focus for idol worshippers. However, they were undoubtedly landmarks in the cityscape and as such a source of civic pride. Temples also controlled vast estates, which had ensured their maintenance and continued functioning. When these estates were appropriated by the state or by the church, the temples began to decay and repairs were not carried out. This in the long run was more damaging than the assaults by bands of zealous monks, the sort of thing that spelled the end of the Serapaeum in Alexandria in 386, much publicised in late antique pagan literature.

Approaches to temple conversion were varied as temples normally consisted of a small inner cella (just large enough to house the image of the divinity) surrounded or fronted by a colonnade. This did not readily lend itself to the needs of a church, which requires space for a congregation and where the altar is inside. Some temples were large enough for a 'cella conversion' i.e. putting the church inside the cella, as in the case of the Parthenon or the Temple of Apollo at Didyma (*covered in Blue Guide Aegean Turkey*). The only additional requirement was an apse and, in the case of the Temple of Roma and Augustus at Ankara, which had already lost its columns, a rearrangement of the roof structure. Another approach was to fill in the spaces between the columns to create walls, thus including the entire temple podium in the church floor plan. This gave a large enough space which then had to be re-roofed, as at Diocaesarea (*see above*). A similar example on a grander scale can be seen at Aphrodisias (*covered in Blue Guide Aegean Turkey*), where the Temple of Aphrodite, measuring 8.5m by 31m, was replaced by the Cathedral of St Michael (26m by 60m). This was achieved by, as the excavators put it, 'turning the temple inside out'. Most of the columns stayed put; aisles were added on either side. Such instances are very rare.

When direct conversion was not suitable, for example in cases where the temple was damaged, the temple was plundered in bulk for its building stones (good ashlars and decorative elements). This is the case of the two churches at Castabala (*p. 230*), believed to be reincarnations of the Temple of Artemis Perasia.

Church orientation (with apses required to face east and the entrance to the west) does not appear to have been a serious problem to start with. In the small church that was created in the agora temple at Assos the apse points west. It was only later that strict requirements regarding orientation were introduced. On the whole, when faced with a pile of valuable rubble or a structure not always the right shape, the Byzantine architects showed imagination and problem-solving skills. We have them to thank for fobbing off the lime-burners who obliterated so much of the past by turning marble into lime.

KUMKUYU

At Kumkuyu (*map D, 7*), c. 6km east of Elaioussa, there are things to see either inland or by the sea. Inland (take the turning in the direction of Esenpınar) there is the **sinkhole of Kanytelis**, where a subterranean water course has dissolved the weak limestone and caused its collapse. The site (*open daily April–Oct 9–7, Nov–March 8–5; charge*) has been equipped for visitors with the provision of walkways but bear in mind that there are a number of unprotected cisterns around, so watch where you put your feet if you stray off the beaten path.

The remains of the settlement are 4km on, by the edge of the spectacular **Kanlıdivane chasm**. Its name is either a corruption of an original name pointing to bloody deeds (*kan* means blood in Turkish) or was perhaps inspired by the red tinge of the rock. Kanytelis was a Hellenistic settlement in the orbit of the king-priests of Olba (*p. 191*), devoted to the worship of Zeus Olbios. It prospered through Roman times and flourished under the Byzantines at the time of Theodosius II, at the end of the 5th century, when it became an important **religious and pilgrimage centre**. At that time it changed its name to Neapolis. It was abandoned in the 11th century as the Seljuks occupied the area.

There are doubts as to whether this was a true town since there seems to be no trace of civic buildings. It has been compared appropriately to Lourdes. The **Hellenistic tower** in polygonal masonry guarded the approaches to the settlement. The remains are quite tall, over 17m in height. According to an inscription it was dedicated by Teucros, a priest of Zeus Olbios, in 200 BC. Note the triskele on the lintel above the entrance, confirming its Olban connection. On the edge of the sinkhole are the impressive remains of four large **Byzantine basilicas**, suggesting that by the 5th century the new religion had taken a firm hold. Nevertheless, the holy aura of the site still lingered on after the Byzantines departed, as indicated by the **Muslim cemetery**, still in use. Sinkholes held a special power for Cilicians, suggesting communication with the other world. The chasm measures 90m by 70m and is 60m deep with a healthy growth of trees at the bottom. On the south side a **relief of a family** of six is believed to be Roman, according to the style of the work and the togas. Another **relief with a soldier** is lower down and can be seen from the eastern rim.

AKKALE

Akkale, the 'White Castle', is between Route 400 and the sea. Take the turn marked Kumkuyu Marina: you will see the buildings after 200m. The ruins were first noticed by Beaufort (*p. 23*) in 1812. He saw the **cisterns** and the rock-cut **harbour** and its structures, and inland the remains of the buildings with arcades, turrets, balconies and winding stairs. These days, because of the overgrowth, you can explore the outside of the main building, one cistern, the mausoleum and a stretch of the paved access road. For a long time Akkale (a modern name) was neglected. Talk of restoration by the Mersin municipality is somewhat premature as the site so far has only been cursorily surveyed, not excavated.

The purpose of this settlement is still debated. It is not a town; it is more like a grand country villa at the centre of an agricultural region and provided with its own harbour facilities. Gertrude Bell (*p. 28*) thought it a fortified monastery, but there is no large church. It is too close to the coast for safety to have been a village and the style of the buildings does not quite tally. The **Main Building**, with a 65m-long façade, was U-shaped with wings facing the sea. The main body of the structure consisted of two or possibly three long, barrel-vaulted halls running east–west. The north façade, over two storeys high, had a long continuous balcony and four windows. To the west it had a tower in large ashlars and to the east a domed room, accessed via a spiral staircase, protruded slightly. Measuring 9m by 10m, this domed room was entered from the south. The two wings, of which only the east one was able to be surveyed, contain large barrel-vaulted rooms. The construction is of rubble faced with ashlar and partly stands on substantial substructures.

The **Great Cistern** is nearby. It measured 33m by 20m and is 10m deep, with steps in the southwest corner. Its roof was supported by two rows of six pillars. It was partly cut out of the rock, partly built. The vaulted ceiling has vents (unprotected) at regular intervals. The surface was waterproofed. On the outside, given the great weight of the building and the lie of the land, it was strengthened with pillars on the east side. It is not clear how such a large cistern was filled but it fed the nearby **baths**, which had apsidal rooms and marble panelling.

The **harbour** is about 1km south of the Main Building. A rock-cut channel conducted water to a small cistern. A **signal tower** and a rock-cut **ramp** have been identified. The stonework is 5th century, which rules out suggestions that have made this the gilded retreat of deposed kings such as Tarcondimotus Philantonius, as he lived earlier, at the turn of the millennium. Three **inscriptions**, two in the baths and one in the residence, mention an Illous, who has been identified with the chief minister (*magister officiorum* and *patricius*) of the emperor Zeno. He died in 488 and is known to have had a country villa somewhere on the Mediterranean coast. There are several examples of such extravaganzas all over the Roman Empire in the late antique/early Byzantine period. To paraphrase Olympiodorus of Thebes, a contemporary, these fine residences contained all the things that could be found in a medium-sized city. He goes on to list them: a hippodrome, piazzas, temples, fountains and baths. He was talking of late antique Rome. Perhaps here, Illous had to make do without the hippodrome.

PRACTICAL INFORMATION

GETTING THERE AND AROUND

Gazipaşa-Alanya Airport is located very near the city centre of Gazipaşa and 1hr drive from Alanya. A shuttle service is available. The Gazipaşa *otogar* is in town by Route 400.

WHERE TO STAY

Accommodation in Rough Cilicia is mainly in Alanya and Gazipaşa. There is no tradition of small *pansiyons* in the stretch in between because the coast is still comparatively empty. The few establishments that have recently sprung up inland are huge luxury hotels.

In **Alanya** the **Öğretmen evi** on Atatürk Blv at the west end of Cleopatra beach (*alanyaogretmenevi. com; T: 90 242 512 57 92*) offers fine views of the Mediterranean (ask for a sea-facing room). All the rooms are decent, however, and prices are very reasonable. You will be able to reach the peninsula with any of the buses that serve the busy Atatürk Blv. On the peninsula (the Tophane Mahalle) are fine boutique hotels overlooking the harbour; you will pay for the view but it is worth it. Try the **Lemon Villa Boutique Hotel**, very close to the Red

Tower (*lemonvillahotel.com*; T: 90 242 513 44 61) or the **Centauera Boutique Hotel** (*centauera.com*; T: 90 242 519 00 16) right above the old shipyards. Both have interesting stone architecture coping creatively with the slope. The interiors are a bit overdone, but nothing can spoil the magnificent view that will accompany your breakfast.

In **Gazipaşa** the **Guven Hotel** (*T: 90 242 572 48 48*) is in the centre of town on Route 400 and close to the *otogar*. No breakfast is served: go to the Dedeoğlu bakery, 150m northwest along the same road, for baklava and Turkish coffee.

In **Anamur**, accommodation is outside the centre of town to the southeast, by the beach. You can try the **Tayfun Hotel** (*T: 90 324 814 11 61*) which has good-sized rooms and an interesting restaurant. Leave town going east and take the right turn (Anamur Ehmenek Yolu), marked İskele at the roundabout, with the statue of a woman holding a bunch of bananas (ask for '*muzlu kadın heykeli*').

The rest of the coast, to Silifke and beyond, does not have much to offer since tourism is still undeveloped. **Taşucu** may be preferable to Silifke. But if you want to stop in **Silifke**, the Silifke Öğretmenevi (*T: 90 324 714 70 16*) is central, on İnönü Blvd.

Further east you will find big, soulless modern blocks (sometimes with underpasses to get to the beach), with the exception possibly of **Kızkalesi/Korikos**. There the **Kilikya Hotel** (*kilikyahotel.com*; T: 90 324 523 21 15) is right in front of castle, which you can admire while floating on the blue waters.

If you happen to be in the hinterland, rely on the network of Öğretmen evi (*p. 13*) in **Mut**, on Sıktı Soylu Sk (*T: 90 324 774 16 29*), near the edge of town and clearly signed.

WHAT TO EAT

The standard fare will always be available, but Cilicia offers you a chance to get to grips with the varied aspects of Turkish cuisine and to try something different, for instance **Tantuni** (a wrap with a tasty filling of vegetables and cut-up meat) said to have first developed in Mersin. The bread looks like lavash, so perhaps one can detect Syrian or Armenian influences here. Give **Batırık** a try if you come across it; it is a bulgur-based mix with tomatoes (fresh and dried), sesame, onion, mint and chopped pistachios, rolled into balls and served on a bed of salad and sliced cucumber. Delicious.

WHAT TO DO

For a day out in a stunning natural setting try the **Sapadere Canyon** (*sapaderekanyonu.com*; map C, 7) well inland 20km southeast of Alanya. Some 800m long, the canyon is a great gash in the rock with numerous waterfalls and natural wonders; it will keep you in its spell for a whole day. It is situated well inland. To get there, take the coastal road from Alanya (going east) and turn inland at Demirtaş, just after crossing the stream. From there it is c. 14km inland, signposted. You can go there by yourself (it is always accessible) or better, join a guided tour from Alanya. The facilities are still quite basic, though there is restaurant at the entrance and a café later on; remember to take water and suncream with you and some mosquito repellent.

SMOOTH CILICIA

The **Limonlu Çay**, the river anciently known as the Lamas, marks the border between Rough and Smooth Cilicia according to Strabo (*14, 5, 6*); later on it was the border between the Byzantine Empire to the west and the Arabs, well established in Tarsus. Here they exchanged prisoners in the 8th–9th centuries. The point of transition was marked by the **Lamas Kale**, a castle on top of a hill near the river, with good visibility of the Mediterranean; it later fell into the hands of the Armenians. From Silifke to here, settlement has been on the coast and only slightly inland as the mountains are close to the sea and the interior is rugged and unattractive. This does not mean it was not explored in antiquity. Remains deep in the Taurus mountains, 47km northwest of Mersin and well above the present tree line at 2437m, belong to a **signal station** and a settlement not far from it. The signal station was a well-constructed tower identified with the **Tetrapyrga** of the *Tabula Peutingeriana* (whose name, Tetrapyrga or 'Four Towers', suggests that there should be three further towers somewhere). Not far from it, a **settlement** of some 100–150 houses with stone walls, monolithic doorposts and tiled roofs set in a network of wide streets has been surveyed. The few column drums are puzzling. Admittedly today or in the recent past these high lands were used as summer pastures (*yaylas*) and in antiquity the treeline was a couple of hundred metres higher. Deforestation has taken its toll on the Taurus. Even so, this looks like an all-year-round settlement. It probably controlled the route from Soli (*see below*) to Lycaonia. Here at the watershed, the high reaches of the Taurus join the Anatolian Plateau.

MEZİTLİ (SOLI)

Soli, now Mezitli (*map D, 5*) or Solin, the 'City of the Sun', to which it holds a yearly festival with plenty of music and dance, is today looking for its place in the sun. The trouble is that Mersin has significantly expanded westwards. Ancient Soli, to give it its original name, is no more than an enclave surrounded by high-rise buildings. Beaches are scarce and tourists even scarcer. The ancient settlement within the walled area, as surveyed by Beaufort (*p. 23*) in 1812, was about 240m by 90m. A larger area has been set aside by the local municipality for archaeologists but land that is not built over tends to be under cultivation and in private hands. The so-called **Tomb of Aratus**, a Greek poet born in the late 4th century BC, has highlighted the problem. Though a 'monumental tomb of Aratus' has recently been discovered, it cannot be touched because it is under a greenhouse, on private land. Add to this the fact that Aratus died in Pella (Macedonia) and you can see the magnitude of Soli's struggle to meet its ambitions.

HISTORY OF SOLI

Soli has a long past going back to the **Neolithic**. Work on the mound to the east, against which the Roman theatre was later built, has shown Neolithic structures followed by evidence of **Hittite involvement**, possibly in their desire to gain a foothold on the sea in order to operate in Syria and Cyprus. Hittite material from a burial context, including seals and weapons, is now in the Berlin State Museum. There appears to have been a **Greek presence** from 700 BC, developing into a fully-fledged city controlled by Athens. This brought its advantages since Soli's famous citizens Chrysippus (a Stoic philosopher), Aratus (a poet) and Philemon (a dramatist) all moved to Athens for their education. They must have arrived there speaking fractured Greek, full of mistakes, if the etymology of **solecism** (from the name of the town) is correct. The architectural terracottas (simas, antefixes and roof tiles) found on the mound, with Greek and orientalising motifs, may have belonged to a temple of Athena, meaning a Greek presence as the Assyrians waned c. 600 BC.

Alexander the Great came past on his way east and later the **Seleucids** took control of Soli. As their power dimmed, Soli suffered at the hands of Tigranes, King of Armenia, who destroyed it in 83 BC. Pompey the Great was magnanimous in his handling of repentant pirates and settled a colony of them here as well as providing funds for rebuilding. Soli was now **Pompeiopolis** and never looked back—at least until 525, when a powerful earthquake shook it; by then it had a **bishop**. Worse was to come, however, as the city was very vulnerable to sea attacks by the Persians and the Arabs. Then came the **Yürüks**. They settled here and toppled the columns to get to the lead dowels that kept the drums together. Finally, in the late 19th century, the growing city of Mersin used it as a quarry. In the medieval Italian portulans, the harbour was called Bombolizo and was still serviceable. Laborde's (*p. 28*) drawings of 1828 show twelve columns standing in a marshy plain against a soundscape (described in his memoirs) provided by boar, jackals and foxes.

REMAINS OF ANCIENT SOLI

The two main sights of Soli are the harbour and the colonnaded street, which are dated to the 2nd century AD. Beaufort (*p. 23*) saw stumps of city walls and evidence of buildings inside the circuit. What was not removed is now probably buried. The deltas to the east of the Cydnus and the Sarus, as well as the strong westerly currents, are responsible for a lot of deposition of lime and silt.

The **colonnaded street** is the most visible remaining structure of Soli, its visiting card so to speak. It runs north–south from the north gate to the harbour, to which it was connected by an arch that Beaufort saw and which has now disappeared. According to Beaufort, a paved road continued east outside the walls and crossed a river. The street was 450m long at its full extent and 14m wide, with **shops** on either side, some with mosaic and *opus sectile* floors. It has been calculated that the columns numbered 200 in total. Today there are just 33 left which are endlessly photographed, usually with a wide-angle lens which makes them appear to lean (which they do not). The local stone is rather coarse and rough, which means that the honorific inscriptions have corroded badly and can no longer be read. The capitals are Corinthian and most of the columns have consoles, which would once have held statues and busts. According to Hellenkemper, the columns were all the same; today they are a little bit disparate. The passage of time, reuse and re-erection must account for this.

The **harbour**, at the south end of the colonnaded street but with an entrance for some reason not perfectly aligned with it, is a structure with an elegant design that is both interesting and new. Built partly on a natural reef, it is an oblong feature with straight sides curving into two semicircles at either end. It was built with cemented rubble, an aggregate of tuff and travertine, covered by clamped ashlars (as many as six clamps per block) to form a quay 320m long and 180m wide. Study of the binding material has concluded that the pozzolana came from its original source in the Phlegraean Fields near Naples and was used here for a strong bond. The harbour mouth is depicted on an 2nd-century AD coin as being due south but it is thought that in reality it was to the southeast, more protected against the prevailing winds. At present the harbour is filled with lime and rubble. When Beaufort saw it, he noted a **petrified beach**, with the pebbles glued together by the hard water. The date of the construction is AD 130–150.

Soli was serviced by **two aqueducts** bringing water down from the hills. They still functioned in Byzantine times, when Bishop Theodorus repaired them.

MERSİN & THE ÇUKUROVA

Mersin (*map D, 5*), now a city of one million, is a recent creation of the mid-19th century. It came about with the stabilisation of the environment, both physical and social, of the land to the east, the Cilicia Pedias of antiquity, now the Çukurova (something like 'the land of pits'). Mersin was developed as a harbour to trade the produce of the reclaimed land, e.g. cotton and rice, with the world at large. The driving force behind this was the Levantine community, tightly knit and entrepreneurial, aptly described by Joseph O'Neill in his *Blood-Dark Track*. Freya Stark (*p. 32*) found the city squalid and at the same time rich, and she refers to the large foreign presence. Most active among them was the Greek-Cypriot Mauromatis family (merchants, producers and bankers) as well as a sizeable French contingent, well integrated in the circles of world commerce. They traded and contributed extensively to the modernising of agricultural practices. With this came important investment in the transport infrastructure. Today's Cilicia Pedias has changed beyond recognition (*see below*).

The 23m-high mound of **Yumruktepe**, overlooking the Kızıl Deresi in the centre of Mersin, a couple of kilometres from the present coastline, shows a very early occupation (7000 BC) lasting until medieval times, when it stops. However, the occupation is not continuous and it is difficult to make this mound the ancestor of modern Mersin.

LOOKING BACK IN TIME: THE ÇUKUROVA
After Soli the mountains recede, turning northeast and leaving a huge basin edged

to the east by the Amanus Mountains. The summits are still high, rising to over 3750m (Demirkazık Tepe), 87km north of Adana. Over the millennia **three large rivers** have done their work, relentlessly carrying and depositing sediment and pushing the coastline outwards. From the west, these rivers are the **Cydnus** (Tarsus Çay), the **Sarus** (Seyhan) and the **Pyramus** (Ceyhan). The last two especially are huge, turbulent watercourses; they have over time changed beds and merged deltas, adding to the **environmental instability**.

The region itself is not very large nor particularly well endowed: the sea is shallow and the coast unsuited to harbour facilities. However, in antiquity it occupied a crucial space between East and West, connecting Anatolia to Mesopotamia via the Syrian Desert's north edge or following the coast to Syria and leading ultimately to Egypt. North of Tarsus was the lowest pass across the Taurus, the **Cilician Gates** (Gülek Boğazı), opening the door to armies and traders to and from the East. Other routes had to cross higher passes. An **east–west route** was therefore essential from time immemorial. It was developed on the very north edge of the river marshes, at the foot of the hills and taking advantage of providential rocky outcrops to the east (the Misis Mountains), which allowed a safe passage to the top end of the gulf of İskenderun. Here the route was barred by another obstacle, the Amanus.

In her detailed study of the development of the Çukurova, the Roman Aleius Campus (*Strabo 14,5,17*), Meltem Toksöz charts its 19th-century history in detail; before that the story is provided by archaeology. There is not a lot to see since agriculture has ploughed over the evidence and modern development has buried it. Suffice it to say that a number of **Neolithic mounds** in the plain have been identified. They gave way in Hellenistic and Roman times to a **line of cities** along the foothills. Some of them did not survive the Arab onslaught. The **Arabs** settled here for about 300 years, making it their base for raids deep into Anatolia. The number of strongholds was reduced. The later **Armenian occupation** added a successful harbour to the area's amenities, as will be explained below.

In the 19th century, a long time after the Armenians had tried to impose some order (they lost control of their kingdom in 1375), the Çukurova was a **marshy plain** barred by dunes to the south, full of malaria and inhabited by nomads: they did not pay tax and lived outside the law: in the Ottoman Empire it was a grey zone between Anatolia and the Arab world. In 1671 Evliya Çelebi (*p. 25*) had already contrasted 'lively Adana' with the surrounding countryside, which in his view was impassable by humans.

The **Kütahya Agreement** (1833) was one of the attempts by the sultan to take the situation in hand. Adana province became part of Egypt, then ruled by Muhammad Ali, only nominally a vassal of the sultan. This made sense. Egypt had a tradition of land reclamation, a prosperous cotton industry and long experience of dealing with a nomad population. The arrangement did not quite work but it pointed the way for further developments with the **Tanzimat** (reform movement) of the 1870s. Settlement was enforced, the population increased by successive waves of **migrants and refugees** from the shrinking Ottoman Empire; security was improved, **new towns** were founded, a land code ensured property rights, a strain of cotton adapted to the local conditions was developed and mechanisation was introduced, doubling the amount of land under cultivation between 1871 and 1918. By then the Çukurova was one of the most productive areas of the Ottoman Empire. It suffered with the Armenian troubles and, judging by Yaşar Kemal's *Iron Earth Copper Sky*, published in 1963, life here was far from easy. His description of **forgotten communities** deep in the valleys, oppressed by debt and leading precarious existences as seasonal cotton pickers down in the plain, is telling. The Çukurova today has reinvented itself, presenting to the outside world a face that bears little witness to its troubled past.

TARSUS

Tarsus (*map D, 5*) is the first of three stepping-stones across the marshes and it has a long history because it is in a sensitive zone. It is 70km from the Cilician Gates, the best pass across the Taurus, and it is on a river, the Cydnus (now the Tarsus Çay), at the point where it could be reached from the sea and formed a lagoon that was used as a harbour. Whether it was at the time of the **Hittites** who came from the north to get to the sea and the southeast, or conversely of the **Assyrians** who came in the other direction, first as traders and then as conquerors, Tarsus was always at the forefront because of its position. And when it was not conquest or the passage of armies, it was trade that came through Tarsus, passing along the same route.

Tarsus's fortunes only waned when the Cilician Gates lost their primacy. That happened in the 13th century: the pass leading into the Sultanate of Rum lost its pre-eminence when the sultanate collapsed under Mongol pressure. The power in Cilicia at the time were the **Armenians** and their trading pattern was different. For a start they put their capital, Sis (*p. 226*), up in the mountains rather than at Tarsus, and secondly they opened up a different trade route, operated by Latin merchants and based in the harbour of Lajazzo (Yumurtalık; *p. 216*). Tarsus was bypassed and declined. It has only recently revived, on the coat-tails of Mersin and the regeneration of the Çukurova.

A SHORT HISTORY OF TARSUS

The mound of Gözlükule to the south of town was investigated by an American team before WWII and again recently by Turkish archaeologists. The results have been spectacular, confirming that Tarsus has a **Hittite past**. A large building dated c. 15th century BC, completely different in style and technique from constructions in the earlier levels, has been interpreted as an administrative building or a temple. A number of seals and bullae have been found. The Hittite presence is therefore proved but the lack of an archive means that this was not a capital but a major centre dealing with high-ranking officials. It must be the Hittite Tarsa mentioned in a tablet.

The **Assyrians** left their mark by destroying the town in 696 BC, after which Sennacherib, according to the source, 'rebuilt it in the image of Babylon with a temple where the gods could live'. We have no way of confirming this; however, it is notable that Tarsus's coinage from the 2nd century BC to the end of the 3rd century AD had an Assyrian appearance, with gods standing on horned animals and wearing Assyrian-style headdresses. It has been suggested that there was a meeting of minds between the locals and the occupiers conflating Marduk, the chief Assyrian god, with Sanda, a local deity. It is thought that under the Assyrians Tarsus was a provincial capital and a naval base. The mound has little to say about the Roman period, when the occupation was lower down. The sources mention **St Paul**, a native of Tarsus and proud of it: his was 'no mean city' (*Acts 21,39*). Plutarch (*Life of Anthony 25*) regales us with a possibly somewhat fanciful description of **Cleopatra** sailing upstream on a gilded barge propelled by silver oars and graced with a complement of young ladies playing the flute and scattering incense and other perfumes. She does have a gate to her name here (*see below*) but it is only fair to say that the gate is also known as Kancık Gate, meaning 'bitch'.

There must have been a **wall circuit** in the mid-4th century since according to Ammianus, Julian the Apostate was buried outside its north gate following his own wishes; he probably did not want to be buried in Constantinople, in a Christian setting. The other two gates pointed south to the harbour and east to Adana. Tarsus was still prospering in the 6th century and attracted Justinian's attention. He redirected the river to the east, so that it would no longer cross the town and create havoc when full and turbulent, and built a new bridge across it (*see below*).

Tarsus came again to the fore at the time of the **Arab conquest**. It became the capital of the frontier zone (the Thughur) between the Caliphate and the Byzantine Empire and developed into an Arab town in which warriors lived, ready for the next campaign. This brought with it a certain degree of modification. For a start, the river was renamed Al Baradan, after the waters flowing at the time through Damascus. The town was refortified with a double wall, 87 towers, six gates and a ditch. The figure quoted by the historian Ibn Hawqal, of 100,000 mounted warriors living inside the circuit, is perhaps an exaggeration but certainly, going by the quantity of material found on Gözlükule, it appears that Tarsus was then an Abassid city with distant contacts. It is possible that at this point Tarsus lost its grid, if it ever had one.

The transition from polis to medina, as Hugh Kennedy has cogently argued, has to do with the form of local administration. If there is no central civic authority to clear the roads and supervise building operations, street patterns will change. If a neighbourhood feels close, it will turn itself into a gated community by controlling access. Streets could become cluttered and narrow, houses would extend by means of first-floor bridges. The transition from wheeled transport to pack animals would not require wide avenues. The authorities would not intervene. One could only hope to get redress by obtaining access to a *kadi* (a judge), which could be a cumbersome process. Besides, if an informal plan suits everyone, why bother? From Tarsus the Arabs defied the Byzantines by land, raiding Anatolia; and by sea, launching assaults on Antalya, Salonica, Egypt and Cyprus.

In 965 Tarsus reverted to the Byzantines for a brief interlude (most of the population moved to Antioch, which at the time was firmly in Arab hands) before falling to the Seljuks and later to the Armenians, then to the Mamluks and finally the Ottomans.

Piecing together the sources, pre-WWI Tarsus occupied the area within the Arab wall circuit, which was still visible in the street pattern, a roundish shape about 1km across. Today the urban spread is 5km across; builders have been busy. Archaeologists do what they can but while valuable work continues on the large mound of Gözlükule, there is practically no research archaeology being conducted on the urban spread below. The beautiful finds in Tarsus Museum (*see below*) have no context or at least they are presented without any and publication is scarce. Moreover, talk of illegal excavations 300m deep (sic), of treasure and even international involvement is rife. The Vatican recently felt the need to issue an official denial that it was sponsoring a dig in Tarsus to look for 'St Paul's Bible'.

WHAT TO SEE IN TARSUS

According to Helen Gibbons, the wife of Herbert Gibbons, then a teacher at Robert College in Istanbul in early 1900s, the Roman city was vast, an inexhaustible quarry for local housing. Defaced and mutilated remains were strewn around. She goes on to paint a vivid portrait of Tarsus at the time of the Armenian troubles in the early 20th century, which is the core of her *The Red Rags of Tarsus*. The city then was surrounded by about a dozen branches of the Tarsus Çay, used for irrigation, washing, mills and drinking water. Turtles swam about in it. Swamps were the domain of boar and buffalo. One hundred years on, there is little left of that.

The **Kancık Kapısı** on Ismet Paşa Blv, not far from Gözlükule, has been hastily linked to Cleopatra in popular lore (*see above*). The analysis of the structure and the building technique has shown that it is a medieval structure. The outer skin has recently been completely renovated. You can only see the original building work in a small area. The inscription next to it, dated to the first half of the 3rd century AD, has been moved from its original setting.

Stroll to **Gözlükule** and you may see the archaeologists at work and have a cool drink. Enjoy the view south over the plain, where in the past was the Rhegma (a Greek word meaning 'fissure, crack', a possible allusion to the many waterways), the **harbour of Tarsus**, with docks, quays and stores. Somewhere against the slope of the mound was the **Roman theatre**.

Following Abdi İpekçi Cd. and across Atatürk Cd., a fine example of 2nd-century BC **road building** has been exposed. It is paved with basalt slabs with a sewer running beneath it. The **stoa** beside it was the gift of the Seleucids, who held Tarsus at the time. It was then that the city received a new name: Antiocheia ad Cydnum. The **well of St Paul** is not far to the northeast, after the market. There is little to say beyond that fact that it is a well. Its connection to St Paul is unsubstantiated and according to recent accounts, its water is not safe to drink.

Another St Paul connection can be found right in the centre of town, at the crossing of Adana Blvd and Menteşoğlu Cd. The **Eski Cami** or **Kilise Cami** is said originally to be the church that St Paul built with his own hands. The three-aisled structure stands 1.2m below street level and has the right orientation for a church. Its stout architecture is medieval Romanesque. There are no spolia; the Armenian inscriptions are hard to read, the capitals have muqarnas and the arches are pointed. Many hands have been at work here; it is difficult to see those of St Paul. Spolia on the other hand can be seen in the **Ulu Cami** a couple of hundred metres to the south. There are some Roman columns and capitals. Attempts have been made to link this building with Aya Sofia, the church where the papal legate Konrad von

Wittelsbach, Archbishop of Mainz, crowned Leon II king of Armenia on 6th January 1199 but the evidence is highly inconclusive.

The **Kırkkaşık Bedesten** nearby is worthy of your attention. It has recently been restored and given over to shops. Its curious name (the '40 Spoons') is apparently a misinterpretation of the frieze of carved lotus buds in the portico. To the untrained eye they may look like spoons. While you shop, go back mentally some 800 years. According to some this was the location of Venetian or Genoese warehouses (their *fondaci*), back in the time when trade was in the hands of the Latins, with whom the Armenians enjoyed cordial relations.

Outside the old town circuit, due east of the bedesten, is a very intriguing monument, the **Donuktaş**. It is a construction 115m long and 43m wide with massive walls. Giosafat Barbaro, a 15th-century Venetian patrician, thought it was a palace; there may have been more to see of it then. Langlois (*p. 29*) later decided that it was the tomb of Sardanapalus, the last king of Assyria. In 1913 the Italian archaeologist Paribeni (*p. 30*) recognised that it was neither palace nor monumental tomb: it was just the foundation in mortared rubble of an unknown monument. It has been excavated recently and dated from the finds to the 2nd century AD. It is now presented as Donuktaş Mektebi. Donuktaş means 'dull stone' (not an inapposite name for the core of a foundation structure). Mektep is meant here as a place of worship (it normally refers to a school), so it could be the remains of a huge temple to Zeus, possibly unfinished but going by its size, in a league with that at Didyma (*see Blue Guide Aegean Turkey*). It could be the Koinon of Cilicia that appears on 2nd-century AD coinage. It was probably plundered by the Arabs when they strengthened Tarsus's defences.

Further east along Adana Blvd, in the **Kuva-i Milliye Parkı**, are the remains of **Justinian's Bridge** (*see above*), a few forlorn arches standing in the dry since the river has changed course to the east. It was known in the Ottoman period as the Baç-Köprüsü, since the caravans paid their duties (*baç*) here.

The newly refurbished **Tarsus Museum** (*open Tues–Sun 8.30–5.30; free*) is at the west end of 3501 Sk in the 75th Anniversary Culture Complex. There you can see the material from Gözlükule as well as chance finds from the town and the region. The finds from graves and an 8th-century AD gold coin hoard show you how rich the town was. Some fine mosaics are also shown. The huge 7m by 8m mosaic with satyrs and maenads, which came to light some years ago during the construction of the courts, awaits you in Antakya. The ethnographic section has material on the traditional dresses and crafts of the nomads that long dominated Smooth Cilicia. There are some beautiful carpets and kilims.

ADANA

Adana (*map D, 6*) would have been the second stopping point in the crossing of the Çukurova. The river Saros, now the Seyhan, spread out and was, according to some, fordable in the dry season. This must remain in the realm of conjecture since a dam has now been built immediately north of town. **Early settlement** (as early as the 3rd millennium BC) is attested in Adana on **Tepebağ**, a mound on the right bank of the river not far from the Taşköprü, for centuries the only fixed crossing point. On the mound, evidence of Bronze Age occupation has been identified. However, a continuous thread is elusive. Adana's trajectory has been different from that of Tarsus. For a start it has been subject to the unruly course of the river and its frequent floods. It is also on a **triple geological fault**. Its houses are traditionally made of wood and mud brick, which does not preserve well. In addition, one has to take into account an explosive urban development. Adana had a population of 45,000 in 1890; now it is the fifth most populous city in Turkey, with 1.75 million. It is not surprising that hard evidence is scarce.

ADANA THROUGH THE CENTURIES

An ancient Egyptian statuette of Sitsnefru dated to the 18th century BC testifies to the far-flung contacts that Adana enjoyed in the Bronze Age. According to the inscription, Sitsnefru was a nurse and believed that if she died here and was not buried with her effigy, her soul would not be able to return to Egypt. **Hittite tablets** mention a 'land of Adaniya'; the Hittites would necessarily have come past here on their way to Syria.

Later on, Iron Age Adanawa entered the Hellenistic era under the Seleucids as **Antiocheia ad Sarum**. In the Roman Province of Cilicia it maintained its strategic importance. Hadrian willed the Taşköprü (stone bridge), a solid fixed link very much in the style of the Romans, master bridge builders. It marked the river's furthest navigable point. The town was probably defended on both sides of the river by the **wall** that Kinneir (*p. 27*) saw still standing in 1818. The extent of the **Roman city** is not known, nor are its public buildings, although it appears that by the time it fell into Arab hands it was still an important city (but not as significant as Tarsus). **Harun al Rashid** in the 8th century built a castle on Tepebağ and, according to sources, a wall with a ditch and eight towers around it, enclosing a smaller area. Adana at that time was **Qasr-Saihan** (the city by the Sayhan).

For a long time Adana remained a settlement of lesser importance than Tarsus (*see above*) and Misis (*see below*). This was true for the 10th-century **Byzantines**, for the **Crusaders** ('a nice place by the river but the inhabitants are poor') and for the **Venetian traders**, who are attested here in the 14th century. Urban development came in the late 15th century, when a local emir of the Razamanoğulları dynasty built baths as well as places of worship and of learning. A good part of the Roman stone must have been used for that. The rest possibly went into the building of the Geçitli Han on the left bank of the river, willed by the Ottoman Sultan Mehmet IV in 1661. At the end of the 19th century, Adana was a small oriental town with winding lanes and a small and a mixed population of Armenian Greeks, Turks and Persians. In the 1830s the city stretched between the river and today's Zia Paşa Blvd to the west. There, a marshy ravine was spanned by a bridge (Kuruköprü, the 'dry bridge'). Both bridges (Taşköprü and Kuruköprü) were closed at night.

Expansion came with the **reclamation of the Çukurova**, the **cotton boom** and the **railway link**, part of the Berlin-to-Baghdad project. At the centre of a prosperous region, Adana has never looked back.

WHAT TO SEE IN ADANA

For all its long history, Adana does not have much to show. Indeed, the new **Adana Archaeology Museum** (at the west end of Cumhuriyet Cd; *open daily 9–5; charge*), housed in a revamped textile factory, rich as it is in artefacts, helps little with an understanding of the history of the town. A lot of the exhibits come from the broader region and have no context. Even so, it is a fine place to visit, not least to pay one's respects to the Hittite god Tarhunt. Alas, Sitsnefru the Egyptian nurse (*see above*) is now in the Metropolitan Museum, New York.

In town you can also have a look at **Tepebağ**, soon to be turned into an archaeological park. Adana's climate can be quite humid and oppressive; you will be able to enjoy a breath of fresh air up there. Apart from this, there is the stone bridge or **Taşköprü**, still in use today (though sharing the honour of crossing the Seyhan with nine other bridges). It is a solid construction that was admired by the Arabs. Traditionally it is attributed to Hadrian and Langlois (*p. 29*), who was here in 1852, mentions a dedicatory inscription to the emperor which was still in place then but is now lost. The attribution to Auxentius (an attested bridge-builder in Rome in the 4th century), also based on an inscription now exhibited in the Archaeology Museum (after spending some time in Adana's Greek church as part of an altar), is problematic. A careful reading of the damaged text suggests that Auxentius built an aqueduct, not a bridge. It is possible to walk the full 310m of the bridge, which is now pedestrianised and hosts cultural events; the two lion reliefs were willed by Sultan Ahmet III in 1713. It is worth finding a good viewpoint to admire the elegant line of the structure and the arches reflected in the water, now that the Seyhan has been tamed. Structurally the bridge shows that many hands have been at work, from Justinian in the 6th century to the Arabs and indeed to anyone who has ever used this vital link.

MİSİS (YAKAPINAR)

Right by the river Ceyhan is the rather insignificant village of Yakapınar (*map D, 6*), marking a site of great importance in the past: here was—and still is—the bridge crossing the river. This was the meeting point of the caravan route up the valley, which was used for traffic from Trabzon and Erzurum destined for Lajazzo (*p. 216*), or going along the main east–west axis. This is also the site of Misis, known in antiquity by a variety of names depending in whose hands it was: Mopsuetia to the Seleucids, Romans and Byzantines (3rd century BC to the 7th century AD), Al Massisa to the Arabs (8th–10th centuries), Mamisra to the Crusaders, Armenians and Mamluks (10th–14th centuries). Misis is the name given it by the Ottomans, when they finally wrested it from its latest owner.

Going by travellers' accounts, it seems that much of the evidence of Misis's past has been lost comparatively recently, thanks to economic development and road building. Now it is trying to catch up and put Yakapınar on the tourist map. Turkish and Italian archaeologists have been working hard to unravel a past that stretches back such a long way that the moniker 'the infinite city' has been coined.

Misis's destiny is determined by its **topography**. It has mountains, although not very high ones (the ridge running north–south does not exceed 700m). A large river, the ancient Pyramus (now the Ceyhan), runs through a gap in the ridge, and it is here that Misis is situated. The river was navigable up to Misis for large craft and beyond it for smaller ones. This superb connectivity largely made up for the problem of shaky tectonics, as the area is prone to earthquakes, being located on the Kyrenia Fault Zone.

Archaeologists working at Misis, both in the 1950s and currently, have been excavating the mound situated to the west of the bridge on the right bank of the river. This is a **natural rocky height** at the point where in antiquity the river was fordable in the summer. Deep trenches have shown **continuous occupation** from the Neolithic (as far back as 6th millennium BC) to the Ottomans. In due course the settlement spread to the flat ground below where the modern village is.

An analysis of the stray finds and of travellers' accounts has concluded that the settlement peaked in early **Byzantine** times. It was defended by a **wall** with towers and bastions. The line of the wall, defining a rough trapezium 800m by 500m fronting the river, could still be made out in the 19th century. The **gate** leading to Adana was demolished and obliterated in the 1970s. There is evidence, going by the spolia, of a **colonnaded street** and of a **theatre**, 72m in diameter with the cavea resting on the slope of the mound. **Baths** and a **stadium** partly cut in the rock and partly resting on substructures have been identified to the east. An **aqueduct** came in from the northwest beyond the motorway and was integrated into the defences; it has been traced for 1.5km. It was supplemented by the three **barrel-vaulted cisterns** on the *hüyük*. Temples remain elusive (unless the red granite columns from Egypt belonged to one of them); on the other hand Misis was a **bishopric** by the end of the 4th century, with Theodore the Interpreter noted for his innumerable books on Christian doctrine. He may have officiated in the **three-aisled basilica** found just outside the wall, with its beautiful mosaic of Noah's Ark. Alternatively Theodore could have officiated in the church on the mound, over which a mosque was later built. The **necropolis** extended to the north on the hills; it has numerous inscriptions.

Under the **Romans**, Mopsuetia acquired a **stone bridge** (the crossing must have been previously of wood). The present bridge looks very restored but the basic shape and location are the same. This crossing point maintained its importance up to the 1960s, when a motorway was built to the north.

Trouble—or rather some profound changes still not fully understood—came in the 7th century with the **Arabs**, who settled for centuries in Al Massisa when they were at the height of their power. The defences were overhauled and the settlement occupied both sides of the river. From travellers' accounts, the walls of the settlements were as different in style as they were in name: Al Massisa and Al Kafarbayya. It has been suggested that the Arab occupiers lived in Al Kafarbayya, the 'little Baghdad' of the Arab sources, from where they conducted raids into Byzantine territory just as they did from Tarsus. The Muslim cemetery was separate to the northwest, with Classical spolia used as grave markers. Al Kafarbayya has not yet been excavated. According to an Arab geographer it had a triple wall circuit and dividing walls inside.

In subsequent centuries, because of its strategic position, Misis was disputed by the **Armenians**, the **Crusaders** and the **Muslims**. All the while, Western traders went on with their business handling the caravan traffic. Following total destruction by the **Mamluks** in 1374, Misis lost its primacy as an administrative centre. Even so, in late medieval times it was still renowned for its silk products and figured on portulans as being connected to the sea. When it finally came under **Ottoman** control in 1515, a caravansaray was built on the left bank (Kafirbina Han), still extant in 1830 with a mosque next to it. Nothing now remains of either. It is significant that Misis has now ceased to be a vital commercial node, its mountains are no longer significant; they are being quarried instead.

Misis has been at the centre of things for too many centuries not to stage a comeback, however. The Ottoman watermills are now being restored and a **museum** (*erratic opening hours*) was built to showcase *in situ* the beautiful mosaic of the Christian basilica; however at the time of writing the mosaic had been removed to Adana's new museum. Archaeological work continues.

KARATAŞ

South of Misis, the limestone conglomerate ridge continues to the sea at Cape Karataş (*map D, 8*) with its 40m cliff. The location is forever linked to the expedition of Alexander the Great: Arrian (5,9) clearly states that on his way east, Alexander paused somewhere here, first at **Megarsos** where he sacrificed to Athena Megarsia, then at **Mallos** where he propitiated a demigod by the name of Amphilocus, a renowned seer. One should not be surprised at this sudden bout of piety since the Persians were not far off and Issus, where Alexander finally met and crushed them, was about three days' march away. Antiquarians and archaeologists have been looking for these two sites ever since.

According to recent geophysical work, Megarsos was a triangular shaped settlement edged by the Karataş cliffs to the south and closed by a wall with towers, about 1km long and running east–west. It was gridded and had a colonnaded street. Presently one can only make out the shape of a theatre and of a stadium. The temple remains elusive. As for Mallos, which should be a fraction inland on the west side of the Ceyhan, it is not very clear where it was or if indeed it was a separate entity from Megarsos.

YUMURTALIK

Before you leave the Çukurova, pay a visit to Yumurtalık (*map D, 6*), a fishing village that was at some point, for a short time and for contingent reasons, the centre of east–west traffic. There may not be much to see, but that also means that whatever remains there were, were allowed to blend into the fabric of the village. If you know the history of this place, you can make sense of what you find. Read on.

HISTORY OF YUMURTALIK
Yumurtalık was formerly known as **Ayas** and further back still it was **Lajazzo** or La

Giazza, a name from which Ayas obviously derives. Back in Hellenistic and Roman times it was known as Aigai. Its main assets were a **deep harbour** and a 40-day fair that attracted many merchants. Alongisde this it also ran a famous **oracle of Aesculapius**. The Temple of Aesculapius was closed by Constantine, who ordered its columns to be used for a church. This decision was reversed by Julian the Apostate when he came past in AD 362, on his way to Persia. The temple went up again (though not with the same columns, which could not be removed from the church) and the cult evidently continued: Libanius, a Greek sophist from Antioch, clearly still trusted the pagan gods and was cured of his ills here c. 367. Later, in the mid-5th century, Aigai branched into a new form of divination with **Anthusa**, who could read the future in the shape of the clouds. Beyond that, Roman and Byzantine Aigai is a closed book (but note by the castle entrance a row of typical Roman grain mills in basalt; where do they come from?). The ruins were reused as spolia. Recently, however, four **mosaics** have been uncovered (one very appealing scene shows putti braving the waves sitting astride tritons). They have been taken to the new Adana museum and the local people of Yumurtalık are none too pleased. All four are dated stylistically to the 4th century; there is no context otherwise.

After the **Arabs** destroyed Ayas, it temporarily disappeared from the scene but resurfaced in the 12th century when the area was in the hands of the **Armenians**. They had excellent relations with the Latin traders, who paid them hefty royalties for capitulations. Aigai was in a particularly felicitous location, especially after the fall of Acre in 1291. With that event the merchants lost their last foothold in the East and Aigai offered an alternative route, going north via Misis-Kadırlı-Geben-Sivas. From there it was possible to access the valley of the Kızılırmak (the ancient Halys) in about eight days, and go east to Trabzon and Erzurum and then to Persia and China. Ayas was at the time the **point of entry to the East**.

Our only information of this turn of events comes from the written sources, for example **Marco Polo** at the beginning of his *Milione*, when he is about to start his trip to the Far East in 1271. He calls the town Laiassus and describes it as 'a place of considerable traffic...trading in spices and other luxuries'. In the town itself he came across the Armenians and their beautiful carpets. In the countryside he met the Türkmen and castigated them for their barbarous language while admiring their beautiful animals. Other written sources mention **foreign consuls** from Venice, Genoa, Pisa, Barcelona and Piacenza. The **merchants** are even more of a motley crew, from Florence, Greece, Corsica, Seville, Montpelier and so on. The two main players, the Venetians and the Genoese, had their loggias and their churches, to St Mark and St Lawrence respectively. The merchandise was mostly stored in Misis, 20km to the north and accessible either by river or via a defended, paved road. Surveys have found little evidence of the buildings of the foreign communities nor of the Armenians, who were collecting taxes here and must have had some administrative structures as well as a number of churches, built with Roman and Byzantine spolia.

The settlement did not have a circuit of walls. Defence instead was a **moated land castle** (which is what Marco Polo meant when he talked of Laiassus as a defended place) which the Ottomans in due course rebuilt, following the original outline and adding a sea wall (destroyed in the 19th century). The castle's polygonal structure, with vaulted rooms and a domed hall, was Armenian although there has been a lot of rebuilding. One can assume that the Armenian officials, or possibly the king himself, lived here and that the foreign loggias were inside the circuit. With time the land castle was quarried for stone by the locals, who also settled inside it and built against the standing walls. The main attraction of the ruins today is that they have been allowed to age with limited interference. With their patchwork of different stones (basalt, limestone, sandstone) and spolia (whole column drums), they have defied time.

The **sea castle**, called Kız Kalesi (as tall structures beside water so often are in Turkey), is an elongated limestone mass c. 100m long and some 400m from the shore. The building style is Armenian and there has been no further work. The quay is made of Roman spolia. Perhaps the merchants hired Armenian masons. The relationship between the two defences is not clear. They were not connected by a causeway as at Corycus, for example. Excavations have shown evidence of earlier buildings.

The polygonal, Ottoman **Suleyman Kule**, a couple of kilometres to the west, was a watchtower with vaulted rooms and a crenellated terrace on top, all built with spolia; it has survived being isolated.

Aigai was destroyed by the Mamluks in 1337, after which the port declined. When Beaufort (*p. 23*) came past in the early 19th century, he found the village inside the castle and a very unfriendly welcome. Shots were fired and he was hit in the hip. As a result his survey work came to an end.

PRACTICAL INFORMATION

GETTING THERE AND AROUND

By air: The main airport is Adana Şakirpaşa, which handles mainly domestic flights. It is located to the west of town, only 2km from the centre. Local buses (135 and 159) will get you there. A new airport (the Çukurova Regional Airport) in the Tarsus area was under construction at the time of writing.

By bus: From Mersin-Tarsus-Adana you will be able to get anywhere by bus. The service from their *otogars* is quite extensive. Bear in mind though that these bus stations have been relocated a way away from the centre of town due to urban development, Adana's *dolmuş* services go from the Yureğir *Otogar* on the east side of the river.

By train: Adana had an early start in railway connections but unfortunately the train services today are poor. Generally it makes sense to travel by coach; however, the 204km ride from Mersin to İskenderun (three and a half hours using 1970s' rail technology) can be a fun experience.

WHERE TO STAY

Tourist accommodation is not in large supply in Smooth Cilicia as this area has come late to tourism, but you can rely on the network of **Öğretmen evi** (*p. 13*). The one in Adana (*ogretmenevine.com/sehir/adana; T: 90 322 453 31 58*), conveniently near the station, is clean and tidy. The one in Tarsus is not yet modernised but **Mersin's** (*suphionerogretmenevi.com; T: 90 324 328 81 11*) is now up to date. It pays to look out for the signposting as you enter towns, big or small.

For something less impersonal, the Mavi Deniz Pansiyon in **Erdemli** (*mavidenizpansiyon.com; T: 90 324 515 33 80*) is a handy place to stay.

In **Tarsus** try the Fırat Otel in the old town, Şehitkerim Mahallesi, at 13, 3404 Sk and in **Adana** the Hotel Bosnali (*hotelbosnali.com; T: 90 322 359 80 00*) overlooking the Taşköprü in the old town on the east edge of Tepebağ.

If you prefer to avoid big towns (and it makes sense to do so), then go to **Yumurtalık** at the south end of Route 817 and follow the line of Pompeii-style Roman basalt grain mills to find the Erzin Pansiyon (*T: 90 538 277 13 58/ 90 322 671 28 09*) inside the castle grounds and possibly built with spolia from it.

Karataş has a number of holiday accommodation options but lacks character. Moreover the access road, Route 815, is really difficult to find and blocked on a Sunday by a market. Inland settlement is more sparse, meaning that accommodation gets scarcer as you go north.

WHAT TO EAT

For fish definitely go to **Karataş**. There is quite a choice of places here, following the increase in tourist accommodation.

Away from the sea, start looking out for **Adana kebab**, one of the glories of Turkish cuisine. It should be made of minced beef and lamb mixed with peppers, onions and spices then grilled on a spit and served on a flat bread with yoghurt, fresh salad and slim little peppers that look harmless but can kill your insides.

If you come across **haydari**, give it a try. You will be captivated by this mix of yoghurt, white cheese, chopped walnuts, garlic and olive oil. Technically it is a *meze*, but one can have it at any time.

Wash it all down with a glass of **şalgam**. This concoction of fermented carrots, turnip, bulgur and various aromas is the speciality of Adana and you should try it at least once in your life—although it is very much an acquired taste.

WHAT TO DO

The **Mersin international Music Festival** has been going for several years, offering a variety of genres from pop to classical in a variety of venues including on the edge of the sinkhole at Kanlıdivane (*p. 202*). It is a novel approach.

INLAND CILICIA: EXPLORING THE VALLEYS

As the Anti-Taurus mountains turn northeast, there are valleys to the north to explore, carved out by the Ceyhan and its tributaries. This was congenial land for the Armenians, who liked high ground for their castles, but it was also a transit route from early times, as the Sirkeli relief shows.

THE SİRKELİ RELIEF & YILANKALE

To see the **Sirkeli relief**, follow the Yılankale sign on Route 400, north of Yakapınar (*map D, 6*). After the castle (*see below*), an unmade road will lead you to the bank of the river opposite the Sirkeli *hüyük*. The relief is at the base of the *hüyük* and barely 5m above the water level. The relief represents, according to the inscription, King Muwatalli II (1306–1282 BC), who moved the Hittite capital south from Hattuşa to Tarhutnassa, a location not yet identified, and defeated Ramesses at the battle of Kadesh (1285 BC). He was quite a key international figure. This is the oldest Hittite rock relief currently known. Here the king is dressed in ceremonial garb with the curved staff, the lituus, and the royal insignia, suggesting that he was performing a religious ceremony or encountering the divine. Another relief discovered later, 13m downstream, has a figure wearing the same attire. Unfortunately the inscription appears to have been erased in antiquity. The *hüyük* itself has been excavated and shows occupation from the Chalcolithic onwards. The carving could relate to diplomatic exchanges between the rulers at the time of territorial disputes in the Levant.

YILANKALE

Yılankale, the 'Castle of the Snakes', will be just behind you. This impressive fortress sits on a limestone outcrop, over 200m long with a complete view of its surroundings, today a peaceful agricultural environment with its share of greenhouses. The Armenians or the Byzantines had different concerns. The **medieval road** would have come past the castle on its north edge while the approach to it was to the northwest. It is not surprising that this part of the circuit is the most defended, with four **towers** and a **bastion**, enough to deter anyone. The whole north area is higher, a separate bailey with its own gate guarded by two towers. The defence was further reinforced by the design, as the access route made a sharp right-angled bend. Inside are a chapel and cisterns. In the bastion are more cisterns, making the garrison self-sufficient. The other two baileys are to the south, also protected by towers. The circuit follows the contour of the outcrop, which in places is very jagged. This style of defence would have appealed to an Armenian baron, even to an Armenian king.

Moreover, there are **Armenian symbols** carved in the rock, for example the stylised crosses with the four splayed arms (a little like a Maltese cross). The **relief over the main gateway**, with a seated figure flanked by two worn rampant lions, was originally interpreted as a representation of King Levon I (1180–1219). However, his pose does not match the representations on his coins: he is sitting in an Oriental fashion. There are also details of construction, such as the use of brick in cisterns, that do not correspond to the Armenian manner. This could have been a Byzantine construction reworked by the Armenians.

Access to the ruins is now from the south, where the car park is. Follow the path and prepare for a scramble. There are many stones about and a lot of loose rubble. Remember that the moniker 'Yilankalesi', which introduces the idea of snakes, may have some foundation in truth. Wear good shoes, watch where you walk and take care where you put your hands.

ANAVARZA

For Anavarza (*map D, 6*), continue north on Route 817 and take the marked right-hand turn at Ayşehoca in the direction of Dilekkaya. You will soon be staring at the big rock.

Anavarza is all about this rock: the name derives from the Persian *nabarza*, meaning something like 'it cannot be conquered', a boast which clearly refers to this great cliff, over 1km long, with a sheer west side and an east face that is slightly more approachable but not much. It is situated up the basin of the Ceyhan, where the Çukurova penetrates the Anti-Taurus mountains next to one of its tributaries. The site is on the way to Cappadocia and Malatya and enjoys maximum **intervisibility** with other surrounding heights. It must have attracted attention from early on.

HISTORY OF ANAVARZA

A Hittite and Assyrian presence is not backed up by hard evidence but must be taken into account. However, the earliest material we have is **Hellenistic** and should be considered in the light of the Karasis Kale, 20km to the north and now overlooking the Kazan dam. This has proven Seleucid origins dated to the early 3rd century BC. At Anavarza, where building and rebuilding, earthquakes and destruction have obliterated a lot of evidence, the Hellenistic presence is mainly attested by coins, suggesting that minting began in the mid-2nd century BC, when Anavarza was still Seleucid or in the hands of the Egyptian Ptolemies. There is a strong possibility that this was then a **veteran settlement** in which military duties were combined with agricultural development. The extent of the Hellenistic occupation is not known. On the rock, Hellenistic pottery has been found and there is evidence on the east side—which is more exposed and has a gentler slope—of a defensive wall. Spolia have been interpreted as the remains of a temple that appears on coins and was possibly dedicated to Zeus. No earlier material has been found. But the rock has not yet been excavated, only surveyed.

Later, in the turbulent times of the 1st century BC, the town came into the orbit of the **Tarcondimotan dynasty** (*see below*). It was then Anavarza Caesarea, but direct **Roman rule** was soon to come and it brought with it a dramatic change in the appearance of the settlement. It developed on the flat land to the west and acquired all the accoutrements of a proper Roman town, remaining **unwalled** for a long while. Remote sensing and other geophysical surveys have established that it was laid out on a grid pattern, with the the two main axes (both of them colonnaded streets) meeting roughly in the middle. It had a theatre (*for a plan of the ruins, see overleaf*) partly carved out of the west slope of the rock, an amphitheatre further to the south and a circus (or according to some, a stadium) between the two. These two last features suggest an important **military presence**, people who needed to be entertained between tours of duty with gladiatorial games and the like. This was not, however, a purely military town, as the peristyle houses and suburban villas with mosaics testify. Other public buildings were obliterated by subsequent events.

Anavarza Caesarea possibly reached its pinnacle when it was promoted to **capital of Cilicia Secunda** by Theodosius II in the early 5th century. Beyond that we know of destructive earthquakes and plagues which prompted imperial assistance. In the 6th century, out of gratitude, it dubbed itself Justinopolis and then Justinianopolis.

The **Byzantines** felt rightly concerned about this strategic node, now so exposed. A **city wall** with 80 towers, a ditch and a second lower wall went up around the lower town, leaving out the theatre, circus and amphitheatre. It made use of a great deal of spolia, suggesting widespread destruction by natural events but also a renewed zeal in obliterating the pagan past. The Byzantines also built a second **aqueduct** to supplement the Roman one, dated to the 1st century of the present era. Both aqueducts came in from the north, partly on arches, from a source some 10km away. On top of the rock, the Byzantine defences were almost completely obliterated by the Armenians but can be seen in the lower courses of the south defences, where a round Armenian tower by the south gate stands on top of a square Byzantine one. The defensive circuit was of no avail when the **Arab raids** began. Anavarza was in Arab hands between the 8th and the 10th centuries, reverting to the Byzantines in 962.

In 1111 it was incorporated into the **Armenian Kingdom** and was contested by the Crusaders until the **Mamluks** swept everything away in 1375. Anavarza fell off the pages of history and became no more than a village.

At some point in this period a **new wall** went up, reducing the town in size by one third. This wall incorporated large spolia blocks, including whole theatre seats. It cut off the top end of the colonnaded street. The town changed character and lost its grid; it was no longer a Roman town; however, it shows continuous occupation to the 12th century, beyond which the lower town was abandoned. It has not been firmly established who built this cross wall: the Byzantines or the Abassid Arabs. If it was the Byzantines, one might be tempted to think of a major destructive event and confusion in its aftermath which prompted a shift in priorities. If it was the Arabs, it would be perfectly normal: the population had shrunk and they had to import settlers from Egypt. The town became more compact: the polis turned into a medina. The Armenians are left out of the equation as there is no trace of them down here:

they only occupied the top of the rock, where their Naversa, as they called it, was an administrative centre and for a time a royal residence, the very place where in 1307 the Mongol emir Bilarghu murdered the Armenian king. There was no room for a permanent civilian population.

EXPLORING ANAVARZA: THE LOWER AND UPPER TOWNS

Anavarza has not been excavated, so do not expect to see large standing monuments (at least, not yet; *see below*). At present you can get a feeling of the place by seeing the towering rock with the lower town nestling beneath it, 200m down. It is quite unique. The modern road, Dilekkaya Yolu, marks the extent of the lower town; beyond it is the modern village of Dilekkaya.

In the lower town, roughly halfway across it, are the remains of the **later walls**, with the gate to the east where the wall meets the rock. The line of the main wall can be followed: just imagine it with 80 towers and five gates. One of them, the south gate, was originally a **triumphal arch**, possibly for Emperor Macrinus after he made peace with the Parthians in AD 218. It originally had five arches, reduced to three when it was incorporated into the wall circuit. In due course the decorative friezes from the inside face were removed to the Church of the Apostles (*see below*). The outside was left unchanged to keep up appearances.

About 500m south of the gate, the shape of the **amphitheatre** (83m by 62m) partly on a slope and partly on substructures, can be made out by the side of the modern road. The **circus** (or stadium), with its spina which had Corinthian columns, is in a field on the way from here to the theatre. It was partly on built substructures and had wooden seats. The main entrance was to the south. It was in use until the 4th century.

On the way to the theatre you cross the modern road, which follows an ancient pathway cut deep in the rock and leading to Castabala (*see p. 230*). The **theatre**, as yet unexcavated, is 58m in diameter. The scena had red granite columns sourced from the imperial quarry of Syene, deep in Egypt near Aswan, a mark of great imperial favour.

Inside the town you can follow the line of the **colonnaded street**, which according to remote sensing was 1.75km long and 34m wide with shops on both sides and archways at both ends. The colonnaded decumanus, which crossed it at right angles, was narrower. The Roman town is otherwise not visible; there has been too much destruction and too much reuse. From the epigraphy and from coins we know of a number of temples with a variety of dedications including Zeus Keranios (storms), Zeus Halazeos (prosperity) and Zeus Soter (earthquakes). Zeus Olybris and Aphrodite Kasalitis, both mountain divinities, apparently had their temples on the rock. They have not been identified but there are many large stones up there which could have belonged to them.

Six church complexes are known. Of key significance among them is the **Church of the Apostles**, in a very prominent position in the centre of town. It may occupy the site of an older temple; it certainly made liberal use of spolia. With its polygonal apse with large windows, its ambulatory and what we know of its decoration, it seems to have been closely parallel to churches in Syria. Measuring 58m by 30m,

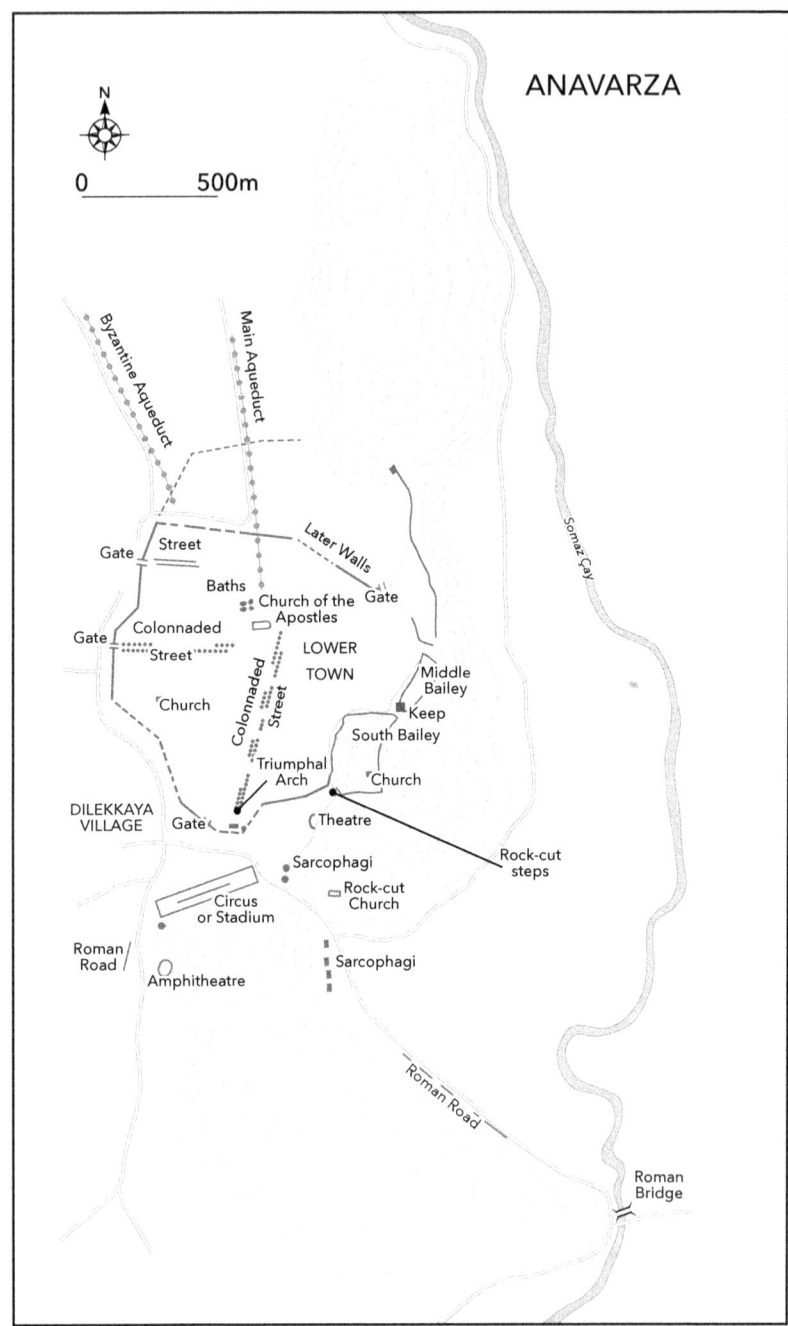

it had a nave and two aisles separated by granite columns and was set in a precinct entered from the colonnaded street. It is dated to AD 500. A Byzantine **baths complex** is nearby.

At the time of writing the lower town was in large part grassed over. However, plans were afoot for a restoration programme: a lot of newly-quarried stark white limestone was to be seen piled up at the entrance to the lower town (where for some reason photography was not allowed). Some pieces had been fashioned to imitate Roman/Byzantine architectural elements. Everything seemed set for a substantial reconstruction programme.

EXPLORING ANAVARZA: THE NORTH–SOUTH RIDGE

The north–south ridge is 4.5km long and dominates the town from its 200m sheer cliff. The key section is in the middle, directly overlooking the lower town. There is scant trace of pre-Byzantine activity up here. The Seleucids may have fortified the exposed east edge; the Romans appear only to have used it for a necropolis, with sarcophagi cut in the rock and possibly a temple. After them, however, many hands were at work: Byzantines, Armenians, Crusaders and Mamluks. Opinions about who did what still differ.

The portion of the ridge that is significant in terms of remains is c. 1250m long and divided into three baileys. It is accessed via **rock-cut steps** beginning in the south by the theatre; on the way up, look out on your right for a short column, possibly an altar. The climb, totally unshaded, is quite demanding as the steps are uneven and tend to disappear when you most need them.

The south and middle baileys have been surveyed. The north bailey, where some walls and towers can be seen on the east flank, has not been examined. There have been no licit excavations. The **south bailey**, which was defended on the east and south sides with towers and bastions, is a roughly rectangular space, 250m by 400m, intended as a refuge for the population in times of danger. A **cistern** in the bastion in the southeast corner was unwittingly discovered by some treasure hunters. The imposing **remains of the defences** show many hands at work: Byzantines, Armenians, Arabs and Mamluks. The wall had a walkway, accessible from the inside by cantilevered stairs. The north and west edges were precipitous enough not to require any defence. Not far from the east wall are the remains of a small church with a nave and two aisles and three apses (13m by 10m), which Gertrude Bell (p. 24) surveyed in the early 1900s. It was built by the Armenian ruler Toros I, at the time when Anavarza was an Armenian royal residence. After the first Mamluk attack, the king moved inland to Sis (*see below*). In the 19th century Langlois (p. 29) saw frescoes and a long Armenian inscription here. The inscription, now lost, mentioned members of the Armenian royal family and Langlois concluded that this was a funerary chapel of the Rubenid dynasty.

To the northeast, the outline of a Byzantine chapel can be made out. To the north, the escarpment grows narrow and it is on this slim **isthmus**, c. 15m wide and cut off from the south and middle baileys by a man-made ditch (look out for the tool marks in the rock), that a square **keep** (12m by 12m and a maximum of 15m tall) was built, according to Robert Edwards originally by the Crusaders. Edwards recognised parallels with Crusader architecture in the interior layout as well as noting evidence of several reconstructions after earthquakes, and Armenian work from the time when it came into their hands. The keep was accessed by a drawbridge.

The **middle bailey** was walled all around, including on the west side, with work attributed to the Byzantines and the Armenians. This bailey, which had a number of buildings and a chapel, was the centre of power and administration.

KOZAN (ANCIENT SIS)

From Anavarza you can go up the valley to Kozan, the old Armenian Sis or Sision, on a route affording a passage to the interior from the coast. Some have linked Sis to the Assyrian town of Sizu, attested in the written sources. However, this seems an ambitious attribution, since the first attested occupation is Byzantine. It was then called Sisin and was a kastron which proved unable to resist an Arab onslaught in the mid-9th century. The **Arabs** settled here and reconstructed the defences as Sis became part of the Abassid frontier until the Arabs were expelled by the Byzantine emperor Phocas in 962.

The Armenian occupation came after the battle of Manzikert (1071), when the Byzantines lost control of their peripheral territory to the east and south. Sis soon became the **Armenian capital**. They had earlier attempted to place their centre of control in Tarsus but they found it too exposed and preferred the mountains. **Genoese and Venetian traders** were soon active here and built their churches. The head of the Armenian Church, the Catholicos, also settled here in 1295. Leo VI and his wife Margaret of Soissons were crowned here in 1374, under the protection of the right hand of Gregory the Illuminator, a relic which the Armenians had wrested from the Mamluks, who had stolen it from Rum Kale (*see Blue Guide Southeastern Turkey*). The Armenian ascendancy could not last, however. Sis soon began to feel the pressure of raids by the Mamluks, who controlled the countryside, and it duly fell in 1375. Nevertheless, the Catholicate managed to remain here until 1915, when the Ottoman authorities ordered the Armenian clergy to leave within two days (*see below*).

SIS CASTLE

The castle of Sis (*open daily winter 8–8, summer 8–10pm; free*) is to the south of Kozan on a narrow limestone ridge, stretching into the plain for 680m. Sis's lower town extended on its east flank. From the top there is good **intervisibility** with Anavarza and other Armenian strongholds: Tumlu to the south and Andil to the north. The **wall circuit** (this was a refuge not a settlement) follows the terrain for a total of 3km. The **entrance** corridor to the east bears an elaborate Arab inscription on the archway, thought to belong to the Mamluks' rebuilding. The passage led to a semicircular **tower**, possibly the original Byzantine entrance. Inside it is divided into **three baileys** with Armenian inscriptions, remains of buildings, stores and cisterns. According to Robert Edwards, the masonry style and the plan are mainly Armenian, with Byzantine and Mamluk elements.

The castle has not yet been fully surveyed or excavated. It is now a public park, partly landscaped, with vehicle access to halfway up, followed for a while by steps and clear paths but quite wild on top, where safety rules seem not to apply. The municipality has recently created an artificial waterfall on the west side to embellish a picnic spot named after the **Armenian monastery**, of which some ruins remain on the slopes; according to Langlois (*p. 29*), the monastery was built on the site of the royal palace and using its spolia. This happened in the late 14th century, after the Mamluk conquest of 1375. Initially the Armenians had fled into the mountains but their religions authorities obtained permission from the conquerors to return to Sis and build a monastery. They were finally ousted by the Ottomans in 1915. In 2015, on the anniversary of the expulsion, the Armenian Catholicate, now based in the Lebanon, filed a suit to regain their lost property.

FEKE CASTLE

Further north on Route 815, about 6km northeast of Feke (*map D, 4*), is **Vahga Kale**, signposted ('Feke Kalesi') along a narrow but acceptable road. This is another daring piece of Armenian construction, controlling the upper reaches of the Seyhan and the road leading to the Bazat Geçidi pass just north of Feke on Route 815. At 1650m, it affords access to Cappadocia and north Mesopotamia. Vahga was one of the earliest seats of Armenian power in Cilicia. Originally the town occupied the southwest slope of the fort. When the castle was abandoned, the village moved inside. About 100 years ago, the population transferred to present day Feke to the southwest (Feke is a corruption of Vahga). The move is perfectly understandable since the castle stands at 1270m and the town, in a sheltered valley, is at a mere 620m. Even so, a small community remains up on the heights, among the olive trees.

The castle is situated on a limestone spine running north–south and surrounded by higher peaks. The approach is from the west. The east side is very steep. The **defences** follow the contour of the rock, with **round towers** and **bastions** especially to the west, which is more vulnerable. Inside are a number of **vaulted rooms** and **cisterns**. The complex, which has only been cursorily surveyed, was recently enthusiastically restored. It seems to have been a Byzantine foundation which the Armenians took over. A path from the access road leads to the entrance. Not far from it is a fine Armenian church, a beautiful construction contemporary with the castle and locally known as **Kara Kilise** ('Black Church'). It has been restored.

KADİRLİ

Kadirli (*map D, 6*), the site of the ancient Flaviopolis, lies on the bank of the Savrun Deresi. It may have grown up around an ancient ford but recent intense development has erased a lot of evidence. However, mosaics and architectural elements such as architraves and columns, as well as a bronze statue of Hadrian, testify to an important Roman phase. However, Kadirli is better known to early church cognoscenti for its **Alacami**. This former mosque was originally a late antique church in a necropolis. The building has been intensely studied and has set the parameters for a kind of church that is found in eastern Cilicia and northern Syria. The building, recently restored and opened to the public, was secularised in 1924.

The Alacami once stood on a low hill overlooking the town but urban expansion means that it is now in the centre of Kadirli, close to the park. Recent excavations have established that originally there was a **hypogeum** here, a fine limestone barrel-vaulted construction measuring 6m by 3m. The passageway to the hypogeum was later filled with mortar and this underground feature became the crypt of the subsequent church. The original stepped entrance to the hypogeum was obliterated. The **late antique basilica** built on top measured 33m by 21m and had a nave and two aisles divided by columns, galleries and a clerestory, mosaic floors, a tiled roof and a porch to the west. According to early travellers' accounts it stood in a precinct. The spolia appear to have come from a single source. It was built in ashlars well smoothed outside but still rough inside, as if they were intended to be plastered and frescoed. The combination of Syrian characteristics (mixing clerestory and galleries) with indigenous traits (the protruding apse) is the hallmark of the Alacami group. On the whole this kind of building is seen as a sign of the prosperity of eastern Cilicia in late antiquity. In due course, however, the church became a chapel, shrinking to just 17m by 11m and using the perimeter wall of the church as a precinct. In 1489 the chapel was turned into a **mosque**, hence the minaret. It was abandoned when the village received a new mosque.

KARATEPE

From Kadirli it is only a short way to Karatepe (*open daily April–Oct 10–7, Nov–March 10–5; charge*), along the Arslantaş Yolu to the east. The road takes you towards the artificial lake formed by the Arslantaş dam (a favourite spot for local families, so avoid weekends if possible), which would have drowned some very fine antiquities had it not been for the archaeologists' determination. The water level was lowered and Karatepe Arslantaş is now an open-air museum in the national park of the same name.

A SHORT HISTORY OF KARATEPE
Karatepe is located on an elevation overlooking the Ceyhan between the Anti-Taurus mountains and the north reaches of the Amanus, on the line of an old trade route connecting Misis to the north to the Anatolian Plateau's metal resources via Andirin and Göksun. It is also on the way to the Bahçe Pass across the Amanus but this is thought to be of less importance. In front of it on the other side of the river stood another site guarding the same spot. This is **Domuztepe**, now submerged, which is thought to have been the antecedent of Karatepe. They are both single-period sites

dating from the time after the demise of the Hittites and their empire centred on Hattuşa, when their holdings in Syria broke up into smaller principalities still using Hittite iconography with some Near Eastern additions.

Karatepe represents a peripheral site of one such power centre, thought to have been based in Adana (then called Adanawa) around Tepebağ, the *hüyük* in the centre of town which has not been fully investigated. We owe the information about Karatepe to the **inscribed orthostats** in which the petty ruler Azatiwata speaks in the first person detailing his ancestry, his deeds (including the construction of the citadel) and ending with a dire warning to anyone threatening his power. It is on the whole a manifesto by which the present power is legitimised and validated by divine sanction. In spite of these defiant declarations the petty rulers here only lasted about a century, from the early 9th to the 8th century BC, at which time either the Cimmerians from the north or the Assyrians from the south put an end to their rule. There are two salient aspects in these inscriptions: the use of two languages and the choice of material.

All the inscribed items, orthostats and statues, are in **basalt**. Karatepe is a limestone hill and basalt is only available across the river at Domuztepe. The basalt came from there, either as worked or raw material; the river was fordable in the summer. This fact may explain some of the inconsistencies in the Luwian inscriptions which may have been recycled from there. Two languages are used: Luwian hieroglyphs and Phoenician, but while the Phoenician texts are compact and consistent, the Luwian inscriptions are arranged in a random fashion. As most of the people were illiterate, the written text was supplemented with appropriate imagery. In addition, the writing itself had a message beyond its intrinsic meaning. It combines a reference to the new and upcoming power of the Phoenicians and their new revolutionary alphabet as well as the strength of tradition represented by the Luwian hieroglyphs, which were by then almost 1500 years old and would have looked much as medieval Latin might appear to us today. The juxtaposition would still speak to illiterate people. It did not matter that the Luwian hieroglyphs were placed at random since at that point in time it was probable that no one could read them anyway.

As for the **iconography**, it is a mix of Middle Eastern imagery (sun disc, lions and sphinxes, the last two guarding gateways) combined with traditional Greek themes such as funerary banquets; it does not appear to relate to the adjacent text. There is no undisputed representation of the ruler though there is a clear distinction between 'them and us'. Gods and rulers are full-size, mere mortals half-size.

EXPLORING KARATEPE

From the car park you walk about 200m to the site. You have to imagine the citadel towering over the river and faced by its erstwhile rival on Domuztepe.

The citadel is fortified. **Defences** at a lower level on the east, south and west side are almost under water. The walls, about 2–4m thick and standing in places to 6m, were made of boulders topped with mud-brick architecture. A number of **towers** and **bastions** have been identified. There are **two main gates**, to the southwest and northeast. The southwest gate was accessed by a **ramp**, cut in the rock and protected by a separate wall. The walls of the two gatehouses are lined with orthostats depicting a banquet scene with attendants fanning the ruler while his pet monkey is under the table. From the gate you enter a **cult area** centred around the **statue of the storm god**, over life-size and now under a canopy, clutching his defaced attributes and standing on a basalt pedestal with two bulls. The **palace** of the ruler was close by. Situated on the highest point of the hill, it could be accessed via a postern to the west. It measured approximately 20m by 50m and is of the bit-hilani type, popular in the Levant at that time, with a porch in front leading to a courtyard with a large hall and other smaller rooms; you can see a model of it in the visitors' centre at the end of the visit. The northwest gate is similar to the other gate in that it has a right-angle entrance for extra security; there you can read the '**Karatepe bilingual**', all 34 lines of it—if your Phoenician is good enough. In the last line, the ruler Azatiwata (who built this fortress and brought prosperity to the people and sacrificed appropriately) claims that his name is 'eternal as the sun and the moon'. This proved to be not entirely the case since Karatepe went up in flames, putting an end to Azatiwata or whoever came after him. The inside of the walled enclosure has not yet been fully investigated; it seems unlikely that it acted as a refuge for the local population. Archaeologists have so far concentrated on the iconographical material—which was broken into a thousand pieces—and on its conservation. You can see some of it *in situ* and some in the visitors' centre.

HIERAPOLIS CASTABALA

A few kilometres south of Karatepe is the town of **Hierapolis Castabala** (or Kastabala; *open daily 8–5; free*), which 50 years ago might have benefited, as Karatepe did, from the threat of being drowned by a dam and the resistance of a couple of visionary archaeologists. That would have focused attention on its past, which is known from the sources, whereas on the ground now, all evidence is disappearing as we speak. The local authorities want to promote Castabala as 'the Ephesus of East Cilicia', a tall order given the constant ploughing, stone robbing and illegal digging, as well as the persistent threat of encroaching industrial development.

In the sources, Castabala is the **land of Tarcondimotus** (*see box*). However, the recent find of a border stone in Aramaic, dated to the 5th–4th century BC and with the name Kashtabalay, pushes its history back to the time when the place was ruled by the **Persians**. It seems that they brought the goddess Kubaba with them when they settled. In Hellenistic times, this deity was assimilated with Artemis as Artemis Persike and then **Artemis Perasia**. Castabala was the centre of her cult and as such it became a holy city, adding Hierapolis to its name. Castabala at this time was a polis centred around the acropolis (where the castle now is).

After the heyday of the early Roman Empire and the short-lived Tarcondimotan dynasty (which brought Castabala to the fore in Roman history, as noted in the box opposite), the town flourished with the *Pax Romana*, although not without some hiccups, being destroyed by **Shapur** (206) and then **Balbinus** (380). Castabala was still thriving in late antiquity, expanding onto the plain and on the terraces below the acropolis. The area was agriculturally very productive, with wine and oil. The cult of its form of Artemis also brought in revenue but it remained local. Castabala was probably walled by this time, although no certain, dated traces have been found. It suffered badly when Emperor Heraclius evacuated the garrisons east of Tarsus because of the **Arab raids**. The town sank into obscurity and lost whatever population was left to the new foundation of Haruniye, willed by the Caliph Harun al Rashid in 799.

The Byzantines in the 10th–11th century built a castle on the acropolis hill, which in due course was reworked by the Armenians. Castabala was a **bishopric** in the late antique period. The bishop soon went to live in the safety of Byzantium but the seat, however, has never been vacant in the church annals. The current Bishop of Castabala lives in Brazil.

BEING A RULER IN DIFFICULT TIMES: TARCONDIMOTUS

In the troubled times of the 1st century BC, when Seleucid power was on the wane and the Romans were extending their hegemony to the east, the better to control the Parthians, one cannot but pity the fate of the small local princes in east Cilicia who found themselves caught up in the turmoil. One we know of reasonably well is the short-lived Tarcondimotan dynasty, whose capital was Castabala. Our sources are the private letter written by Cicero when he was an official there, and later accounts of the Roman civil war after the death of Caesar. Piecing all the evidence together, with the help of some meagre archaeological finds, mainly coins and inscribed statue bases, it has been possible to trace the colourful trajectory of a family with an uncanny ability to back the wrong party and still land on its feet.

The first we hear about Tarcondimotus, the founder of the dynasty in 51 BC, is from Cicero, who in a letter to his family back home describes him as a 'true friend and ally of Rome'. Tarcondimotus at that time was a local ruler, not a king, in the area north of the Gulf of İskenderun, in the foothills of the Amanus. It is not clear how he came to power: his father, Strato, is mentioned without any titles. As for Tarcondimotus himself, he was a local as revealed by his Luwian name, which is ultimtately derived from the storm god Tarhunt, although twisted and turned to give it a Hellenistic sound. According to inscriptions, he adopted Greek-style institutions, at least in name. He also gave his children Roman names, as we shall see. His territory included Anavarza (*see above*), possibly some parts of the northern slopes of the Amanus, but not the south, which was out of his control; the coast was occupied by the Roman army. Even so, this friendly king was still able to give the Romans early warning of Parthian movements, a circumstance which earned him Cicero's gratitude. In the civil war between Caesar and Pompey, Tarcondimotus chose badly, backing Pompey. However, when Pompey was defeated in 48 BC, Caesar pardoned Tarcondimotus. In gratitude—or perhaps also because, together with the pardon, Tarcondimotus was awarded Roman citizenship—he called his newborn baby daughter Julia. A few years later, however, he found himself in trouble with the Romans again. According to Dio Cassius (47,26), after the murder of Caesar in 44 BC, Tarcondimotus backed Antony against Octavian. For a time, all went well and it seems that, with Antony's patronage, Tarcondimotus became a king, a title that could only be conferred by the Roman senate and which required a powerful backer. In his coinage of this period he appears as King Tarcondimotus Philantonius; his demeanour and hairstyle are truly Roman and he now looks tough, quite a way from the idealised Hellenistic ruler. His leanings are clearly indicated: the newly-appointed king was planning to assist Antony by leading his own fleet in the forthcoming confrontation with Octavian. However, he was killed in a skirmish a short time before. His son Tarcondimotus Philopator, initially deposed by Octavian, was reinstated by him ten years later when Parthia had been beaten and the East looked settled. Duly grateful, Tarcondimotus Philopator renamed Anavarza, adding Caesarea to it, and one of his freedmen erected a statue to Tiberius' son Drusus in Castabala. After the death of Philopator in AD 17, the end came pretty soon. The kingdom was absorbed into the Roman Empire, a move made to ensure that the population sensed the distant presence in the West more keenly than the power of the local dynasty.

EXPLORING CASTABALA

Castabala has been legally excavated since 2009, in the hope of putting it on the tourist circuit. However, the results have been meagre and there is no detailed published plan beyond a sketch by two German archaeologists dated 1990. At present Castabala is in a confused state, with little published research and wild speculation in the press. One of the most recent examples was the assertion that the visible stretch of **colonnaded street** was medieval while the original Roman feature was 8m deeper. It makes little sense. Meanwhile, the red breccia columns with consoles for statuary have been re-erected. Capitals found in people's gardens have been repossessed to create more things to see. The colonnaded street is Castabala's main feature, endlessly photographed although none too stable (and one is not allowed to get close to the columns). Other no-go areas (there is a list at the entrance) include the theatre, the castle and the excavation areas presently covered with plastic. Meanwhile, the site is regularly visited by local people as part of a day out. The best advice is to do as they do and just enjoy the scenery, which is truly beautiful.

You enter the site at the west end of the colonnaded street, next to a stretch of the city wall. The street led east to the **Temple of Artemis Perasia**, a huge construction on vaulted substructures set in a temenos which is represented on coins and mentioned by Strabo, confirming the eastern location (12,2,7). Here the rites would take place. The priestess would have mystic visions, go into ecstasies and perform feats such as walking on red hot coals or on water, all the while looking like her standard image, holding a torch in one hand and a frond in the other. The temple is only known from the sources and the coinage. The stadium and the theatre, which would have been needed for the **Severia Perasia games** attested under Macrinus in AD 217, are not far from the supposed location of the temple. The **theatre**, dedicated to Hadrian (80m in diameter), is halfway through facing south. It could accommodate 5,000 people and had a two-storey scena; it could easily have had a Hellenistic antecedent. The **stadium** has been tentatively located to the east of the theatre. North of the colonnaded street the rising land was terraced, with evidence for fine housing and civic buildings, possibly including a temple for the worship of the emperor; these buildings were paid for by local worthies. There is no sign of imperial involvement.

Two churches have been identified so far. One very close to the colonnaded street, immediately to its south near the west end, and another, slightly smaller, 350m due south of it. The style, with beautiful polygonal apses, is 5th century. The quality of the workmanship is high but not as high as that at Anavarza. The consistent use of large blocks has suggested that it may have been built of masonry recycled from the pagan temple, which could explain why it is so thoroughly obliterated. **Water supply** was ensured by cisterns and by an aqueduct coming in from the northeast; there are some beautiful arches left. The **Roman necropolis**, with some fine monumental tombs, extended east, north and south.

The **territory of Castabala** is not known but in its heyday it must have had a harbour, since Tarcondimotus had a fleet there, which Pompey used in 48 BC. The harbour of Catabolo in the Gulf of İskenderun, which features on the *Tabula Peutingeriana*, the copy of a Roman map, is a possibility.

The hill to the north, the supposed seat of the **Hellenistic acropolis**, has been little investigated; it is known as Bodrum ('Castle'). Geologically the hill, 35m high, belongs to the Taurus mountains. T.A. Sinclair, who surveyed the castle, thought it was Byzantine, its masonry later reworked by the Armenians; they made liberal use of spolia and used it as a citadel. In their time there was no settlement. The castle has two wards and is partly cut deep into the rock.

PRACTICAL INFORMATION

GETTING THERE AND AROUND

For transport details, see the relevant section in the previous chapter.

WHERE TO STAY

Accommodation is scarce in this part of Cilicia, but you can rely on the network of **Öğretmen evi** (*p. 13*). **Kozan** (*T: 90 322 515 85 13*) has one just north of the Kale on Teknisyen Sk; **Kadirli** has new one behind the new Belediye (*T: 90 382 718 11 68*). It pays to look out for the signposting as you enter towns, big or small. Note also, for **Kozan**, the Avşaroğlu Otel (*avsarogluotel.com; T: 90*

322 515 16 75), a perfectly adequate place on the east side of town.

WHAT TO EAT

In **Kozan**, go to Mahmut Usta on Saimbeyli Cd.; you will not be disappointed.

WHAT TO DO

Hire a car and drive to **Zeytun**, an important place in Armenian history. In this village (now Süleymanlı, off Route 825; *map D, 4*) the Armenians held out successfully to the very end. Today nothing is left of them. But the scenery has not changed. The Berlit Dağı (3027m) still looks down on the valley, bisected by roaring torrents. The Armenian presence in Cilicia came to an end here in 1924, when the last remaining members of its population were sent to the region of Thessaloniki. The history of this village explains why there is a Kenaker-Zeytun district in Yerevan. Today what remains are the old fountain, the extraordinary bridges and the shrunken village.

BLACK CILICIA

Black Cilicia is a new term used by academics to describe the area around the Gulf of İskenderun, the tail end of Cilicia. The Ceyhan river (the ancient Pyramus) flows between the Taurus mountains and the Amanus, a mountain chain which is not part of the Taurus and which marks Black Cilicia to the east. Amanus is the Classical name. The range is now poetically called Nur Dağları ('Mountains of Light') and in the recent past it was Gavurdağları (the 'Mountains of the Infidels', probably a reference to the Greeks and Armenians living there). Running north–south, these peaks have always marked the eastern border of Cilicia. Since antiquity a source of shipbuilding timber, the wooded slopes are now showing clear signs of environmental degradation. The beautiful cedar stands seem to be a thing of the past. The massif, reaching over 2000m in height, is cut by two main passes. To the north is the Bahçe Geçidi (anciently the Armenian Gates), roughly where today's motorways go through after Osmaniye. The pass provided a way east to the upper reaches of Mesopotamia, keeping to the northern edge of the Syrian desert. To the south, the Belen Geçidi (the Syrian Gates, also called the Amanus Gates) led on to Syria.

The mountain chain is geologically complex and to the present day active, growing some 10cm every thousand years. It has faults on either side, creating the condition for eruptions of black basalt. The rock at Karatepe (*p. 228*) is one example and you can also observe the phenomenon at Tilmen Hüyük and Zincirli (*see Blue Guide Southeastern Turkey*) on the east side of the mountains. It is probably the presence of the basalt that inspired Jennifer Tobin to coin the term 'Black Cilicia'.

KİNET HÜYÜK & THE SITE OF THE BATTLE OF ISSUS

Over the millennia this area has been much contested. It is a true bottleneck. Anyone wishing to go east or south or vice-versa has had to negotiate it. Perhaps the most famous—though certainly not the first—clash to take place here was the Battle of Issus (photogenically depicted in the fabulous mosaic in the Archaeological Museum in Naples) when, on November 5th, 333 BC, a young man barely 23 years old took on the mighty king of Persia and won. For centuries people were in search of the exact location of that battle. It was a natural conclusion to the mania for 'following in Alexander's footsteps', a favourite occupation of antiquaries and archaeologists alike. Now we know where it is.

Although the site of the great battle may have been located, the problem is that in recent years the Gulf of İskenderun has seen rapid industrial development. The site now lies on the edge of a huge petroleum storage area, 35km north of İskenderun. You will also find that the environment has changed.

Kinet Hüyük (*map D, 6*) is now 700m inland but it was originally by the sea, a promontory with two harbours. As for the river, the Pinarus, that crops up in Arrian's narrative in Book 2, do bear in mind that rivers silt up or change course and that this is an earthquake zone. So read on.

Kinet Hüyük is one of a number of mounds that have been spotted on the edge of the gulf. Some have been studied, others have been ploughed up or built over. Kinet Hüyük has been recently excavated by Marie Henriette and Charles Gates. They have identified a number phases starting form the late Neolithic (3000 BC) through the Bronze Age and to the mid-1st century BC, when it was abandoned. The Arabs used the harbour, which they called Hisn at-Tinat (the present name may derive from this denomination or from Issus). Later the Armenians or the Crusaders (or both) built a stronghold on top.

For most of its life Kinet Hüyük was a **transit point** for conveying goods to consumers and raw material to producers. The 26m high mound had a particularly important **Hittite phase**, when it was called Izziya, with large-scale architecture and pottery that is not local but Anatolian. This was the time when the Hittites had incorporated the state of Kizzuwatna into their empire. When the Hittites met their fate and bowed out of history, there was a lull before things picked up again c. 900 BC, showing contacts with Cyprus and the Aegean. Kinet was then part of a much smaller **neo-Hittite** state. In due course the **Assyrians** left evidence of their presence with their wafer-thin prestige pottery (the so-called palace ware), suggesting that some official lived here. Later, in the 4th century BC, the **Achaemenids** built a massive mud-brick building and defensive walls. Decline set in towards the end of the Hellenistic period. When Kinet was abandoned, it was no more than a village.

AROUND THE BAY OF İSKENDERUN

KURTKULAĞI, TOPRAKKALE & SAVRANDA CASTLE

At Kurtkulağı (*map D, 6*), off Route 817 south of Ceyhan, there is a recently restored **caravansaray** built by the Ottomans in 1659 to service the road to Aleppo. It stands on the site of an earlier Roman post station (*mansio*) which is attested in the sources and measures 23m by 45m with large pillar halls. It is now used for weddings and other functions. The restoration has used a lot of limestone but if you look at the original masonry (e.g. the lower courses of the walls) there is a fair amount of basalt. This caravansaray may have lost its original function but it has kept its surroundings. It sits in beautiful greenery.

Toprakkale (*map D, 6*) has not been so lucky. Lying 10km west of Osmaniye, it is now situated in a spaghetti junction sandwiched between routes 400 and 817 and a slipway connecting the two. To add to its woes it sits directly on a fault, from where in geological times volcanoes have spewed basalt, much of which has gone on to form Toprakkale: it is on a hump of basalt made higher by the deposition of human debris. Sixty-five metres tall, it affords excellent visibility. From prehistoric times the location guarded the corridor to the Bahçe Pass and Aleppo. Bronze Age tumuli have also been noted in the area and investigations have revealed a small defended Roman settlement at the foot of the mound. The origins of the present construction are obscure. According to Hellenkemper, there could be a Byzantine core onto which Caliph Harun al Rashid built his castle in 786. The Arabs called it Kanisah al Sawda ('Black Church', unless that name refers to Epiphania; *see below*). Later, when it was contested by Crusaders, Byzantines, Seljuks, Kurds, Armenians, Mongols and Mamluks, it was known as Thila or Castellum Nigrum, 'Black Castle', a reference to the basalt. Set on two terraces built on the rock and measuring 150m by 105m, it has two baileys: the **lower bailey** (with circular and pentagonal towers) and the **upper bailey** in its southeastern corner, defended by thickly-set towers and bastions with vaulted rooms beneath the battlements. Up until the 17th century there was a village inside, of which no traces remain. However, we must remember that earthquakes and collapses have been frequent.

SAVRANDA CASTLE

Two castles guarding important crossing points over the Amanus should retain your attention. One of these, Bagras Kalesi, is described below. The other is east of Osmaniye, on Route 400, south of Kalecik Köyü. This is the Castle of Savranda (*map D, 6*), on the south flank of a pass that leads southeast and was therefore an access to Antioch. The castle is in fairly good condition, having been lived in until 1830. These days it overlooks an artificial lake. With the building of the dam came a road but even so, you have to make the ascent on foot. Originally a **Byzantine construction** (though this did not stop the Seljuks getting through from the 11th century, coming from Syria), it became in due course the **eastern border of Armenia**, the last of a defensive chain stretching across Cilicia. Here Armenian barons resided with their garrisons. The Mamluks conquered it in 1337. The complex occupies the summit of a limestone outcrop and developed its circuit in a roughly triangular shape following the contour. The sides are steep and in places the defences are reinforced by a talus. The entrance through the **gate house**, guarded by a bulging tower, is to the northeast. This led to the **lower bailey** where a **chapel** has been identified. A ramp led to the **upper bailey** to the south, much smaller and very heavily fortified with huge bastions.

EPIPHANIA

The location of Epiphania (*map D, 6*) is, according to some, in a narrow corridor edged on either side by two motorways and the railway line serving İskenderun. If you really want to see the spot, your reference point is Erzin railway station, 3km west of the town. For a long time the location of Epiphania was a mystery. It is mentioned in the sources. Apart from a letter from Cicero to Cato the Younger one can refer to Pliny (*5,101*), who gives the original name of the city: Oiniandos, later changed to Epiphania upon refoundation by the Seleucid ruler Antiochus IV Epiphanes (mid-2nd century BC).

Epiphania had the **right of asylum**, according to its coins, and Pompey established some repentant and reformed pirates there, turning their attention to the virtues of agriculture. The Romans used it as a **military base**. In due course it obtained a **bishop**. By the 9th century it was in **Arab** hands and was for them a border town, appearing in their itineraries. They apparently gave it the name of Kanisah al Sawda. Later, under the **Armenians**, it was Kanisah al Yahud, a reference to the **Jewish presence**. After this, Epiphania sank into historical oblivion.

Recent travellers' accounts mention various ruins with lots of basalt. Among them were a **defensive wall**; a **theatre**, 87m in diameter, on the slopes of the acropolis; a **colonnaded street**; a **temple**; a large **Byzantine basilica**; **inscriptions** and an **aqueduct**, of which 116 arches could still be seen in 1906 by the Germans who came here to build the Berlin-to-Baghdad railway. Today there is really nothing left. Epiphania was deeply ploughed and robbed to extinction before it could be studied and recorded.

YAKACIK (PAYAS)

The road to İskenderun, the ancient Alexandretta, occupies a narrow strip of land between the Amanus Mountains and the sea. Two motorways and a railway now run through this slim corridor, which leads to the important Belen Pass, the gateway to Syria. **Payas** now Yakacık (*map D, 6*), the Baiae of old, a flourishing port in the medieval period when it had entrepôts of Venetian and other Latin merchants, was restored by the Ottomans who rebuilt the medieval defences c. 1575. One enterprising emir in the 18th century made a bid for independence: he seized the castle and proceeded to take tolls from the caravans. From then on the town declined and eventually lost out to İskenderun.

Payas castle and the külliye, which have been restored, are worth a visit. The complex is enormous and includes a mosque and medrese, a very long bedesten, a hospice and a large han, as well as a double hamam which is now home to shops and cafés. The castle, immediately to the west of this and surrounded by a pentagonal moat, was meant to ensure the safety of traders and pilgrims. The entrance to the east is guarded by a barbican. All around are seven towers; the one to the northeast is the keep, with three storeys. According to Robert Edwards, the prevalence of Armenian masonry does not mean that it was an Armenian castle but rather that the Ottomans employed Armenians to build or rebuild the fort, which may originally have been linked to the Latin traders.

THE PILLAR OF JONAH

The narrow strip of land south of Payas was an ideal place for a gate that could be used to control the movements of armies, goods and pilgrims. One kilometre south of Sarıseki, a sign at the side of the road marks the Yunus Sütunu or Pillar of Jonah, on the extreme west edge of the coast beyond the railway line, built on top of the old road. Here, in 1211, Wilbrand of Oldenburg (*p. 33*) saw a stone and marble structure marking the passage from Armenia to Syria; he mused that the bones of Alexander might be buried on the top of it. In 1774 Edward Pococke (*p. 30*) observed an arch,

Severan in style, then ruinous. The name 'Pillar of Jonah' is derived from the belief that the whale had regurgitated the prophet somewhere in the vicinity. At the time of the Crusaders it was a toll station, an important transit point then called Portella. There is very little left.

İSKENDERUN

İskenderun (*map D, 6*), the old Alexandria Minoris, Alexandretta or Scanderoon, has not had an easy life. It certainly occupies a brilliant location next to the Belen Pass but the area has been plagued with malaria since time immemorial, to the extent that the **Romans** centred their settlement inland, on the slopes and summit of a hill now called Esentepe (something like 'Healthy Hill'). The remains of cisterns, mosaics, columns, walls and roof tiles are reported in the area but there has never been a thorough survey so to all intents and purposes, İskenderun has no past. When it fell to the **Arabs** it was remodelled and moved close to the sea; that is where Wilbrand of Oldenburg found it in 1211. Later, the **Ottomans** were keen to revitalise the area and improve port facilities. They built a **castle** at the foot of the hill at the time of Süleyman the Magnificent. With time the swampy areas were drained. The city, which in those days was the port of Aleppo, grew but was still vulnerable. It had no road connection to the plains of Cilicia. When the Suez Canal opened it declined. It was boosted by the **Berlin-to-Baghdad railway**, to which it was linked by a branch line. At the turn of the last century the foreign population, the consuls and the major traders, still lived on the inland heights. The plain was not completely safe. After WWII the city expanded and boomed with the construction of road links (routes 53 and 817) to the north. It is thought that in the process they obliterated some of the Roman evidence.

BAGRAS CASTLE
At the south end of the Amanus is Bagras Kalesi (*map D, 8*), 500m west of Ötençay Köyü off Route 825 (*signposted*). It was the ancient Greek city of Pagrai. The role of the defence here was to guard the eastern approach of the Belen Pass connecting Antioch (Antakya) to İskenderun. The line of the road today is different since the Amuq Plain has been drained. In the past, because of the marshes, the road was closer to the mountains. The construction, sitting on a limestone outcrop, is thought at the earliest to be Arab. Caliph Hisham, who built it in the 8th century, wanted a garrison here for 50 men. In the 10th century it fell into the hands of the Byzantines during their reconquest under Emperor Phocas. The garrison now was 1,000 men. After a spell in which it was contended by the Armenians and the Crusaders and was known as Gaston (a reference to the Byzantine kastron), it fell to the Mamluks in 1268; but by then the Crusaders had set fire to it.

Robert Edwards in his survey noted that the complex did not appear at all Armenian. For a start it is in an isolated position. There are no lines of intervisibility with other defences. The plan, with two baileys, is extremely compact, with none of the long wards to which the Armenians were partial. Distinctive Armenian masonry is scarce. This state of affairs reflects the Armenians' position. For them, Antioch was peripheral. They held it for a short while between 1198 and 1222 under Raymond Rupen. It is possible that they felt overstretched at this point and let it go. There are some very fine remains and the access from the west is not too taxing.

At the south end of the Amanus Mountains, the 1281m **Musa Dağ** towers over a peaceful shingle beach. There is nothing to mark the memory of the events of 1915.

PRACTICAL INFORMATION

GETTING THERE AND AROUND

By air: **Hatay Airport**, 25km northeast of Antakya, serves mainly domestic flights; international connections are with Cyprus and the Middle East. Transfer *dolmuş* services are available from İskenderun (on Route 817 near the City Courthouse).

WHERE TO STAY

The area is still new to tourism and there not a great deal of choice. In **İskenderun** try the Anılife Hotel (*anilhotels.com; T: 90 326 618 18 18*), close to Route 817 and therefore easy to find.

ANTAKYA & THE HATAY DISTRICT

Beyond the Amanus mountains it is no longer Cilicia. Antakya (*map D, 8*), the main city of the district of Hatay, has been for the largest part of its existence a settlement in Syria, only recently incorporated into the Turkish Republic. The history of Antakya must be viewed in its physical and geopolitical context.

ANTAKYA

The city of Antakya is not far from the point where the Asi Çay (the Orontes) takes a sharp turn south through a gap in the Amanus mountains and reaches the Mediterranean. This last stretch of water was navigable in antiquity. To the north of the bend, today's beautiful arrangement of perfect fields was once a marsh with a lake at the south end. This is the **Amuq Valley**, sitting directly on the Karasu Fault, a northern extension of the Rift Valley Fault. A number of tells have been excavated in the valley and have shown that it was an **important pathway** connecting Egypt to Anatolia (north–south) and Mesopotamia to the sea (east–west). Excavations have revealed that the area was not an agricultural backwater but the home of active political centres. Finds of **large buildings** have been made, as well as **tablets** and **statues** from the Early Bronze Age. It is here that an urban settlement was founded on the shore of Lake Amuq (drained a few decades ago). This was called **Antigonea**, from the name of its founder, Antigonus Monophthalmus. We know very little about it because its life was cut short by events. Antigonus Monophthalmus was the loser of the battle of Ipsus (301 BC), in which the heirs to Alexander's empire fought over the spoils. Antigonus died in the battle and this part of the world came to the **Seleucids**, who found themselves at the head of an empire stretching from the Indus to the Mediterranean. An urban centre was needed and the new ruler, Seleucus I Nicator, wanted a fresh start. He opted for a location at the mouth of the Orontes, looking for connections to Cilicia to the north, and to Palestine and Egypt to the south. The new foundation was called **Seleucia Pieria** (*see below*) but it proved a short-lived choice as soon afterwards Antioch (the future Antakya) was founded as part of a tetrapolis that included Apamea, Seleucia and Laodicea. The **inland location** proved more attractive. The river was navigable and water plentiful. Antioch, named after Seleucus I Nicator's father, has never looked back. It has had its ups and downs but the 'fair crown of the Orient', to quote the 4th-century AD historian Ammianus Marcellinus (*22,9,14*), is still with us. The choice proved inspired, certainly in late antiquity when Antioch rose to be the third city of the Empire after Byzantium and Alexandria. Its territory, hemmed in by Aleppo to the east and Apamea to the south, fitted well into the local economy, providing transport down the Orontes. It made some people rich, as their mosaic-adorned villas testify. The limestone slopes were exploited for wine, oil and livestock until the soil was exhausted in early Byzantine times.

FROM ANTIOCH TO ANTAKYA

When the Treaty of Sèvres (signed in 1920), which signalled the end of the Ottoman Empire and of its rights over Arab Asia, was supplanted by the subsequent Treaty of Lausanne (1923), supposedly an arrangement more favourable to the successor states of the Ottoman Empire, the border of the future Turkish Republic still ran north of İskenderun. Antioch on the Orontes was part of the French Mandate in Syria and Lebanon and as had been the case in Ottoman times, it still belonged to the Province of Aleppo.

The population of Antioch was heterogeneous, a mix of Turks, Syrians, Armenians, Greeks, Kurds, Circassians and others. Divisions cut across the religious spectrum with Muslims (Sunni and Alawi) and Christians of various denominations. Things seemed settled as long as the French Mandate looked stable. But by the mid-1930s, as Europe was facing up to oncoming events and the Front Populaire (an alliance of left-wing parties) was keeping French diplomats and politicians busy with domestic issues, Atatürk saw a window of opportunity.

His leverage was the undertaking by the French authorities to protect Turkish culture in the district of Alexandretta (the name for İskenderun at the time), which had been signed in 1921. In 1933, according to a census, there were more Arabs than Turks in the district but Turkish culture did not appear threatened. This was a hotchpotch of a place, with many people cutting across different cultures and languages. But Atatürk decided to make this cause his own and it was his determination that brought it to fruition.

He first pitched for an independent state under Turkish guarantee. Bloody riots erupted as the fire of nationalism was lit. Armenians, most of whom had fled Cilicia at the time of the troubles, were as opposed as the Arabs to the plan. Turkish troops moved close to the border.

Atatürk kept the pressure on, coining a new name for the territory and indulging in a well-judged piece of theatre. The district was to become Hatay, which sounded either like a medieval or Turkic (or perhaps Mongol?) tribe of Khitai, or the mythical land of Khatay and the mythical connection (very dear to the great man) between the Turks and their ancestral Hittites. As for the piece of theatre, he persuaded his adopted daughter Sabiha Gökçen to express her patriotism by wearing her full Air Force pilot's uniform and firing a shot in the air in an Ankara restaurant in the presence of the French ambassador. This was duly reported by the press, who were already whipped up to a near frenzy. The young lady spent a night in jail, where she was joined by Atatürk's sister Makbule.

Pressure was kept on and, while the League of Nations proved ineffective, it was agreed to hold elections under international supervision. In the end, the elections were held in a tense atmosphere with riots and clashes, a heavy Turkish military presence, talk of voters bussed in from the north, beyond the border, and the total indifference of the international community. The resulting assembly, not surprisingly, returned a Turkish majority. The territory was absorbed into the Turkish Republic in 1939. A number of Arabs moved out; the Armenians left for Lebanon. This was to be Atatürk's last gift to the nation. He died on 10th November 1938.

A SHORT HISTORY OF ANTAKYA

Because the archaeological evidence is so scarce, we have no idea if the site was inhabited in any way before the set date for the **foundation**, which must be in the early 3rd century BC. The population was a mix of Macedonian settlers and veterans; local people were transferred here from nearby communities and the population in Antigonea probably followed the spolia, as building material was required for the new city. The new foundation was positioned on the left bank of the Asi (Orontes), bordering the north–south through road connecting Laodicea with today's Aleppo. According to legend, its urban perimeter was traced by elephants. Hellenistic Antioch was walled and had separate districts. On the east side Mt Silpius, rising 510m above the plain (*see map on p. 247*), was steep, giving an impression of defence. But there were problems. For a start, after torrential winter rains the river Parmenius (then locally known as Onopnictes, the 'Donkey-drowner') would bring down enormous quantities of debris. Secondly, the ascent of the other side of the mountain was very easy, shattering any illusion of safety; the Persians used this entrance successfully twice. Within a sort time Antioch was in the hands of the **Ptolemies**.

The **first historical mention** of Antioch is on a papyrus dated 246 BC. After it reverted to the **Seleucids**, the city expanded onto an island formed by two arms of the Orontes, to settle veterans of the latest campaign, as well as along the terraced slopes of Mt Silpius to the north. That island has been joined to the mainland at least since Crusader times, the eastern portion of the river bed having filled up with debris and silt. On a Google map you can still pinpoint its location, though, c. 2km north of the Ata Köprüsü bridge. Look for a patch of undeveloped land east of the present course of the river. When in 64 BC Antioch became the **capital of the Roman province of Syria**, though remaining a free city, various rulers left their mark as the city grew into an administrative, military (the starting point of the Persian campaigns) and commercial centre.

Caesar left a basilica, an aqueduct, a theatre and a monomacheion for gladiatorial combats. **Tiberius** provided an improved wall circuit, **Herod the Great** the first colonnaded street, the emperor **Valens** a forum (he would rather stay here than in Constantinople, which had supported his rival in the competition for the throne). On the island, **Diocletian** built a palace in the style of his other palace at Split. Nearby were a stadium, a circus and baths. A tetrapylon with elephants went up in front of the palace. Here in March 363 Emperor Julian posted his *Misopogon*, in which he castigated the Antiocheans for being disrespectful to the old gods.

The list is not exhaustive. However we have very scarce hard evidence for these buildings, as well as for others of the late antique period described by historians such as Procopius and Malalas and orators like Libanius. Nor is there any trace of the statues that were spirited away to Constantinople in 387. Going by what evidence is available (the mosaics), Antioch was a very wealthy place in late antique/early Byzantine times: people enjoyed high living standards. But then a series of disasters struck: earthquakes, sometimes followed by fires, and plagues prompted **Justinian's intervention**. A new set of walls went up, protecting a smaller area but defending the eastern heights that were far too exposed. Landmarks were rebuilt as well as a new church to the Mother of God (Theotokos).

The reprieve was not long-lasting. In the 6th century, **Persian attacks** resulted in the enslavement of the population. In due course the Arabs began pressing from the south and the situation got worse after the Battle of Yarmouk in 636, when they defeated the Byzantines. The Arab forces took Antioch in 641; it was then a destroyed city. It became an important Arab military base and it was possibly at this point that it lost its Classical identity, as the polis transitioned to a medina: it was **rebuilt as an Arab city**.

Antioch was retaken by Phocas in 969, only to be lost to the Seljuks in 1094. The **Crusaders** had a principality here from 1098 (after an eight-month siege) until 1130. After that it was the turn of the **Mamluks**. Finally the **Ottomans** settled in what was left, in 1516. This turn of events fuelled a diaspora (*see box below*), especially in the earlier years. Otherwise the city settled into survival mode, hitting a low point around 1625, according to the description by the well-travelled polymath Pietro della Valle. The only thing he saw still standing when he visited were the city walls, but in a terrible condition; towers were being used as animal pens; the circuit had been breached in places. Inside, by a gate, he found a square '*pescheria*', which from the context sounds like a built fish tank. In addition he described vegetable patches, hovels and a much reduced population. He did not see any structure he could call a house and yet the place was strewn with spolia. A street paved with 'white marble' caught his attention. It must have been the colonnaded street, the main artery around which the city had been built. But he does not mention any columns. In fact, not one of the estimated 1,400 which the city once boasted, nor their bases or their capitals, has ever been traced. At that point Antioch only had one bridge left of its original five. It was probably the Roman bridge, which was replaced in the 1950s by the Ata Köprüsü.

Antioch's woes came to an end after WWII. From a town of 35,000 in 1935, it now has a population approaching 220,000 and has expanded well beyond its ancient limits, especially to the west.

FINDING ANTIOCHIA

The sources about Roman and early Byzantine Antioch are so abundant and detailed that in the 19th century antiquarians set about making a plan of the city without bothering to excavate it. One of them was General Lewis Wallace (of *Ben Hur* fame).

Moreover, 18th-century prints showed portions of the walls and gates still standing almost to full height.

ANTIOCHIA'S DIASPORA

The year 540 was a turning point for Antioch, as the forces of nature joined with the power of the Persians lead by Chosroes. The destruction was immense. Indeed, the excavators found little in the way of hard evidence for 6th-century Antioch but instead came across a thick layer of silt and broken-up material. The people left, at least, those that had not been led into slavery in Persia.

Traces of the refugees have been found around the Mediterranean, adding to other diasporas like the Cilician community in Rome, in the area known as 'ad Aquas Salvias' where the abbey of Tre Fontane is today. Antioch had a flourishing building industry and in it we can include painters and mosaicists.

While none of the mosaics from Antioch is signed, one from Chania in Crete is, by a worker from Daphne (*p. 249*). With no standing walls of any ancient structure, we have no frescoes but we have no reason to rule out painters altogether. In 1944 a cycle of frescoes dated to the 9th century was discovered beneath later artworks at the rural church of Santa Maria Foris Portas at Castelseprio in Lombardy. In style, technique and the choice of topics, the artwork does not fit with what was going on in the area at the time. The work has clear Byzantine traits. This is not an isolated find. In Milan, 34km to the southeast of Castelseprio, the round plan of the church of San Lorenzo Maggiore, with four apses and an ambulatory, is close to the plan of the martyrion in Seleucia (*see below*). The same idea, with Syrian elements, eventually fused with the Armenian tradition and resulted in the churches of Zvartnots (in today's Armenia) and Bana (*see Blue Guide Eastern Turkey*). These are slim threads but on the other hand, in the more general context of northern Italy at the time, they show sustained contacts with the East. Milan itself is home to cults that have an Antiochean flavour. The Church of San Babila, dedicated to Antioch's St Babylas (*p. 249*), a stone's throw from the Duomo, seems to show that Milan was the home of early Eastern cults that are not found outside its diocese. As well as San Babila there is San Romano, Santa Pelagia and Santa Tecla, who are not known elsewhere in Italy or anywhere in the West. Moreover, certain aspects of the Ambrosian rite (an alternative form of Catholic liturgy), which is specific to this geographical area, show contacts with the East of around the 4th–6th century.

The **American-led excavation team** that set about looking for the archaeological evidence in the 1930s, was soon in trouble. The palaces, like the one mentioned by St John Chrysostom, in which bishop Euphrasius came to grief during the earthquake in 526, drowning in a cauldron of hot pitch; Constantine's octagonal church on the island; or any of the churches that go with Antioch's solid Christian tradition, refused to come to light. What was found instead, in unexpected abundance, were **mosaic floors** and soon the excavations became a mosaic hunt. Locals would alert the archaeologists to a newly discovered mosaic, and the artwork would be lifted and saved for posterity. Financially this system kept the dig going and it also explains why the mosaics are so scattered around the world. A good number are in the Hatay Archaeological Museum but one got as far as Honolulu; artworks belonging to the same building have been similarly separated. Unfortunately, because of the pressure of time, the complex political situation (*see box above*) and financial problems, the record of the context of the artworks is extremely scanty; houses with mosaics were not excavated in full. Much information was lost at the time. The only feature that was stratigraphically investigated was the **colonnaded street** (*see below*). These days, as the city has expanded and more concrete has been poured on it, new methods of research such as geophysics and aerial photography have been put to use. However, the changed topography, with the possible shifting of the river bed, the very thick blanket of alluvium, the ups and downs endured by the urban fabric may defeat attempts to recover a credible plan of the old city.

EXPLORING ANTAKYA

A good place to start is **Kurtuluş Cd.**, now slightly peripheral as the town has expanded west, beginning at the Antakya Evi café and restaurant on Silahlı Kuvvetler Cd. and heading north for about 3km. You will be walking between two of the city gates of Antioch, the Daphne Gate to the south and the Aleppo Gate to the north. The name of the third gate (Philonauta) is thought to have referred to the harbour and it was possibly in the vicinity of the Ata Köprüsü bridge. Kurtuluş Cd. is roughly the location of the original pathway connecting the Mediterranean to Syria, on which Antioch's commercial fortunes were based; it was also the locus of the military and religious life of the city. It was unpaved in Hellenistic times, made of beaten earth on virgin soil. In 6 BC Herod the Great monumentalised by it adding a continuous colonnade on either side; it was then 29m wide, including the side porticoes with shops. The idea was to join, in a single sweep, the porches that ornamented the front of Hellenistic houses. It was a concept that was to gain great currency in the Roman world, from Palmyra to Gaul. Excavations have revealed nine phases, with a depth of deposit nearing 10m. At the time of Justinian the street had narrowed. It had gutters and terracotta pipes below the pavement of the porticoes. The present-day Kurtuluş Cd. runs on top of the old west portico. The layout of the ancient street had a kink roughly halfway along it, which is still faintly apparent where Kurtuluş Cd. meets Hacılar Sk. The reason for it is little understood. Here in the past was a nymphaeum and a statue of Tiberius on a column, possibly marking a central point. To the east was the Forum of Valens, offered to the town by the Roman emperor in the 4th century. In mid-Byzantine times the troublesome Parmenius river (which originally flowed into the Orontes) was channelled beneath it in two vaulted tunnels, putting an end to the flooding.

St Peter's Church (*open Tues–Sun 9.30–12 & 1.30–6; charge; Mass on Sun 3–4.30*) is on the slope of Mt Silpius, not far along İzmir Cd. to the east. Many legends

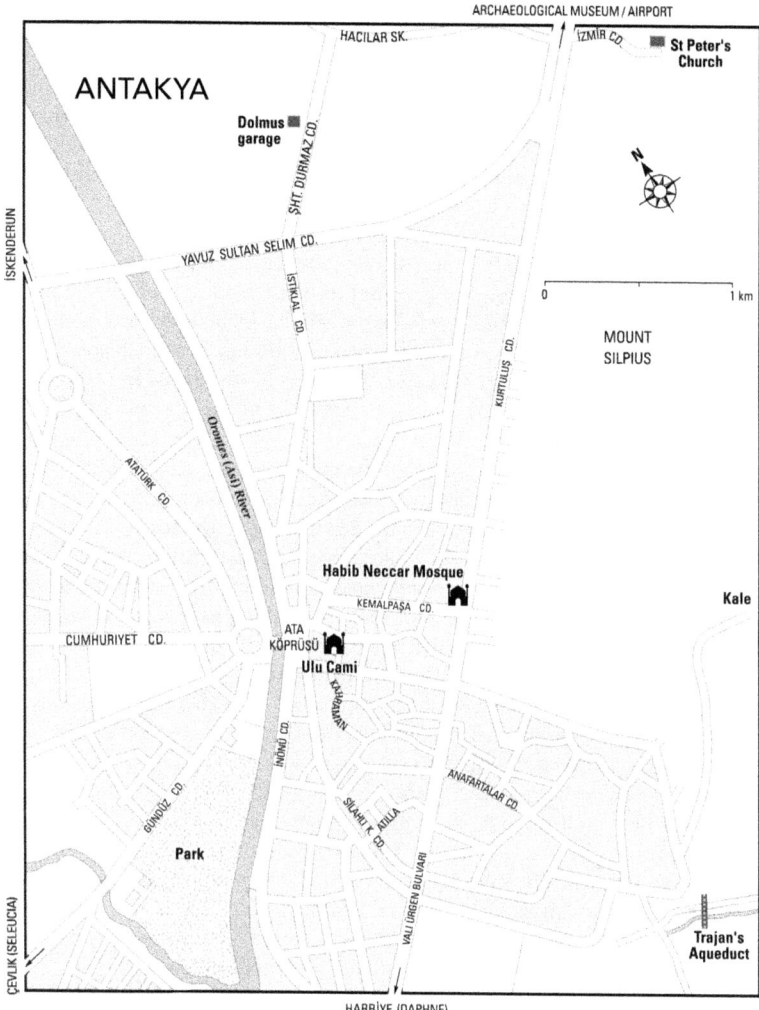

have grown up around this **cave church**, conveniently supported by an imaginative reading of the relevant early Christian literature. It is entirely possible that St Peter preached in Antioch and there was certainly an early Christian community here. It is more difficult to link this building to him. The fine façade in local style is the work of 19th-century Capuchin monks. Behind it a large grotto, measuring 9m by 13m and 7m high, has been carved out. There is no way to date the work. This is the only ancient church known in Antakya. Churches turned into mosques are not confirmed and no mosaic pavement has been attributed to a Christian building. And yet the Church owned large estates and Antioch developed as a cornerstone of Christianity.

About 200m northwest of St Peter's is the **Charonion**, an unfinished figure cut in the rock about which legends abound. It is attributed by Malalas (writing several centuries later) to Antiochus IV (175–163 BC) and interpreted by him as a talisman against the plague. A talisman that did not work very successfully, one might add. According to Hatice Pamir, the figure in the badly eroded relief is actually a woman, a mother goddess in Anatolian style, with a figure of Tyche on her right shoulder.

As for the **walls**, what you see now is mainly reconstructed. After an earthquake in the 19th century, what was left was used as building stone.

Fortunately this meagre crop of remains is not all that Antakya has to offer. There are two more places where you can get a feel for what it meant to live here in the old days. One of them is Daphne (*see below*), where the inhabitants once built their beautiful villas and where today's inhabitants go to find some cool on a hot day. The other is the **Hatay Archaeology Museum**. Antioch is justly famous for its mosaics. Here in the museum, on Atatürk Cd. (*open daily 9–6.30; charge*), you can admire some 300 of them.

Beyond the sheer aesthetic pleasure that the mosaics afford, other aspects should retain your attention. Antioch has always been a crucible: it is really a place where East meets West, where Hellenism fused with the Semitic world. The result is a stunning mix of standard mythological themes, philosophical meditation, street scenes and a touch of humour. Take the ***Megalopsychia* mosaic** from Yatko, a nearby village. Ever since its discovery, academics have been busy unravelling its allegorical meaning: does the figure in the central roundel represent a virtue, therefore magnanimity; or not, in which case it can be interpreted as depicting arrogance? Such a dilemma fits well with the image of the indigenous population through antiquity, who were believed to be unruly, individualistic, rebellious and prone to loose living. But there is more to come. The border of this vast mosaic features a number of buildings which those same academics have been trying to match with the written sources. Is this a genuine stroll through late antique Antioch or an imaginary landscape? Opinions differ.

A later find, unearthed in town during construction work for a cableway, features a skeleton holding a cup with the caption 'Be happy-Enjoy life', another brand of philosophy. And just as minds met and fused here, so techniques also came together, revealing Greek influence side by side with Persian contributions, especially in the mosaic borders and in some details such as the abundance of birds, lions with red ribbons and in heraldic patterns. Also new is the use of *sfumato* techniques, avoiding sudden breaks between colour, so that the mosaics behave almost like paintings. Early works c. the 2nd century AD have particularly fine panels: up to 500 tesserae per 10cm square in a glass mosaic head of Dionysus, for instance.

Here in the museum you can also admire the **Tyche of Antioch**, a divinity who was the heart and soul of the city, just as important as Athena was to Athens. Other cities had such a symbol: you can see four of them (from Rome, Byzantium, Alexandria and Antioch) at the British Museum in London. The Tyche of Antioch was the most imaginative. The draped goddess, with a crown looking like a circlet of city walls, has a young man doing a perfect crawl at her feet. He is the personification of the river, of the Orontes, which is just as rebellious as the population was purported to be. Over the centuries the 600km-long river has had at least three names. To the Greeks it was the Orontes, either from the name of an Indian prince who defied Dionysus and then committed suicide in the river or, more prosaically according to Strabo (*16,7*), from the name of the first man who built a bridge across it. To the Arabs it was al Maklub, 'the overturned', because it flowed towards the north, or al Asi, from which the present Turkish name, Asi Çay, is derived. Here is a clear reference to unruliness, in this case meaning the frequent changes of course and subsequent floods. But Antioch's Tyche has her foot on the young man and she controls him.

HARBİYE: ANCIENT DAPHNE

On a hot day, leave the Orontes-induced mists in the plain and do as the locals do, go up to Harbiye, the ancient Daphne (*map D, 8*). The limestone plateau, with water oozing from myriad **springs**, overlooks the Mediterranean, 240m down to the west. Families come here for a day out by the murmuring **waterfalls** that dot the slope, which is enveloped in a refreshing green cover; there are many little restaurants and plenty of refreshing pools. Some people come here with picnics and BBQs.

In antiquity the site was developed at the same time as Antioch, first with **scattered villas** and later possibly with a **gridded settlement**. In later times, as wealth became more concentrated, Daphne became the home of **large dwellings with extravagant mosaic floors**. Such is the dearth of information about the local archaeology, however, that conclusions about town planning have been drawn by observing sections of the hydraulic system as the mosaics were lifted. There is certainly water here, enough for Daphne and plenty to spare for Antioch, 8km away. Daphne was connected to Antioch by an **aqueduct**, one of several since there were at least five baths and a city of approximately 200,000 people to service; moreover, according to Libanius, water was delivered to all the houses.

The plateau is a rectangle, measuring roughly 1.7km by 1.3km and originally with a thick cypress cover. There is a dense mythological thicket to accompany it, too. Here Paris is said to have pronounced his momentous judgement and here **Apollo** spied a beautiful nymph and ran after her. She asked for divine help to repel his advances and was turned into a laurel tree: it is from this story that Daphne (which means laurel in Greek) got its name. Apollo was very much at home here. He had his oracle by a spring and a temple with the right of asylum, which went up in flames on 22nd October 362. A year later, when Julian the Apostate visited, he was none too pleased with the state of it; he ordered the **relics of St Babylas** (Antioch's principal saint) to be removed so that Apollo could speak once again. The Christians grumbled, as they had brought the relics up to Daphne with the precise intention of silencing Apollo, whom they equated with the devil. Nevertheless, the relics of St Babylas were taken to a purpose-built martyrium on the plain, on the right bank of the river.

Daphne, according to Polybius (*30,2,25*), was by the 2nd century BC already the locus of **military celebrations**, those triumphs with elephants, thousands of chained captives and a profusion of gold and exquisite perfumes that unfortunately leave no material trace. With the *Pax Romana* came the age of **games and festivals**. The **theatre** was partially excavated in the 1930s: it proved to be quite luxurious, with monolithic granite columns from Aswan and a fair amount of marble. Built partly into the hillside, it measured 106m in diameter and had an orchestra that could be flooded for special games. The style is of the late 1st century AD, with repairs dating from after the 341 earthquake. But it was really Justinian who sounded its death knell, when he prohibited theatrical spectacles.

SELEUCIA PIERIA & AL MINA

When Seleucus I Nicator founded Seleucia, soon to be superseded by Antioch, there had been a harbour at the mouth of the Orontes since very early times.

Al Mina (an Arab word meaning 'the harbour'; *map D, 8*) was excavated in the 1930s and revealed at least ten levels of occupation, plus earlier ones that appear to have been lost. It was an **emporium**, with its settlement (Sabouni) higher up on the slope of Mt Casius (now Kel Dağı), which overlooks it from the south. The location of the harbour itself was not considered very healthy. However, it had a long life and according to recent investigations, its beginnings go back at least to the times of the Mycenaeans in the 12th century BC (pottery and Mycenaean seals have been found in the fields). It serviced the Amuq Valley in the hinterland and from there Mesopotamia, including its northernmost reaches in the land of Urartu, south of Lake Van. In due course the **Phoenicians** used it, disseminating their alphabet. It was a reference point for the **Greeks** and the **Egyptians**. Al Mina declined in the 4th century BC for reasons that are not clear. Its replacement, Seleucia Pieria, only came into being after the Battle of Ipsus (301 BC). By then Al Mina was already on the wane. The question remains open.

Although inspired by divine intervention in the form of a sacrifice to Zeus on Mt Casius, which had been a sacred mountain since time immemorial, the choice of a new capital for the Seleucid ruler proved fickle. Zeus's bird, the eagle, may have snatched the sacrificial victim from the hands of the king and taken it to the location of the future Seleucia, but very shortly afterwards that same king changed his mind and started work on Antioch. Whatever worked stone had accumulated in Seleucia was taken to Antioch via the Orontes. Depite this shaky start, Seleucia in due course caught up and was soon an important harbour, developing commercially and militarily.

It was neglected under the Ptolemies but from 50 BC to about the end of the 1st century AD the **Romans** were busy here, adding plenty of public works. Seleucia was the main harbour for an embarkation to Rome (27 days) and it was also the point of entry for commercial transactions, as the large storehouses show. From the 2nd century it was the base of the Syrian fleet and later of the fleet known as the *Classis Seleucena*. Although a military camp has not been located, a number of soldiers lived and died here.

Although beset by problems (*see below*), the harbour kept going into early Byzantine times, only giving in after another earthquake; and then the **Persians** devastated it in 540. Walls toppled and were fed to the lime kilns. At that point the dormant Al Mina took over once again, as material from the 4th–9th/10th centuries appears to suggest. The **Arabs and Crusaders** used it (the latter called it St Simeon). The port facilities lost their importance when the Caliphate was transferred from Damascus further east to Samarra. Today the area is home to a military base and some tourist infrastructure. The ground has been drained and the coastline has progressed.

VISITING SELEUCIA

Seleucia, now near the town of Çevlik, was set out on the slopes of Mt Coryphaeus, which from a height of 322m descends steeply to the sea (with a gradient comparable to that at Pergamon), roughly northeast to southwest. It was **naturally defended** by a couple of streams, the Burnaz and the Sakiat, running on either side in ravines. There may have been a previous settlement, the **acropolis**, right at the top end; otherwise the remains are Hellenistic and Roman. The **wall circuit**, about 5km long, took in the harbour and the east side and possibly—according to McNicoll—went around the acropolis, though the stones have disappeared. There were at least nine towers. Three gates in the south portion of the wall afforded communication towards the Orontes Valley. The **Market Gate**, with two semicircular towers that are later than the wall itself, is Roman-medieval in style, similar to what you see in Trier or İznik. It is comparatively narrow: under three metres. It remains difficult to date the defences with any precision because they belong to different periods.

It seems that the **public area** was to the north of the Market Gate: a peristyle **temple**, possibly Hellenistic, and the location of the **agora** with shops, storehouses and granaries, as well as traces of a **colonnaded street** running roughly east–west, have been identified. The **residential area** was on terraces along the slope. The two areas were separated by a cliff that could be negotiated by winding **rock-cut steps**— steps which Polybius mentions (*2,59*) and which have been identified.

The **harbour** was Seleucia's perennial headache. These days there is not much to see since the land has been drained and is under intensive cultivation, but it could still be made out in the 1960s in aerial photographs. It was a cothon, an inner harbour, Phoenician in style, whose prototype was Carthage, with its command-and-control island in the middle and a chain to control access from the sea. Seleucia's harbour was a simpler affair: a body of water about 400m in diameter with an exit channel to the northwest. It early on developed a serious problem of silting. Being placed at the end of a steep slope, it accumulated a lot of hillwash and the unruly Burnaz Çay did the rest. In the 1st century AD the Flavian emperors took action by building the famous **tunnel** (*see below*), later completed by the Antonines. Only two Flavian emperors (Vespasian and his son Titus) figure in the relevant inscription, which can be seen at the entrance. Vepasian's other son, the emperor Domitian, was posthumously damned (*damnatio memoriae*) and his name was erased from monuments, literally chiselled away, across the Roman world. This might well have happened here too.

Gigantic as the tunnel was, it did not completely solve the problem. As Libanius reported in one of this letters, the army was still (in the early 4th century) employed in deepening the mouth of the channel, which was forever getting blocked up by silt. They mutinied and a full-scale riot ensued. The work was left unfinished.

It is entirely possible that the soldiers preferred to spend their time at the **circus**, which has been identified to the east, just outside the city walls not far from the necropolis.

By the end of the century, Seleucia acquired an **outer harbour**, with two artificial moles that have been identified. This also ran into trouble, from adverse winds and currents, and frequent gales that made loading and unloading problematic. Tectonic shifts caused the sea level to drop, affecting the functioning of the Orontes delta and resulting in yet more silt.

The **tunnel** (to be precise there are two of them) takes the form of a deep trench cut in the rock, intended to channel the Burnaz away from the inner harbour. The work is 1380m long and makes use of a combination of natural features in the rock, such as gorges, as well as man-made cuts, to achieve a passage 6 to 7m wide and 7m deep. A **dam** and a **wall** were intended to force the stream to take a westerly course, away from the enclosed harbour. Provisions were made to accommodate an **aqueduct** coming from springs higher up, then running along the gap and crossing it. In the end, the silt got the upper hand. Earthquakes damaged the work and trade returned to Al Mina (*see above*).

Seleucia had its share of **mosaics**, uncovered in the torrential rains and lifted to museum safety by the 1930s expedition. Some of them can be admired in the Hatay Archaeology Museum (*p. 248*). A number belonged to the upper town, showing a degree of prosperity. Lower down, not far from the Market Gate to the west, was the so-called **martyrium**, a building dated to the late 5th century and found razed to the ground. Roughly 36m in diameter, its shape indicates a colonnaded quatrefoil surrounded by an ambulatory. It would have been covered by a timber roof. The deep chancel or baptistery to the east seems to be a later addition. The ambulatory was richly decorated with marble panelled walls in *opus sectile* and a fine mosaic in the peribolos, a bestiary illustrating the tale of Noah's Ark.

THE STYLITES OF ANTIOCH

The individuality and rebelliousness of the Antiochean character is well illustrated by some of the goings-on in the countryside. Like the rest of Syria, Antioch was fertile ground for Christianity, which was tempered here by a spirited pagan resistance in which the philosopher, writer and orator Libanius took the lead. Here, as in other parts of the East especially, **religious extremism** took root. But it was not of the ascetic sort, with hermits seeking contact with the divine in desert retreats (though close enough to a settlement so they could benefit from offerings). In this region, asceticism was very public and meant to be seen. It took place on top of a column, with the ascetic very much the centre of attention as he preached and fasted and firmly remained there, in a very confined space, for years. It was a spectacle of extreme religion, almost a stunt. It also attracted pilgrims, something the hermits in the desert could only hope for after their death, if an aura of sanctity around their memory could be contrived.

One of the famous stylites of the Antioch region was St Simeon the Elder, whose monastery is now across the border in Syria. **St Simeon the Younger**, a monk inspired by his namesake, adopted his style in 541. Around him a monastery was built on the Samandağ, which for some time after that was known as **Mons Mirabilis** (the 'Mountain of Wonders'). St Simeon the Younger remained on his column until his death in 592. The place developed into a **pilgrimage centre** and buildings to accommodate the pilgrims were added to the three churches. Weathering the disruption caused by the Arab occupation, the complex grew very rich in the 10th–11th centuries and was only abandoned around the mid-13th century, when the Principality of Antioch came to an end and the Mamluks took over from the Crusaders. The remains, surveyed but not yet excavated, can be visited. They are near Uzunbağ, on Route 420 some 15km southwest of Antakya. There you can see some fine architecture and the octagonal base of the column on which St Simeon lived, which is said to have been 10.5m tall.

PRACTICAL INFORMATION

GETTING THERE AND AROUND

By air: Hatay Airport, in the area of the ancient Lake Amuq, is 25km northeast of Antakya. It serves mainly domestic flights; international connections are with Cyprus and the Middle East. Transfer *dolmuş* services are available from Antakya (south end of Kurtuluş Cd.) and from İskenderun (on Route 817 near the City Courthouse).

By bus: Antakya *otogar*, where there are coaches to and from a wide variety of places, is on the north edge of town, 7km from the city centre. There is a shuttle service. *Dolmuş* services for Harbiye (Daphne) and other destinations depart from the Köy Garajları, to the north of town on Şehit Durmaz Cd. (but you can also hail them on Yavuz Sultan Selim Blvd and on Kurtuluş Cd.). When you get to Daphne, get off opposite the Hotel Çağlayan and walk down into the wooded valley on the left, which is usually full of local people enjoying the greenery and the cool water.

WHERE TO STAY

The area is still new to tourism and there not a great deal of choice outside Antakya or Çevlik. In **Antakya**, the Fi Hostel (*fihostel.com; T: 90 326 216 20 06*) in the heart of the old town on Silahlı Kuvvetler Cd., will offer you a bed and plenty of information to make the most of your stay. It is a hostel, so expect male/female dorms. The Antakya Öğretmenevi (*T: 90 326 216 11 56*) is on Cumhuriyet Cd. (west of the Ata Köprüsü). For something more upmarket, try the Kavinn Butik

Otel (*kavinnbutikotel.com; T: 90 532 167 64 94*) in Prof. Ataman Demir Sk off Kahraman Sk. Or, to experience a night like an upper-class Antiochean of old, book at the **Museum Hotel**, a stone's throw from St Peter's grotto at Hacılar Sk 26/1 (*themuseumhotelantakya.com, T: 326 290 00 00*). It stands on stilts on a very large and beautiful mosaic (which is also accessible as a museum, by a separate entrance). The hotel is an example of a case where archaeology won the day, as the building plans had to be redrawn from scratch.

In **Harbiye** (Daphne), the Çağlayan Hotel (*caglayanotel.com.tr; T: 90 539 400 66 97*) is not too close to the main road and is quiet. The Harbiye Sara Hotel (*T: 90 326 231 26 26*) has a fine view overlooking the waterfalls, a good 500m off the main road. You will hear the water rather than the traffic.

In **Çevlik** (Seleucia) try the Çevlik Öğretmen Evi (*T: 90 326 512 24 11*), which is on the sea front next to the modern harbour. There are a couple of pansiyons to the south of it, but they may be closed out of season.

WHERE TO EAT

On the whole, in the Hatay region you will find the same basic Turkish cuisine, with lovely soups and kebabs, but you can also clearly see that you are moving east. *Lahmacun* (the Turkish answer to pizza but made with meat) is popular here. You will also find its miniature version (*fındık lahmacun*): the topping is the same but the base is a little bit thicker and therefore softer, and it is bite-sized.

There is also a fair amount of *ciğer kebap* (liver on a spit) on offer, to remind you that you are getting closer to Diyarbakır, the national capital of *ciğer kebap*.

For fish go to **Çevlik**, to the **Ekmek Arası Balık** by the harbour.

In **Antakya**, the **Affan Coffee House** in the old town towards the south end of the main thoroughfare on Anafartalar Cd., is a good place to take a break. Try their interesting ice creams. For a meal go to **Beyzade Konağı** café and restaurant on Atilla Cd. to the west. They have a good spread of mezes. Alternatively, a good value place for traditional Turkish food is the Özdeniz Saray Lokanta near the *dolmuş* garage.

In **Harbiye**, explore the little restaurants by the waterfalls. They may all serve the same fare but it all seems to taste better in such lovely green surroundings.

INDEX

Accommodation 13
Adamkayalar 197
Adana 212
Akkale 202
Akyaka 35
Al Massisa (see Misis)
Al Mina 250
Alahan 189
Alanya 167ff
Alarahan 166
Alcetas of Termessus 124
Alexander the Great (Battle of Issus) 235
Alexandretta (see İskenderun)
Altınkaya 138
Anamur headland 178
Anavarza 221
Andriake 97
Anemurium 179
Antakya 241ff
Antalya 126ff
Anthony the Younger, St 149
Antigonus Monophthalmus 241
Antioch (see Antakya)
Antiochia ad Cragum 177
Antiphellos 84
Aperlae 85, 86
Aphrodite of Cnidus 39
Apollo and Daphne, myth of 249
Apollonia 89
Apollonius of Selge 142
Ariassos 135
Arif 106
Armenians 168, 234; (ancient capital of) 226
Arneai 100
Arslantaş dam 228
Artemidoros of Cnidus 42
Arykanda 105
Aspendos 150

Atatürk 153, 242
Attalus II of Pergamon 121, 126
Ayaş 197
Ayas 216
Ayatekla 187
Aydıncık 182
Bagras castle 239
Balboura 60
Barbarossa, Frederick, death of 185
Bean, George 23, 61, 124, 126, 141, 175
Beaufort, Francis 23, 40, 72, 116, 156, 170, 177, 179, 181, 183, 196, 205, 206, 207, 218
Bell, Gertrude 24, 202, 225
Black Cilicia 235ff
Boğsak island 184
Boyazı 181
Bozburun Peninsula 43ff
Bubon 60
Burgaz 38
Bybassos 44
Cadyanda 57
Caretta caretta turtle 46, 49
Carter, Robert and Cynthia 86
Castabala 230
Caunus 45
Cedreae 36
Çelebi, Evliya 25, 36, 147, 208
Cennet and Cehennem 194
Ceramic Gulf 35
Chimaera, the 116
Cibyra 61
Cilicia 164ff
Cilician Gates 208
Cilicians 7
Cleopatra 36, 167, 210
Cnidus 38
Cnidus Peninsula 37ff
Corycian Cave 194

Corycus 195
Corydalla 108
Ctesias, historian 39
Çukurova 207ff
Cyaneae 89
Dalyan 45
Daphne 249
Datça 38
Demre 91
Dereağzı 100
Dilek Mağarası cave 195
Diogenes of Oenoanda 58
Domuztepe 228
Dorian, Dorians 37
Döşeme Boğazı 136
Düden waterfall 134
Echimos, John 149
Elaioussa 197
Emecik 38
Epiphania 237
Ernez 100
Eski Anamur 179
Eudoxos, astronomer 39
Evdir Hanı 124
Feke castle 227
Fellows, Charles 8, 26, 50, 52, 53, 57, 63, 67, 73, 96, 153
Fethiye 53
Finike 101
Frederick Barbarossa, emperor, death of 185
Gagai 110
Gaius Caesar, cenotaph of 105
Gazipaşa 176
Gelemiş 78
Gelidonya, Cape 113
Gemiler Adası 56
Gibbons, Helen 211
Gökçen, Sabiha 242
Gökova Körfezi 35
Göksu river 185
Göl Ada 61
Gölhisar 62
Güllük Dağı Termessos Milli Parkı 120
Hadrian, emperor 130

Haimoff, June 49
Harbiye 249
Harpy Monument (Xanthus) 73
Harun al Rashid 213, 231, 237
Hatay district 241ff
'Heaven' and 'Hell' 194
Hermogenes of Xanthus 80
Hierapolis Castabala 230
Hittite, Hittites 220, 229, 236
Ibn Battuta 22, 53, 62, 128, 170
Ibn Hawqal 210
Idebessus 107
Idrisi, geographer 160
Idyma 35
İnan, Jale 61
Iotape 175
Isaurians 7, 165
Isinda 89
İskenderun 239
Islamic presence in Asia Minor, earliest evidence of 43
Issium 96
Issus, battle of 235
İztuzu beach (Dalyan) 49
Izzedin Keykavus 124
Jonah, Pillar of 238
Julian the Apostate 217; (burial place of) 210
Kadirli 227
Kanlıdivane chasm 202
Kanytelis sinkhole 201
Karain Cave 125
Karataş 216
Karatepe 228
Kargıhan 154
Kaş 84
Kastabala 230
Kastabos 44
Kayaköy 56
Kekova island 88
Kelenderis 182
Kinet Hüyük 236
Kinneir, John 27, 213
Kırlangıç Burnu 113
Kızkalesi 195

Köprülü Canyon 163
Köyceğiz, Lake 46, 50
Kozan 226
Kumkuyu 201
Kumluca 108
Kurtkulağı 236
Kydna (see Pydnae)
Laborde, Léon de 28 185, 186, 206
Laertes 174
Lajazzo 216
Lamas Kale 205
Lanckoroński, Karol 28, 129, 130, 132, 135, 144, 147, 156
Langlois, Victor 29, 212, 214, 225, 227
Letoön (Xanthus) 76
Limonlu river 205
Limyra 8, 101
Loryma Peninsula 43ff
Love, Iris 40
Lycia 52ff
Lycian League 80
Lycian Way 13
Lydae 55
Lyrbe 155
Lysander 36
Magydos 126
Mallos 216
Mamisra (see Misis)
Mamure Kalesi 181
Manavgat waterfalls 156
Marcian, emperor 67
Mark Antony 36, 167
Marmaris 36
Mausolus of Halicarnassus 38, 48
Megarsos 216
Melli 137
Mersin 207
Meryemlık 187
Meydancık Kale 183
Mezgit Kale 194
Mezitli 205
Misis 214
Mopsuetia (see Misis)
Muğla 35

Mut 189
Myra 91
Nagidos 181
Nagidoussa 182
Narlıkuyu 194
Nereid Monument (Xanthus) 73
Newton, Charles 36, 40, 42
Nicholas of Myra, St 93
Nicholas of Sion, St 66, 94
Oenoanda 57
Olba Diocaesarea 190
Ölüdeniz Milli Parkı 56
Olympus 114
Opramoas 59, 61, 65, 83, 102, 108, 109; (mausoleum of) 110
Orontes, river 248
Pamphylia 113ff
Pamphylians 7
Paribeni, Roberto 30, 128, 156, 175, 212
Patara 78
Paul, St 92, 142, 210
Payas 238
Pednelissos 138
Perge 141
Perikles of Limyra 102
Peter, St 247
Phaselis 117
Phellos 85
Physcus 36
Pillar of Jonah 238
Pinara 65
Pirates, piracy 165
Pisidia Heritage Trail 135ff
Pisidians 7
Plancia Magna 144
Pococke, Edward 30, 238
Polo, Marco 217
Pompey the Great 165
Pydnae 78
Reşadiye Peninsula 37
Rhodes, Rhodian Peraea 43
Rhodiapolis 108
Rough Cilicia 164ff
Saklıkent Milli Parkı 112

Sandak Dağı 67
Sapadere Canyon 204
Şarapsa Han 167
Savranda castle 237
Sebeda 85
Seleucia Pieria 250
Seleucus I Nicator 186, 191, 241
Selge 138
Selinus 176
Seljuks 127, 153, 168, 170
Sertavul Geçidi 189
Sia 136
Sıcakyarımadası 86
Side 156
Sideyri island 36
Sidyma 67
Silifke 185
Sillyon 147
Simena 88
Simeon the Younger, St 253
Sion Treasure 94
Sirkeli relief 220
Sis 226
Smooth Cilicia 205ff
Softa Kalesi 182
Soli 205
Solymians 121
Sostratos of Cnidus 39
Spratt, Captain T.A.B. 31, 37, 44, 52, 60, 61, 84, 90, 108, 110, 116
Stadiasmus (Patara) 83
Stamira 99
Stark, Freya 8, 32, 36, 45, 65, 93, 177, 207
Stylites 252
Suleyman the Magnificent 36
Sura 90
Syedra 174
Tarcondimotus 231
Tarsus 209
Taşdibi 99
Teimioussa 89
Tekke Oğlu Osman Bey 129
Telmessus 53
Termessus 120
Tersane Ada 55
Tetrapyrga 205
Texier, Charles 32, 52, 55, 82
Thecla, St 187
Tlos 63
Toksöz, Meltem 208
Toprakkale 236
Trajan, site of death of 176
Trebenna 120
Üçağız 85
Uluburun, Cape 85
Uzuncaburç 190
Vahga Kale 227
Valle, Pietro della 244
Varus the Stork 142
Verres, Roman governor 142
Via Sebaste 136
Vulso, Gn. Manlius 62
Wallace, Lew 244
Wilbrand of Oldenburg 33, 238
Xanthus 8, 68
Yakacık 238
Yakapınar 214
Yanartaş 116
Yılankale 220
Yumruktepe 207
Yumurtalık 216
Yunus Sütunu 238
Zeniketes 114, 165
Zeno, emperor 166, 188
Zeytun 234

ATLAS OF MEDITERRANEAN TURKEY 259

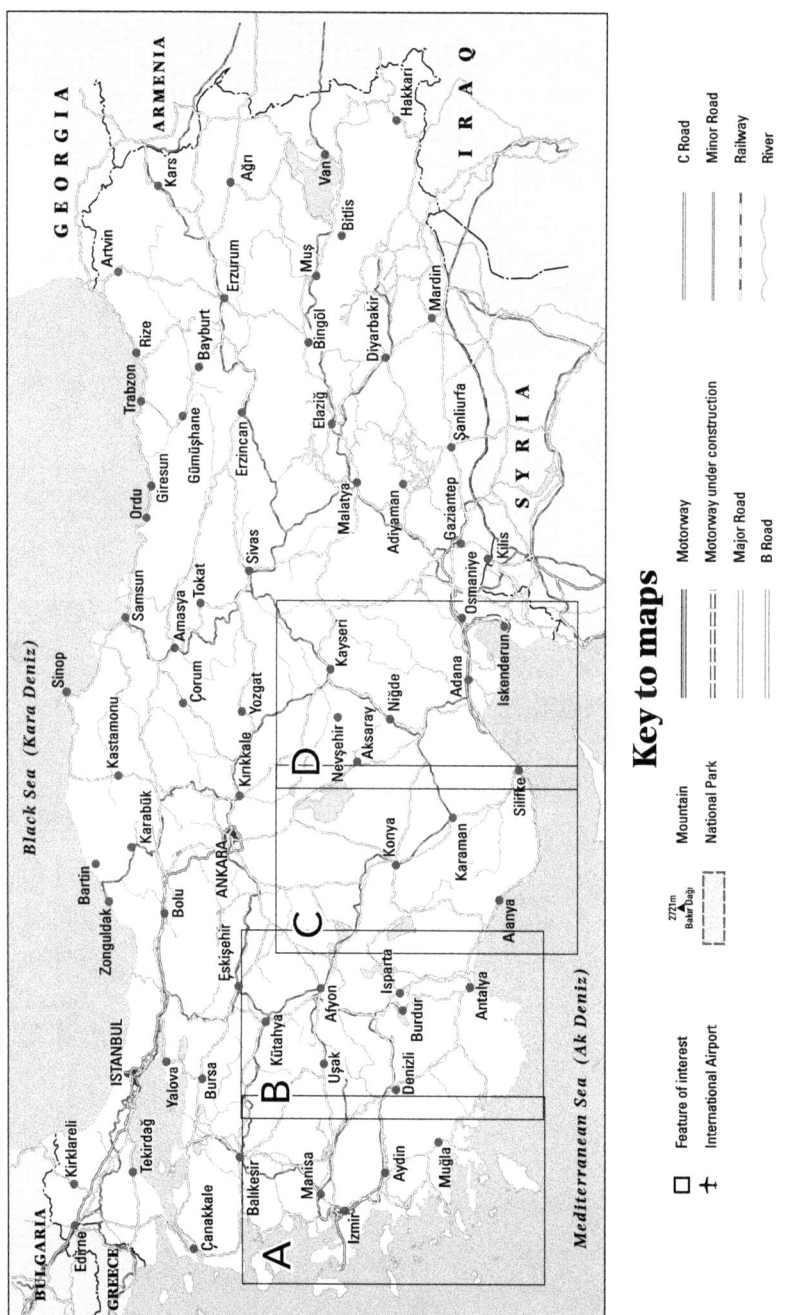

MAP A

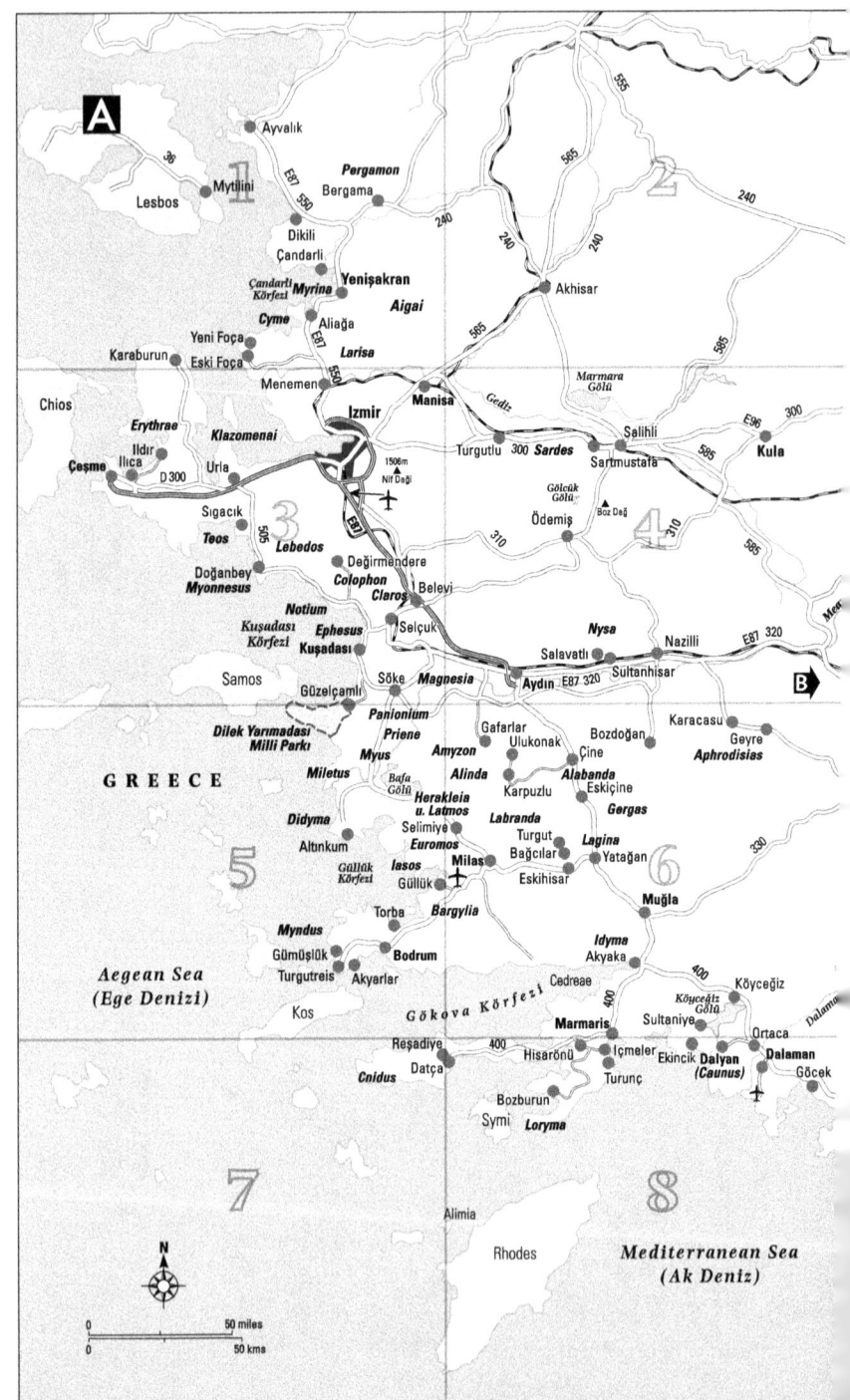

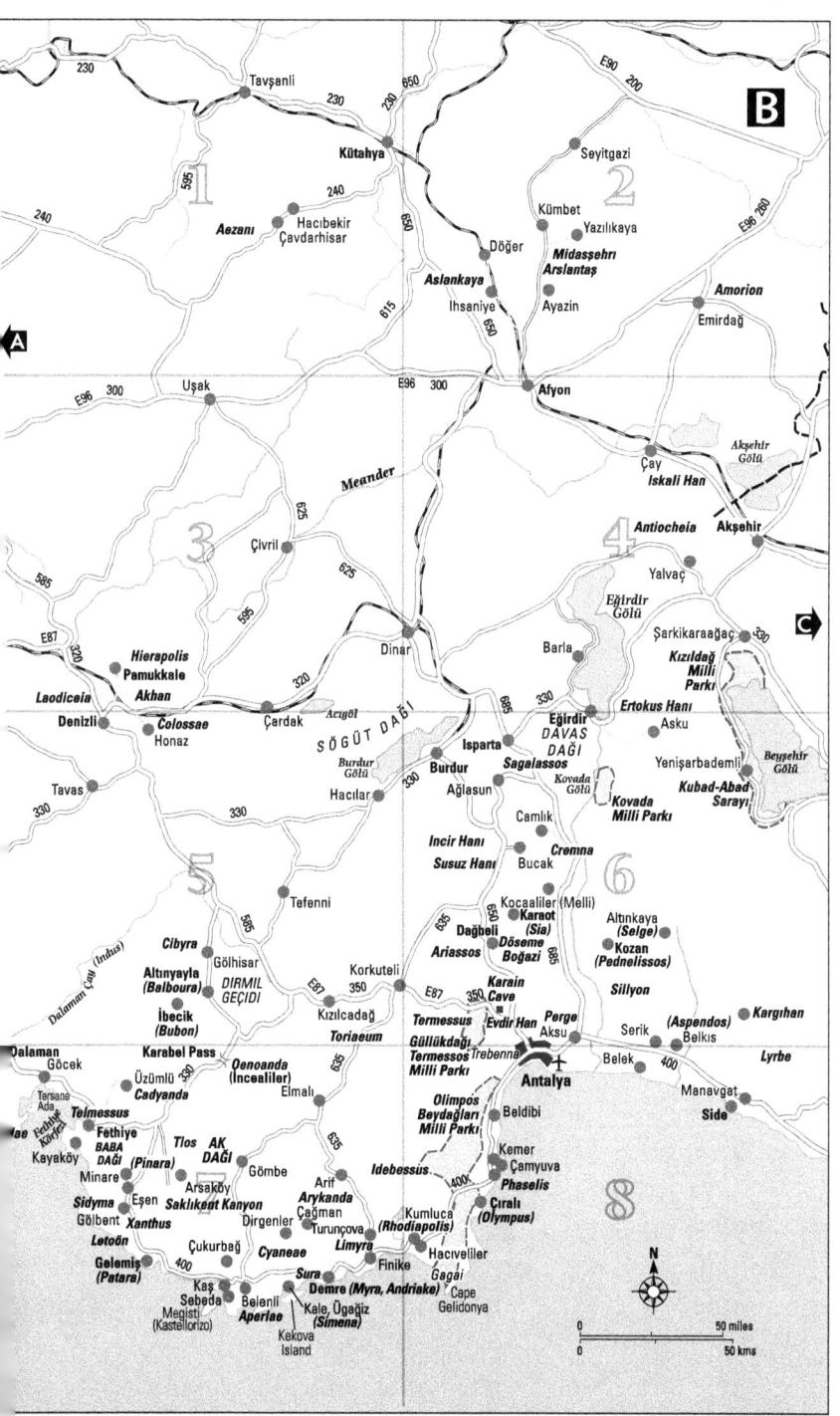

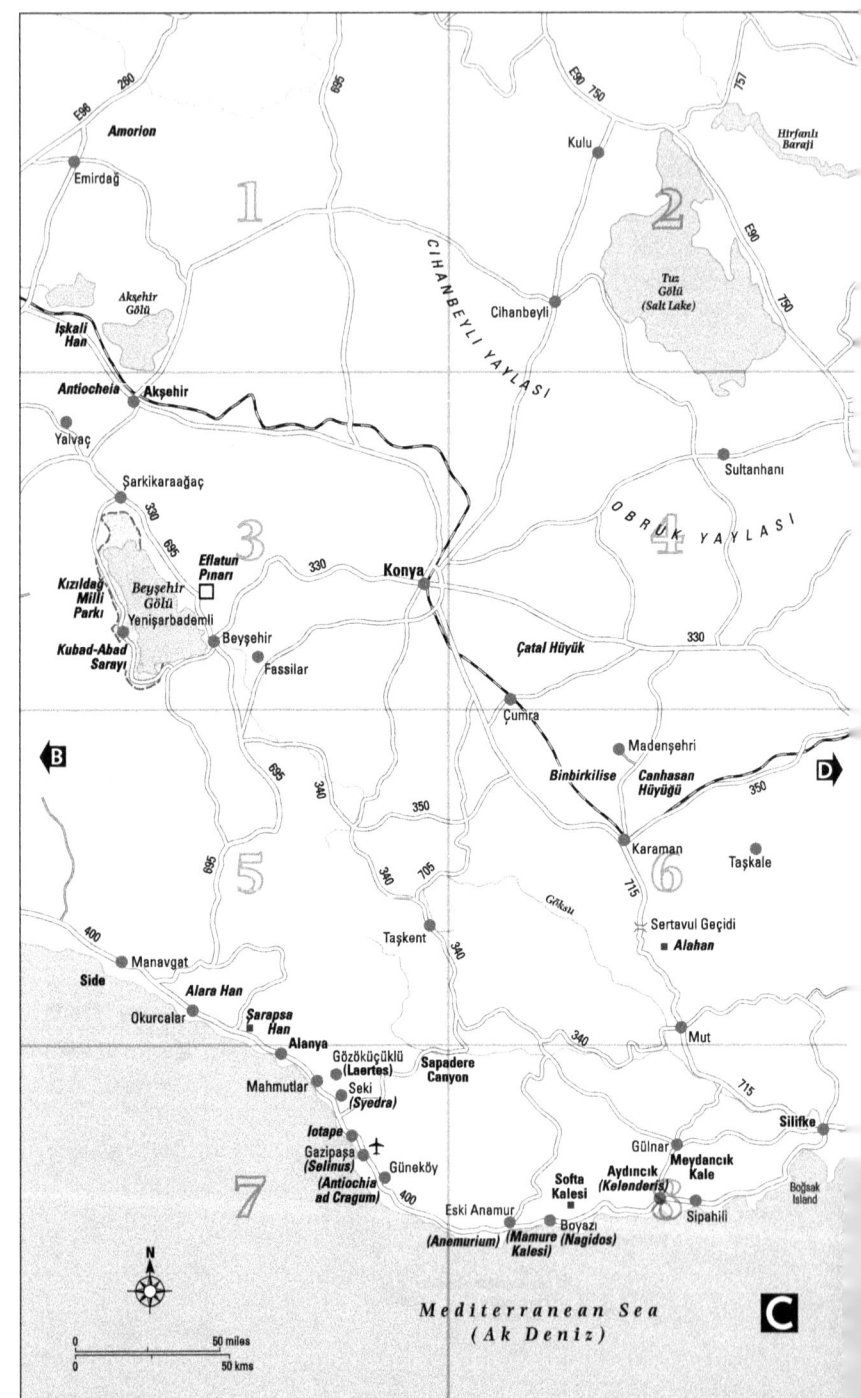

MAP D 263

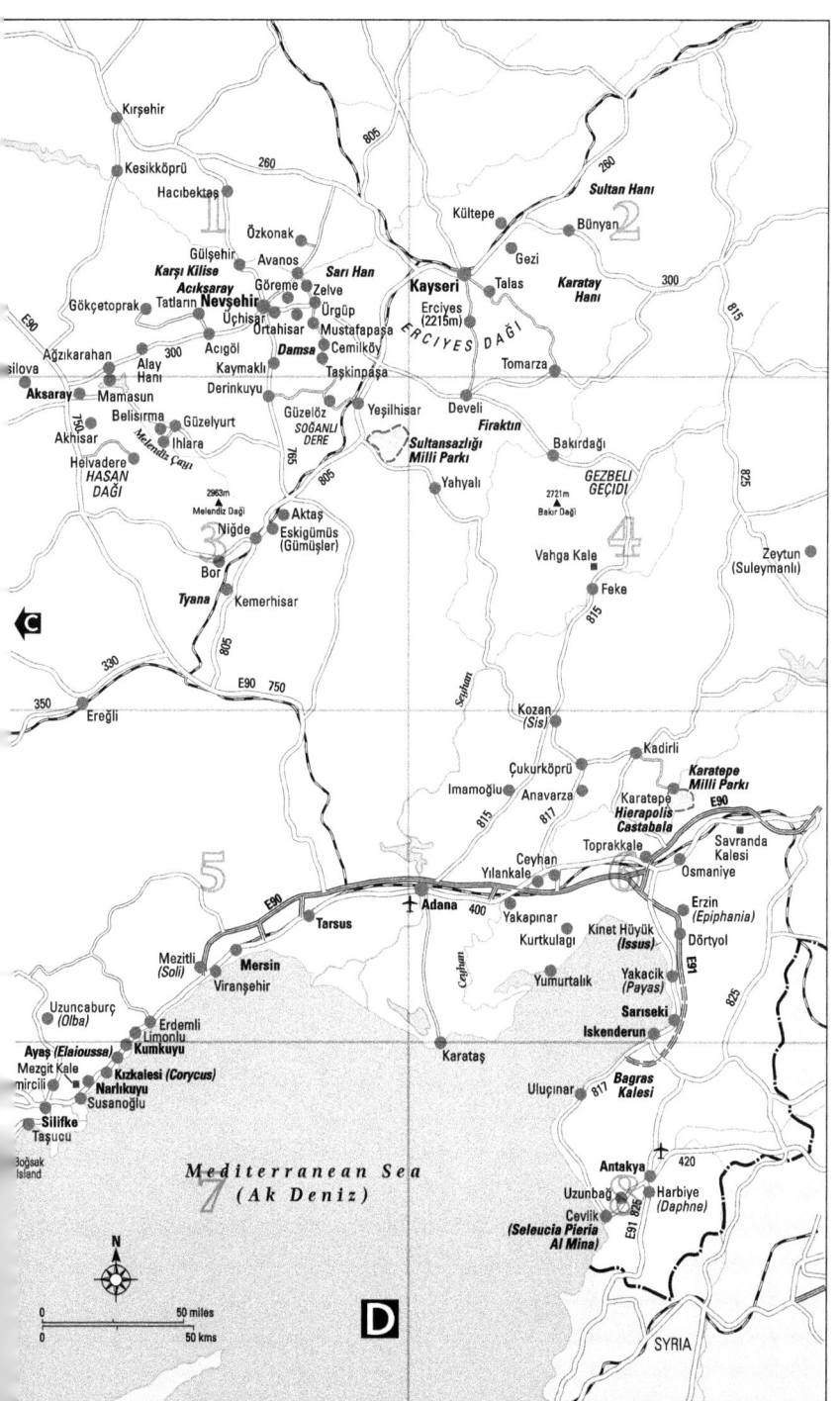

ANCIENT PROVINCES OF TURKEY

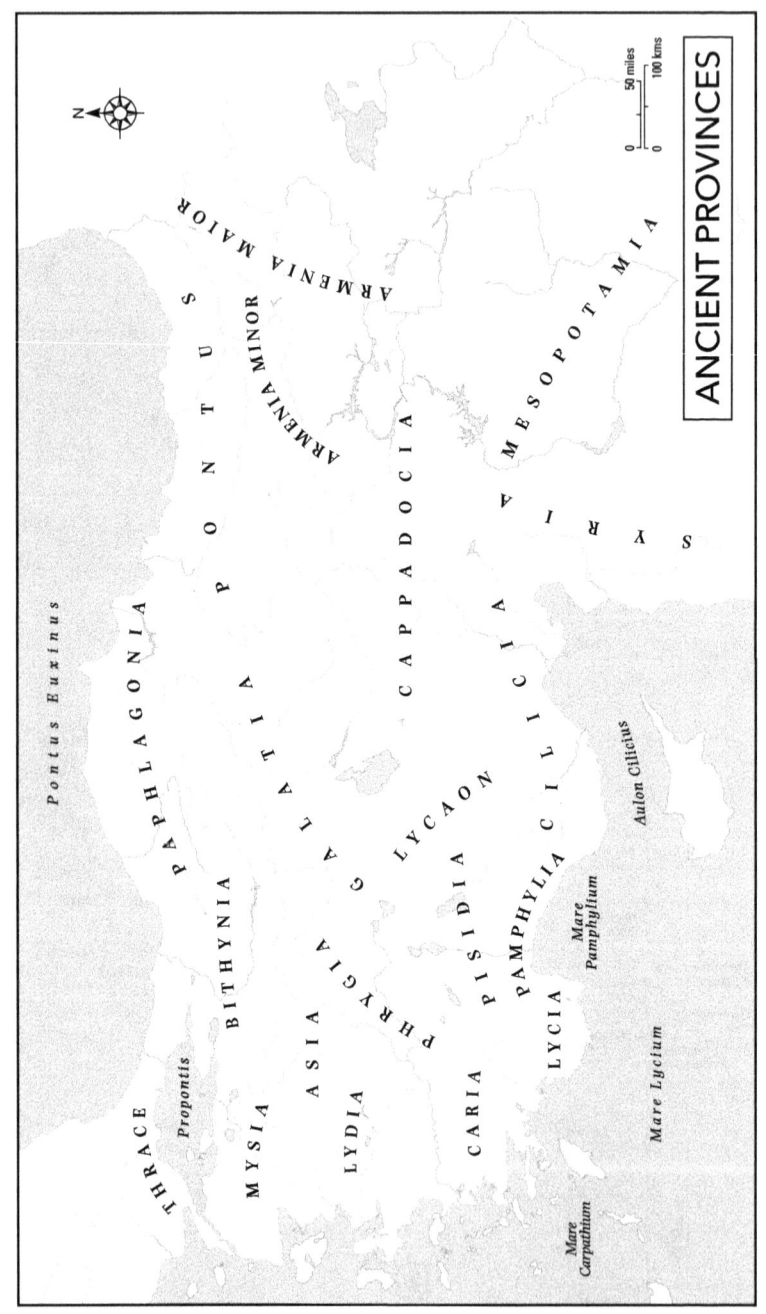

www.ingramcontent.com/pod-product-compliance
Lightning Source LLC
Chambersburg PA
CBHW060501090426
42735CB00011B/2072